Research Methods in Social Work

Eighth Edition

David Royse

University of Kentucky

cognella®

SAN DIEGO

Bassim Hamadeh, CEO and Publisher
Amy Smith, Project Editor
Abbey Hastings, Associate Production Editor
Jess Estrella, Senior Graphic Designer
Alexa Lucido, Licensing Associate
Natalie Piccotti, Director of Marketing
Kassie Graves, Vice President of Editorial
Jamie Giganti, Director of Academic Publishing

cognella® | ACADEMIC PUBLISHING
3970 Sorrento Valley Blvd., Ste. 500, San Diego, CA 92121

Research Methods
in Social Work

Brief Contents

Detailed Contents

Preface

Dear Students and Instructors,

THANK YOU IN advance for taking the time to examine or purchase this text. Of course, maybe it is required and you have no choice but to buy it or use it. However you arrived here, I'm glad to give you a little information about the design of this book. And I want to involve you as a partner. I hope you will feel free to contact me to let me know what parts of the book work for you and those that don't.

Having taught research methods for many years, I know that many students aren't interested in the topic, others fear the subject matter, and others want to get on with the business of learning how to help those who are in tough life situations. Sometimes, these attitudes make it challenging for the student to learn and the faculty member to communicate how a knowledge of research can benefit the practitioner and his or her clients.

To maneuver around attitudes opposed to learning research methods, I have tried something in this text that makes it unique and different from other texts. I'm introducing two characters, Sophia and Bill, who are social work students in an internship—perhaps just like you. There is not a lot of personal information about what they look like, so you can fill in the blanks and see them as you want them to be. Perhaps Sophia has silky black hair and Bill's is cut military style. At any rate, they differ somewhat in their style and approach to things. But most importantly, they will be exploring the research methods content the same as every reader. Occasionally, I will have them share literature that they found or an instrument they created (of course, I did all the work). I'm hoping this will make the book more interesting for you.

Research Methods in Social Work attempts to make direct applications to social work practice, to prepare you to think in terms of evidence-based practice, and most importantly, to show you recent and relevant studies that you can read on your own to further your knowledge about research methodology. I don't believe any other research text provides as many references to current and actual research in every chapter as this one does. I've spent a great deal of time locating research examples, and I hope you take the time to investigate some of them—it just might convince you that research can be interesting and relevant. Useful studies are almost always available if one makes the effort to find them.

Also, in this edition you'll find that, unlike previous editions of this book, the emphasis of Chapter 13 has changed slightly. It is now focused on your understanding the statistical symbols and findings that you are likely to encounter in research publications. Some instructors may wish to supplement the material in Chapter 13 by having you also learn how to enter data or analyze it with the IBM Statistical Program for Social Services (SPSS). And I fully support that idea. However, other instructors may simply see the importance of that chapter as helping you to become an intelligent *consumer* of research and statistical findings. These instructors may not emphasize hands-on practice with statistical software. I have tried to make the book friendly and useful for whichever way your instructor wants you to learn about basic statistical procedures and what they communicate.

While it may not be all that unique, I have also tried to help you master the contents of this book by providing self-review questions and anxiety checks in most chapters. You can test your knowledge of the material by responding to these items and checking your answers at the end of the book.

Last, I've used the APA format for listing the references used. In many, if not most, of the papers you will be required to write in your social work courses, APA is the expected style. I have followed it with this exception: when I have known the issue number of a journal, I have shown it in parentheses, as I believe that it makes it easier for the reader to locate the article he or she is looking for. A good resource if you have questions about APA formatting is the Purdue Online Writing Lab (**https://owl.english.purdue.edu/owl/resource/560/01/**). You might also want to consult the American Psychological Association's website for free assistance: **https://apastyle.apa.org/?_ga=2.23989619.898651929.1564431171-374531821.1564431171**.

I trust your research course will make an important contribution to your thinking and knowledge as a social worker. Don't forget to let me know what parts of the book you enjoy and what parts you'd like to see expanded or explained better.

Best wishes,
David Royse
droyse@uky.edu

CHAPTER 1

Introduction: Where Does Research Start?

S OPHIA AND BILL met at the coffee shop before starting the first day in their new practicum. She, always the early one, was checking her phone to see why he might be running late as he sat down with his cup.

"How's it going?" he asked, as he stirred copious amounts of sugar into his coffee.

"I'm fine," she said. Just a little nervous. There's a lot I don't know about incarcerated women."

"Guess we'll learn together." Bill tried a sip of his coffee. "They can't be all that different. Can they?"

"Well, unlike last semester, we won't be creating activities for their children."

"I'm okay with that," Bill said, pulling a crayon out of one of his jacket pockets. "I find them everywhere."

"Finish your coffee, Bill. I'm anxious to get there and meet the new field instructor and learn what we might be assigned to do."

After a short walk, Bill and Sophia arrived at the city's prison. They emptied their pockets, walked through a metal detector, and presented their identification to the guard, who then escorted them to a small room where they waited for their field instructor.

"It feels like *we've* been locked up, doesn't it?" Bill said as he paced the room. "That click of the security door behind us gave me the chills."

After a few minutes, Mrs. Simpson, a licensed clinical social worker with a sunny smile, greeted them and shook their hands with a surprisingly strong grip. "Let's go to my conference room," she said. "Have any trouble getting in?"

"Nope," said Bill with a grin. "And I hope we don't have any getting out."

Once they were settled in what looked like a small classroom with tiny shatterproof windows and bars, Mrs. Simpson said simply, "What I need for you to do this semester is to design an evidence-based HIV/STI prevention program for our women."

"What's STI?" Bill blurted.

"Sexually transmitted infection." Sophia quickly responded, not wanting Mrs. Simpson to think that she was as uninformed as her friend and classmate.

"Chlamydia, gonorrhea, syphilis, and others. We're especially concerned about sex workers and those injecting drugs being exposed to and transmitting HIV." Mrs. Simpson added, looking at Bill.

"A lot of your prisoners are sex workers?"

"Not *currently*, Bill." Mrs. Simpson smiled. "But many of them have worked in the trade and have substance abuse issues—which, as you can imagine, complicates HIV/STI prevention programs."

She paused for a moment and then asked, "What do you think? Could you design a program for our inmates during the semester? We'd like to implement it around the first of the year."

Bill nervously glanced at his watch as if it could help answer the question. It was 8:50 a.m.

Sophia took charge. "Sure, we can do it. Right, Bill?"

"Uh, well ... I'm thinking that maybe ... okay, sure. We can, uh, at least outline a program for you."

"Great!" said Mrs. Simpson, pushing her chair back from the table. "We want to do it right—evidence-based practice and all that. Do a thorough literature review, then make a recommendation for an intervention. When that's agreed upon, you'll need to prepare an evaluation design. If we do a good job, maybe there will be a conference presentation in your future, or perhaps an article we can write."

"Will we have individual clients, too?" Sophia asked.

"I'm not thinking you will," said Mrs. Simpson. "But we'll see how things go."

"When do people eat lunch around here?" Bill asked, almost immediately feeling Sophia's scowl.

"Whenever you want. Some staff go early, and some go late," Mrs. Simpson said. "Sorry I can't stay longer to help you get started, but I'm slammed with meetings this week." She again smiled at the interns as she started walking toward the door. She turned, then said, "Let's meet each Friday at 1:00 and you can update me with your progress. Of course, come see me before that if you have questions."

As soon as she closed the door, Bill turned to Sophia and said, "What do we do? Where do we start?"

Where Would You Start?

Take a few seconds to actually think about how you might respond to this question. Problems like this are often presented to social workers in real life. Sometimes, even students are asked to design a research project or a new intervention because they have access to resources (e.g., the university's library and faculty) and time that other staff don't. Truthfully, there is more than one way to start, but ... what would you do first? Here are a couple of options:

Path 1: Sophia and Bill could get on the Internet with the idea of trying to find an expert who has already created an HIV/STI prevention program for incarcerated women. They could then talk to that person and request information on the program or see if the expert has written any articles on the program. Sadly, sometimes agencies have created programs but failed to really evaluate them so that it is difficult to know how successful they are or whether they have good results, say, for longer than two or three months. They might consider knocking on Mrs. Simpson's door and asking if she knows of someone who has created a program like she's envisioned that they could talk to. However, if she knew of that person already, wouldn't she have told them? She didn't seem like someone who was trying to trick them.

Path 2: Sophia and Bill could have a discussion about evidence-based practice (EBP) and what it would entail. In their research methods class just yesterday, the instructor had spent the whole period talking about EBP. Here were the steps they knew they needed to begin right away. Other steps would be taken a bit later.

- Step 1—developing an answerable question.
- Step 2—looking for the best evidence to answer their question.
- Step 3—critically evaluating the evidence and then conferring with practitioners with expertise in the area. After that, they could involve potential program participants to learn about their values and expectations before putting the finishing touches on the program design.

Sophia and Bill knew they would need to do a thorough literature review at a minimum. Before beginning, they decided to pool their knowledge and begin to discuss evidence-based practice. However, before we dig into that content, you may recall that this section began with the question "Where does research start?" It should be apparent to you from Bill and Sophia's story that sometimes we encounter the necessity for research when we are in our practicums and on the job. It may initially have little to do with someone aspiring to be a research scientist and much more with just wanting to be a good practitioner of social work or wanting to develop a sound program. As we'll see in the coming chapters, research starts with individuals like Sophia and Bill—with persons like you! Questions needing answers can come from life experiences, work experiences, problems that family members or friends have faced, or even a special interest that you've developed from reading or learning about a social problem. Unanswered problems, riddles, and mysteries surround us and provide the stimulus for research. Who creates knowledge for social workers? Individuals like you.

Evidence-Based Practice

What is it? Sophia and Bill learned that **EBP** is a process, ideally a systematic process, in which social workers or other professionals gather evidence to apply to a particular problem—such as identifying the best treatment or intervention for a certain practice issue. Typically, it starts with a question. For instance: Is an individual psychoeducational approach for this problem better than a group therapy approach? Or pragmatically, someone might look at agency data on readmissions or rearrests and ask: Is there a better way to minimize these? Anyone can pose a problem. It could be the clinical director, the director of the agency, your immediate supervisor, a coworker, or even you. The question could arise from frustration with seeing the same clients again and again.

BOX 1.1   STEPS IN EVIDENCE-BASED PRACTICE

Step 1: Develop a Well-Built Question
Step 2: Search for Evidence/Literature
Step 3: Evaluate the Evidence Found on an Intervention
Step 4: Consider Evidence Conjointly with Client Preferences and Practitioner Expertise and Launch Intervention
Step 5: Evaluate the Intervention's Outcomes

The individual given the most credit for the popularizing of the concept of EBP is Sackett and his colleagues (1997) in the book *Evidence-Based Medicine: How to Practice and Teach EBM*. Social worker Leonard Gibbs was also instrumental in our field, and many know him for his 2007 article "Applying Research to Making Life-Affecting Judgments and Decisions." In that article, he drew upon the earlier work of Sackett and colleagues and outlined a process that is very useful for those learning about evidence-based practice. In his article, we learn how to start the first step of the evidence-based practice process by developing a well-built question. Here is a schematic for developing a **well-built question** that could be answerable and could guide a search for EBP literature that would ultimately result in good practice information for their program design.

Specify the Problem/and Client Population	Possible Approach or Solution	Alternative Course of Action	Successful Outcome for Evaluating

FIGURE 1.1 Schematic for a Well-Built Question

Specifying the Problem   Mrs. Simpson presented Sophia and Bill with more of a request than a problem. However, underlying the request is the problem that HIV is a life-threatening issue if not treated and it, as well as STIs, is a public health threat. As Ben Franklin noted, "An ounce of prevention is worth a pound of cure." Investing a little time and effort to try to prevent the problem is both more humane and a better use of taxpayers' money than treating it years later with hospitalization and expensive medications. Mrs. Simpson identified the population as incarcerated females; Bill and Sophia will refine their understanding of the client population in need of the program as they spend more time in the practicum. They might decide to focus on female inmates between the ages of 18 and 45, for instance. Or they might identify the client population as female inmates who had worked as sex workers or had addiction problems within two years of their arrest.

Possible Approach to the Problem   Since the prison holds several hundred women prisoners, it would not be possible to try to educate those most at risk for STI/HIV on an individual, one-on-one basis. Therefore, other modalities must be considered. Could a group modality of some kind work? It would be important to keep the groups relatively small so that there could be a good amount of interaction among participants, possibly role-plays, and avoidance of dry lecturing. What might the literature suggest?

Alternative Approach to the Problem Could educational videos be made and shown to the inmates? Educational brochures handed to them? Sophia and Bill were feeling pretty confident that while these options existed, their instincts told them they should go with a small-group approach. However, looking at the research evidence more in-depth could suggest even other approaches are more effective. Bill and Sophia couldn't be closed-minded, but had to be open to the best practices supported by evidence.

Successful Outcome/Success Measure   Clearly, if the proposed program was able to prevent these women from obtaining any diagnoses of STI or HIV once they are released back into the community, this would be a fantastic accomplishment. However, Bill and Sophia listed a number of questions they had about measuring success. For instance, how do you track the program participants when they are no longer in prison? How do you get them interested in the program and cooperating with the research effort after they leave prison? What kinds of incentives might be needed to encourage participation in the program and cooperation later? How much time should pass before contacting them once they are back in the community? Once they had listed their initial questions, they decided to put these aside for a while. The success/outcome indicator could change, depending on what they discovered when they actually began trying to find prevention programs in the literature.

Steps in an Evidence-Based Practice Process

Step 1 in any EBP process is to formulate, as was suggested above, a question that can be answered—a well-built question. What might an example be of a question that can't be answered? These tend to be philosophical concerns like: What is truth? What is beauty? Other questions that aren't well built tend to be poorly specified. For example: Is hunger increasing? Are people drinking more? Are married couples having fewer problems? A question that is poorly specified is one that can be misinterpreted. To examine just one of these: Does drinking refer to any beverage? Is the concern whether people are drinking enough liquids to keep hydrated and their kidneys healthy? Does it refer only to alcoholic beverages? Does the term *people* include teenagers or just legal-age adults? Is there a geographic focus: Inner city? Rural? People residing in Illinois? It is very easy to develop questions—and a lot more effort is required to formulate one that can contribute to evidence-based practice.

Not all questions can be answered; for those that can be investigated, research seeks to generate information that can be verified by others. "Why is there suffering?" is an example of a question best left to philosophers or theologians. Social scientists in the quantitative tradition are interested in concrete, tangible, objective findings that can be **replicated** (reproduced) by others.

Sometimes, however, it is possible to give a slightly different emphasis to an expansive question like "Why is there suffering?" and make it a researchable question. "How do children with leukemia explain the origin of their illnesses?" is a question that could be investigated. Often, very broad questions can be narrowed by considering specific manifestations of the problem or how one would go about collecting the data.

There is a definite knack to developing a good question. If too few words are used, the question tends to be too large to investigate. "What causes child abuse?" is an example of a research question that needs to be narrowed. There is nothing wrong with wanting to provide answers to such questions, but practically speaking, the research needed to answer them would be well beyond the resources available to most undergraduate or graduate students. As you read about child abuse, you will discover that the role of certain factors has already been demonstrated. It is usually better to ask questions that will allow you to examine a specific theory or perhaps a small part of the problem. A better question might be "Were child abusers abused themselves as children?" or "Do adult perpetrators of child physical abuse tend to be chemically dependent?" Questions that are asked in research studies usually are very specific.

Before reading the answerable (well-built) question that Sophia and Bill fleshed out their first morning, do you want to try writing one before reading any further? Here is what they came up with prior to searching for literature:

For incarcerated women returning to the community, would a psychoeducational program delivered through a group modality in prison be effective in reducing HIV/STI diagnoses at one year post-release?

You may have written a slightly different question or had a different focus. This next question is also answerable (well built):

Will a prison-based psychoeducational program for female inmates with a prior history of drug addiction be successful in reducing future arrests after their release from prison?

Note that the two questions focus on two different outcomes. All of those involved in planning the program will, at some point, have to decide if the prison program will have one true emphasis and outcome indicator or will be broader and address both aspects.

Step 2, searching for evidence on the best approach to the problem, can be a great deal of fun—but also a little intimidating.

Fortunately, the university where Sophia and Bill attend has a wealth of databases available such as *EBSCOhost, ProQuest, PsycINFO, Medline, Web of Science*, and *Social Service Abstracts*. Starting with an electronic database is an efficient way to search for information. A note here about the choice of databases: *PsycINFO* is a comprehensive database and has good coverage of a number of topics that would interest social workers. That makes it a good place to begin searching for just about any topic in the social sciences.

Social Work Abstracts and *Social Service Abstracts* are good sources of articles on topics that are of special interest to social workers—such as adoption and foster care. However, they don't have quite the breadth of some of the other databases. *Medline* also provides broad coverage but specializes in research focusing on a medical-related problem. So, one wouldn't expect it to be as good a source for certain kinds of subjects (e.g., high school dropouts, racial disparities in prison, etc.) as another database.

Don't assume that all databases are the same. Databases vary in terms of the number of relevant hits they produce and the number of journals that are associated with the database. If you don't obtain a respectable number of hits from one database, check a second one. Students often experience two types of problems in searching for literature. One is the use of too many key words in the search box. For instance, typing *high school dropouts prone to incarceration in Texas* might not return any hits. However, using *high school* in one search box and *dropouts* in another will yield many, many more. Using three search boxes with *high school*, *dropouts*, and *prison* will locate some articles to get you started.

Use the category *All text* until you have a feel for the number of articles on your topic in the database. If there is a large number, then use the category *Title* to obtain possibly fewer, but more relevant, articles. If you are still overwhelmed with the number of articles at that point, you might want to add another search box with another key word.

Sometimes, students start looking for literature with terms that are too broad. For instance, searching for *female prisoners* will completely overwhelm you with thousands of hits if you use the *All text* category. To produce a more manageable number, try using the *Title* category. Here are some other strategies:

- Add key words (for example, to *female prisoners* in one box, add *HIV* in another).
- Skim some of the current titles to determine if other key words may be more productive than the ones you are using. For instance, *HIV* produces more literature in association with female inmates than *STI*.
- Limit the search by language, year, or type of publication. With some topics, you may find all that you need in the way of literature by going back only 10 years or so. However, with that strategy, you may miss the older "classic studies," but they likely could still be found in the references of the articles you do read.
- Look for titles and/or abstracts of articles that are themselves reviews of the literature on your topic. A **systematic review** on the topic is a thorough, comprehensive attempt to collect all of the information available to answer a single, well-built question. The focus will be narrow and precise, and the studies will be examined in-depth and critiqued (some will have stronger research designs than others), and then the authors will summarize what the studies point to. They may have the same general findings (for instance, that studies are inconclusive about a particular intervention). Finding a systematic review or a meta-analysis is often a tremendous boost to gaining an understanding about how others have conducted their research and what they have learned about an intervention, program, or problem. (A **meta-analysis** is also a focused collection of studies on a topic and examines only those studies reporting enough *statistical data* that the amount of change from before the study starts to sometime after the intervention was delivered can be determined. The meta-analysis usually tries to conclude that an intervention had a small, medium, or large effect. In other words, it attempts to summarize the effectiveness of the intervention using statistical methods.)

Here are a few examples of the systematic reviews that could be quickly located using the key words *female*, *prisoners*, and *systematic* in the *All text* category:

✓ Tripodi et al. (2011). Effects of Correctional-Based Programs for Female Inmates: A Systematic Review. *Research on Social Work Practice, 21*(1), 15–31.

✓ Kouyoumdjian et al. (2012). A Systematic Review and Meta-Analysis of the Prevalence of Chlamydia, Gonorrhea, and Syphilis in Incarcerated Persons. *International Journal of STD & AIDS, 23*(4), 248–254.

✓ Fazel et al. (2006). Substance Abuse and Dependence in Prisoners: A Systematic Review. *Addiction, 101*(2), 181–191.

If your searching doesn't provide enough literature of the kind you need, here are a few tips:

- Substitute synonyms (for example, *female inmates* instead of *female prisoners*; substitute *women* for *female* and *jail* or *correctional facility* for *prison*). Keep notes on the terms that you use in your search.
- Use the smallest stem of the word possible. More hits will be obtained with *jail* than *jails* and more with *prison* than *prisons* in a title search.
- Go further than the most recent three years (for example, ten years).
- Check your spelling (for example, *incarcerated* and not *incarrcerated*).
- Look in a different database.
- Consult a faculty member or the reference librarian in your college or university library.
- Check out the Cochrane Collaboration (**www.cochrane.org**) for a library of systematic reviews and meta-analyses focusing largely on interventions related to health. Although you may not be able to find information on a particular intervention, the reviews that you do find will be thorough and scholarly. The Campbell Collaboration (**www.campbellcollaboration.org**) is another valuable resource that centers its efforts in the social sciences (social welfare, education, and criminal justice). The Campbell Collaboration also houses prepared systematic reviews and meta-analyses on selected interventions that could be of interest to social workers. Of the two, the Cochrane contains more studies. And you may want to go there to see such examples as "Advocacy interventions to reduce or eliminate violence and promote the physical and psychosocial well-being of women who experience intimate partner abuse" by Rivas, Ramsay, Sadowski, Davidson, Dunne, Eldridge, Hegarty, … & Feder (2015). I think you'll be surprised at how much research still needs to be conducted on topics that will be of interest to you. Both the Cochrane and Campbell collaborations will allow you to quickly assess the evidence available on a topic by reading a summary, or you can choose to read the whole study. While sometimes you may encounter vocabulary that you don't recognize, look up the terms. Reading these reports is a good way to learn how researchers conduct and write about their research.

Step 3, evaluating the evidence, in an EBP process begins when you have found what you consider to be a sufficient number of studies or articles on your topic. If you started looking for information on the Internet, you know that you may find some scholarly articles that have used credible research approaches—and you may find some impressive-looking documents that *give the appearance* of being based on research. So how do you know the difference?

BOX 1.2   WAYS TO EVALUATE INTERNET INFORMATION

- Who is the author? Does he or she have credibility? (Sometimes academic degrees lend respectability, but they may also be purchased from phony universities on the Internet. More important is whether the author has published findings in respectable academic or scholarly journals. Be suspicious of information where the author's name is not given and where contact information such as street and city addresses are missing.)
- What is the author's perspective? (The author's bias may be readily apparent or subtle. Objective research articles usually mention both sides of an argument.)
- Who or what is the publishing source? Is the document associated with a well-known and respectable organization? (If the author is affiliated with a university or widely recognized organization such as the American Cancer Society, then the source may be more credible than if the domain comes from the .com or corporate world where someone is attempting to make money from readers of the website. Generally, information from sites ending in .edu {educational institutions}, those ending in .gov {government}, and .org {nonprofits} tend to be more reputable.)
- What is the supporting documentation? (Internet studies that do not support their claims with legitimate studies listed in a provided reference list are to be avoided. Scholarly writers know it is important to inform their readers about the pertinent studies and literature on the topic that they have identified. The "evidence" being provided should contain sufficient details so you can conclude that real research was actually conducted. Does the author provide sufficient information that you understand how the study was conducted? Who were the **research subjects** or participants in the study? How was "success" or outcomes of the intervention measured? Were statistical procedures used in analyzing the data?)
- How did you find this information? (If you were surfing for information and were directed to see a website from another site that has dubious origins and doubtful claims, don't be surprised if the content of the second website is also untrustworthy. Websites found by using Internet search engines will not necessarily bring you the most reliable information. When the quality of information is important, specialized search engines associated with university libraries {e.g., Medline} will supply scholarly articles that have been reviewed by professionals in the field—a process called **peer review**—that serves as a quality check of good scholarship.) Unlike magazines that are written for public entertainment, professional journals report studies for students, professionals, and scholars. As a rule, articles always contain a reference list and sometimes statistical analysis. You seldom find multicolor advertisements or pictures that are common in magazines.

Faculty often caution students against using unreliable data from websites, self-published sources, and even Wikipedia (although some of the information can be quite good). Most faculty prefer that your information gathering comes from professional journals and not magazines or untrustworthy sources on the Internet.

Even if you find articles in professional journals, be aware that they differ in quality and in their power to inform you about how their results may **generalize**. The goal of scientific studies is to allow for **generalization** of the results. When a sample is drawn from a larger group, then the findings might generalize back to and represent the larger population—depending on how the sample was drawn (e.g., a random selection method was used). However, as a rule you can generalize only back to the specific population of people who are interviewed, observed, or surveyed in your study. So, if you draw an unbiased national sample, then one could speak to the attitudes or preferences of the nation. Drawing an unbiased sample from all the adults in a given state allows one to speak about the knowledge or attitudes of adults residing in that particular state. An unbiased sample from a large city will allow one to talk only about the citizens of that city. For instance, if you had data from a sample of adults living in Las Vegas, Nevada, concerning their attitudes toward prostitution, it would not be responsible to assume that the data were representative of attitudes in other American cities.

Studies that are relatively free of bias are the wheels that allow science to move forward. By allowing us to generalize the findings, they improve our knowledge and guide our practice. Unfortunately, you will come across studies in journals that did not use rigorous research methods and do not allow for their findings to be generalized.

It is possible to think about sorting all the studies available on a given topic in terms of an evidence hierarchy. At the very bottom (least persuasive evidence) would be anecdotal accounts or qualitative studies based on a very small number of participants (e.g., 5–20). (See Figure 1.2.) The next level up would be surveys (for example, of practitioners being asked their opinion about a particular intervention). There are several layers in between the surveys and the very top of the hierarchy.

We will learn more about these levels of evidence as we move through the book and discover, along the way, credible ways to study a problem and the key decisions to be made when planning a study. Sometimes, pragmatic decisions, such as the amount of time employed to collect a sample of respondents, have a direct effect. Not enough time to develop an adequate sample can make it weaker and less likely to generalize. Can you explain why systematic reviews and meta-analyses are at the top of the hierarchy? We'll learn later in Chapter 5 how strong research designs control the threat of other factors explaining away or confusing the principal findings.

As you read over the articles collected from your literature search, you might feel that the articles aren't a good fit for the type of intervention you were hoping to find. If you've tried some of the strategies suggested previously (e.g., using different synonyms, etc.), you may have to broaden the search by thinking "outside the box." For instance, you could hunt for HIV prevention programs that have been developed for male prisoners. While these studies may not be a perfect fit, it may be that many of the components in that program are relevant for women as well. Or you may find that an STI prevention program designed for adolescents judged to be at high risk—perhaps with some modification—could be adopted for the female

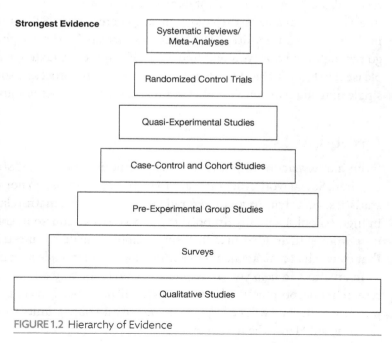

FIGURE 1.2 Hierarchy of Evidence

incarcerated population. Some studies may not be an exact fit because of geographic, ethnic, or age differences, but this is where Sophia and Bill would want to discuss possible alternatives with Mrs. Simpson. Together, the three of them will critically assess the information collected.

Step 4 is a "systematic process that blends current best evidence, client preferences (wherever possible), and clinical expertise resulting in services that are both individualized and empirically sound" (Shlonsky & Gibbs, 2004, p. 137). So, once Sophia and Bill identify possible HIV prevention programs from the literature, read the articles, and evaluate the success of the different programs reported by authors, then it makes sense for Mrs. Simpson to weigh in with her clinical expertise and knowledge of the target population. In this instance, she may or may not wish to involve other knowledgeable social workers in designing the program. Also, she may feel strongly that actual female inmates should provide input and state their preferences regarding any proposed program.

Before finalizing their plans, the interns might wish to contact authors of the studies that they have decided to base their model upon. In the time it takes for a study to be submitted to a journal, reviewed, revised, and then published, one to two years might have passed. In that length of time, the originators of the program may have fine-tuned it or made important changes. Also, the interns might wish to ask if there is a procedure manual or training manual they could acquire. One of the most important things ensuring that a program operates the way it was designed is to train all those involved, and where a manual exists, to provide it to those running the intervention or research. Manuals provide continuity and keep the program from drifting away from its original design when the interns leave at the end of the semester and another set of interns follows them.

When the previous four steps have been completed, then full program planning and development can begin.

Step 5, the last step in an EBP process, is to evaluate and to examine the outcomes for those who have received the program. In this step, the interns (or those who follow them) would want to know if the intervention was successful—did it, in fact, decrease HIV/STI rates once the women prisoners were back in their home communities? Did it decrease arrests for those who struggle with substance abuse? As we go through the book, you will find ideas of ways to evaluate your practice and agency programs. (And please don't lose sight of the fact that this same EBP process also applies when you are working with a single individual or couple and planning treatment. It does not just apply to this one example.)

Anxiety Checks

From many years of teaching research methods, I know that students often wish this course wasn't required. Social work students want to help people—most do not want to have to work with numbers or statistics. I get that. As an undergraduate, I, too, feared math-related topics because of terrible teachers in high school. I actually dropped my first statistics course in college because I was afraid I might fail it—enrolling in another in a different discipline the next semester made all the difference. Fortunately, that course had real, applied problems to solve, and it made a lot more sense to me. I finally got it!

In an effort to help you overcome any worries or concerns you might have about understanding the research concepts presented in this book, I will periodically place an ANXIEY CHECK box in chapters. The purpose of the box will be to provide you with an opportunity to self-assess whether or not you grasped the concept. Here's the first one:

ANXIETY CHECK 1.1

Which statement reflects the correct understanding of the term "generalization?"

 a. Martha said that her 12 clients' experiences at Reach for Recovery in Napa County could well represent and generalize to problem drinkers anywhere in America—they were all between the ages of 18 and 75.
 b. Tyrone argued in a staff meeting that Martha's clients and their treatment success couldn't generalize to problem drinkers anywhere in America because they were the first 12 clients admitted in July and only from Napa County.

[Answers are at the end of the book.]

Research? No Way!

Social work is an exciting career choice. Students select this profession because they like people and want to help them with such problems as domestic abuse, mental illness, alcohol dependence, homelessness, and others. As a consequence, social work students are often eager to learn how to become counselors, therapists, or frontline social workers. Students approach practice-oriented courses with enthusiasm and vigor. All goes well until they learn that they must take a research course (sometimes two courses) as part of the requirements for a degree. Immediately, some students are resentful. "Research!" they say. "Why do I have to take research? I don't want to be a researcher. I want to work with _____" (fill in the blank). Does this sound familiar?

Why, then, must social work students study research? Here are a few of the reasons:

- As we just discussed, social workers must be able to find the best available evidence about interventions, to critically appraise it, and to evaluate the results (Thyer, 2008). As a social worker, you will need to read journal articles and technical reports where research results are presented. You must be able to distinguish good research from bad, and be able to evaluate the strengths and weaknesses of the published research. Research studies can be biased or flawed for a lot of different reasons, and you might not be able to detect these reasons without a basic understanding of research methodology. To make effective use of the research that you encounter as a practitioner, whether it be in social work journals or agency reports, you need to know something about how proper research is conducted.

Like it or not, we are all consumers of research. We hear the results of studies or polls on television and radio, and we read about studies that are reported on the Internet and in newspapers, magazines, and journals. How do you know if these studies are any good? Could you identify a poorly designed study? What criteria would you use? One best-seller that used thousands of questionnaires to support its conclusions has been called the "functional equivalent of malpractice for surveys." Just because something finds its way into print does not mean that it is based on the best methodology or scholarship. Hopefully, as we go further into this text, you will learn to be a skeptical reader—to ask questions of what you read.

Even a little knowledge of research will help you become a more informed consumer of the information you routinely encounter both in print and on the Internet.

Being an *informed consumer* will allow you to evaluate the reported research and enable *you* to make more substantial contributions when you are called on to disseminate knowledge in your everyday practice. Social workers are often required to prepare reports, conduct in-service training, or make workshop presentations. Information you assemble will be shared not only with fellow professionals but also with clients and the community. If you want to be an advocate and recommend policy changes, whether presenting at the local agency level or making a presentation to legislators, you need good data and the ability to interpret it for your audience. As you make greater use of professional journals and databases, you will find that you need an understanding of research to fully comprehend what is being reported.

- Second, social workers are accountable for their interventions. As a professional, you must be able to determine whether the intervention you are using with a client is making any difference. Could you demonstrate that a client is improving? Or, at the very least, could you show that your intervention has not harmed the client? Even if you are not interested in conducting research on a large scale, you owe it to your clients and yourself to be able to evaluate your practice with them.

Accountability is important on another level. Social service agencies vary enormously in size and may employ several to hundreds of social workers. Taxpayers, governmental agencies, and funding sources such as United Way organizations often expect social service agencies to provide data and evaluation research on such issues as client utilization of the agency's services and the effects or outcomes of the services provided. Agencies must show that they are meeting the needs of their target populations, that their clientele feel satisfied with services, and that the agency's operation is productive and efficient.

Suppose you become a program director or manager in a social service organization and the executive director wants you to begin a new program. The director insists that the program must have a good evaluation system built into it. Would you know how to go about evaluating a social service program? Would you recognize a poor evaluation plan if you created it? New programs are sometimes funded with the provision that they demonstrate some impact on the problem. This provision usually means that research in some form or fashion is required. Faced as we are with major social problems and fairly limited amounts of monies that can be applied to these problems, it is incumbent on social workers to create and maintain programs that have the best success rates.

As a new social worker fresh from school, you might be asked to conduct a study to meet some reporting or accreditation requirement. Occasionally, students tell me how surprised they were on their first jobs when they were assigned a research project—especially when it was not even discussed during the initial employment interview. They got the assignment because among the staff, they had most recently completed a research course and therefore should be the most knowledgeable about what to do. Would you be more interested in learning how to design a study if you knew you would be responsible for evaluating a program in your next job?

- Third, two of the nine competencies in the new Educational Policy and Accreditation Standards (EPAS) from the Council of Social Work Education (2015) required of all BSW and MSW programs (and therefore their students) directly speak to the importance of research. Competency 9 states:

Evaluate Practice with Individuals, Families, Groups, Organizations, and Communities. *Social workers understand that evaluation is an ongoing component of the dynamic and interactive process of social work practice with, and on behalf of, diverse individuals, families, groups, organizations and communities. Social workers recognize the importance of evaluating processes and outcomes to advance practice, policy, and service delivery effectiveness. Social workers understand theories of human behavior and the social environment, and critically evaluate and apply this knowledge in evaluating outcomes. Social workers understand qualitative and quantitative methods for evaluating outcomes and practice effectiveness. Social workers:*

- *select and use appropriate methods for evaluation of outcomes;*
- *apply knowledge of human behavior and the social environment, person-in-environment, and other multidisciplinary theoretical frameworks in the evaluation of outcomes;*
- *critically analyze, monitor, and evaluate intervention and program processes and outcomes; and*
- *apply evaluation findings to improve practice effectiveness at the micro, mezzo, and macro levels*

Competency 4 (**Engage in Practice-Informed Research and Research-Informed Practice**) states:

Social workers understand quantitative and qualitative research methods and their respective roles in advancing a science of social work and in evaluating their practice. Social workers know the principles of logic, scientific inquiry, and culturally informed and ethical approaches to building knowledge. Social workers understand that evidence that informs practice derives from multi-disciplinary sources and multiple ways of knowing. They also understand the processes for translating research findings into effective practice. Social workers:

- *use practice experience and theory to inform scientific inquiry and research;*
- *apply critical thinking to engage in analysis of quantitative and qualitative research methods and research findings; and*
- *use and translate research evidence to inform and improve practice, policy, and service delivery.*

- A fourth reason you should make a commitment to learn research skills is because of this language in the National Association of Social Workers' Code of Ethics (2008):

SECTION 5.02

a) *Social workers should monitor and evaluate policies, the implementation of programs, and practice interventions.*

b) *Social workers should promote and facilitate evaluation and research to contribute to the development of knowledge.*

c) *Social workers should critically examine and keep current with emerging knowledge relevant to social work and fully use evaluation and research evidence in their professional practice.*

Selection from 2015 Educational Policy and Accreditation Standards, pp. 8, 9. Copyright © 2015 by Council on Social Work Education.

The Code of Ethics asserts that we have a responsibility for evaluating our practice and programs, as well as building knowledge that will benefit clients. Research improves our practice and allows us to test new innovations.

As professional social workers, we must advocate for our clients by conducting research—not just at the local level, but also at the state and national levels. While it may seem unlikely right now that you would ever be involved in such research, consider for a moment the extent to which most clients are affected not only by state and national policies, but also by a lack of resources. Recently, I learned of an unfortunate situation in another community when a college-age individual wanted help for his substance abuse and attempted to receive detox services on a Saturday night. Although he was motivated to get help at the time, he was informed that the center didn't have an empty bed. What was he supposed to do until one opened up? While a possibly disastrous scenario was adverted that night, I couldn't help but wonder how many times that happens in a week. How many more beds are needed in the community? Is it possible that someone looking at the data on the number of clients turned away from the detox center might then have enough evidence to encourage public officials to either expand the number of beds or find another solution? Can you see the value of having "hard data" to advocate for these and other services?

The profession needs researchers who can show that cuts in social service programs ultimately result in greater tax burdens. Numbers might be scary if you've never liked them, but showing that detox services cost less than ambulance runs and hospitalizations when individuals overdose is certainly data that every social worker should be able to gather, organize, and present. I am convinced that greater funding for social services will come as social workers are better able to demonstrate that adequate levels of social services are cost-effective for reducing or eliminating some of the major social problems facing us today.

- Last but not least, you need to be comfortable with both consuming and conducting research because otherwise you may not be practicing the most effective treatment available. Myers and Thyer (1997) phrased the issue this way a number of years ago:

> *A client sees a clinical social worker about a psychosocial disorder for which there is a treatment that has been demonstrated effective through repeated, well-designed outcome studies. Does the client have the right to receive this validated treatment, or does the social worker have the latitude to provide another, unsupported treatment? (p. 288)*

Most of us would probably agree that clients deserve the best intervention available, not one that is delivered simply because "that's the way I have always treated this problem" or because "this is what I learned 10 years ago in graduate school."

Social workers who do not keep current on the literature and research in their fields are in danger of practicing incompetent social work. Interventions are not equally effective, and newer, improved ones come along from time to time. Social workers must be able to inform clients why, on the basis of empirical studies, one particular treatment is recommended over another.

At the same time, there is still so much that we don't know about what will work with what clients. This is where you come in. As a social worker who can understand as well as conduct research, you will be able to identify those interventions that should be used with specific client groups and those that shouldn't. You have an ethical obligation to do as much. Social work professionals should be consumer advocates for the interventions our clients receive. And how does one advocate for effective programs without the ability to collect and interpret data?

I realize that at this point in your education, evaluating programs and attempting to build knowledge may not interest you, but once you are engaged in practice full time, you may make discoveries—perhaps you will want to report on the effectiveness of some new treatment approach or exciting innovation in your agency. There might be a conference in sunny Miami where you would like to make a presentation, or a journal where you would like to submit your article. In other words, you need competence in research methods to help you achieve your potential as a contributing member of the social work profession. There will be times when even the most thoroughly convinced "I've-always-wanted-to-be-just-a-clinician" wishes that he or she understood a little more about research. By acquiring research skills, you position yourself to reach higher goals—becoming a manager or administrator, by becoming a nationally recognized expert or consultant, by developing copyrighted instruments or interventions that are sold commercially. Who knows, you might even become a faculty member!

Social work educators want their students to be skilled, expert practitioners. Our profession's future depends on you becoming the most competent practitioner possible. Social workers should employ the treatments that have been shown to be clinically relevant because scientific investigations have evaluated them. What we learn or know this year may not be correct at some time in the future. As Mullen, Bellamy, Bledsoe, and Francois (2007) have noted:

> It is widely acknowledged that because of the pace of change all around us, it is not possible to assume that what we learn today will be valid or relevant tomorrow. Gone are the times when social work could assume that it had a manageable and relatively stable knowledge base that could be taught within the limits of a 2-year graduate program. (p. 575)

In choosing interventions, the social worker should ask questions such as "What has been shown to work with this type of problem?" or "What intervention is the most effective with this type of client?" Questions of this type will lead the practitioner to information that has to be assessed in terms of whether it is credible, methodologically sound, from a well-respected source, and convincing in terms of what is known about success and prior interventions with the client group.

ANXIETY CHECK 1.2

Quite a bit of this chapter discussed EBP, and it is important that you understand the logical progression of steps involved. One of the steps listed below doesn't belong. Can you place the others in the correct order?

1. Determining the best intervention based on appraisal of evidence, clinical expertise, etc.
2. Evaluating the intervention.
3. Seeking permission from the National Institute on Drug Abuse.
4. Evaluating the evidence.
5. Forming an answerable question.
6. Searching for evidence.

[Answers at the end of the book.]

Great accountability is expected of today's practitioner. To prepare yourself to be the most conscientious and evidence-based practitioner, you'll need to learn—at a minimum—how to sort the "junk" from the good science so that you can apply the strongest research-supported interventions in your practice. Allow this book to show you how to recognize good and poor data collection methods and research designs. Research *is* a tool that can inform your practice.

Unlike some fields, social work research is applied; it seeks knowledge that will improve the lives of our clients and make this world a little bit better. Research begins when people like you develop questions from real-life situations in agencies and observations of fellow humans and become concerned about the lack of information or answers. If a thorough search of literature does not answer a question, you may have identified a gap in our knowledge base. Whether you take the challenge or not, many opportunities exist for you as a researcher to make important contributions to our field. Social work has no shortage of problems and gaps in our knowledge that need investigation.

If you had the time and the funding to explore one currently unanswered question, what would it be?

Key Terms

evidence-based practice (EBP)	well-built question
generalize; generalization	systematic review
research subjects	meta-analysis
peer review	replicated

SELF-REVIEW
(Answers at the end of the book)

1. List three of the five reasons discussed in this chapter that social work students should study research methods.
2. What is the purpose of the Council on Social Work Education?
   a. accreditation of social work programs
   b. peer training of social work educators
   c. marketing of social work programs
3. T or F. The NASW Code of Ethics requires social workers to monitor and evaluate their practice, their programs, and the policies that shape their interventions.
4. Summarize what "empirically based practice" means.
5. What is the chief characteristic of social work research?
6. What is a well-built question?
7. Is a well-built question required to specify a population associated with the problem?
8. What is a systematic review?

QUESTIONS FOR CLASS DISCUSSION

1. What are your fears about taking a research class?
2. What do you hope to learn from this class?
3. What experiences have you had that might help in this class? Describe any research-related experiences you may have had.
4. What are the problems that might develop when a profession's knowledge base and research lag behind its practice?
5. As a class, make a list of problems and questions that you think need to be researched.
6. Have you ever come across a piece of research you thought was worthless? Why did you have this opinion?
7. Does one have to choose between being a good practitioner and a good researcher?
8. In what ways could research be used to affect a local, state, or national policy that you think needs to be changed?
9. Make a list of reasons that it is important for social workers to engage in empirically based practice.
10. IDEA FOR GROUP PROJECT: Divide the class into groups. Imagine that you have the same assignment given to Sophia and Bill. What specific decisions do you think would have to be made along the way? Refer to steps in the EBP process as necessary and make a list of all the decisions that will have to be made before the program can be implemented and evaluated.
11. *Well-Built Questions*: Alternatively, the group should choose a different problem than the one above and draft not one, but two different well-built questions for the same client population.

RESOURCES AND REFERENCES

Bender, K., Altschul, I., Yoder, J., Parrish, D., & Nickels, S. J. (2014). Training social work graduate students in the Evidence-Based Practice process. *Research on Social Work Practice, 24*(3), 339–348.

Chonody, J. (2015). Addressing ageism in students: A systematic review of the pedagogical intervention literature. *Educational Gerontology, 41*(2), 859–887.

Council on Social Work Education. (2015). *Educational Policy and Accreditation Standards for Baccalaureate and Master's Social Work Programs*. Alexandria, VA.

Epstein, L. (1987). Pedagogy of the perturbed: Teaching research to the reluctants. *Journal of Teaching in Social Work, 1*(1), 71–89.

Gibbs, L. (2007). Applying research to making life-affecting judgments and decisions. *Research on Social Work Practice, 17*(1), 143–150.

McNeece, C. A., & Thyer, B. (2004). Evidence-based practice and social work. *Journal of Evidence-Based Social Work, 1*(1), 7–25.

Mullen, E. J., Bellamy, J. L., Bledsoe, S. E., & Francois, J. J. (2007). Teaching evidence-based practice. *Research on Social Work Practice, 17*(5), 574–582.

Myers, L. L., & Thyer, B. A. (1997). Should social work clients have the right to effective treatment? *Social Work, 42*, 288–298.

National Association of Social Workers. (2008). *Code of ethics*. Washington, DC: Author.

Rivas, C., Ramsay, J., Sadowski, L., Davidson, L. L., Dunne, D., Eldridge, S. ... Feder, G. (2015). Advocacy interventions to reduce or eliminate violence and promote the physical and psychosocial well-being of women who experience intimate partner abuse. *Cochrane Database of Systematic Reviews*, Issue 12, Number CD005043.

Sackett, K. L., Richardson, W. S., Rosenberg, W., & Haynes, R. B. (1997). *Evidence-based medicine: How to practice and teach EBM*. New York, NY: Churchill Livingstone.

Shlonsky, A. & Gibbs, L. (2004). Will the real evidence-based practice please stand up? Teaching the process of evidence-based practice to the helping profession. *Brief Treatment and Crisis Intervention, 4* (2), 137–153.

Thyer, B. (2008). The quest for evidence-based practice? We are all positivists! *Research on Social Work Practice, 18*(4), 339–345.

ASSIGNMENT 1.1

Who Are the Students in This Research Class?

Objective: *To introduce you to each other and to demonstrate, at a beginning level, how patterns and themes exist within a collection of data.*

The Task: Interview two people you don't know from your research class, asking them the following questions. (Your instructor may want to pool all of the responses from class to see if any common elements or themes emerge. Learn the names of those you interview.)

Respondent #1   Respondent #2

1. Have you completed any other research courses? If yes, how many?

2. Name one skill, talent, or life experience you have that could be useful as a researcher.

3. How important would you say it is for social workers to know how to conduct research? (Use a scale from 1 to 10, with 1 equaling *not very important* and 10 equaling *very important*.)

4. Why have you chosen to be a social worker?

5. What is one thing you hope to acquire from this class?

6. What is your favorite food, movie, or song?

ASSIGNMENT 1.2

Evidence-Based Practice and Me

Objective: *To help you apply the EBP in this chapter to a specific problem, population, or intervention.*

Scenario: Imagine that a wealthy philanthropist has agreed to fund your salary for one year, providing that you conduct research about some problem that concerns social workers.

1. What question or problem would you investigate? Why?

2. Develop a well-built question.

3. Where would you start searching for literature?

4. List three facts relating to this problem that you already know. (Or browse an article to get some background on the problem. Mention the source of your information.)

CHAPTER 2

The Research Process Unpacked

Long before evidence-based practice became a popular term, the process for conducting research was called the **scientific method** and was based on the assumption that the natural world is essentially orderly, and that phenomena we observe must have some stimulus or cause. If the laws of nature are not haphazard, then it must follow that there are rules or laws that govern what we observe. It is only when we don't know very much about a phenomenon that there seems to be no discernible laws operating. The more we know about something, the better we can see certain laws or principles in action. Science, then, whether it is in the social sciences or what's referred to as the "bench sciences" (e.g., chemistry, physics, etc.), has as its aim the discovery of factors which might help us to understand, explain, and predict the events and experiences in our world. As researchers create a body of knowledge, this becomes the evidence that social workers and others draw upon for evidence-based practice.

While the steps of the scientific method or research process are similar to those we discussed on EBP in Chapter 1, we will now go more in depth, as these steps are the heart of courses in research methods.

Note that this next section provides an overview of the research process from a **quantitative perspective**—one that relies on numbers and counting things. However, some social work researchers have a **qualitative perspective** or orientation and prefer relying upon words and narratives. These researchers are not locked into the following steps in quite the same way. After discussing the research process steps in the quantitative tradition, we'll then examine the steps from the qualitative perspective.

BOX 2.1 OVERVIEW OF THE RESEARCH PROCESS

Step 1: Observing/experiencing a problem that leads to a question
Step 2: Gathering information about the question. (Does an answer already exist?)
Step 3: A hypothesis (educated guess) is made as to what may be causing or contributing to the problem—or what might resolve it
Step 4: A study is conceptualized
Step 5: The data are collected
Step 6: The data are analyzed and interpreted
Step 7: A report is written

Step 1: Developing a Question

Questions may emerge from a number of different places. Bill and Sophia did not think a lot about the problem of STI/HIV transmission until beginning their internship at the prison. Personal experience with family members, friends, coworkers, and clients can sometimes contribute ideas for investigation.

Questions may emerge from observations of individuals with the problem, discussions with colleagues, or reading the literature pertinent to a certain topic.

Research questions can also stem from wanting to better understand a problem or interest in approaching it from a way different from the "established" way. For instance, almost from the beginning, the conventional interventions for homelessness involved homeless individuals becoming sober before providing them any housing other than emergency shelter for a night. However, that "wisdom" recently has been rejected by vigorous interest in "housing first," where homeless individuals with substance abuse and mental health issues are provided an apartment or other shelter, and little or no attempt is made initially to require that they address their substance abuse, although services are available when they show interest.

Questions can also arise from a story we hear on TV, radio, or read in social media. As I write this, there was a report over the weekend of a three-year-old child who shot himself in the chest and died. Immediately, I had questions racing through my head. What questions might that story raise for you?

At least initially, the question or questions percolating around in your mind might not be of the *well-built* variety that we covered in the last chapter. They could also be broad questions rather than having a specific focus. Broad questions like, "Why do people do drugs?" are often developed when we don't know much about a problem. To narrow the question down a bit so that it may have application to a specific group we are working with, sometimes we bring in other factors (e.g., of the child fatalities occurring last year, how many were associated with a caregiver or parent with substance abuse issues? Or, if we were counselors in substance abuse treatment programs, we might want to know what proportion of substance abusers were reared in homes where a caregiver or parent also had substance abuse issues.)

Without a question of interest, there is no need to start a research process. Bill and Sophia were focused on finding literature to answer the question "What is the best way to educate incarcerated women about STI/HIV so as to prevent them from acquiring it or transmitting it to others?"

Step 2: Gathering Information/Reviewing the Literature

The second step involves reviewing the professional literature to see what is already known about the topic. There are many good reasons for learning as much as possible about your subject before beginning to conduct a study. A careful review of the literature can save a lot of unnecessary work and prevent you from wasting your time studying a problem that has already been thoroughly investigated (e.g., Does smoking cigarettes shorten one's life?)

There are several ways to start a literature review. One of the best ways is to use an electronic data base (e.g., *Medline*, *PsycINFO*, *etc.*) as we discussed in the last chapter. However, sometimes we may know of a journal that specializes in a certain topic and just reviewing its table of contents may be productive. For instance, Sophia discovered that there is a journal called *AIDS Education and Prevention* and another called *AIDS and Behavior*. (For a list of over 60 key social work journals hosted by the website *Information for Practice* (**http://ifp.nyu.edu/**) maintained by Dr. Gary Holden, see **http://ifp.nyu.edu/browse-key-journals**. (By clicking on the link for a specific journal, you can browse the table of contents for the latest issue and back issues. However, you can't access the actual article unless you buy it.)

Bill approached the problem a little differently. He found a relevant article in a different journal and started looking at its references. He made a list of several of them he wanted to read. From there he went to his university library's electronic resources and opened *Web of Science*. From this database, you can enter an article's title or its authors and it will show you all of the articles that have cited the original article you started with.

When the pdf or document is available electronically, it will open those documents for you. Thus, Bill found 37 articles had cited the initial article he started with. While many were not directly relevant, several were.

As Bill looked over the journal articles *Web of Science* had found for him, he realized that he and Sophia should have a discussion about whether there is a particular theoretical approach that should guide the STI/HIV prevention program. For instance, he found one article that talked about an AIDS reduction model and one that talked about a social-cognitive model.

And then he found another and blurted out, "Look, Sophia! Here's an Informational-Motivation-Behavioral Skills (IMB) model."

"Wow," she said. "That sounds interesting—even better than the AIDS reduction model that Mrs. Simpson mentioned at lunch."

Bill nodded, "Yes, but I'd also like to know more about that theory of reasoned action that Dr. Jones mentioned in class yesterday."

The *Web of Science* is a very powerful search engine, and one can conduct searches for key words like *STD* in the title and then add another keyword in another search box (e.g., *IMB*) or *reduction model*. You can also go with a wider search and use the same key words in a "text" search (meaning the key words could appear in the abstract, title, or author's selected key words, for instance). And you can also narrow the search by adding a third box, perhaps *incarcerated* or *prison*.

Bill and Sophia knew that their search should not exclude any theory at this beginning part of their information gathering—it was too early to pick an intervention based on a particular theoretical model. Why do you think discussion about theory is important in choosing an intervention?

BOX 2.2 PROBLEMATIC INTERVENTION IN NEED OF A THEORY

Several years ago, I was leading a weekly field seminar discussion with interns. As was our custom, the students each took about 10 minutes to report the progress of their clients or to share something new they had learned. When it was Marcie's turn, she began describing a client who had been referred for counseling because he had a severe drinking problem and had been told by his physician that he faced significant damage to his physical health if he continued. Each week, the client stated that he "could quit any time he wanted." However, each week he reported no decrease in the amount of alcohol he was consuming.

Because he was a heavy chain smoker, the student seized upon a plan. Knowing that he recognized cigarettes were bad for his health, too, she asked if he could give them up. He said he thought he could. The student then said, "Why don't you show that you could give up alcohol by stopping smoking?" The client agreed to think about it.

The MSW student stopped talking, and I asked, "Where did you get the idea for that approach? Did you talk with your supervisor?" The student admitted that it had just occurred to her during the session. She hadn't discussed it with anyone.

"Well," I said, "nicotine is a very difficult addiction to break. What if the client tries to stop smoking and can't? Have you then convinced him that he can't quit drinking?"

"Oh," she gasped. "I didn't think of that."

Was the student practicing EBP? No, she wasn't. Had she done any real reading to prepare herself for working with alcoholics? Obviously, she hadn't prepared enough. Had she discussed how to work with this particular client with her field instructor? Nope. Would the student have benefited from having a theoretical model that would explain how to work with this type of client? What do you think?

BOX 2.3   HOW THEORY RELATES TO PRACTICE

Theory organizes knowledge and attempts to explain a phenomenon which, if the theory works well, then allows one to make predictions about future actions or behavior. Theories suggest what you might expect in the future and allow you to integrate the facts you already have. A good theory focuses attention, saves effort, and builds on existent knowledge. Theories lead to predictions about the world in which we and our clients live and might be likened to mental maps that suggest avenues or directions. Theories vary considerably in their complexity, their perspective or orientation, and the amount of evidence that can be mustered to support them.

The research you do—or at least the way you go about it—will likely be strongly influenced by your theoretical orientation. If you assume, for example, that addiction is caused by one's genetic inheritance, then the types of questions you'll explore will be vastly different from those you'd employ if your assumption is that people acquire addiction through social learning and acculturation. Your theoretical orientation directs your attention to events that are assumed to be important and allows you to ignore those that are expected to be irrelevant.

A thorough literature review will help you find those theories that are empirically supported and thus applicable as a basis for developing or justifying practice approaches.

Sophia and Bill discovered that while some databases may contain book titles, do not be surprised if most of the sources produced from a computer search are from journals (many of which you may not have known existed). New knowledge in a field is often first introduced or reported in journal articles. Journals tend to be specialized and to allow for precise reporting and discussion of a topic written for a specific audience. Typically, a journal article starts with a question or problem to be investigated, provides a historical overview of the problem, and then explains the current study. At the end of the article, the findings are discussed in terms of implications for professionals. An article may also identify areas where future research should be directed. A careful literature review could produce all of the following for you:

- A nice summary of our knowledge about the problem, program, or topic (including a discussion of other studies)
- A range of theoretical approaches that have been applied
- Examples of interventions or programs, how they have been conceptualized and developed
- Measures for assessing change in clients or participants (e.g., changes in knowledge, attitudes, or behavior)
- Suggestions for how the next set of studies should be tweaked or focused
- Data to compare with your own findings. (Particularly if you are planning an intervention or evaluating one, you will want to know how successful other approaches have been.)

As you become more familiar with the literature relevant to your research question, you will be able to refine your question and might even decide to modify it. You may be delighted to discover that researchers have suggested that the study you are planning is desperately needed. Even if it is not so directly stated, you may find gaps in our knowledge about the problem that interests you. These are fertile areas where you as a social worker can make an important contribution with your research.

The necessity of immersing yourself in the literature cannot be emphasized enough. Research builds on the accumulated efforts of all those laboring to expand our knowledge and correct our misconceptions.

But to make a contribution in the social sciences, we first must be familiar with what is known about the problem. When you read the literature on a topic as a social work researcher, you are reading for a purpose. You are trying to discover:

- What do the majority of the studies conclude?
- What theories have attempted to explain the phenomenon?
- What interventions have been tried?
- What instruments have been used to assess the problem?
- What are the gaps in our knowledge about the problem?
- What suggestions have been made for future research?

As you discover how others have studied the problem, approaches that you hadn't considered may be suggested. In sum, there are many benefits to conducting a thorough review of the literature. Sometimes one gets lucky and finds an article which reviews the article on the topic for you. Here's an example: Wang, D., & Chonody, J. (2013). Social workers' attitudes toward older adults: A review of the literature. *Journal of Social Work Education, 49*(1), 150–172.

Step 3: Forming a Hypothesis

Research starts with a problem or question that needs to be answered. As we discussed previously, these need to be specific questions that can be answered with data. Especially in **exploratory studies** (where not much is known about a phenomenon), research questions are in an early formative state—they don't have to be perfectly worded. As more information is obtained about a topic, the research question can be refined. The question or questions may be restated as a hypothesis. A **hypothesis** is simply a formal version of a hunch or speculation about what the data may reveal. Hypotheses are often derived from a theoretical perspective. A good hypothesis is one that clearly expresses a statement that can be empirically tested about the relationship of two or more variables. (More discussion about types of variables is presented a little later.) Data are gathered to see if they will *support* the hypothesis—hypotheses are either accepted or rejected. (Social scientists don't *prove* hypotheses.)

Hypotheses and research questions are both legitimate starting points for the research process, as long as they are not frivolous or unethical. One's hypothesis can be converted into a research question and vice versa, as seen here:

> *Example of a research question:* Are children without nurturing parents more often incarcerated as adults than children who describe having "close emotional relationships" with their parents?
>
> *Hypothesis 1(a):* Ninth-grade boys without a father or stepfather living in their homes are more likely to commit a felony by age 25 than other ninth-grade boys with a father or stepfather residing in the home.
>
> *Hypothesis 1(b):* Ninth-grade girls without a father or stepfather living in their homes are more likely to commit a felony by age 25 than other ninth-grade girls with a father or stepfather residing in the home.

Note that Hypothesis 1(a) and Hypothesis 1(b) examine the same basic issue but allow the researcher to look for possible differences by gender. Also note that as a researcher, one has a choice of what to measure.

For instance, maybe the researcher thought it would be easier or would result in more reliable data if she didn't ask about close emotional relationships, but about whether or not the father or stepfather lived in the home. Another researcher might attempt to measure the emotional closeness of the father-child relationship.

If you think about Hypotheses 1(a) and 1(b), you probably have an idea about improving them. How might a researcher view these hypotheses? Before reading the next paragraph, take a moment to read them again and give them a healthy critique.

Here are some issues with them that I see: with 1(a), the hypothesis doesn't help us to know how long the father or stepfather has been absent from the home or how long he actually lived in the home. These men could be absent because they are in prison, in the military, or work some distance from home and visit as often as they can, or they could be divorced/separated from the child's mother and not residing in the home at all; also, we don't know anything about the relationship of the child to the father or stepfather. A man can be emotionally cold or impaired and not at all close to the child (or anyone else), but reside in the home. Finally, might it be important to know the age of the child when the father became absent? And the age of the child when the study was being conducted? Maybe you are not done yet—we don't know anything about the mother or whether her child or children are living with her or with another relative, and so forth.

Hypotheses sometimes get refined as the researcher begins thinking about what data to collect and how to collect them when the researcher begins to discuss his or her plans with others and considers how to make the project feasible (not too expensive, not taking too long, etc.) as it is being planned.

Occasionally, **null hypotheses** are used. These state that there is no difference between the groups being compared (for example, adolescent males are no more likely to be incarcerated than adolescent females). Researchers sometimes hope to find sufficient evidence to allow for *rejection* of the null hypothesis. The researcher does not have to believe that there is no difference or no relationship to state a null hypothesis.

> *Example of a null hypothesis:* Female adolescents without a father in the home, but who participate in organized sports, are no more likely to be incarcerated as adults than female adolescents without a father in the home who are not involved in athletics.

When you write hypotheses, aim for precision, and avoid the "you" construction shown in this example:

> *Poor:* The lower the education level, the more likely you are to be unhappy. *Better:* Adults with less than 12 years of education will have lower life satisfaction scores than adults who have completed 12 or more years of education.

Hypotheses, like research questions, may be developed from literature, interactions with colleagues or clients, or theory. Although the term *hypothesis* (from Latin, meaning foundation or groundwork) may seem like a complicated concept to grasp, it is actually very simple. Here is the typical structure for developing a hypothesis:

BOX 2.4   FORMAT FOR WRITING A HYPOTHESIS

_____ decreases/increases or affects _____ _____
(Variable #1)   (Variable #2)   (In what way?)

ANXIETY CHECK 2.1

Using the format shown above, do Hypotheses 1a) and 1b) discussed earlier in this chapter conform to that model?

[Answers found at the end of the book.]

Don't interpret the structure in Box 2.4 too literally. That is, researchers usually write hypotheses without using the specific terms *increases* or *decreases*, as in these examples:

Hypothesis 1c): Men are more likely to be incarcerated than women.

Hypothesis 1d): Incarceration rates for both genders are higher for adults residing in urban areas than for adults residing in rural areas.

BOX 2.5   CHECKLIST FOR EVALUATING HYPOTHESES

- ☐   Does it make a clear statement that suggests what data will be collected? (Poor hypothesis: *Prison inmates will have different feelings about the relationships in their lives.*)
- ☐   Is it specific, not vague? Can you determine who the research subjects will be and how the relationship will be tested? (Poor hypothesis: *Previous accident victims will demonstrate a more conservative approach.*)
- ☐   Does one variable seem to influence or affect another variable? (Poor hypothesis: *There will be a difference in motivation scores and length of time on the job.*)
- ☐   Would a research project testing the hypothesis be realistic and feasible to conduct? (Poor hypothesis: *The amount of verbal abuse that older adults have received in their lifetimes will be proportionate to the self-images they draw while doodling at restaurants waiting for their food to arrive.*)
- ☐   Would an investigation of the hypothesis add important new information to our knowledge base? (Poor hypothesis: *The minutes spent in real, meaningful conversation among first-year college students will be directly related to the minutes spent dreaming the night before.*)

Hypotheses identify connections among key variables. They state a hunch about what might be causing, linked to, or associated with a problem or condition. They can be decided upon ahead of planning the research or may be revised and refined in the planning process.

Step 4: Conceptualizing a Study

Before we can conduct a study to test our hypotheses, we must create a study design. A **research design** is something like a blueprint. It outlines the approach to be used to collect the data. It describes the conditions under which the data will be collected; how the subjects or respondents will be selected; how the variables will be measured; and generally provides information about the who, what, when, where, and how of the research project.

The research design should be carefully thought out to ensure that the information obtained will be the information you need to accept or reject your hypothesis. In developing a research design, ask, "What do I need to know?" and then "How will I go about gathering the information?" The answers to these two questions will guide the development of a research design.

For now, research designs can be classified as fitting one of three broad categories:

1. **Exploratory designs**
2. **Descriptive designs**
3. **Explanatory designs**

As we learned earlier, exploratory research designs are used with topics about which very little information is available. Because exploratory studies are responsive to new concerns or to areas that have not been subjected to intense research, they tend to be more tentative and small scale (e.g., small samples). Their findings are not conclusive or definitive, and, as a consumer of the information resulting from an exploratory design, you may get ideas about ways to improve the study. Generating research questions and hypotheses for additional investigation, in fact, is the main value of exploratory studies in the quantitative tradition.

A **pilot study** is usually a small-scale type of exploratory study. Practitioners might want to try out a new or different intervention on a handful of clients before adopting it agencywide. The participants in the study may have been selected because they were available or easy to access; they might not represent the full range of clients with that problem or served by the agency, but they may serve as a quick gauge of the ability of the intervention to improve their lives. You may wish to look at the example listed below:

✓ Crawley et al. (2013). Needs of the hidden homeless—no longer hidden: A pilot study. *Public Health, 127*, 674–680.

The idea for conducting an exploratory research project might start when you discover something about a client—say, a homeless street teen reports a history of childhood abuse. From there, you might gather data from a few similar clients to see if they fit the same pattern. If they also affirm childhood abuse, you might then want to expand your inquiry and conduct a descriptive study to provide a profile of these clients that allows you to generalize your findings.

Descriptive studies are larger-scale efforts that attempt to characterize a population group (for example, the homeless) in a definitive way. They may aim to provide precise information, for instance, on what proportion of the homeless are single women, women with children, veterans, persons of color, and so on. These studies may be concerned with questions like "How many clients are incapacitated because of mental illness or substance abuse?" An agency may want a descriptive study to understand its client population better, to compare its caseload today with the "typical client" from five years ago, or to make comparisons with client groups in other agencies or other parts of the country. These studies are often concerned with the issue of **representativeness** (the extent to which the smaller sample resembles the larger population).

They may also involve a much smaller group of individuals as in these three examples:

✓ Kropp et al. (2013). Characteristics of Northern Plains American Indians seeking substance abuse treatment in an urban, non-tribal clinic: A descriptive study. *Community Mental Health Journal, 49*(6), 714–721.

✓ Nakase-Richardson et al. (2013). Descriptive characteristics and rehabilitation outcomes in active duty military personnel and veterans with disorders of consciousness with combat- and noncombat-related brain injury. *Archives of Physical Medicine and Rehabilitation, 94*, 1861–1869.

✓ Vigen, M. P., & Woods, S. D. (2011). Serious assaults on prison staff: A descriptive analysis. *Journal of Criminal Justice, 39*, 143–150.

ANXIETY CHECK 2.2

Kay has proposed the hypothesis that high school juniors in the state of Washington are reading fewer books in the summer before their senior year now than they did 10 years ago. If you were her research instructor, would you rate the hypothesis as acceptable or tell her to revise it?

(Answer at the end of the book.)

Explanatory studies are basically experiments in which hypotheses from certain theories are tested, and control or comparison groups are often used. An explanatory study might be conducted, for instance, to investigate whether cognitive behavior therapy is more effective than prescription medicine for persons with anxiety disorders. Hypotheses are usually stated in explanatory studies.

Frequently, the studies we want to conduct as social workers are exploratory. We may read about or attend a workshop on some new treatment approach and want to implement it. However, because we're not entirely sure that it will work with our clients, we realize the importance of initially involving only a small group of clients—and then, if it is effective, expanding the number of clients who would receive it. On other occasions, it makes sense to conduct a small-scale exploratory study to collect some beginning data before committing a lot of resources. If the smaller-scale study provides interesting findings, we may want to seek funding to launch a more thorough descriptive or explanatory study.

Sometimes, it is difficult to know how many subjects are required by a particular type of research design. Although this is an issue we will discuss in more depth later (Chapter 8), for now, the best advice is to plan your study to be roughly comparable to similar studies being reported in the journals you have been reading. Having a small number of subjects is not likely to jeopardize the potential of your manuscript being published if your project explores a topic with little in the way of previous investigation. If, however, you are planning a more elaborate study in an area where a good deal of research exists, then sample size is much more crucial.

Group research designs are discussed in Chapter 5. In that chapter, we'll learn about the importance of designs employing random assignment of subjects and control groups and why the information they produce is so strong. You'll also learn about situations that rob us of the ability to determine if it was our intervention or some other factor that made a difference in the lives of our clients. But first, we have to give a lot of thought to the key variables in our study. The next section will explain the importance of defining our variables well.

Operationalizing Variables

Once a design has been settled upon, researchers must precisely define the concepts to be employed in their studies; this is called developing operational definitions. In everyday conversation, for instance, we easily understand terms like *heavy drinker, frequent drinker*, and *problem drinker* to mean approximately the same thing. However, the way one researcher defines problem drinking for the purposes of a study may be quite different from the way another investigator defines the concept.

One study might define binge drinker as a male who has five or more drinks within two hours; another may identify problem drinkers in terms of the presence of two or more negative consequences (for example, arrests for drunken driving, loss of relationships, trouble at work or school). A third study could focus on the number of times an individual drinks per day or week or on the symptoms normally associated with alcoholism (drinking to the point of memory lapse, drinking before noon). Still another study may ask significant others to rate their loved ones' drinking on a continuum, with numerical values representing low and high levels of the behavior.

So, if you are planning a study of problem drinkers, the way you define the variable called Problem Drinking impacts the participants included or excluded from your study. Just to be clear, a **variable** is a concept that we attempt to measure and it is assumed to have the ability to change. So, if you were working with couples in therapy because of problems with their relationship, you might wish to measure a variable like Marital Satisfaction. On another occasion, you might measure depression levels with individuals in therapy because of a transient situation like the loss of a loved one, relationship, or job—or even with individuals referred because of clinical depression.

To be able to compare and make sense of the data you collect, it is often a good idea to use the operational definitions employed by other researchers. When you use the same methodology, operational definitions, and data-gathering instruments, you are replicating (reproducing) that study for the purpose of comparison with your local clients—and this is often a useful strategy.

Always in a quantitative study, you must *operationally define* your variables so precisely that no one would have any problem understanding exactly what is being measured or observed before you begin to collect data.

Bill asked Sophia the other day if she thought that the prison inmates had good self-esteem. "How could they?" she asked. "Locked up all day, unable to wear street clothes, unable to be with their families or loved ones. I think they feel terrible about themselves."

"Well," said Bill, "maybe they are thinking, 'Okay, I made a mistake, but I won't do it again.' Maybe they are thinking that when they get out they have a chance to start all over again—and they feel good about that."

"Is feeling good about yourself the same as feeling confident about the future?" Mrs. Simpson sat down at the table. "Sorry," she said. "I don't mean to interrupt—I was on my way to the copier and this is so interesting. However you decide, the question will have a direct bearing on what the research can potentially reveal. Right?"

"Can't we just look at an inmate and see that she has good self-esteem?" Bill asked.

"What if you and Sophia don't agree? Would that be a problem?" Mrs. Simpson looked at Bill and then turned to Sophia.

"A major one," said Sophia. "We can't even agree where to go for lunch."

ANXIETY CHECK 2.3

What do you think about looking at a client to determine if she has healthy self-esteem? Would that always give a precise and dependable measure?

[Answers found at the end of the book.]

Imagine you have designed a new intervention for persons with a gambling addiction. It would be easy to claim success if your clients had absolutely no relapses over a five-year period. Unfortunately, most social workers cannot wait that long to conclude that an intervention is effective. We need results quicker than that. What if we were to use a 14- or 30-day follow-up period?

It is entirely possible there would be no relapses if our observation period is narrow enough. But suppose we define successful intervention as meaning no relapses within 60 days? Or should it be 90 days? Within a year? Might we discover that the longer the time frame we observe for relapses, the more will be discovered? Would it be possible to conclude that the intervention was a total success—when it was not—if we observe for too brief a period? What is a reasonable time frame? This is where your knowledge of the subject and of the literature comes in. Other studies will provide benchmarks that can help with operationalizing your variable and deciding upon criteria to measure improvement.

Constructing operational definitions requires us to think conceptually about what we want to measure with our variables. Homelessness is a topic that often needs to be better defined. Anybody can be locked out of a house and have to sleep in a car for a night. That's not homelessness as we usually think about it. What about the 16-year-old adolescent whose stepfather throws him out and who has to live with friends for five or six days? To take another situation, what about the impoverished person who lives in a dilapidated house, but with no running water or electricity? Is that homelessness?

Social workers deal with a lot of intangible concepts. We have to deal with differences in intelligence and motivation, power, social status, and pathology. All abstract concepts must become operationalized if they are to be employed as variables in research projects. But how do we go about that?

Let's start with variables such as gender, race, marital status, and political affiliation, to take a few examples; these tend to be easy for us to operationalize. That's because we can usually think of natural groupings or categories with these variables. For instance,

- Gender: Male or Female
- Race: American Indian or Alaska Native, Asian, Black/African American, Native Hawaiian or Pacific Islander, White

- Marital Status: Never Married, Married, Separated, Divorced, Widowed
- Political Affiliation: Democrat, Independent, Republican

The researcher may wish to fine-tune even categorical variables. For instance, it is possible that someone could identify as Transgender, Multiracial, or Socialist. In a lot of surveys that social workers conduct, categorical variables are often called independent variables. (It might help you to remember this by realizing that Bill's gender is independent of Sophia's gender.)

Independent variables are variables that are either descriptive (like Hispanic/Latino or Not Hispanic/Latino) or those that the researcher can manipulate (like the frequency, modality/type, or length of an intervention). For example, clients could be in Individual or Group Therapy, or Both; they could have appointments once weekly or more or less often. Here's what you need to remember about independent variables—they may influence, affect, or somehow be associated with the situation that you are studying. For example, the number of prior hospitalizations for alcoholism or mental illness might be an important independent variable for predicting homelessness.

It is useful to remember that independent variables generally *precede* the dependent variable in time. If we were investigating how hours of sleep (independent) affect test performance (dependent), the number of hours of sleep the night *before* an exam occurs before the exam itself. Do you think there could be an association between amount of sleep before an exam and test scores?

Amount of Sleep before an exam might be categorized: a) less than 4 hours; b) 5 to 8 hours; or c) 9 hours or more. Or the researcher might decide to have an open-ended question so the respondent could record the exact amount of time that he or she slept. Researchers usually have the discretion to decide how their variables should be measured. In a carefully controlled experiment, a researcher might allow some of the research subjects to have 2 hours of sleep, 4 hours of sleep, and 8 hours of sleep to see which group achieved the highest scores.

Dependent variables are those that result from the independent variable. Think of the independent variable as the stimulus and the dependent variable as the response—what the researcher is attempting to examine, explain, or predict. For instance, a student intern in a health care setting might wonder whether participation in support groups (independent variable) helps cancer survivors live longer than those who don't participate. The dependent variable might be called Longevity or Survivability and could be operationalized as the months or years that the cancer patient lived with the disease. The researcher does not control how long the research participants live (dependent) but could control the independent variable (e.g., whether they get a support group as an intervention, or receive an informational video, or perhaps a recipe book for healthy eating).

Variables are like a potter's clay in that they can be shaped in different ways. Dependent variables in one study may be used as independent variables in another study. For instance, Survivability (the number of years one has lived after a cancer diagnosis) might be used as an independent variable in a new study that looks at level of depression (dependent variable) among persons living with cancer. It is not always easy to determine whether a variable pulled out of a study is independent or dependent without knowing more about the study.

Operationalizing Involves Measurement One of the keys to understanding social science research is the notion that if a thing can be defined, then it can be measured. If we can precisely define concepts such as depression and anxiety, for example, then we can measure how much less a client is depressed or anxious before and after an intervention. Just how anxious is the client? How severe is the depression?

Social workers design or use instruments to measure the extent of such problems. These instruments provide quantifiable (numerical) values for problems like depression so that we can discuss relative levels of depression and talk more precisely about those who are very depressed and those who are somewhat less depressed. Simply stated, **measurement** is the process of quantifying states, traits, attitudes, behaviors, knowledge, or theoretical concepts.

The importance of measurement is revealed in two axioms of treatment formulated by social worker Walt Hudson (1978). The first states: "If you cannot measure the client's problem, it does not exist." The second, a corollary of the first, states: "If you cannot measure the client's problem, you cannot treat it" (p. 65). Clinicians and researchers alike must be able to precisely assess (measure) clients' problems. Without precise measurement, it may be impossible to show that clients have improved as a result of intervention. Researchers often attempt to obtain this precision by using scales and instruments when they operationalize their variables.

A **scale** is a cluster or group of statements or questions (items) that are designed to measure a single concept. Social scientists constantly work on and develop new scales to accurately measure concepts of interest to them. Because investigators may approach a concept in different ways, scales measuring the same concept may vary in length, in the type of item used, and in the response categories available to the subject. For example, it is possible to find a 10-item self-esteem inventory, a 25-item one, and others even longer.

Fortunately, social workers Kevin Corcoran and Joel Fischer (2013) in *Measures for Clinical Practice* have collected hundreds of scales, which they refer to as "rapid assessment instruments," for social workers to use with problems commonly encountered in clinical practice. In other words, you can operationalize most concepts by choosing a scale already in existence. Complete scales—as well as information on the scales' availability, primary reference, scoring, and other essential information—are found in their reference book, which contains many interesting and useful scales to use for research projects and for evaluating one's practice. For illustrative purposes, several examples of scales can be found in Chapter 6 and in the appendixes.

It is likely that sometime in your life you have been asked to complete a questionnaire that used a **Likert response scale** (sometimes referred to as a five-point scale). A Likert scale is a *standard set of response choices* usually in this format:

5	=	Strongly Agree
4	=	Agree
3	=	Undecided
2	=	Disagree
I	=	Strongly Disagree

There is nothing sacred about these particular categories. For instance, you may encounter a scale where clients self-reporting on how much various symptoms bother them might use:

0	=	Not at all
I	=	Slightly
2	=	Somewhat

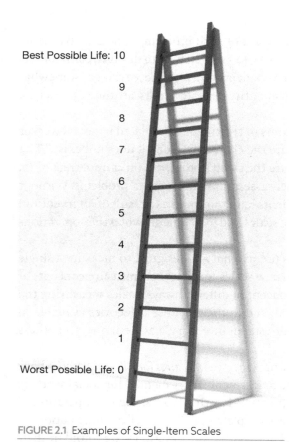

Best Possible Life: 10

9

8

7

6

5

4

3

2

1

Worst Possible Life: 0

FIGURE 2.1 Examples of Single-Item Scales

3 = Very much

4 = Extremely

Likert scales are not limited to only five response choices, and although they usually contain an odd number of categories, they can contain an even number. What characterizes a Likert scale is the attempt to standardize categories. By employing the same descriptors each time and assigning them numerical values, responses to multiple items on a scale can be summed to create a single overall score (e.g., a score on a depression measure).

As a researcher, when you begin to look at scales that have been constructed to measure abstract concepts like marital satisfaction and emotional abuse, you will discover that scales vary enormously in how well they measure the concept they were designed to assess. We'll discuss this topic further in Chapter 6; however, social workers sometimes operationalize a concept in terms of a single-item scale when they don't have more standardized instruments available. This option involves naming the concept and then anchoring it at both ends. (See the three examples in Figure 2.1)

Even children can respond to single-item scales. A colleague once told me that when her children were small and wanted to stay home from school, she would ask, "On a scale from one to ten, how sick are you?" She said they soon learned that saying eight, nine, or ten would probably mean a visit to the doctor. A six or seven would probably result in getting their temperature taken, and maybe a Tylenol or two. If they said "four" or "five," then Mom might give them some special attention or ask what was going on at school (for example, maybe the child had a special report due and was experiencing some butterflies) and they would likely still go to school.

Emotional Abuse
Rate how much you have felt "put down" by your partner in the last week:

None   *Some*   *Quite a Bit*
1   2   3   4   5   6   7   8   9   10

Fear of Injury
Rate the extent to which you fear injury from your partner:

No Fear   *Moderate*   *Extreme Fear*
1   2   3   4   5   6   7   8   9   10

Many social workers first realize that they must operationalize their concepts when they begin to develop a questionnaire for use within their agencies. Here's some advice for when you have to operationalize such common variables as age, education, and income—try to think ahead to the use you will be making of the data. Will you need to report average age and average income? If you use *categories* instead of asking for actual age or income with open-ended questions, then you are precluded from getting averages. So, if you would like to know that the average client was 26.4 years old and earned $17,585 per year, then *don't* capture categorical data, but allow respondents to tell you their actual age and income. And don't set up overlapping response categories like the following examples:

WHAT WAS YOUR FAMILY'S INCOME LAST YEAR?

Under $10,000
Under $25,000
Under $40,000
Under $50,000

WHAT IS YOUR PRESENT AGE?

Adolescent (18 and under)
Young Adult (18 to 30)
Adult (30 to 45)
Middle-Aged Adult (45 to 65)

ANXIETY CHECK 2.4

Do you see any problem with the response choices shown in the two examples in the boxes above?

[Answers are found at the end of the book.]

Any operationalizing or measurement of a concept should meet the test of clarity. It would do little good to create an age category, for instance, of "pre-middle age" or "old-old" if there was confusion as to what ages went into these groupings. A concept like emotional exhaustion has not been operationally well defined if you don't know or can't tell who is and who isn't emotionally exhausted.

Often, behaviors are indicative of the concepts we want to measure. For instance, a racist could attend white supremacist meetings, frequently visit their websites, or tell ethnic jokes. Some students find it helpful to think about operationalizing concepts in terms of behaviors that you could detect from watching a video. A "good" student might be one who studies at his or her desk at least two hours a day; an emotionally neglectful mother might be one who never touches, hugs, or kisses a young child.

You don't have to look for or create a scale to operationally define a concept: it's just that scales tend to allow for more possibilities so that gradations (think of a continuum running from low to high) of the concept can be measured. Does it make sense to try to distinguish persons who lack a few parenting skills from those who have superb parenting skills? We'll talk more about creating good measurement items in Chapters 6 and 7.

Step 5: Collecting the Data

This step is sometimes referred to as conducting the study. Depending on your research design, you will interview people, mail out questionnaires, or begin to procure data that have already been published (such as suicide rates, marriages, divorces, or births by county and year).

This phase of the research process is obviously important. Without data, you will have nothing to analyze or report. If your choice of methodology is poorly planned, it will allow a lot of bias to creep in and influence your findings. A lot rides on your research design and data collection procedures!

Researchers strive to eliminate **bias** from their studies. Bias is an outside contaminant that tends to produce some distortion from what is actually occurring in the data, causing us to make erroneous conclusions. For instance, a client asked to evaluate the agency may fear loss of his or her therapist if their comments are too critical. Clients might tell the researcher that they have no issues or problems with the counseling services when they really have issues. This results in inaccuracy. Bias can be conscious or unconscious, glaring or subtle, and may sneak in and affect the research process at various points. For instance, in developing a questionnaire, you might inadvertently use all masculine pronouns and offend female readers. Offended respondents, if they are angry, may not respond to the questionnaire as you had intended. Complex instructions or questionnaires using sophisticated vocabularies might make responding difficult for those with low levels of education. While we all have values and biases of our own, researchers should strive to keep their studies as free from bias as possible. A biased data collection instrument can give information that does not produce a true picture or representation of the attitudes, knowledge, or behaviors you are investigating.

Bias can also result from the way we select interviewees or respondents. This type of bias commonly happens when not enough thought has been given to the sampling design. For example, suppose you are interested in getting social work majors to evaluate their undergraduate program. Because you are a male and it is convenient for you, you decide to go to a nearby men's dormitory and interview all of the social work majors you can find. Obviously, if you base your study on just the interviews from that one dorm, you will have ignored all female social work majors. Your study, then, will be biased, as female social work students may have different experiences and evaluations of the social work program.

The way, the time of day, and the place you collect your data can have major effects on the outcome of your study. Suppose you go to a neighborhood supermarket to conduct a survey on attitudes about abortion. You choose to do your interviewing on Mondays, Wednesdays, and Fridays for two weeks from 9:00 A.M. to 4:00 P.M. However, a friend tells you that a better day to go is Saturday because everyone is more talkative. When should you collect your data?

If you interview solely on Mondays, Wednesdays, and Fridays from 9:00 A.M. until 3:00 P.M., you may discover that your study underrepresents those persons who are generally at work during those hours. If you choose to interview only on Sunday mornings between 10:00 A.M. and noon, what segment of the population might be underrepresented?

Some research questions or populations of interest determine how the data will be collected. Because homeless persons do not have telephones and may not have an address where mail could be sent, it would be ludicrous to attempt a mail or telephone data collection procedure with this population. Pragmatic considerations such as the amount of time available for conducting the study, the amount of money that can be spent, the availability of subjects, and the ease of locating them all have a direct bearing on the way researchers go about collecting their data and the research design chosen.

Bias is generally minimized as survey samples approach representativeness; that is, as samples more closely resemble the larger population being studied. Typically, we try to draw respondents **randomly** (without bias so that everyone has a chance of being selected) in order to create representative samples and minimize bias. There can be many sources of bias, but in the conduct of research, **objectivity** is the proper and necessary stance. You want your data to be as free from bias as possible.

Studies that are free from bias typically have much greater generalizability than those with overt bias. Generalizability means how well the findings from a specific study fit another situation. Let's say that I think my spaghetti sauce is the greatest in the world. I invite my aunt Bessie over to try it. She agrees that it is the best she has ever tasted. My wife also agrees. Even the kids like it. I then decide to quit my day job in order to sell the sauce across the whole country. Is it reasonable to assume from this small sample of family members that enough of the American public would buy my spaghetti sauce to justify quitting my job and spending all my savings to market it? Probably not—in this instance I would have been guilty of **overgeneralization**. In other words, I would be assuming too much and going beyond what the data would support.

As a rule, you can generalize only to the specific universe of people who are interviewed, observed, or surveyed in your study. If you draw an unbiased *national* sample, then you can speak to the attitudes or preferences of the nation. If you draw an unbiased sample from all the adults in a given *state*, then you can speak about the knowledge or attitudes of adults residing in that particular state. An unbiased sample from a large *city* will allow you to speak only about the citizens of that city. For instance, if you had data from a sample of adults living in Las Vegas, Nevada, concerning their attitudes toward prostitution, it would not be responsible to assume that the data were representative of attitudes in other American cities.

Studies that are relatively free of bias are the wheels that allow science to move forward. By allowing us to generalize our findings, they improve our knowledge and guide our practice. And while the goal of most researchers is to have a bias-free study, in reality many (if not most) studies often have some possible bias. Researchers identify these in the discussion section of the article as limitations—these can be shortcomings, flaws, or ways the data collection method was unexpectedly compromised.

I once attended a conference that brought together researchers and chronically mentally ill consumers of services who had been studied for four years as part of a special project that provided them with peer support and other measures to keep them from being rehospitalized. The principal investigator, armed with charts and transparencies, began explaining that the battery of eight different psychological tests administered before and after the project began showed no significant changes. He stated he was a little perplexed by the clients' lack of improvement. There were a couple of snickers from the audience, and after a few minutes, one of the consumers revealed a possible reason the psychological tests hadn't found any changes. He said that participants had been afraid that if they answered honestly, they could ultimately lose their disability checks! So, they responded in a way suggesting that none of their symptoms had improved.

While the investigators had gone to great lengths to protect their study from known sources of bias by such procedures as random assignment of consumers to the different intervention groups and sensitive instruments were used to measure symptoms, some of the subjects, acting in their own self-interest, appeared to have biased the findings on their own. The researchers had not prepared for this turn of events. They knew that the information they were collecting from individuals in the study would not be shared with the government and disability checks would not be affected. They may even have explained this to their subjects. However, to individuals who had much less education and were not informed about what researchers actually do with their data, integrity of the research was less important than preserving the few resources available to them.

Keep this story in mind as you plan your research projects. At each stage of the research process, consider how bias might creep into your study and what you could do to minimize it. If you anticipate problems, you may wish to strengthen your design or change the way you collect your data or operationalize your dependent variables.

Step 6: Analyzing and Interpreting the Data

Once you have finished collecting the data, you are then ready to analyze it. One of the purposes of analysis is to express the data in a way that is mentally digestible. It may be easy to present detailed observations or responses from three or four individuals, but when you have more than five responses, full descriptions become cumbersome. Further, it is awkward, if not impossible, to display information from a large number of persons without summarizing the data in some fashion.

Why summarize the data? Let's look at the following statements. Which do you find easier to understand?

1. The ages of respondents in Group A were: 22, 24, 25, 22, 23, 24, 22, 23, and 24.
2. The average age of respondents in Group A was 23 years.

Fundamentally, with analysis, we try to condense information in order to better comprehend the data we have gathered. Your hypothesis may suggest ways that you can summarize, categorize, or organize your data. For instance, if your hypothesis is that women voters are more supportive than men of tax policies that directly benefit persons with low income, your data naturally suggest two divisions: male and female voters. Your analysis would compare and contrast the voting sentiments of males and females on specific election issues.

Analysis is a logical process that begins with looking at the **raw data**—the responses or data before it is processed or transformed. For example, you may want to determine how many persons of each sex, race, or age grouping completed your questionnaires. Most likely, you will then want to order or arrange your data in some fashion. If you looked at several local or state elections in different years, you might array the data by year of the election. You may begin to notice a trend, for example, of women being more supportive of social service issues, or you may identify patterns or directions that have not been suggested in the literature.

Interpreting the data is made easier by comparing your findings with those of other studies. Perhaps your respondents are more knowledgeable than those in a study that you found during the literature search. To switch examples, published program evaluations might provide useful benchmarks for comparing the success of your local agency's program.

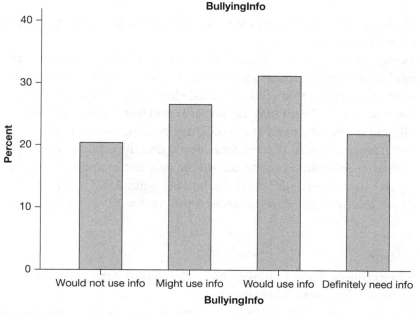

FIGURE 2.2 Example of a Bar Chart

Occasionally, research findings are portrayed as pie or bar charts (see Figure 2.2 and Figure 2.3) or even maps shaded to indicate high or low densities of one variable or another. These graphic representations can be useful for helping others understand the results of your study. However, statistical methods may also be needed to determine if there is a significant difference between two or more groups. Statistics aid in the interpretation of data. With the software available, the computation of statistical tests has become quite easy.

Chapter 13 highlights most of the statistics you'll need to know to begin to analyze your data. That chapter will present a quick overview of descriptive statistics (e.g., measures of central tendency like mean and median) and inferential statistics (e.g., t-tests and one-way analysis of variance). **Descriptive statistics** help us understand how much our variables vary (like the range of years between the oldest and youngest participants). **Inferential statistics** are used to test hypotheses about differences between groups and aid us in understanding the probabilities of

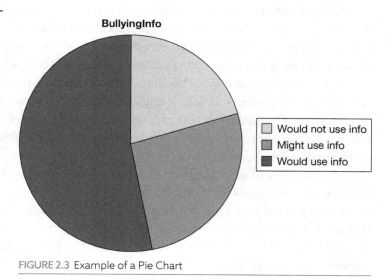

FIGURE 2.3 Example of a Pie Chart

obtaining our results by chance. Graphs and charts are descriptive in nature and help readers quickly digest some fact or trend in the data.

Sophia was showing Bill the results of a small study she conducted in an elementary school last year. She asked two classes of sixth graders about whether they wanted information to counter bullying. The four response categories that students could choose were: *Definitely Need the Information*, *Would Use the Information*, *Might Use the Information*, or *Would Not Use the Information*. The bar chart in Figure 2.2 visually shows that the percent of students choosing each category was pretty similar. However, two of the categories suggest that students would find the information helpful. Sophia then combined *Definitely Need the Information* and *Would Use the Information* and produced a pie chart for the teachers and principal to help them understand the data more quickly. This can be seen in Figure 2.3. These examples show that one can begin to understand data without being all that mired down in statistics.

Step 7: Writing the Report

Once the data have been collected and analyzed, the final step is preparing your findings in such a way that they can be understood by others. There may be times when a memorandum to your supervisor or director summarizing the results of a study will be adequate. If you received funding for the research, you likely will be required to write a report of your findings. If what you found was especially interesting, you may want to submit your findings to a professional journal. Journals, even those in different fields, tend to be organized in the same basic format as research reports.

The first part of a research report, the **Introduction**, puts the research question or hypothesis in context (a description of the extent or severity of the problem, the length of time it has been a problem, what is generally known or believed about the problem) and reviews the important studies found in the literature.

The next section, **Methods**, is an explanation of the research methodology—how the data were collected; which variables were included and how they were operationalized; who the subjects were, their characteristics, and how they were recruited. Enough information should be presented so that others can follow what you did and replicate the study.

The third section, **Results**, presents what was actually learned from the study. Tables and graphs may be employed to visually demonstrate differences and to help with comparisons. Findings from statistical tests are often reported. Qualitative researchers may use tables or graphs but seldom report statistical results. Instead, qualitative reports will be characterized by thick, descriptive detail and actual quotations from those they've talked with that illuminate or characterize the participants in their studies. (More on the differences between qualitative and quantitative research a bit later in this chapter.)

Finally, the **Discussion** section addresses the implications of your findings for other social workers (or other audience), speculates why those particular results were obtained, and suggests ways future research on the topic might be conducted.

It almost goes without saying that many fine research reports are filed away or relegated to dusty shelves because the social work investigators failed to exert a little extra effort and prepare the report for publication in a journal or as a paper for a professional symposium. However, I hope that as we move through this text you will gain knowledge and ability so that you might someday submit to a professional journal or conference. The last chapter of this textbook, Chapter 14, focuses on developing research proposals, reports, and other professional writing.

A Qualitative Approach

Thus far in the book, the research process has been presented from a quantitative orientation—one that relies upon numbers and values the counting of things. Now it is time to view the same process from the perspective of a qualitatively oriented researcher.

Step 1: Posing a Question

Qualitative researchers tend to explore questions about lifestyle or membership in little-known groups or subgroups. For instance, they may want to interview refugees from Sudan's Darfur region to learn what conditions were like in the refugee camps. Or the qualitative researchers may be interested in documenting the atrocities that occurred and forced people to leave their homes. If we change locations, a qualitative researcher may want to know what it is like to be a member of a gang in Los Angles, how prisoners with long-term sentences adjust to life behind bars, what discrimination mothers with special-needs children experience, what it's like to live with a heart transplant, or with a partner diagnosed with dementia. Qualitative researchers are often said to be interested in the stories and experiences of living. Unlike quantitative researchers, qualitative researchers have little interest in counting or computing statistics.

In qualitative research, the first step involves identifying a topic, a problem, a phenomenon, or a group of people of interest. Generally, an initial question or small set of questions may serve as the core or catalyst. The qualitative investigator may start with several questions that may give rise to other (often unplanned) questions during an interview. In contrast, the quantitative researcher usually has a well-defined set of questions or a prepared standardized instrument and typically does not deviate from these.

Qualitative interviewers tend to ask broad, open-ended questions like "What is the hardest thing about living in a refugee camp?" or "How did you maintain your mental health in a refugee camp? What strategies do you employ?" These questions produce lots of narrative and don't lend themselves to precise measurement (e.g., average scores on the Beck Depression Inventory) that could be analyzed using statistical procedures.

Step 2: Gathering Information/Reviewing the Literature

While the quantitative researcher would normally never begin a research project without becoming very familiar with the relevant body of literature, the qualitative researcher is less constrained. In qualitative research, there is no requirement that a literature review come before data collection. Some qualitative researchers consult the literature after they have collected their data so that previous studies don't "cloud" or influence the new study with the possible misconceptions or erroneous conclusions of others. Agar (1980) notes that a thorough literature review "introduced a lot of unnecessary noise into my mind as I tried to learn about being a heroin addict from 'patients' in the institution" (p. 25). Qualitative researchers try to empty their minds of preconceptions and prejudices—to become open to alternative ways of thinking about and viewing the world.

Instead of attempting to read journal articles and books to become more informed about the topic of the proposed research, the qualitative researcher may become more familiar with the topic by talking with others who have worked with the group of interest or who are knowledgeable about them. They also could decide to dip into the literature and to read the quantitatively researched reports skeptically, looking for questions that weren't answered or explored well. Similarly, qualitative researchers may be guided by some underlying theory (for example, black feminist theory), but, unlike quantitatively oriented researchers, they are not required or as likely to test aspects of a given theory. That may come later, as a qualitative study could precede a larger quantitative study. Typically, qualitative studies involve many *fewer* participants than quantitative studies.

Step 3: Forming a Hypothesis

Qualitative researchers often do not state hypotheses ahead of time, and their research questions are not as specific or as narrowly focused as those of quantitative researchers. While qualitative researchers may have hypotheses in the back of their minds, these hypotheses are not always stated or prominent. For example, the qualitative researcher may suspect that armed militias were purposely conducting genocide rather than just battling over disputed territory. Interviews with refugees could confirm that assumption. Qualitative researchers can have hypotheses, but they tend to be more informal, sometimes emerging from the study rather than coming at the beginning of one's own data collection. The qualitative study may generate hypotheses for a quantitative study.

Step 4: Designing a Study

Qualitative researchers tend to rely heavily on personal interviews and participant observation. They tend to not have a great deal of concern about the number of respondents and obtaining a representative sample and typically do not use the group research designs with the random assignment and pre- and posttesting that will be explained further in Chapter 5. It is not that qualitative researchers are forbidden from using these procedures; it is that as a rule, they aren't interested in the same kinds of questions that their quantitative counterparts want to explore.

How research participants are recruited is an issue that both qualitative and quantitative researchers have to explain. Similarly, both types of researchers are concerned with informing participants about their rights as research subjects and receiving the participants' consent. (There will be more about this in Chapter 3 when we discuss ethical research practices.)

The qualitative researcher may choose to be an observer, to be a participant-observer, or to read letters, journals, diaries, or other source material. For instance, if the researcher were investigating life in a homeless shelter, the choice of strategy as a data collector could involve several options as these: (1) securing permission to *observe* the homeless individuals as they come into the shelter and listening to their conversations—say, at meals; (2) securing permission to *interview* residents residing in the shelter; (3) deciding to give the appearance of being homeless to request services there and obtain firsthand *experience* about the shelter; or 4) reading letters that homeless individuals have written or received. Or the qualitative researcher might volunteer to work in the shelter or even obtain employment there— providing a legitimate role for interacting with the residents. If the researcher were exceptionally brave, he or she might spend several weeks out on the streets and sleeping in shelters to get a real feel for the problems and life of the homeless. Of course, the ethical researcher will want to have his or her project approved by the relevant IRB prior to beginning the qualitative or quantitative study.

Operationalizing

Instead of operationalizing dependent and independent variables and trying to find instruments that would allow for precise measurement of these variables, the qualitative researcher would likely go into detail specifying the site where the data collection will take place. The site can consist of a particular geographic location (e.g., the place where a street gang gathers) or a facility (e.g., a hospital emergency room or homeless shelter). Often, the site is described in narrative form in terms of its history or significance and the participants or residents found in that place. These **informants** are the inside "experts" on the culture or group who share their everyday experiences and interpret events for the qualitative researcher. Sometimes, it is necessary to build a rapport and long-term relationships with insiders before meaningful data collection can begin. Could a qualitative researcher use a standardized instrument if he or she wanted to? The answer is yes, of course. However, the use of paper-and-pencil data collection instruments (as discussed later in Chapter 6) is much more characteristic of the quantitative researcher than the qualitative one.

Step 5: Collecting the Data

Data collection involves virtually everything the qualitative researcher sees, hears, or smells—information from all the senses can be recorded to describe informants, location, etc. The interviews that are conducted can be structured, but more commonly they are not and could occur on the street or wherever the informants gather or reside. The answers received to a question might lead to an entirely different set of questions than originally planned as the qualitative researcher attempts to learn about a particular lifestyle or set of experiences. The research processes of qualitative researchers have much more fluidity than those of quantitative researchers.

One important issue for qualitative researchers is whether the interviews can or should be recorded. As you can imagine, sometimes the informants might be uncomfortable or extremely suspicious of the qualitative researcher's motives in wanting to record conversations—particularly if these informants are engaged in illegal activities. Unlike the quantitative researcher who usually obtains written responses to questionnaires that could be completed anonymously, the qualitative researcher herself is most often the data collection instrument and usually meets the informants face to face. Names are often exchanged. The qualitative researcher may take notes (called **field notes**) in order to remember discussions. Recorded interviews are usually prepared as written transcriptions, and these serve, too, as the data to be analyzed.

Qualitative researchers do not expend much energy worrying about representativeness of the sample; sample size also is not an issue. The quantitative researcher is often looking for statistical significance; she wants to have confidence in the numbers produced. The quantitative researcher relies on counting, measuring, and analyzing numbers. Unlike the quantitative researchers' focus on numbers, qualitative researchers desire to explore the detail, richness, and depth of the human experience with the activities and words used by their informants. They want to know the answers to questions like "What would it be like to live as a homeless person?" "To be a social worker assigned to a psychiatric emergency room?" "To be an undocumented immigrant trying to find employment?" The qualitative researcher seeks to understand social relationships and patterns of interaction. Many times, it is the conversations and the explanations provided by the participants or informants that matter most.

For the qualitative researcher, generalizability comes from the trustworthiness of the informants and the thick, descriptive detail that is provided. **Triangulation** (collecting information using multiple techniques or from a variety of sources) is also a way to ensure that the findings are credible and accurate and that they have validity. There are other ways that qualitative investigators attempt to eliminate bias and improve generalizability in their studies; these will be discussed in Chapter 6.

Step 6: Analyzing and Interpreting the Data

In some ways, the qualitative researcher analyzes her data as it is being collected. The qualitative researcher looks for themes or patterns, transcribing interviews and reading field notes to look for categories, themes, or topics that allow for grouping and organizing the information. For instance, if you had conducted interviews with street gang members, you might logically begin to group together relevant parts of their conversations on such topics as their views about the police, guns, drugs, family, friendships, and school. The qualitative researcher might also be seeking to learn their **norms of behavior**—unwritten rules of conduct that govern the gang members. The qualitative researcher is never really sure what the interviews or observations might turn up, and so the data being analyzed usually are not the type that would allow for statistical analysis. When there is a certain redundancy of information, when the researcher feels that no new information is likely to be forthcoming, then she will be ready to stop data collection. Computer software exists to help the researcher organize and analyze the text of interviews, recorded conversations, or documents, although themes and patterns can be identified without the use of software. There will be more on qualitative analysis in Chapter 11.

Step 7: Writing the Report

Qualitative research is generally reported in a much more narrative style than quantitative research. The reports usually do not contain statistics or averages—very few numbers are involved in qualitative research reports. Instead, they read more like an in-depth journalistic account, such as you might find in a newspaper. Many details describing the participants or their world will be present, as will many of their quotations. Unlike the tradition of quantitative research, the qualitative researcher may use a lot of "I" language, as in this brief sample from a student's account:

> My first night in the homeless shelter was the worst. Besides the overpowering body odor from those lying beside me on the floor, someone stole my shoes after I lapsed into a light sleep around 2:00 A.M. That's why most of the men used their shoes for pillows—to keep others from taking them.

Research Process	Problem-Solving Process
Starts with a problem, question or hypothesis	Starts with a client's problem
Review of the literature	Social worker takes client's history, identifies strengths, resources, networks
Conceptualization of a research plan; operationalizing key variables	Developing a treatment plan and negotiating a contract with client with a specific aim
Data collection for study	Begin client intervention
Data analysis	Evaluation of client progress
Final Report	Process recording; case closed?

FIGURE 2.4 Comparison of the Research Process and A Social Worker's Problem-Solving Process

Social Work Research and Practice

While it is often the case that we think of social work practice and research as completely separate and distinct, they both share a logical problem-solving process. They both, for instance, start with a focus on a problem, proceed through some review of its extent and history, develop a plan for addressing it, implement the plan, and then evaluate the research process. In Figure 2.4, you can see for yourself the similarities between the research process and the task-centered or problem-solving process used by social workers.

Even the third step, which might seem the strangest to you—conceptualizing and operationalizing—is part and parcel of what social workers must do in everyday practice. A young man and his wife came into a mental health center after a physician couldn't find anything wrong with him. However, the young man was unable to articulate any specific concern—just vague issues that didn't seem to have any real substance. His social worker's challenge was to identify those times when the patient felt most troubled and hope that the precipitating event could be pinpointed. This is a form of operationalizing that happens a lot in counseling, as the counselor may have to help the client recognize and associate specific feelings with what is going on at the time. Perhaps the next example is a better one. I was once assigned a client whose presenting problem was that her husband was a volunteer firefighter. Whenever there was a fire alarm in the evening, he never came back home. Usually, the next morning he arrived back at breakfast time and acted as if everything was fine. No explanation was ever offered. The wife didn't know what to think about the situation, but she never quizzed him about it. What would you be feeling if this happened every time there was a fire? Do you think she needed to become a little more assertive? To let him know how his actions made her feel? And wouldn't you like to know how to evaluate their progress in treatment?

If you look for areas of overlap between research and practice, you surely will find them—because they use the same general approach. The research process is no more complicated than the problem-solving model you will use as a social worker. It is not an artificial contrivance designed to make life difficult, but an orderly and logical process that can become almost second nature to you.

Key Terms

scientific method	pilot study
quantitative	variable
qualitative	field notes
hypothesis	objectivity
null hypotheses	research design
dependent variable	exploratory study
descriptive study	norms of behavior
operational definitions	explanatory study
representativeness	descriptive statistics
independent variables	inferential statistics
measurement	Introduction section
scale	triangulation
Likert response scale	overgeneralization
bias	random
raw data	Methods section
Results section	Discussion section
informants	

SELF-REVIEW

(Answers at the end of the book.)

1. List the steps in the research process.
2. T or F. The following is a null hypothesis: Math majors do not have higher grade point averages than chemistry majors.
3. In the following hypothesis, what is the dependent variable? "Men arrested for assault and battery are more impulsive than men arrested for public intoxication."
4. What is the major characteristic of descriptive studies?
5. Operationally define "good student" using different criteria than the example provided in the chapter.
6. In a study of men arrested for assault and battery, what would be some logical independent variables that would describe this group?
7. A scale is designed to measure a single _____.
8. T or F. A true/false response set on a questionnaire is an example of a Likert scale.
9. Researchers strive to eliminate which of the following from their studies?

    a. theories
    b. dependent variables
    c. bias
    d. representativeness

10. T or F. Betsy interviewed 10 students from her research methods class about the president's job performance. As a result of this study, she thinks she can speak to what most Americans think about the topic. This is a case of overgeneralizing.
11. Identify which of the following are good and which are poor hypotheses; state a reason for each of your answers.

    a. Altruism varies in different groups of people.
    b. In terms of values, there is no comparison between MSW and BSW students.
    c. High levels of gun ownership are associated with high levels of homicide in this country.
    d. Fatalistic attitudes about the benefit of treating cancer affect survivability rates.

12. T or F. Qualitative researchers demand hypotheses of each other.
13. Briefly explain the role that a literature review would have for the qualitative researcher.
14. T or F. Qualitative researchers are extremely concerned about sample size in their studies.
15. T or F. The quantitative researcher is more concerned with operationalizing than the qualitative researcher.
16. Which group of researchers (qualitative or quantitative) is more likely to use unstructured personal interviews?
17. Which group of researchers is more likely to use statistical analysis?
18. Which type of researcher is more likely to write a report that reads like a lengthy newspaper story?
19. Cleo, a recent graduate, wants to assess the depression in the newly admitted ambulatory residents of his nursing home. What is the dependent variable?

QUESTIONS FOR CLASS DISCUSSION

1. Practice developing hypotheses and research questions on the following list of topics:

    a. alcoholism
    b. effective psychotherapy
    c. fear of open spaces
    d. depression
    e. social drinkers
    f. racist attitudes
    g. exercise addicts

2. Take a hypothesis or research question from Question 1 above and convert it into a null hypothesis.

3. Identify as many theories used by social work practitioners as you can.

4. Identify the dependent variables in the following studies:

    a. Alcoholism in Young Adults: The Role of Parents' Drinking Behavior
    b. Repeat Pregnancies Among Unmarried Teen Parents
    c. Increasing Child Support Payments with Two New Interventions
    d. Do All-Nighters Pay Off? An Examination of Test Scores and Cram-Studying Techniques in First-Year College Students
    e. Weight Gain in a Sample of Anorexics Receiving Cognitive Therapy

5. Operationally define a "bad marriage" so that a clinical social worker could locate couples who might benefit from a new 12-week intervention designed to help those with troubled marriages.

6. Operationally define each of the following:

    a. a humorous television program
    b. an educational television program
    c. an offensive television program

7. What do you like about how a qualitative researcher might go about conducting a study?

8. Brainstorm examples of how bias could affect a study.

9. Look around the classroom. In how many different ways do your classmates vary? Make a list of as many different independent variables as may be represented by the diversity of characteristics found among your classmates.

10. Discuss the similarities that you see between a research process and the kind of work you would like to do as a practitioner of social work.

11. Make a side-by-side comparison of the differences between qualitative and quantitative research.

RESOURCES AND REFERENCES

Agar, M. (1980). *The professional stranger: An informal introduction to ethnography.* New York, NY: Academic Press.

Corcoran, K., & Fischer, J. (2013). *Measures for clinical practice* (2nd ed.). New York, NY: Free Press.

Crawley, J., Kane, D., Atkinson-Plato, L., Hamilton, M., Dobson, K., & Watson, J. (2013). Needs of the hidden homeless—no longer hidden: A pilot study.

Hudson, W. W. (1978). Notes for practice: First axioms of treatment. *Social Work, 23*(1), 65–66.

Pockett, R., Dzidowska, M., Hobbs, K. (2015). Social work intervention research with adult cancer patients: A literature review and reflection on knowledge-building for practice. *Social Work in Health Care, 54*, 582–614.

Credit

ASSIGNMENT 2.1

Developing Hypotheses and Research Questions

Objective: *To develop competency in recognizing and writing good hypotheses and research questions.*

Once you have a topic in mind that you want to explore, an early step in the research process is to state a formal hypothesis or research question. It cannot be vague or unclear, but must tell the reader precisely what you would like to investigate. In the space provided here, take an idea and state it so that it would be capable of guiding a research project.

My hypothesis is:

The dependent variable in the hypothesis is:

The dependent variable would be operationally defined as:

One independent variable that I would use to understand the dependent variable would be:

ASSIGNMENT 2.2

Conducting a Literature Review

Objective: *To acquire experience in searching for relevant professional literature.*

Go into one of the databases that specializes in professional journal articles: PsycINFO, Social Work Abstracts, Medline, and so on. Look for five articles that would help you with your hypothesis in Assignment 2.1. Look for such things as theories that attempt to explain why the social problem exists, gaps in our knowledge about the problem, approaches that have been used to study the problem, or results of interventions that have been tried. You may have to skim or read more than five articles to find useful ones for your area of interest.

1. What is the topic on which you want to find literature?

2. What key word(s) will you use? _____ (the initial term)
    List all other key words you will use:

3. *On another sheet of paper* that you will attach to this one, list the full citations of the articles that you found. Use APA style (author, year, title of article, title of journal, etc.). In the space below, write a brief summary that explains what each article contributes to *your* knowledge about a topic you might want to conduct someday.

Article 1:

Article 2:

Article 3:

Article 4:

Article 5:

4. Which database(s) did you use in your literature search?

ASSIGNMENT 2.3

Impressions from Conducting Literature Searches

Objective: *To help you learn about differences in databases and search engines; to allow the instructor opportunity to address difficulties and problems in locating pertinent literature.*

1. What was the most important thing you learned from conducting your literature search in Assignment 2.2?

2. What did you find frustrating?

3. How was searching for professional literature different from going into a search engine such as Google?

4. Did you discover it was necessary to narrow your research topic? How did you do this?

5. Did you see any patterns or themes in the literature? What were they?

6. What journals tend to publish the articles most relevant to your topic?

ASSIGNMENT 2.4

Reading a Professional Journal Article

Objective: *To acquire experience in reading and using professional journal articles.*

Evaluate one of the journal articles that you found in your literature search, doing it along the following lines. (*Note:* Your instructor may want you to attach a photocopy of your article to this page.)

Give the full citation of the article.

1. Does the article state a research question or hypothesis? What is it?

2. Is there an obvious dependent variable? How is it operationalized?

3. Does the article mention at least one theory? Which one(s)?

4. In your opinion, is there a solid literature review? How many references are there?

5. Does it describe a research design? What is the research design?

6. Are statistical procedures used to analyze the data? What procedures were used?

CHAPTER 3

Ethical Thinking and Research

BEFORE GOING MUCH further in learning how to conduct research, we must have a good understanding about what does and does not constitute ethical research practice. Without this foundation, researchers run the risk of unintentionally harming their research subjects, being embarrassed, or even ruining their reputations and generating public disapproval for the agencies that employ them. While most social workers would never do anything that they knew was clearly unethical, problems can and do arise on occasion. This chapter will provide you with essential information that should help you avoid ever being accused of unethical research conduct.

Bill had a filling in one of his molars last week that broke apart and required an emergency visit to his dentist. As a consequence, he missed the research methods class. He knew what topic was going to be covered and asked Sophia how class went.

"Actually," she said, "it was pretty interesting. I really hadn't thought much about ethical dilemmas in a research context."

"Whoa," said Bill, "me neither. I don't even know how to wrap my mind around that. What's an ethical dilemma—and do I have one?"

"Bill, you crack me up. Here, take my notes and see what you missed."

An **ethical dilemma** develops anytime we have to choose between two compelling choices that conflict. For instance, we might know that clients have the right to refuse to participate in a study, but when only a few of them have volunteered to become research subjects and it looks like *our* study is going to be a failure, we might be tempted to not correct a group facilitator who informs her clients that they *have to participate*. Or if we overhear a family member pressuring another family member to participate, would we decide to step in and emphasize the client's right to choose—or simply allow the beleaguered client to complete the questionnaire?

While we all know that it is generally wrong to lie, what if it is important to the study that our human subjects don't know the true objectives of the study so that they can't misrepresent their real behavior or attitudes? Can ethical researchers ever deceive research participants? Here are a couple of examples involving deception. Decide if you think the researcher is doing something unethical.

1. Maria wants to learn experientially how society treats our senior citizens. She has a friend who can create latex wrinkles on her face, and they've found clothing and a wig that guarantee she'll look like an 80-year-old woman. Is Maria being unethical if she doesn't tell the people at the Senior Citizens Center that she is really only 23 years old? When a kind person offers to help her carry groceries up two flights of stairs?

2. Wellons (1973) engaged in some brilliant, creative research. Knowing about the powerful effect of negative labeling (sometimes known as the self-fulfilling prophecy), Wellons wondered if positive

labels also could have strong effects. He gave workshop supervisors *positive*—but untruthful—labels for a group of trainees with mental retardation. He told the supervisors certain supervisees could be expected to "blossom" in intelligence and workshop performance. And sure enough, one month later, the experimental group of adult trainees not only had a higher level of productivity but also showed gains in intelligence. There were no changes in the control group. Even though deception was used, was this research unethical?

You begin to see the problem. Ethical dilemmas thrive in those gray areas that are in between totally right and totally wrong. Sometimes, research cannot be conducted without deception. The purist might argue that deception should never be used, but what if the research could benefit society? Should we prevent research in instances where subjects are not informed precisely of the study's purpose? And before you answer that, consider this question—are we obligated to inform those participating in medical research that they will be receiving a **placebo** (an inert or nonreactive substance, a "sugar pill"), not the new experimental drug? Placebos work because individuals believe they are receiving a new or effective treatment for their problem.

ANXIETY CHECK 3.1

Assume that you are a social worker in a health setting and a medical researcher is evaluating a new drug for persons with anxiety. Could the study be affected if you told participants whether they would be receiving the new drug or the placebo?

[Answer at the end of the book.]

Heated controversies occasionally arise because of disagreements over what constitutes an unethical act. A final example involves a researcher (Coughlin, 1988) who submitted to 146 journals in social work and related fields a fabricated study of the benefits of temporarily separating asthmatic children. One version of the article claimed that social work intervention benefited the children. Another version indicated that the intervention had no effect. On acceptance or rejection of the manuscript, the study's investigator notified the journal of the real purpose of his study—to collect data on whether there was a tendency among journals to accept articles that confirm the value of social work intervention.

The controversy arose when an editor of the *Social Service Review* lodged a formal complaint against the author with the National Association of Social Workers. The author believed that the review procedures of journals ought to be investigated because of their potential influence in determining what will be printed. Some argue that the author should not have initiated such a large-scale deception of journals, but how does one investigate the hypothesis that professional journals have a bias that constitutes "prior censorship" without using a little deception? In many instances of unethical research, harm or potential for harm is apparent. Yet, who was injured in this example? (To read more about this episode and Coughlin's subsequent research, see Epstein, 1990, 2004.)

Historical Context

Guidelines to protect the subjects of research originated with the Nuremberg trials after World War II, which, among other areas of concern, examined the Nazis' medical experiments on prisoners. Nazi physicians conducted cruel and harmful experiments on human subjects. Some of their experiments, for example, were designed to determine how long it was possible for human subjects to live in ice water. Prisoners were subjected to conditions that literally froze them. Female prisoners were ordered to warm the frozen subjects with their naked bodies to determine if more subjects lived with slow thawing than with quick thawing. To test vaccines, other prisoners (including children) were injected with diseases such as typhus, malaria, and epidemic jaundice. To test antibiotics, human beings were wounded and had limbs amputated. Grass, dirt, gangrene cultures, and other debris were rubbed into the wounds so that the injuries would simulate those received on the battlefield. To simulate the problems of high-altitude flying, test chambers were created, where oxygen was removed and the effect of oxygen starvation on humans was studied. Other prisoners of the Nazis were given intravenous injections of gasoline or various forms of poison to study how long it would take them to die. These involuntary subjects experienced extreme pain, and of those few who lived, most suffered permanent injury or mutilation.

These and other atrocities resulted in what became known as the **Nuremberg Code**—a set of ethical guidelines to govern research with human subjects named after the 1947 Nuremberg Military Tribunals, which tried war criminals. Organizations such as the World Medical Association subsequently developed their own guidelines (the Declaration of Helsinki) for distinguishing ethical from unethical clinical research. The American Medical Association and many other groups endorsed the declaration or developed similar guidelines.

Despite awareness of Nazi atrocities and the development of ethical guidelines for research by a number of organizations and professional associations, unfortunate incidents in this country have occurred in which subjects were experimented on without their permission. For example, the US Department of Energy (DOE) has acknowledged that between 1945 and 1947, Americans were involved in government-sponsored human radiation experiments without their permission. The government paid the one survivor and the 11 other families $400,000 each to settle a lawsuit brought because plutonium injections were given without the recipient's knowledge or consent. In some instances, more than 600 rads of radiation were given—enough to cause bone cancer. Many other covert studies were conducted by the government in the Cold War era. (Search *human radiation experiments* for the DOE report and sources of information about unethical research in the United States.)

In the 1960s in New York, a physician injected cancer cells into 22 geriatric patients. Some were verbally informed that they were involved in an experiment but were not told that they were being given injections of cancer cells. No written consent was acquired, and some patients were not competent to give informed consent. Later, it was learned that the study had not been presented to the hospital's research committee and that several physicians directly responsible for the care of the patients involved in the study had not been consulted (Faden & Beauchamp, 1986).

Another notorious case involved a sample of men with syphilis. In 1932, 400 mostly poor and illiterate black males with tertiary-stage syphilis—most of whom lived in Tuskegee, Alabama—were informed that they would receive free treatment for their "bad blood." In actuality, these men received no treatment for syphilis. They received free physical exams, periodic blood testing, hot meals on examination days, free treatment for minor disorders, and a modest burial fee for cooperating with the investigators.

The researchers (supported by the US Public Health Service) were interested only in tracing the pathological evolution of syphilis. Although the study was reviewed several times by Public Health Service officials and was reported in 13 articles in prestigious medical and public health journals, it continued uninterrupted until 1972, when a reporter exposed the study in the *New York Times*. The survivors were given treatment for their disease only after this publicity. After the story broke, the US Department of Health, Education, and Welfare (HEW) appointed an advisory panel to review the study. Not until 1975 did the government extend treatment to the subjects' wives who had contracted syphilis and their children who had been born with congenital syphilis (Jones, 1981).

Public outcry over the Tuskegee Syphilis Study and other abuses led Congress in 1974 to pass the National Research Act (Public Law 93-348), which requires any organization involved in the conduct of biomedical or behavioral research involving human subjects to establish an institutional review board (IRB) to review the research to be conducted or sponsored. This act also created the National Commission for the Protection of Human Subjects of Biomedical and Behavioral Research. In October 1978, this commission produced recommendations for public comment. The National Commission for the Protection of Human Subjects of Biomedical and Behavioral Research (*The Belmont Report*) identified these three ethical principles for research on humans in 1978:

> **Beneficence**—Maximizing good outcomes for humanity and research subjects while minimizing or avoiding risk or harm
>
> **Respect**—Protecting the autonomy of all persons and treating them with courtesy and respect, including those who are not completely autonomous (for example, children, the mentally incompetent)
>
> **Justice**—Ensuring that reasonable, nonexploitative, and well-considered procedures are administered fairly; that the distribution of costs and benefits is fair (for example, those bearing the risks of research should receive the benefit).
> (Sieber, 1992, p. 18)

The US Department of Health, Education, and Welfare refined the recommendations and in 1981 issued them as regulations for research being conducted with its funds. In 1983, specific regulations protecting children were incorporated.

The impact of these regulations is that all colleges, universities, hospitals, and other organizations engaging in research and receiving federal funds from HEW (the Department of Health and Human Services) and other selected federal departments had to establish **institutional review boards** (sometimes called human subjects committees) to review and oversee research conducted by investigators affiliated with their organizations. Depending upon the project, IRBs review students' proposed research as well. These review boards have the authority to approve, disapprove, or modify research activities covered by the regulations; to conduct a continuing review of research involving human subjects; to ensure that there is an informed consent process; and to suspend or terminate the approval of any research being conducted at that institution or agency.

Institutional Review Boards

Institutional review boards are now firmly established as our society's watchdogs, protecting human subjects from unethical, risky, or harmful research. This policy does not mean that IRBs prevent all unethical research practices. They cannot oversee research that is covert or not brought to their attention. However, research today is monitored much more rigorously than it was 20 years ago, and IRBs have grown in power and clout. IRBs also have the responsibility to ensure that any projects they approve are scientifically sound. A project can be ethical (e.g., it causes no harm), but it could also be trivial and inconsequential. Such projects, depending on the local IRB, might not be approved.

Researchers begin the process of getting IRB approval by obtaining an application and preparing a description of their project. This narrative containing the research methods and procedures, the benefits and risks, the hypotheses, the recruitment of subjects, the consent form, and so forth is called the **protocol**. Protocols vary in length and format, depending on the planned research and the procedures established by the local IRB. There are three levels of review, from the most cursory (the exempt status), to expedited, to full review.

Federal regulations allow for some kinds of research to be exempted from a full review by the whole IRB set of members. (Exempt status does not mean "no review," but generally is limited to a review by one or two IRB members.) Research projects that qualify for **exempt status** are those that contain very little or no risk to the research subjects.

Those exempt activities most applicable to social work are:

1. Research conducted in educational settings, such as research on normal educational practices involving instructional strategies or effectiveness of instructional techniques, curricula, or classroom management methods;
2. Research involving the use of educational tests (cognitive, diagnostic, aptitude, achievement) if information taken from these sources is recorded in such a manner that subjects cannot be identified directly or through identifiers—and if any disclosure of the subjects' responses outside the research would not place the subjects at risk of criminal or civil liability or be damaging to the subjects' financial standing, employability, or reputation;
3. Research involving survey or interview procedures and observation of public behavior, if such research meets the conditions specified in (2);
4. Research involving the collection or study of existing data, documents, or records if these sources are publicly available or if the information is recorded by the investigator in such a manner that subjects cannot be identified directly or through identifiers linked to the subjects;
5. Research and demonstration projects approved by the department or agency heads that examine public benefit of service programs;
6. Research involving survey or interview procedures when the respondents are elected or appointed public officials or candidates for public office.

These criteria mean that most survey research is exempt from IRB review unless identifying information is collected and unless the disclosure of such information may cause harm to the subjects (Oakes, 2006).

When research activities are of minimal risk—defined as "the probability and magnitude of harm or discomfort anticipated in the research are not greater in and of themselves than those ordinarily encountered in the daily life or during performance of routine physical or psychological examinations or tests" (Oki & Zaia, 2006)—then they may qualify for **expedited review**. Expedited reviews are usually conducted by a single member of the IRB. The protocol must not be greater than minimal risk and fit into one of the eight expedited categories. The category where social workers most often seem to apply is when the research involves individual or group characteristics or behavior employing survey, interview, oral history, focus group, program evaluation, human factors evaluation, or quality assurance methodologies.

Proposed research activities that do not fit into the exempted or expedited review categories discussed previously are then subjected to a full committee review.

The **full review**, the highest level of review from the IRB, requires a slightly lengthier application and the principal investigator may be required to appear before a meeting of the IRB to respond to questions. The full review will be necessitated if the investigator's research involves **vulnerable populations** (for example, children, prisoners, persons with intellectual disabilities) who cannot give informed consent to participate in research or when there is deception of subjects or use of techniques that expose subjects to discomfort or harassment beyond levels normally encountered in daily life. Further, exemption is not usually available when the information obtained from medical records is recorded in such a way that subjects can be identified directly or through identifiers linked to the subjects.

Generally speaking, students are not required to seek approval from institutional review boards when their research projects are primarily for educational purposes (e.g., having a course assignment to interview a small sample of people to learn about interviewing and recording data or to acquire a small sample of data for analysis when no publication is expected). However, if the project involves living human subjects and is likely to contribute to **generalizable knowledge** (that is, research that could be published or presented to a professional conference), students need to seek IRB approval. Normally, student projects with the greatest potential for generating generalizable knowledge are doctoral dissertations and some master's theses. The criteria that IRBs apply to research projects are these: (1) is the proposed study designed to be a systematic investigation? and (2) is the goal of the proposed study to add to or produce generalizable knowledge? The proposed data-gathering activity must meet both of these tests to be appropriate for IRB review (Amdur, Speers, & Bankert, 2006).

BOX 3.1   PRACTICE NOTE: THE HEALTH INSURANCE PORTABILITY AND ACCOUNTABILITY ACT (HIPAA)

The Health Insurance Portability and Accountability Act, better known by the acronym of HIPAA, has changed the way research data are collected and how individuals in health care settings are informed about research efforts and their right to privacy. The "Privacy Rule" is that portion of HIPAA that addresses the protection of individually identifiable health information and regulates access and disclosure of this information. Protected health information (PHI) as defined by HIPAA amounts to all personally identifiable health information that is kept, held, and transmitted by health care providers, insurance providers/payers, or clearinghouses (referred to as covered entity [CE]). This federal law is specific and has large penalties for those who violate its requirements (ranging from $100 per violation to up to $250,000 in fines and 10 years in jail for those who sell, transfer, or use PHI for commercial advantage, personal gain, or malicious harm).

HIPAA defines 18 data elements as individually identifiable health information. Examples are admission and discharge dates, date of death, birth date, medical record numbers, account numbers, photographic images, and any other unique identifying number, characteristic, or code. Access to these and other protected health information items must be obtained through a disclosure authorization unless the information is de-identified by removing names, telephone numbers, and all individually identifiable health information,

BOX 3.1   PRACTICE NOTE: THE HEALTH INSURANCE PORTABILITY
AND ACCOUNTABILITY ACT (HIPAA) (CONTINUED)

including all geographic subdivisions smaller than a state. (The first three digits of a zip code may be used if at least 20,000 people live in that area.)

The written authorization form must provide a description of the protected health information that is to be used or disclosed, the names of those making the request to disclose the information, the purpose of the research, the expiration date of the research effort, signatures of both parties (researcher and participant), information about the participant's right to revoke the authorization, and a statement that health care or service delivery is not contingent upon signing the authorization. Under HIPAA, participants in research from health care facilities have a right to access information about themselves.

HIPAA requirements mean that the health care researcher must often obtain what amounts to two separate informed consents: one that meets the IRB's standards and one that conforms to HIPAA requirements for the authorization of disclosure of information for a specific purpose. According to Muhlbaier (2006), about 50% of the time authorization and consent documents are separated, and 50% of the time they can be combined—but this is an institutional decision and not the researcher's decision. In some instances, the IRB may grant a waiver for authorization (for instance, to conduct research on decedents).

In summary, here is a quick overview of HIPAA as it relates to research:

- Contacting health care patients to recruit them as participants in a study requires a partial waiver from the appropriate IRB.
- Medical information without identifiers (de-identified data) must be collected and stored in a database by the hospital or health facility—not by the researcher who wants to access the data.
- Limited databases can contain ages, dates, and zip codes when no other personally identifiable items are obtained, but a limited data-use agreement with the facility must be created.
- When it is not possible or practical to contact those eligible to participate in a study, a waiver of individual informed consent must be sought from the IRB.
- When you want to contact individual consumers of health care services to interview them or review their medical information, they must sign individual authorizations that have been approved by the appropriate IRB.

More information on HIPAA can be found at **http://privacyruleandresearch.nih.gov** and **http://www. hhs.gov/ocr/hipaa/guidelines/research.pdf**.

General Guidelines for Ethical Research

Social workers do not, as a rule, get involved in biomedical or other research where invasive procedures or physical harm to subjects is likely to occur. Research conducted by social workers typically involves surveys and interviews that require a certain amount of cooperation from the participants in the study. The risks to the subjects of social work research generally derive from the possibility that a third party will violate **confidentiality** and cause the subject physical, psychological, social, or economic harm. This threat is particularly acute for those research subjects engaged in or with past histories of illegal acts.

When questionnaires are used or interviews are conducted with adults who are not in a vulnerable population, the principle of **implied consent** is applied. That means choosing to participate is seen as giving informed consent. In these instances, IRBs do not require written documentation that subjects gave their consent. However, a problem arises when potential subjects feel that they cannot refuse to participate. If these subjects are clients (especially persons on probation or parole, or recipients of some form of public assistance), they may not feel free to refuse without putting themselves in some jeopardy. Consultation with an institutional review board can come in handy in this type of situation. The IRB may suggest alternative ways to collect data or to reduce any implied coercion by informing potential subjects of their rights in writing. One of the things the written consent form does is to state clearly that the potential subject has the right to refuse participation without any penalty or loss of service. Social workers must be alert to the possibility that encouraging their clients to participate in research could be perceived as coercion. Because social workers are often the gatekeepers of services, clients could feel pressured into participating to gain access to or continue receiving services.

If you are employed at a small agency that does not have its own IRB and you have questions about a proposed research or evaluation project, you might try consulting with the IRB at the nearest university. To help you understand how IRBs make decisions and go about the process of weighing risks against benefits, the following guidelines are presented.

Guideline 1: Research Subjects Must Be Volunteers

Social work research is not something that can be imposed on involuntary subjects. All of those participating in a research effort should freely decide to participate. No coercion of any kind should be used to secure participants for a study.

All subjects must be competent enough to understand their choice. If they are not able to comprehend fully (e.g., if they are under the age of majority), then their legal caretakers must give permission, and the subjects must also **assent**. Even if parents give permission for their children to participate in a research project, the children may still refuse to participate. The subject's right to self-determination is respected, and any research subject is free to withdraw from a study at any time.

The use of written consent forms helps ensure that research subjects know that they are volunteers. These forms provide brief, general information about the nature of the research, the procedures to be followed, and any foreseeable risks, discomforts, or benefits; and they indicate that the research subject is free to withdraw consent and to discontinue participation in the project at any time without penalty or loss of benefits. Consent forms generally contain the name of someone to contact should there be questions about the research or the subject's rights.

Although the details of the psychoeducational program that Bill and Sophia have been asked to help plan are still rudimentary, Sophia had some time over the weekend and quickly sketched out an informed consent form while the topic of research ethics was still fresh on her mind. She made some assumptions about incentives they could provide, about the follow-up data they might want to collect, and so forth. Her rough draft lays out a number of the important aspects of a consent form. Is anything left out? Anything that you would want to add?

Guideline 2: Potential Research Subjects Should Be Given Sufficient Information About the Study to Determine Any Possible Risks or Discomfort as Well as Benefits

Sufficient information includes an explanation of the purpose of the research, the expected duration of the subject's participation, the procedures to be followed, and the identification of those procedures

---

I have been asked to participate in a research study under the direction of Ellen Simpson, M.S.W., the Principal Investigator, whose phone number is (231) 333-0000.

Purpose: I understand that the purpose of this study is to examine the success of the HIV Risk Abatement Program (HRAP) in which I am participating—to keep myself healthy and free of illegal drugs once I am back in the community.

Duration and Location: I understand the study will take place in the group room at my facility and I will be asked to complete questionnaires requiring about 30 minutes on two occasions while still in prison and three times once I am released. I will be asked to provide a urine sample on three occasions as well in one of two locations in my community.

Procedures: I will be asked to answer questions about my social and psychological well-being, relationships, employment, drug use, and illegal activities. In addition, I will be asked to provide a urine sample to test for evidence of drugs in my system.

Risks/Discomforts: It has been explained to me that the interview questions are very personal, involving drugs and criminal behavior.

Benefits: I understand that the benefits from participating in this study may help researchers and those involved in public policy better understand the factors that may keep future incarcerated women from continual involvement with drugs and additional incarceration.

Confidentiality: I understand that a research code number will be used to identify my responses from those of other clients and that my name, address, and other identifying information will not be directly associated with any information obtained from me. A master listing of persons participating in the study and their identifying information will be kept in a secure location under lock and key except when being used by select staff. Further, I understand that a certificate of confidentiality has been obtained from the Department of Health and Human Services (DHHS) that protects investigators from being forced to release any of my data, even under a court order or a subpoena. When results of this study are published, my name or other identifying information will not be used.

Payments: I will be paid nothing for my participation while in prison but $50 for each time I cooperate by submitting a urine sample and completing a question after release. If I quit participating early, I understand that I will be paid an amount appropriate to the time I have spent on the evaluation.

Right to Withdraw: I understand that I do not have to take part in this study, and my refusal to participate will involve no penalty or loss of rights to which I am entitled. I may withdraw from the study at any time without fear of losing any services or benefits to which I am entitled.

Consent: I have read this entire form, completely understand my rights, and voluntarily consent to participate in this research. I will receive a copy of this consent should questions arise and I wish to contact the researcher or the University of Somewhere's Institutional Review Board (555-555-5555) to discuss my rights as a research subject.

FIGURE 3.1 HIV Risk Abatement Program (HRAP) Evaluation Consent Form

that might be experimental. The exact hypothesis does not have to be given away; it can be stated generally. However, the researcher must be specific about procedures that will involve the research subjects. If there are potential risks, these must be identified. Subjects should be given the opportunity to raise and receive answers to any questions at any time about the study or procedures that will be used.

The types of risks resulting from social work research might be psychological, physical, legal, or economic. Psychological risks could result from any procedures that cause research subjects to leave with lowered self-esteem and a sense that they aren't as smart as others (for example, feeling "stupid" to have been a victim of abuse). Similarly, researchers must be cognizant that certain participants might become depressed if questions awaken painful memories. As they deem it appropriate, IRBs may ask researchers to provide information to research subjects about whom they can contact if they have intrusive or recurring memories (for example, the local community mental health center's phone number).

Physical harm might occur to research subjects. For instance, if questionnaires were mailed to the homes of women who had secretly attended a support group for battered spouses, their violent partners could discover this and punish them for their efforts to get help.

Legal risks are possible for research participants involved with illegal behaviors—drug use, child abuse, stealing, or other illegal activities. Just as a social worker would do at the beginning of treatment, researchers must inform adults of the "rules." For instance, if during an interview an adult reveals abusing a child, the social work practitioner/researcher is obligated to report it to the appropriate authorities. The most common risk here, however, is that a subject's confidentiality may be compromised if personal identifiers are used and the topic involves illegal behaviors. If the researcher receives a subpoena, the research subject's confidentiality may no longer be protected.

Economic risks could occur if, for example, employees reveal that they are taking drugs or if they are surveyed about the work climate within their agency—particularly if they criticize a supervisor or boss and this information isn't carefully protected. The IRB's job is to think not only about the direct risks but also about the indirect or remote possibilities.

Here are some of the questions that a written informed consent must address for the potential participants of research:

- Who is conducting the study, and what is its purpose?
- Where will the study take place, how long will it last, and what will I be asked to do?
- What are the possible risks or discomforts (if any)?
- Are there any benefits to participation?
- Do I have to take part in the study? Are there other choices if I'm not interested?
- Who will see the information I submit?
- Will I receive any compensation for participating?
- What if I have questions, suggestions, concerns, or complaints?

Depending on the nature of the study, IRBs may ask the researcher to obtain signatures from all participants on the informed consent showing that they understood the project and agreed to participate.

BOX 3.2   PRACTICE NOTE: ANONYMITY AND CONFIDENTIALITY

Anonymous responding means that the research participant cannot be identified by any means or by any person. When anonymity is promised, not even the researcher should be able to associate a response with a particular individual. Researchers need to be sensitive to the issue that participants can sometimes be recognized not just from their personal identifiers like addresses and social security numbers, but also from sociodemographic information. For instance, a small agency might employ one female Asian American or only one PhD who is 50 years of age. With small samples of research subjects, researchers might want to use broad categories for such variables as age, education, ethnic groupings, and years of experience to keep from identifying persons with unique characteristics.

Confidentiality means that the potentially sensitive or private information is being supplied with the understanding that the research participant's identity, although known to the researcher, will be protected. Sometimes, it is necessary to know a research participant's name, address, phone number, or social security number to match current information with medical records, prior offenses, or when pre- and post-testing of an intervention are being done. Where it is necessary to know the identities of research subjects, investigators routinely use a coding scheme so that personally identifying information is not contained on clients' survey forms, assessment forms, and so on. The listing that links code numbers with individuals' names is always kept in a secure, locked area except when being used.

Benefits of participating in research can include incentives (usually small cash awards but can be much larger, depending on the amount of time the participant might have to spend in testing, traveling, being interviewed, etc.) Benefits of participating can also result in subjects acquiring some type of insight or learning (for example, learning better nutritional habits) or some worthwhile information (e.g., resources the local university makes available to the general public). Researchers quite often appeal to subjects' altruism and state that the project will advance scientific knowledge. Sometimes a final report of the project is offered to those subjects who voluntarily participated.

Finally, note that informed consent means that language used to inform the prospective research subjects should be not only age appropriate (an especially important consideration with children), but also free of jargon and technical/professional terms that an average person might not understand. A good guideline to use might be to try not to exceed a ninth- or tenth-grade reading level with adult client populations. Further, using "I" language seems to make the informed consent easier to understand than use of the second or third person.

Guideline 3: No Harm Shall Result as a Consequence of Participation in the Research

Social work researchers are not likely to propose research that would result in evident harm to their subjects. But one's perspective on harmful effects should not be limited to the active participants in a study.

What if you wanted to study the reactions of police officers to reports of international students being robbed? In this hypothetical study, the researchers would need about 15 international students from different countries to repeat a fabricated story. While data *might* reveal that the police were not as concerned or as sensitive as they should have been, there could be unfortunate effects. First, there could be legal repercussions for filing false police reports. Second, subsequent disclosure that it was only a study might make the police distrustful of researchers. But most important, such a study might have led police to be skeptical of international students who truly have been robbed or threatened. In short, the benefits of the proposed research would not seem to outweigh the risks and the potential harm that could result. Would you approve the research if you were an IRB reviewer?

Unethical research can result in harm to succeeding generations. For instance, many African Americans appear to distrust medical researchers because of the Tuskegee syphilis experiments (for a discussion of the rationalization of unethical research, see Paul and Brookes, 2015). More recently, the publicity given to the case of Henrietta Lacks provides another example that may have made some African Americans suspicious of medical research (Plunk & Grucza, 2013). Henrietta was an African American mother who acquired a fatal form of cancer, and while receiving treatment, the physicians removed samples of her tumor and healthy cervix without her permission or knowledge by her family. Later, researchers discovered that her sample of cells multiplied and could be kept alive—harvested and grown for supplying to other medical researchers. Dr. Salk used samples of the strain of cells known by this time as HeLa to test the polio vaccine. This commercialization of Mrs. Lacks's own cells (she died in 1951) came to the family's attention in the 1970s, when researchers contacted the family and wished to obtain blood samples to better understand the genetics of the sample.

Might other cultural or ethnic groups have trust issues with the medical care system? See if you can find another article besides this one:

✓ McAlearney, A. S., Oliveri, J. M., Post, D. M., Song, P. H., Jacobs, E., Waibel, J., ... & Paskett, E. D. (2012). Trust and distrust among Appalachian women regarding cervical cancer screening: A qualitative study. *Patient Education and Counseling, 86*, 120–126.

Researchers have a responsibility to identify and to minimize harm or risk of harm that might befall the research subjects. And researchers should constantly monitor the subjects for harmful effects of the research. Subjects should not go away from a study feeling they possess undesirable traits. Often, debriefings are used to inform subjects about the study and to neutralize negative feelings once participation in a project has concluded. Sometimes, it is useful to point out that "most subjects" responded in a certain way.

Guideline 4: Sensitive Information Shall Be Protected

This guideline suggests that no harm to research subjects should result from improper handling of information. The privacy of research subjects may be protected in the following ways:

- Allowing subjects to respond anonymously
- Separating identifying information from the research data by using special coding and keeping the master list secure
- Training all staff and stressing the importance of protecting confidential material.

It is not always possible for subjects to respond anonymously—for example, when you have a situation in which participants have completed both pretests and posttests and their scores must be matched to check for improvement. However, it is sometimes possible to invent a special code that is easy for subjects to remember and still protect their anonymity. Such a code might consist of the first four letters of the subject's mother's maiden name and the first four letters of the subject's favorite food. Even a code this simple will help guard against the accidental recognition or identification of your subjects.

> ## BOX 3.3   PRACTICE NOTE: RESEARCH AND PERSONS WITH ALZHEIMER'S DISEASE
>
> Research involving patients with Alzheimer's disease is fraught with ethical problems. Because their illness destroys cognitive abilities, participants may lack the capacity to understand an informed consent process, and even if they do, they may forget that they have given consent. Further, there are no well-accepted standards for determining when individuals with Alzheimer's disease have lost the capacity to give consent. Even mild cognitive impairment in older subjects can cause them to experience difficulty in understanding consent information.
>
> If the patient with Alzheimer's disease is unable to understand the consent process, informed consent is generally obtained from the next-of-kin or legal guardian. In any case, assent from the subject is still sought.

ANXIETY CHECK 3.2

If you were working with persons with Alzheimer's or cognitive decline who might have some difficulty understanding the consent process, do you think an IRB might still expect that the participants would need to assent?

[Answer at the end of the book.]

Quantitative researchers report their research findings in summaries (e.g., group means and totals), which offer a great deal of protection to subjects who would not want to be connected to their responses. However, sometimes researchers wish to use a particularly apt comment (especially when open-ended questions have been employed) to summarize or illustrate the sentiments of the respondents. The caution here is to never report anything that would allow an individual participant to be identified. For instance, it would be a serious mistake to use the following quotation to show the depth of employees' feelings about a new director in a job satisfaction study at a local social service agency:

> I've been working abuse investigation longer than anyone else here—22 years—and I can say without any doubt in my mind that our new executive director is all fluff and no substance. He doesn't have a clue about how to do his job; I'm not sure he would even recognize an abused child if he saw one.

Another protection available to clients when an outside researcher makes a request to collect information from clients is for the agency instead of the researcher to contact former or present clients and ask about their interest in participating. That way, client names, addresses, and/or phone numbers are not disclosed to the researcher. Sometimes, agencies ask researchers and those working with privileged communications to sign a written pledge of confidentiality.

Research and Boundary Issues

Besides these basic guidelines, most IRBs insist that researchers keep the research project role separate from the direct service role so that clients will not be confused. To help maintain clarity, service providers are usually required to not recruit research subjects directly and to not administer questionnaires or conduct research interviews with their clients, for example, but instead to use another researcher or assistants for data collection. This separation prevents clients from feeling subtle coercion to participate in a study and thus avoids placing the professional helper in a **dual relationship** of being both a researcher and a direct service provider. This kind of dual role can create misunderstanding in clients as to the nature of the "true" interest of the social worker. As a practitioner working with individuals who have been traumatized, trust is a key part of the relationship. However, clients who are unfamiliar with research procedures may not understand why their empathic, kind counselor becomes more aloof and objective in collecting data for a study.

Imagine, if you will, the sensitivity required of a qualitative researcher interviewing the non-offending partners of female rape victims within 14 days of the event. Van Wijk and Harrison (2013) have written about the ethical issues involved with recruiting and safeguarding the safety of their participants while conducting a pilot study in South Africa.

✓ Van Wijk, E., & Harrison, T. (2013). Managing ethical problems in qualitative research involving vulnerable populations using a pilot study. *International Journal of Qualitative Methods, 12*, 570–586.

ANXIETY CHECK 3.3

In the psychoeducational project that Mrs. Simpson has been discussing with Sophia and Bill, do you foresee any dual relationship issues? When might they arise? How might they resolve them?

[Answer at the end of the book.]

BOX 3.4   PRACTICE NOTE: CLINICAL TRIALS AND AFRICAN AMERICANS

Social workers in health care settings may have patients who are interested in or involved in clinical trials. Clinical trials are medical research projects where volunteers are randomly assigned to groups so that researchers can test the effectiveness and safety of new medicines and medical interventions. The control group generally does not receive the new intervention but gets a placebo (inert substance or activity) or the customary treatment. Participants do not know which group they are in until the end of the study. One can't choose to be in the group receiving the new treatment or to be in any other group. Some participants might be unhappy to learn that they did not receive the most effective treatment for their problem, but a possible benefit could be that they may receive the new treatment at no cost. They may also feel that they are making a contribution to science and knowledge about treatment of the problem. Because there are race-related differences in responses to drugs for both medical and psychiatric symptoms, there has been a growing awareness of the need to recruit persons of color and to ensure that they are represented in clinical trials research. However, many African Americans display a lack of trust with the white research establishment because of such historical events as the Tuskegee Syphilis Study.

If you are interested in successful approaches to recruiting and retaining African Americans into clinical trials, you may wish to review the following article:

✓ Otado et al. (2015). Culturally competent strategies for recruitment and retention of African American populations into clinical trials. *CTS-Clinical and Translational Science, 8*(5), 460–466.

Potential Ethical Problems in Research

It is not uncommon to find that students and practitioners who have been out in the field for a few years have misconceptions about what is proper and not allowed in conducting research involving patients, clients, or other individuals. This section will address several issues that arise from time to time.

Deception

One of the thorniest ethical problems facing researchers in the social sciences has to do with deception. Generally speaking, deception should not be employed unless there is no other way to collect the necessary data or to study the phenomenon. Thus, deception might be acceptable if without it, respondents would be too embarrassed, ashamed, or defensive to respond truthfully.

Some researchers avoid deception of clients or vulnerable populations by the creative use of simulations in which subjects (such as college students) are asked to imagine themselves in a particular role or setting—and then to respond as if the situation were real. In a study of the qualities that make someone a "good" therapist, subjects might, for instance, be shown video clips of "therapists" in action and then be asked to choose the one they would want if they had a problem that could benefit from counseling. In such a study, actors might be used to simulate actual therapists and clients.

At times, the informed consent document that subjects must read and sign alerts them to the possibility that some deception may be involved. At other times, the IRB can decide to waive the right of subjects to be fully informed until after data have been obtained from the subject(s). IRBs generally require debriefing the research subjects whenever any deception is employed.

Because it is important that the deception not cause subjects to lose confidence in science or the scientific process, IRBs also expect that subjects should be given ample opportunity to have their questions answered about the project at the time of the debriefing, and if they choose to do so, subjects are allowed to withdraw their own data from the study.

Should you use deception? Clearly, you should not if someone could be harmed or could go away from the study with a feeling of having been degraded or exploited. For this reason, the decision to use deception should not be made without consultation with others. As part of this process, alternative methodologies for studying the problem should be considered. But as indicated earlier, sometimes the best way to study a problem depends on deception. An example comes to mind: Suppose you want to study racism, but you know that if you approach the topic directly, most individuals would see your intent and construct their answers to minimize their racist opinions. However, suppose you inform your subjects that you are conducting a study on humor and will be giving them 30 different jokes to see which ones they think are the funniest. Couldn't this mild deception allow you to investigate racist values without alerting subjects to your real intent? The answer, of course, is yes.

Denial of Treatment

Another potential ethical problem is that sometimes social workers who contemplate research think that using a control group may be unethical because clients would be denied services. It would indeed be unethical to deny beneficial services to clients strictly for the purpose of research. But there are ways to obtain control groups without being unethical. For instance, if we wanted to evaluate a new program or intervention, we could compare clients receiving the new or experimental intervention against those who receive the usual set of services. In this scenario, there would be no denial of services. Some clients would

> ## BOX 3.5   PRACTICE NOTE: CONDUCTING RESEARCH WITH CHILDREN
>
> A host of ethical problems can be associated with conducting research with children. Gensheimer, Ayers, and Roosa (1993) identify several of these in discussing a prevention program designed for children of alcoholics. They point out that the very act of recruiting these children, whether by teacher referral or child self-selection after viewing a special film, places them in a situation where "labeling is almost assured." Another problem is that requiring informed consent from parents may prevent at-risk children from entering the program, because such children might fear being harmed by a parent who would be opposed to their participation. Still another question is: How much coaching or prompting is ethical? Could children—even with parental permission—truly feel they could choose not to participate when teachers and other adults in the school were encouraging them to be involved?

get a slightly different intervention or set of services than those clients normally receive. This situation could be to their advantage.

In those agencies or programs with long waiting lists, researchers might consider as a control group those clients next in line for services. Clients on a waiting list might appreciate periodic contact with an agency representative (even if it is limited to the administration of a pretest and posttest) because it would indicate they have not been forgotten by the agency and that they are still actively queued for services. If these clients had similar problems, it might be possible to distribute educational pamphlets or materials to them while they were waiting for service. This group of clients could be considered to be receiving an educational intervention. While it may be a weaker or milder intervention than they would later receive, it would be better than nothing and may help the researcher feel better about gathering data from them. Comparisons could be made to the waiting-list clients (the control group) and those who received the new intervention (the experimental group).

Another way to obtain a control group is to compare your program participants with the clientele of a similar program or agency. While the groups would not be equivalent, at least you would have some beginning evaluative data. Still another "natural" comparison group could be found in that group of clients who keep one or two appointments and then drop out of treatment. This group could be compared with those individuals who complete the intervention. These examples are only some of the ways in which control groups can be identified without denying treatment.

Compensation

Is the practice of paying respondents or research subjects unethical? While reimbursing subjects for costs incurred (such as babysitting, time away from work, transportation) seems reasonable, questions arise whenever participation includes a *large* financial incentive. The guideline here is to avoid giving incentives so large that they constitute "undue inducement." When large financial rewards are offered to research subjects, the risk increases that some individuals may fabricate information to become eligible for the study and qualify for the incentive. Should you reimburse subjects for time lost from work and their time spent commuting to the agency to participate in research? This level of compensation is not generally viewed as excessive. Sometimes, when subjects are followed over several years (longitudinal design), an incentive is built in (for example, a $50 bonus) if they participate in all of the scheduled follow-ups. Increasingly, lotteries have become popular as incentives. Typically, there is a cash prize that every respondent or participant becomes eligible to win.

Existing Data—Records Research Without Clients' Consent

Although many community mental health centers and other such agencies routinely request that clients sign consent forms at intake in the event that a researcher or program evaluator would look at their records sometime, many agencies do not use consent forms unless their clients will be actively participating in a specific study.

Suppose you wanted to conduct research within a state psychiatric hospital to determine if more bipolar personality disorders were being diagnosed in a recent year than 10 years ago. In such a situation, would you be prevented from conducting research because clients did not give permission for you to perform archival research involving their records? Probably not, if you are a legitimate researcher and have approval from the hospital and the IRB.

As a student or faculty member, you would go first to your own university's institutional review board and complete the appropriate forms. The IRB would likely request that you submit a letter of support from the state hospital. Then, you might still need to contact the hospital's human subjects committee. The study ought to be approved if it is to be viewed as having scientific merit or useful for those professionals working in the mental health area.

Archival research of this type is not generally viewed as having any real potential for harming subjects. Further, in some localities, the information you want might even be a matter of public record. Even so, some agencies may have you sign an agreement of confidentiality before allowing you access to their records. Remember that existing data is viewed by IRBs as data that are or have been routinely collected. It does *not* refer to data that may be collected at some time in the future.

Conducting Ethical Internet Research

Given that the vast majority of Americans use the Internet, it makes sense that using electronic forms of communication would be used for social science research. And there are a number of advantages for researchers (and sometimes offsetting disadvantages) when conducting online surveys. Keim-Malpass, Steeves, and Kennedy (2014) present some advantages and limitations of online research. Take a look at these and see if you can add to the list.

Do the advantages outweigh the disadvantages? Do you see more or less research being conducted online in the future? Whether we conduct online research or use other approaches, we must always be cognizant of the purpose of research in the social sciences and the reason why you are learning research methodology. Mahon (2014) phrases it well: "human participants' research must provide benefit either to the participants or to scientific understanding, and there can be no benefit unless data are valid and reliable" (p. 125). If online research interests you, you may wish to read this article:

✓ Sharkey, S., Jones, R., Smithson, J., Hewis, E., Emmens, T., Ford, T., & Owens, C. (2011). Ethical practice internet research involving vulnerable people: Lessons from a self-harm discussion forum study (SharpTalk). *Journal of Medical Ethics, 37,* 752–758.

Internet Resources for Conducting Ethical Research

Several federal offices provide tutorials for the purpose of educating researchers about protecting human subjects. The National Institutes of Health (**https://phrp.nihtraining.com/users/login.php**) and the US Department of Health and Human Services (**www.hrsa.gov/humansubjects**) both have self-guided instructional tutorials that provide a certificate of completion when one is finished with the brief courses. Some IRBs require these certificates before granting approval to research applications. You can also find human subjects training or tutorials on the websites of most large universities. Sometimes, the universities subscribe to the CITI Program for the tutorial and certificate process. You might want to see if you can access their human subjects training at **www.citiprogram.org/**.

ANXIETY CHECK 3.4

What ethical issues do you think could arise when Sophia and Bill attempt to conduct research with an incarcerated population? How are prisoners vulnerable? If you are stumped, you may want to look at the following website: **https://humansubjects.nih.gov/prisoners**

[Answer is at the end of the book.]

Internet Advantages	Internet Disadvantages
Ability to reach possible participants anywhere in the world	Possible loss of control of who receives or forwards the data collection instrument on to others. Someone under-age could respond. Could an individual respond multiple times?
Ability to reach participants who could be stigmatized or not want to be recognized in other settings	Loss of ability to confirm identity, diagnosis, symptoms, etc.
Ease of access, not burdensome to clients or participants; surveys can be completed 24/7	Findings may not be generalizable; self-selected sample of respondents may not resemble the target population
Automatic data entry (the researcher doesn't have to key the data into a spreadsheet)	Typically, there are low response rates
Anonymity is usually possible	Could a hacker break into a site or the software and learn personal information?

FIGURE 3.2. Advantages and Disadvantages of Conducting Surveys and Research Online

Qualitative Research Note

At this point, you probably have enough knowledge about qualitative research to know that it is a different perspective from the quantitative view with regard to data gathering and research design. For instance, qualitative researchers seldom use the term *research subjects*, but much more often speak of *research participants*. Thus, qualitative researchers do not want to view another human being as some kind of guinea pig. Rather, they prefer to observe and interview and to allow the data to flow from whatever stories or accounts the participants or key informers choose to tell. The research then is an elevation of these stories or explanations. Along this line, the collection of personal stories and oral history interviews may not require IRB review, as they may not be considered "science" and able to contribute generalizable knowledge.

The potential risks that participants in qualitative research might experience are ordinarily negligible because there is little possibility of result in injury or harm. However, among the risks might be violation of privacy; breach of confidentiality; sanctioning bad or illegal behavior (that is, an adult studying adolescent drug use may convey the attitude that their behavior is acceptable); harm to self-image, dignity, or data collection; or presentation of results in such a way that the individual being studied does not feel respected (Gallant & Bliss, 2006).

A special uniqueness of qualitative research is that even with an **interview schedule** (a list of questions the interviewer wants to use), responses to questions may well lead to other questions that weren't anticipated at the beginning of the study—and so the issue of informed consent and subjects' knowing exactly what they'll be asked can be problematic. Thus, it is possible that a social work interviewer could uncover a reportable event such as child or elder abuse, even though that was not the intent of the interviewing or participant observation.

An interesting qualitative article by Bell and Salmon (2011) explores what female drug users think about ethical research. As a vulnerable population, there has been debate whether drugs users have the capacity to give informed consent and about whether cash incentives amount to undue inducement and exploit this population. When asked about their views on the research process, they spoke about researchers acting superior, talking down to them, being treated disrespectfully, and feeling used. While one issue that researchers struggle with is whether to include or exclude possible informants who are high, the focus group attendees spoke of exclusion as a form of discrimination. They were critical of the claim that drug users lacked the capacity to consent to research. Another issue was whether incentives should be offered because they could be spent on drugs. And one participant volunteered that "No one asks what they [the researchers] do with their money ..." (p. 90). Incentives seemed to be viewed as "ethical and respectful acknowledgment of their time and expertise" (p. 92).

What ethical issues do you see in conducting research with addicted persons? Are there power differences between researchers and their participants? Is capturing data from clients or patients a privilege that requires our most respectful treatment of the other person?

If you find the notion of power differentials in the conduct of research thought provoking, you may wish to read the following article:

✓ Pyles, L. (2015). Participation and other ethical considerations in participatory action research in post-earthquake rural Haiti. *International Social Work, 58*(5), 628–645.

Final Thoughts

Even though students and university staff usually must seek approval for their research from an institutional review board, sometimes grumbling is heard that it is a waste of time for the knowledgeable and ethical researcher who will not be doing any harm. However, to bypass review boards entails a certain risk—as revealed in the following case of a university-based investigator who did not get approval for a controversial questionnaire administered within a school district. Although a lot of data had already been collected, to avoid hostile parental reaction and a possible lawsuit, a school official shredded several

(a) Social workers should monitor and evaluate policies, the implementation of programs, and practice interventions.

(b) Social workers should promote and facilitate evaluation and research to contribute to the development of knowledge.

(c) Social workers should critically examine and keep current with emerging knowledge relevant to social work and fully use evaluation and research evidence in their professional practice.

(d) Social workers engaged in evaluation or research should carefully consider possible consequences and should follow guidelines developed for the protection of evaluation and research participants. Appropriate institutional review boards should be consulted.

(e) Social workers engaged in evaluation or research should obtain voluntary and written informed consent from participants, when appropriate, without any implied or actual deprivation or penalty for refusal to participate; without undue inducement to participate; and with due regard for participants' well-being, privacy, and dignity. Informed consent should include information about the nature, extent, and duration of the participation requested and disclosure of the risks and benefits of participation in the research.

(f) When evaluation or research participants are incapable of giving informed consent, social workers should provide an appropriate explanation to the participants, obtain the participants' assent to the extent they are able, and obtain written consent from an appropriate proxy.

(g) Social workers should never design or conduct evaluation or research that does not use consent procedures, such as certain forms of naturalistic observation and archival research, unless rigorous and responsible review of the research has found it to be justified because of its prospective scientific, educational, or applied value and unless equally effective alternative procedures that do not involve waiver of consent are not feasible.

(h) Social workers should inform participants of their right to withdraw from evaluation and research at any time without penalty.

(i) Social workers should take appropriate steps to ensure that participants in evaluation and research have access to appropriate supportive services.

(j) Social workers engaged in evaluation or research should protect participants from unwarranted physical or mental distress, harm, danger, or deprivation.

(k) Social workers engaged in the evaluation of services should discuss collected information only for professional purposes and only with people professionally concerned with this information.

(l) Social workers engaged in evaluation or research should ensure the anonymity or confidentiality of participants and of the data obtained from them. Social workers should inform participants of any limits of confidentiality, the measures that will be taken to ensure confidentiality, and when any records containing research data will be destroyed.

(m) Social workers who report evaluation and research results should protect participants' confidentiality by omitting identifying information unless proper consent has been obtained authorizing disclosure.

(n) Social workers should report evaluation and research findings accurately. They should not fabricate or falsify results and should take steps to correct any errors later found in published data using standard publication methods.

(o) Social workers engaged in evaluation or research should be alert to and avoid conflicts of interest and dual relationships with participants, should inform participants when a real or potential conflict of interest arises, and should take steps to resolve the issue in a manner that makes participants' interests primary.

(p) Social workers should educate themselves, their students, and their colleagues about responsible research practices.

Source: **https://www.socialworkers.org/pubs/code/code.asp**

FIGURE 3.3 NASW Code of Ethics Regarding Evaluation and Research (Section 5.02)

hundred already completed questionnaires (Schilling, Schinke, Kirkham, Meltzer, & Norelius, 1988). You can imagine how much time was lost—to say nothing about damage to the research project and possibly someone's career. Ultimately, the researcher is responsible for the ethics of the research effort. Even with the approval of an institutional review board or other advisory group, the researcher must constantly be vigilant to prevent any harm or potentially unethical act from occurring.

While the thought of preparing a research protocol or appearing before an institutional review board might be somewhat intimidating, another way to see the process is as a review by concerned peers—individuals who really want good research to be produced. Their suggestions and comments may well improve your project.

As social workers, we really don't have the option not to engage in research and evaluation activities. The National Association of Social Workers' Code of Ethics requires us to evaluate our policies, programs, and interventions—to develop professional knowledge while protecting our research participants. A relevant section of the code addressing ethics in research and evaluation is reproduced in Figure 3.3.

Although it is not uncommon to worry whenever one is seeking IRB approval, if you have been open and honest about how the study will be conducted, you should have nothing to fear. If the IRB wants certain procedures to be tightened up, they will make recommendations in writing. While it is true that investigations asking for certain sensitive information could be stressful for some clients, rarely is that a problem. When a protocol involves a vulnerable population, for example, interviewing sexual assault victims, IRBs may ask that researchers provide their subjects with the phone numbers and addresses of counseling agencies or rape crisis centers. The vast majority of studies proposed by social work researchers poses little risk to research subjects.

Although the majority of this chapter has been cautionary about the ethical problems that can arise in conducting research, the positive benefits of being a research subject should not be overlooked. In clinical interventions, subjects may gain from new therapeutic procedures. Even if that doesn't occur, subjects may feel that the research is important and that they have made a contribution that will be of help to others. Participants may experience an increase in self-worth because they feel honored to have been selected to participate in "research." Sometimes, participants receive some form of remuneration, and they appreciate it—even inconsequential amounts. Another consideration is that some research projects are interesting. Participants may enjoy giving their opinions or sharing their insights. These examples are just some of the positive effects that could be associated with participating in research.

Key Terms

protocol	HIPAA
ethical dilemma	respect
Nuremberg Code	full review
assent	implied consent
exempt status	interview schedule
institutional review board	placebo

anonymous

confidentiality

beneficence

vulnerable population

expedited review

dual relationship

justice

generalizable knowledge

clinical trials

SELF-REVIEW

(Answers at the end of the book)

1. T or F. Legitimate researchers using archival or existing data pose little risk of causing harm.
2. T or F. Social workers are required by their code of ethics to evaluate programs and interventions.
3. T or F. When parents grant permission for their children to be interviewed or tested in a research project, these children cannot refuse to participate.
4. T or F. Institutional review boards cannot refuse to grant permission for researchers if there is no harm to participants and also no scientific merit.
5. T or F. Deception can never be used in a research study involving participants under the age of 21.
6. T or F. Separate signed informed consent statements are always required—even with brief mailed surveys.
7. The research proposal describing the methods and procedures, recruitment of subjects, the consent form, and so forth is called the _____.
8. _____ means the research participant cannot be identified by any means or any person.
9. _____ means that sensitive or private information may be linked to personally identifying information but is supplied with the understanding that the participant's identity will be protected.
10. T or F. Every potential research subject has the right to refuse to participate and may even choose to quit in the middle of a project without being assessed any penalty or losing any benefits.
11. Name one way that qualitative research might vary from quantitative research when viewed from an ethics perspective.
12. T or F. Under the HIPAA regulations, research participants can give verbal consent over the phone for their medical records to be released to a qualified and legitimate researcher affiliated with a hospital.

QUESTIONS FOR CLASS DISCUSSION

1. Would it ever be appropriate for a researcher, while collecting data, to offer unsolicited advice to a participant regarding the need to obtain individual counseling or therapy?
2. Discuss situations in which it would be acceptable to involve people in research without their knowledge.
3. A researcher wants to interview children in families where there has been a hospitalization for mental illness within the past three years. Discuss the potential ethical issues that will have to be addressed.

4. A researcher is interested in observing family functioning in families that have experienced a recent suicide. What precautions would the researcher need to take to ensure that no psychological or emotional harm resulted from the interviews?

5. A doctoral student conducting a confidential study of terminally ill patients in a hospice program finds that 15% of the patients are contemplating suicide. Discuss what can and should be done with this information. For instance, should family members be informed?

6. A researcher wants to investigate the emotional consequences of abortion. Because of the difficulty in getting access to the names and addresses of women who have had abortions, the researcher proposes a sampling design based on referrals from women who know of other women who have had abortions. What are the ethical issues involved in the use of this design?

7. Which of the four guidelines for conducting ethical research is of paramount importance? Why?

8. What might be some of the ethical issues with regard to obtaining research participants from the Internet?

9. Discuss HIPAA regulations from a researcher's perspective. Does the act greatly complicate data collection? Does the protection it provides for health care information offset the challenges it creates for the researcher?

RESOURCES AND REFERENCES

Amdur, R. J., Speers, M., & Bankert, E. (2006). Identifying intent: Is this project research? In Elizabeth A. Bankert and Robert J. Amdur (Eds.), *Institutional review board: Management and function*. Sudbury, MA: Jones and Bartlett Publishers.

Bankert, E. A., & Amdur, R. J. (Eds.). (2006). *Institutional review board: Management and function*. Sudbury, MA: Jones and Bartlett Publishers.

Bell, K., & Salmon, A. (2011). What women who use drugs have to say about ethical research: Findings of an exploratory qualitative study. *Journal of Empirical Research on Human Research Ethics: An International Journal, 6*(4), 84–98.

Coughlin, E. K. (1988, Nov. 2). Scholar who submitted bogus article to journals may be disciplined. *Chronicle of Higher Education*, A7.

Epstein, W. M. (1990). Confirmational response bias among social work journals. *Science Technology and Human Values, 15*, 9–38.

Epstein, W. M. (2004). Confirmational response bias and the quality of the editorial processes among American social work journals. *Research on Social Work Practice, 14*(6), 450–458.

Faden, R. R., & Beauchamp, T. L. (1986). *A history and theory of informed consent*. New York, NY: Oxford University Press.

Gallant, D. R., & Bliss, A. (2006). Qualitative social science research. In Elizabeth A. Bankert and Robert J. Amdur (Eds.), *Institutional review board: Management and function*. Sudbury, MA: Jones and Bartlett Publishers.

Gensheimer, L. K., Ayers, I. S., & Roosa, M. W. (1993). School-based prevention interventions for at-risk populations. *Evaluation and Program Planning, 16*, 159–167.

Humphreys, L. (1970). *Tearoom trade: Impersonal sex in public places*. Chicago, IL: Aldine.

Jones, J. H. (1981). *Bad blood: The Tuskegee syphilis experiment*. New York, NY: Free Press.

Keim-Malpass, J., Steeves, R. H., & Kennedy, C. (2014). Internet ethnography: A review of methodological considerations for studying online illness blogs. *International Journal of Nursing Studies, 51,* 1686–1692.

Landau, R. (2008). Social work research ethics: Dual roles and boundary issues. *Families in Society, 89*(4), 571–577.

Mahon, P. Y. (2014). Internet research and ethics: Transformative issues in nursing education research. *Journal of Professional Nursing, 30*(2), 124–129.

Miller, T., Birch, M., Mauthner, M., & Jessop, J. (2012). *Ethics in qualitative research.* Thousand Oaks, CA: Sage.

Muhlbaier, L. H. (2006). Health Insurance Portability and Accountability Act and research. In Elizabeth A. Bankert and Robert J. Amdur (Eds.), *Institutional review board: Management and function.* Sudbury, MA: Jones and Bartlett Publishers.

Noel, M., Boerner, K. E., Birnie, K. A., Caes, L., Parker, J. A., Chambers, C. T., ... & Lee, K. (2015). Acceptability by parents and children of deception in pediatric research. *Journal of Developmental and Behavioral Pediatrics, 36,* 75–85.

Oakes, J. M. (2006). Survey research. In Elizabeth A. Bankert and Robert J. Amdur (Eds.), *Institutional review board: Management and function.* Sudbury, MA: Jones and Bartlett Publishers.

Oki, G. S. F., & Zaia, J. A. (2006). In Elizabeth A. Bankert and Robert J. Amdur (Eds.), *Institutional review board: Management and function.* Sudbury, MA: Jones and Bartlett Publishers.

Paul, C., & Brookes, B. (2015). The rationalization of unethical research: Revisionist accounts of the Tuskegee Syphilis Study and the New Zealand "Unfortunate Experiment." *American Journal of Public Health, 105*(10), e12–e19.

Plunk, A. D., & Grucza, R. A. (2013). Public health research, deception, and distrust. *American Journal of Bioethics, 13*(11), 54–55.

Schilling, R. F., Schinke, S. P, Kirkham, M. A., Meltzer, N. J., & Norelius, K. L. (1988). Social work research in social service agencies: Issues and guidelines. *Journal of Social Service Research, 11*(4), 75–87.

Skloot, R. 2010. *The immortal life of Henrietta Lacks.* New York, NY: Macmillan.

Sieber, J. E. (1992). Planning ethically responsible research: A guide for students and internal review boards. Newbury Park, CA: Sage.

Wellons, K. (1973). The expectancy component in mental retardation. (Doctoral dissertation, University of California, Berkeley.)

Credit

ASSIGNMENT 3.1

Conducting Ethical Research with Vulnerable Populations

Objective: *To provide the experience of reflecting about the ways that data collection can intersect with ethical concerns.*

Some clients of social workers are those who may be vulnerable for many different reasons. One population that we haven't discussed thus far in the chapter consists of people with intellectual disabilities. These may be individuals with congenital developmental conditions like Down syndrome as well as those with acquired brain injuries (e.g., traumatic brain injuries).

Before answering the questions below, your instructor may ask you to read the following article: Northway, R., Howarth, J., & Evans, L. (2014). Participatory research, people with intellectual disabilities and ethical approval: Making reasonable adjustments to enable participation. *Journal of Clinical Nursing, 24*, 573–581.

1. As a researcher, how would you go about explaining a study involving individuals with intellectual disability to the possible participants you would like to recruit?

2. How would you check to make sure the participants understood their rights as research participants?

3. How do you think you might have to modify your data collection procedures from those typically used with persons without intellectual disability?

ASSIGNMENT 3.2

Developing an Informed-Consent Form Draft

Objective: *To obtain practice in writing an informed consent form.*

Check the website of the institutional review board at your college or university and obtain a sample informed-consent form. If they do not make these available, then use the example provided in this chapter to write your own in a "participant-friendly" style. Address the following questions as you think about the safeguards needed for some fictitious study that you could propose.

1. What is the purpose of the study?

2. Why am I being invited to take part in this research?

3. Who is conducting the study?

4. What will I be asked to do?

5. Where is the study going to take place, and how long will it last?

6. Are there any possible risks or discomforts?

7. Will I benefit from taking part in this study?

8. Do I have to take part in this study?

9. Do I receive any payment or rewards for taking part in the study?

10. Who will see the information I give?

ASSIGNMENT 3.3

Preparing an IRB Exemption Request

Objective: *To obtain experience in succinctly explaining research plans on a required form.*

Check the website of the institutional review board at your college or university, and obtain the instructions (or the form) that researchers follow to request permission to have their research exempted from full IRB review. To complete this task, you will need to (1) list research objectives; (2) describe the characteristics of the population from which you will be drawing your subjects; (3) describe your plans for recruiting the research subjects; and (4) detail the activities or procedures that will pertain to the subjects. If there are any potential risks to the subjects, these will also have to be described. Your instructor may want you to write your responses here as a draft before or in lieu of using the IRB form.

1. List your research objectives:

2. Describe the characteristics of the subject population such as gender, age ranges, ethnic background, and whether they have any special status (for example, minors, prisoners, mentally disabled):

3. Describe your plans for recruiting subjects:

4. Briefly describe the research procedures that will be applied to the human subjects:

5. Describe any potential physical, psychological, social, legal, or other risks to the research:

CHAPTER 4

Single-System Research Designs

S INGLE-SYSTEM RESEARCH DESIGNS (SSRDs) are easy to use and understand, even with a limited understanding of research methodology. They provide practitioners with immediate, inexpensive, and practical feedback on whether their clients are improving.

Unlike the quantitative approaches we will study later that involve groups of clients and assist us in understanding the "average" client, single-system research designs typically focus on an individual client and his or her situation. Single-system research designs are easiest to explain when the client has a specific behavior that will be the focus of intervention. For instance, a child with autism spectrum disorder may break things whenever he gets stressed. Parents could ask for your help in managing this behavior.

Besides applying these designs to individual clients, single-system research designs can be used to evaluate the progress being made by a community, an organization, a family, or even a couple receiving marital counseling. The main thing to keep in mind is that the choice of a target behavior or outcome variable must allow for frequent or continuous assessment. This is the chief characteristic of all SSRDs.

Advocates of single-system research designs argue that information about specific clients is often obscured in studies where clients are grouped together, that one might learn little about an individual client—perhaps only whether a client did better or worse than average. However, single-system research designs "personalize" the research by looking at a single client's particular behavior over time. That is, repeated assessments are made of the problem or situation. This makes SSRDs particularly valuable to those concerned with evidence-based practice.

Before we learn how to develop single-system research designs (also known as $N = 1$ research, single-case evaluation, and single-subject designs) for our clients, let's first consider their history.

The Origin of Single-System Research Designs

The study of individual cases has long been a part of the richness of the social sciences. For more than a century, case studies have been conducted in behavioral research. Prior to the development of statistics for group comparisons, research in the social sciences consisted almost entirely of descriptive case studies and reflections on them. Case studies were useful for illustrating to one's colleagues and students how problems requiring remedial action could be approached with specific theories or interventions.

Individual case studies have appeared with some frequency throughout social science literature, and case examples or vignettes of cases are not uncommon today in some journals. However, case studies vary greatly in their format, content, and organization. As statistical tests of comparison were developed and widely accepted, case studies fell out of favor with researchers in the social sciences. The use of control groups and group statistical comparisons is now firmly established in the social sciences, and the objective or quantitative methods of measurement used with these studies have led to changes in those wanting to determine if a single client has improved.

The emergence of single-system research designs in the 1960s and 1970s has been attributed to their use by B. F. Skinner and other practitioners of behavior modification. With a focus on a specific target behavior, single-system research designs are well suited for practitioners interested in demonstrating that their interventions are effective. Unlike the descriptive case studies of prior years, which relied heavily on subjective opinions and assessments of change, SSRDs today use objective measures to document that change has occurred.

ANXIETY CHECK 4.1

What is the difference between an objective and a subjective assessment?

[Answer at the end of the book.]

Single-System Research Designs and Practice

Single-system research designs can be thought of as a bridge between research and practice. How is this possible? Imagine for a moment that it is sometime in the future. You have made it through the social work program and are now employed as a therapist in a mental health agency. The following case presents itself:

> A 20-year-old attending the local university is your second appointment of the day. She is of medium height, on the thin side, and wearing jeans and a wrinkled cotton top. Her intake sheet says that she is unable to sleep, doesn't have much of an appetite, and has been referred by a friend. Once the student begins talking, she describes being unable to focus and is failing most of her classes. Even her employer on campus is threatening to fire her for absenteeism. When asked a few more questions, she reveals that her mother, residing in another state, was recently given a terminal diagnosis.

You have worked with depressed persons before and feel that you can help this woman. You also remember that your new clinical director wants staff to evaluate their practice with clients. So, how would you determine whether your counseling was successful? Would you calculate the number of times she said she cried last week? Could her affect indicate depression? Her inability to focus on courses? Even with an intuition that you could help her, how would you go about evaluating your own practice?

Because the client's symptoms suggest depression, you ask the client to complete a short, 21-item standardized scale, the Beck Depression Inventory (BDI-II). The client scores 35 on this scale, suggesting that she has severe depression. (Here's something you should know about the BDI-II: scores 13 and lower indicate minimal depression, those 14–19 are indicative of mild depression, scores 20–28 represent moderate depression, and 29 and higher suggest severe depression.) Discussion began immediately about ways the client could better manage her course load and part-time job and find a way to spend time with her mother. You decide to track the client's progress by administering the BDI-II each time the client comes for an appointment. When you view these test results on a graph over the several weeks of treatment, it

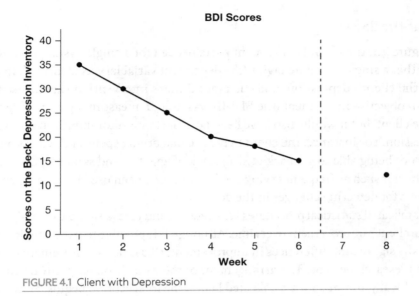

FIGURE 4.1 Client with Depression

is easy to see that the client's level of depression fell during this time and remained low even after not meeting for a week. Figure 4.1 demonstrates this visually in a graph.

Even a cursory glimpse at this graph or at the others in this chapter will convince you that single-system graphs are often easy to comprehend. This simplicity is the essence of single-system research designs—the visual presentation of a client's progress. In Figure 4.1, you will also see the data used to prepare the graph in Excel. Here's an explanation of how to go about creating a graph:

BOX 4.1   CREATING AN SSRD GRAPH WITH EXCEL

Excel is a well-known spreadsheet that has very powerful graphing properties with many more bells and whistles that you may need. You don't have to be an expert to create nice-looking graphs without too much effort—but you may need to experiment a bit. Here is a simple version of steps needed to create an AB design graph.

Step 1: Open Excel and enter your data. In the first column type the name of your variable (e.g., Days—for the horizontal axis) and then enter each day covered by both the baseline and intervention period.

Step 2: In Column B enter the name of your operationalized target behavior (e.g., Nail-biting) and the frequency with which it occurs each day. There should be an enry in Column B for each day in Column A.

Step 3: Highlight the targeted behaviors, then click on the Insert tab. Chose *Graphs* or a graph format to use. (Scatter graphs are best for SSRD designs.) The data should populate the graph.

Step 4. Choose the *Layout* tab or *Design* and label your chart and the horizontal and vertical axes.

Step 5. To add the dotted line separating the A phase from the B phase, go back to *Insert,* choose *Shapes,* then click on a straight line. Place the origin of the line at the top of the chart and take it to the bottom. Either click on the line or choose a *Dash Type* to make it dotted.

Step 6. If you want to label the A and B phases of your SSRD, go to *Insert* and click on *Textbox.* Click in the chart where you want to place it. To remove gridlines, click on your chart or find *Chart Tools* to indicate *No lines.*

A Closer Look at the SSRD

If you examine Figure 4.1, the several component parts needed for a single-system research design can be detected. Note that a single **target behavior** (the dependent variable) was identified. In this instance, the problem was the client's depression, and the practitioner's intervention was focused on reducing that depression. An objective instrument (the BDI-II) was used to measure the level of depression being experienced by the client, but it would also have been possible to monitor improvement with behavioral measures of depression. For instance, the client may have had crying spells or sleepless nights, episodes or waking up and not being able to get back to sleep, lack of appetite and skipped meals, etc. The selection of a target behavior such as frequent crying spells could have been used had there been no objective instrument available for detecting changes in the depression.

Note that no complicated statistical procedures are needed to interpret a single-case design—just a simple graph to record the client's improvement over time. Although it is possible to use statistical procedures to check for statistically significant differences in improvement, this is not a requirement or a necessity for most single-system research designs. The arrangement of the data chronologically on the graph makes it easy to interpret. Ideally, initial data are collected before the intervention begins. However, in the case presented at the beginning of this chapter, the practitioner needed to make an assessment of the client's problem before choosing an instrument to measure the progress in treatment.

The pre-intervention data create the **baseline** and allow for comparisons to be made during treatment and possibly later in a follow-up period.

Retrospective baselines are memory-based estimates of the severity of a problem; or in some instances, they could be based on actual data that already exist, such as grades on a mid-term report or absences from school on a high school student's report card. **Prospective baselines** or concurrent baselines are measurements of the problem that are usually begun at or immediately after an initial assessment and extend into the future. The measurement of a target behavior prior to beginning intervention (the baseline) is the second key characteristic of SSRDs.

Steps in Starting an SSRD

Step 1: The first step in developing an SSRD is to define the problem and choose a behavior to monitor. This may be a difficult decision, but sometimes it is obvious which behavior needs to be targeted: If you have a client who has been arrested for driving while intoxicated, and this is the second arrest in six months, it is clear that you have a client who needs to change his or her drinking behavior. Similarly, it would be apparent that a child with school phobia must decrease the number of days absent from school. Some clients need to demonstrate greater assertiveness; others need to learn to handle their destructive anger. Generally speaking, you will be working with clients to either increase (or acquire) or decrease (possibly to completely suppress) certain behaviors.

There will not be one target behavior that can be selected for all your clients. Here are some examples of problems that clients or their families may bring:

- A child needs to increase positive interactions with peers
- Parents want to reduce a child's fear of the dark and get the child to sleep quicker
- A single woman wants to address her shyness and become more assertive
- Several men have been referred by a judge for anger management

ANXIETY CHECK 4.2

Look at the bullets shown above and think of at least one way that you could measure some behavior connected to each of the problems so that improvement could be graphed.

[Answer at the back of the book.]

- Behaviors to be monitored in a SSRD must necessarily follow from the treatment plan prepared for that individual client. As a practitioner, you most likely will find specific behaviors to target for the SSRD as you work with the client and begin developing treatment goals.
- The selection of the appropriate problem to be influenced by the intervention is obviously important. When choosing a target behavior, keep the following in mind:
- *Target behaviors should come from the client.* Selecting problems that are not aligned with the client's perceptions of their issues may lead to them dropping out of treatment. Although some clients may have problems that are only revealed after a trusting relationship has been established, the best place to start is with the problem the client has identified as being most significant. This may require some prioritizing of the client's problems.

Horner et al. (2005) say that the dependent variable "is perceived as important for the individual participant, those who come in contact with the individual, or for society" (p. 167). Along this line, it may be helpful to use the following criteria to prioritize the problems mentioned by clients.
Problems that:

a. are the most concern to the client or court;
b. have the most negative consequences for the client, the client's significant others, or society if not handled immediately;
c. have a high probability of being corrected quickly and providing an experience of success that may lead to continuing work;
d. problems that require handling before other problems can be addressed.

Ideally, the social worker and the client should reach mutual agreement regarding the major concern and focus of the intervention during treatment planning.
Step 2: Because vaguely stated problems are difficult to measure, select a method that allows you to monitor a concrete and observable behavior. Avoid any behavior that might be difficult to detect or about which there might be disagreement as to whether it is happening.

Choose behaviors that can be counted, observed, or quantified. You may have to help your client move from an ambiguous description of the problem to a more precise definition. For instance, "nervousness" is a vague complaint, but associated with it may be several observable behaviors such as nail biting, over-eating, stuttering, episodes of gastrointestinal attacks, or excessive use of antacids that could be used as surrogate measures of the nervousness. You could count the number of antacids consumed in a day, the number of stuttering episodes, or the number of snacks or calories ingested per day. Whenever possible, target behaviors should be so well defined that others would have little difficulty in observing or recording them. Start with the client's presenting problem and then explore how that problem manifests itself.

Bill dropped heavily into the hard desk before class. The only other student in the classroom was Sophia, studying as usual. "Hey," Bill said. "Have you got a minute? There's something I want to ask you."

"Sure. I've already read the chapter once—just wanted to review it again."

"My sister is having some issues with her husband and they're talking about going into marriage counseling."

"That would be a good first step," said Sophia, closing her book and giving Bill her full attention.

"Anyway, my sister says that her husband has explained their problems as 'Megan doesn't respect him.' However, Megan doesn't have any idea of what he's talking about. Does he mean that Megan is busy cooking or walking away while he is still talking? Is he unhappy when she asks him to change the baby or go buy diapers after he comes home from work? If so, I told her she could try to track it—see how many times it happens."

"Good idea," Sophia said, "but 'lack of respect' doesn't work as a target behavior. The term is too broad and not immediately associated with any specific behavior. In counseling, the therapist will ask what is happening when your brother-in-law experiences feeling not respected. Now, if they were arguing almost daily, then they could keep track of how often they argue—that would be a good target behavior. Does that make sense?"

"It does. Megan was just blindsided and confused by his saying that she doesn't respect him. Of course she does. She loves him. I get it, though. Tom is going to have to tell Megan when he is feeling disrespected so that they can identify whatever is annoying him. Thanks, Sophia. Maybe I could use this example for my SSRD assignment—what do you think?"

"You could, Bill, but be sure to disguise things so that no one knows it's your sister."

"What should the target behavior be?"

"I don't think we know enough to really say at this point," Sophia said.

"Maybe I should look for an instrument that the counselor could administer." Bill pulled a small notebook out of his back pocket and placed it on the desk as three other students walked in to the classroom.

"Fine idea," Sophia said. "You might want to look for a standardized measure to assess something like their marital satisfaction. If the marital counseling is successful, then it is reasonable to assume that their scores on a marital satisfaction scale would improve."

Sometimes, clients describe problems like fear of dying or loneliness that seem to be more of a mental state than a behavior. In instances like these, you may want to consult Corcoran and Fischer's (2013) *Measures for Clinical Practice* to obtain scales that objectively measure the kinds of problems that social workers often encounter. However, even mental states and attitudes are likely to be associated with a set of behaviors. The person who is afraid of dying (perhaps because someone close to them died recently) may be having panic attacks or insomnia, or they may be unable to concentrate at work or school. The individual who is experiencing loneliness may need to change introverted, reclusive behaviors (e.g., staying inside his or her apartment all the time) and increase social contacts by joining clubs, coed volleyball teams, hobby groups, and so on. As a practitioner, you have to decide what behaviors to monitor and how to monitor improvement. The challenge is always to operationalize so specifically that there is little doubt when change or improvement is occurring.

Not only will vaguely stated problems create difficulties when you attempt to measure them, but so can rather specific events (for example, hearing voices or having delusions) if your client doesn't report these or if they are not observable by others. Certainly, most clients are able to self-report on behaviors or problems that are not noticeable to others, but unless the client is strongly motivated to alleviate the problem, these might not be ideal to select for measurement with an SSRD. The easiest problems to measure are those that are easily recognized by others and repetitive. (For instance, I once heard of a client in a residential treatment program who took 10 or more long showers a day—inconveniencing most of the other residents.)

BOX 4.2 THREE WAYS TO MEASURE A BEHAVIOR

Frequency (For example, counting the number of a resident's showers each day. If conducting marital therapy, frequency of arguments or days per month of sexual intimacy. For a family, number of game nights or outings as a family. In a volunteer organization, how often it meets or the number of new members that get added.)

Duration or length of time (For instance, how long the showers typically last. In marital therapy, length of arguments, longest single conversation, or time spent in dinner together in past week.)

Magnitude or intensity (For example, a door-slamming argument over the lack of hot water or a physical altercation. Also, extreme or out-of-bounds behaviors such as punching a hole in the wall, throwing the dinner out, overspending the budget on a shopping spree or gambling episode, destroying something valued by the other person. In an organization, the set objectives that are accomplished, achievements.)

The practitioner has quite a bit of freedom in choosing what to measure, how to measure, and even who should do the recording. However, the target behavior should suggest itself from the client's description of the problem. The behavior should be an activity that a client agrees is important to count or record. Clients should be able to see how change in the target behavior contributes to improving their problem situation.

Step 3: Choose the intervention. The treatment will depend upon the problem and behavior, of course. Following an evidence-based practice approach, you will want to obtain as much information as possible about the effectiveness of various interventions available to you and the client.

Step 4: Select the SSRD to use. There is a wide variety of SSRD designs, and we will discuss those very soon. However, first we need to direct our attention to thinking about the baseline, which will be a key feature in any SSRD we might choose, and developing a graph.

Step 5: Monitor the target behavior over time. Graphs are useful tools for allowing us to visually see and portray changes in behavior. Graphs can be drawn on engineering or graph paper, or you can also create SSRDs in Excel. Figure 4.2 shows the bare-bones basics of an SSRD with two hypothetical axes.

On the *vertical line* (or *y-axis*), plot the number of times (frequency) the target behavior occurs. You must have a rough idea how often the behavior is occurring to devise a scale to show its pattern. For instance, if Juan Pablo misses his bus three times in one week, the vertical axis should record the range of lowest and greatest number possible of these incidents. Because it is unlikely that he could miss his bus more than five mornings a week, the range of these episodes would be 0 to 5.

Some thought needs to go into the selection of the behavior or the problem being counted on the vertical axis. Because missing a bus might be a matter of oversleeping, you might want to target the number of times that Juan Pablo gets to bed on time the night before. Or, if he is a little older and sets his own alarm clock, the number of times that he oversleeps. Both of these could be legitimate target behaviors for intervention. (However, it is also possible that he is reluctant or resistant to going to school because

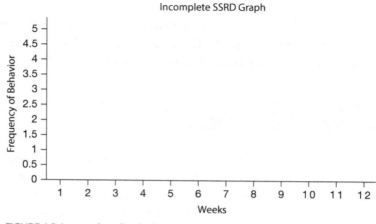

FIGURE 4.2 Incomplete Single-System Graph

he is being bullied—and maybe hasn't revealed that. If that is the explanation for missing the bus, a social worker would have a different intervention and target behavior.)

Notice the emphasis on counting behaviors. It would be less useful to chart the actual time that Juan Pablo gets out of bed because there are too many possibilities (60 minutes in an hour). But one might create categories of something like: less than 9 minutes, 10 to 19 minutes, 20 to 29 minutes, 30 to 39 minutes, and 40 minutes or more. On the other hand, if his difficulty is getting to bed on time, the vertical axis might be constructed to show the number of minutes past his bedtime that he is late each evening. Or if Juan Pablo tends to dawdle, counting intervals of time such as minutes spent dressing or eating breakfast might also be appropriate for the vertical axis. If he is so late that he tends to not have time to eat breakfast, then counting those events could be appropriate.

The *horizontal line* (or *x-axis*) is used to portray the behavior as it occurs over time. Whether you decide to use hours, days, or weeks as the unit of time depends on the behavior itself. If you are working with an eight-year-old who is having stomachaches because of school phobia and this tends to happen once a day, say, 10 minutes before the school bus arrives, it would be better to count the number of times a week that the stomachaches occur than to keep hourly records. A baseline graph of the number of stomachaches in a month prior to the intervention might resemble the one in Figure 4.3.

This graph shows that the child complained of stomach problems five times (corresponding to the five school days) the first week that a record was kept, five times the second and fourth weeks, but only four times in the third week when there was a school holiday. In this example, we know that the symptoms are occurring every school day. The child missed having a stomachache only once on a school day during a 28-day period. This is a well-established, or **stable, pattern**

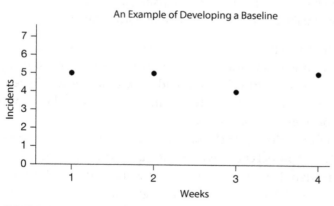

FIGURE 4.3 An Example of Developing a Baseline

of behavior. If intervention is effective, a pattern of improvement will be readily observable. Contrast this pattern with a target behavior that is unpredictable (where there is no discernible pattern). Suppose that the child had three stomachaches the first week, two the second week, three stomachaches during the third week, and none during the fourth week. This would be an erratic pattern where we might want a longer baseline to help us understand what is going on. Instead of school phobia, the child's stomach problems might be due to food allergies that are triggered by specific foods that are not eaten seven days a week. Alternatively, we might want to choose a different target behavior for the SSRD.

ANXIETY CHECK 4.3

What behaviors besides a stomachache do you think a child might exhibit if he or she has school phobia?

[Answer is at the back of the book.]

One rule often heard about the length of the baseline period is that it should contain at least three observations. However, if the behavior is highly variable, three observations may not be enough. You may need five, seven, nine, or more. The issue here is the stability of the pattern. A behavior that occurs relatively infrequently probably is not a useful behavior to choose for monitoring because it will be hard to see any patterns. Similarly, behavior that varies a great deal will not make a good target behavior. Choose a behavior that is fairly dependable in its occurrence. The behavior can vary in frequency, but this variation should not swing wildly.

BOX 4.3   GUIDELINES CONCERNING THE LENGTH OF THE BASELINE

- The baseline should be long enough to provide a "snapshot" of the client's problems.
- It should be stable enough to allow you to understand how often the behavior is occurring (its frequency without intervention).
- Three observations during baseline are considered a minimum, but this number is often insufficient, and ten baseline points are recommended if it is ethically and practically possible.

You don't have to wait five or six weeks to construct a baseline. Suppose a mother comes to you because she is concerned that her five-year-old is still wetting the bed. You ask, "About how often does this happen?" If the mother says, "About every night" or "Almost every night," then the baseline is established, and you can begin with the assumption that bed wetting is occurring about 30 times a month. Even if it is actually happening only 27 or 25 times a month, the obvious goal is to decrease these incidents to zero times per week.

Baseline data can come from various sources. You might find ample reference to the occurrence of the target behavior in the progress notes made during a client intake or therapy session, or the client may have kept some informal records or have a good memory, or there may be official records (for example, school absences). In US society, documentation is often readily available. A baseline for a spouse whose drinking behavior results in days missed from work might be obtained by looking at paycheck stubs. In some instances, clients can keep logs or self-report on the occurrence of the target behavior. In other situations, someone else will need to monitor the behavior. These decisions are individually determined by the practitioner from knowledge of the client's abilities and situation.

A good argument for using existing records or data for the baseline is that the very act of counting or measuring a behavior during the baseline phase may begin to change the client's behavior (especially if the client is self-reporting and motivated to improve), even before the intervention is implemented. This could make it difficult to determine later if the intervention was making a difference. Needless to say, self-monitoring data will give a false picture if the client is motivated to misrepresent the extent or severity of the problem.

As can be seen in Figure 4.4, the behavior during the baseline period is usually separated from the behavior during the intervention phase by a vertical dotted line. Once you have a good idea about how to handle the baseline, then it is time to definitely commit to a design. Of the many single-system research designs from which to choose, only a few of those judged to be the most valuable to practitioners are presented here. As you read the balance of this chapter, you may find yourself liking some designs over others.

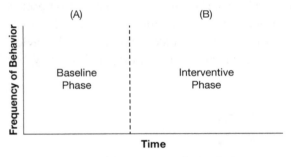

FIGURE 4.4 Essential Components of a Single-System Design

Some designs may strike you as impractical (or worse) because they seem more suited for applications where one has greater control over the client system than you anticipate. One design (the AB) is likely to meet most of your needs. But other designs may be more appropriate for a particular case or for when you want greater assurance that it was your intervention and not some other factor that had the desired effect.

View each of the designs described to gain knowledge about how they could be applied in your practice.

Types of SSRD Designs

There are several ways to conceptualize a single-system research design. That is, there are relatively simple designs and much more complex and involved designs. The choice of design is largely influenced by the extent to which you wish to establish that it was the intervention that truly made the difference. However, the design choice may also be affected by other considerations as well, as we'll see.

The Case Study or B Design

Case studies are familiar to most students. They are detailed descriptions of an individual client, family, group, community, or other "units." Usually, they are selected because of some uniqueness or because they exemplify a situation or problem that is the focus of a study. These may be rare situations or common ones where a new or different hypothesis is being proposed as a way of understanding or treating a type of case or situation. From a case study, one might learn how a certain theoretical approach or intervention is applied.

Case studies are sometimes called uncontrolled case studies because they lack baseline measures and use anecdotal information rather than systematic and objective assessment of the target behavior. These designs are therefore seriously limited in that they do not permit conclusions that the intervention caused the change in the client's behavior. (Other forces or influences may have been at work in addition to the intervention.) What's more, there is no guarantee that the findings from a case study will generalize or fit any other case.

However, case study designs are simple to conceptualize, don't require preplanning, and are possible to start once intervention has begun. Although they can't ascribe causation or rule out competing explanations, they can describe client progress.

With the beginning of intervention, the practitioner begins keeping records on how much the client changes or improves. No attempt is made to compare the behavior at the end of the intervention with its baseline (because there was none). This design is descriptive in nature and can be used with any theoretical orientation. However, the case study has a number of serious limitations: lack of systematic observation and standardization of assessment, no baseline measures, and little control of the treatment variable (the intervention may involve several simultaneous procedures). Furthermore, case studies rely heavily on anecdotal information that may rest on a heavily biased presentation, and because of the focus on one individual, the results cannot be generalized to other situations.

Though they lack scientific rigor, case studies are useful for several reasons: They are a source of hypotheses about human behavior and techniques for working with clients; they have a strong persuasive appeal in illustrating a particular point; and they stimulate us to examine rare phenomena (Yin, 2014).

A fascinating case study is found in Russ Rymer's *Genie: An Abused Child's Flight from Silence* (1993). This book narrates the discovery of a 13-year-old girl who, weighing 59 pounds, was incontinent, could not chew solid food, could not cry or focus her eyes beyond 12 feet, and had no perception of heat and cold. Her productive vocabulary was limited to "Stopit," "Nomore," and several other shorter negatives. And yet she was described as having incredible curiosity, energy, and personality. For most of her life, Genie had been confined alone in a small bedroom, harnessed to an infant's potty chair, and beaten if she made any noise. Case studies like this can be riveting to read. However, often they are devoid of pertinent information that would give us a basis for comparison. In this case, the child's father was convinced that she was mentally retarded and would die before the age of 12, but what was her IQ before she was socially and physically deprived? (You can also read a detailed account of Genie's story online: **https://en.wikipedia. org/wiki/Genie_(feral_child).**)

While case studies are educational and useful from a pedagogic standpoint, they are not able to formally test hypotheses. One does not see that many case studies reported in our professional literature. However, if you want to go beyond their description in this chapter and learn more about them and ways to assess or evaluate their quality, you may wish to read Lee, Mishna, and Brennenstuhl (2010).

When we encounter a complex, difficult, or particularly puzzling client or family, it is often beneficial to build on the simple case study model by constructing a baseline and observing target behaviors. When we add these features, the simple case study becomes an SSRD, capable of providing objective evidence that our treatment did or did not benefit the client.

Should you wish to read an illustration of a case study, two examples in the literature are listed below:

✓ Cree, V. E., Jain, S., & Hillen, D. P. (2016). The challenge of measuring effectiveness in social work: A case study of an evaluation of a drug and alcohol referral service in Scotland. *British Journal of Social Work, 46*(1), 277–293.

✓ Bragin, M., Taaka, J., Adolphs, K., et al. (2015). Measuring difficult-to-measure concepts in clinical social work practice operationalizing psychosocial well-being among war-affected women: A case study in northern Uganda. *Clinical Social Work Journal, 43*(4), 348–361.

AB Design

The basic **AB design** (see Figure 4.5) is the SSRD most often used by social work practitioners and researchers. The *A* portion of the design is the baseline measurement (for example, the client's scores on a scale assessing depression). The *B* part of the design is the data collected during the treatment phase. Because of its simplicity, the AB design is virtually unlimited in its applicability in social work. This is perhaps its greatest strength. It reveals changes in behavior—if they occur. Unfortunately, changes in behavior that are detected with this design do not "prove" that the intervention was responsible. Alternative explanations such as the occurrence of other events during intervention (for example,

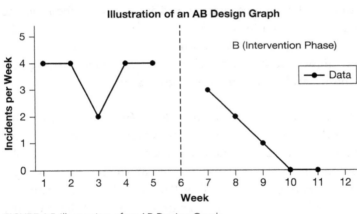

FIGURE 4.5 Illustration of an AB Design Graph

leaving a stressful job, the birth of a child, over-the-fence counseling by a neighbor, or maturation of the client) may account for changes in the client's behavior. These alternative or rival explanations are difficult to rule out with the basic AB design. Most practitioners, however, would be happy with the client's success and would not worry about alternative explanations. While the AB design may not adequately control for competing explanations, it provides a useful way of examining whether there has been an improvement since intervention began.

ABA and ABAB Designs

These two designs are sometimes called **experimental single-system** (also withdrawal or reversal) **research designs** because they employ a second period of nonintervention, another baseline condition, to show that the intervention was responsible for the observed effect on the target behavior. These designs are concerned with whether the effect of the intervention will continue or be maintained. After the intervention (B) has been completed or substantially delivered, treatment is withdrawn or stopped, and the target problem is monitored to see what direction it takes.

The second *A* phase in an **ABA design** is like the first *A* phase in that behavior is recorded during a period of no intervention. This is not to suggest that you as a practitioner should purposely withdraw treatment for "research" purposes—that could be an unethical practice. The second *A* phase could legitimately come about because of any absence or break in treatment—such as an extended Christmas break or illness. Or it could come as a follow-up visit a week or two after the client's treatment has ended.

Each phase of the classical single-system research design (AB) is repeated twice in the **ABAB design**. As in the ABA design, a second baseline allows the practitioner to determine if the target behavior will return to its original level (prior to intervention). There may be valid reasons for a second period of nonintervention, both practical (for example, the client's or therapist's vacation) and therapeutic (for instance, a trial period of three weeks between appointments to wean a "dependent" client away from intervention). After the second baseline period, the treatment is reintroduced. Unlike the ABA design, the study ends during an intervention phase, which may make it more appealing to some practitioners.

Because the client serves as his or her own control, the ABAB design is an experimental design and provides some assurance that the intervention actually was responsible for any changes in behavior. In this sense, the ABAB design is a stronger and more powerful design than the AB and ABA designs. If the same effect (e.g., client improvement) is shown during the second AB (replication) phase, then there is less likelihood that outside influences (alternative explanations) were responsible. The ABAB is a strong design for those who are interested in contributing to the knowledge base by experimentally demonstrating that a new intervention may have promise.

However, use of the ABAB design is not always practical. In fact, if the first treatment phase reduced the behavior to acceptable levels for the client, it is likely that the practitioner would feel that the intervention was a success. Termination would occur, and the therapist would be given a new client to add to his or her caseload. There would be little reason to introduce intervention again unless the client made another request. In fact, the more successful the intervention, the less likely it will be that the behavior will return to its initial baseline (A) level.

The ABAB design may not feel comfortable to many practitioners because they may feel pressure to close cases and address clients on the waiting list for service. Even though the second baseline could come about naturally due to vacations, hospitalizations, and so on, the ABAB design may still seem excessive or a luxury unavailable to many practitioners.

The ABAB design is best thought of as a design to be used for knowledge building. It is a design that enables thorough testing of an intervention and reduction of alternative explanations for the client's improvement. You would use this design if you wanted to make sure that a given intervention worked and you wanted to document or publish your findings. You might want to keep in mind, though, that carryover effects are likely present in this design. That is, what the client has already learned or experienced in the first treatment phase "cannot be unlearned or unexperienced" (Ray, 2015, p. 396).

ABC and ABCD Designs

Practitioners know well that sometimes the intervention you start with doesn't work, is not valued by the client, or does not appear to be working as fast as it should. In these situations, major changes could be made in the treatment plan. Another intervention might be started or additional modalities employed.

The **ABC** or **successive interventions design** permits the practitioner to respond with different interventions when needed and still allows for monitoring the effects of these interventions. In this scheme,

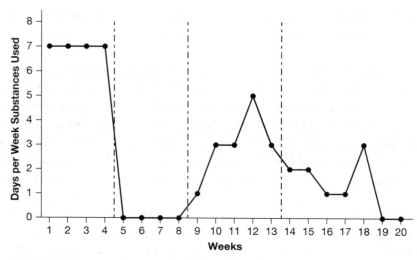

FIGURE 4.6 Treatment Progress of a 25 Year-Old College Dropout

the effects of the second intervention are identified as **C**. The effects of the third intervention are **D**, and so on—a new letter for each different treatment modality. Figure 4.6 shows an example of an **ABCD design**.

Because there is no return to a baseline between the second and third forms of treatment, these successive intervention designs do not allow the practitioner to determine which interventions actually caused the changes in the behavior. Imagine you have a client abusing prescription medication. It appears that inpatient treatment was very successful in the *B* phase when the client couldn't get access to drugs, but without that structure in place, the client relapsed during the outpatient treatment in the *C* phase. The patient begins routinely attending a 12-step program in the *D* phase.

Was it that intervention that made the difference? Or could it be that the accumulative and interactive effects of both *B* and *C* resulted in the client's change? With this design, it is difficult to attribute any successful outcome to a specific intervention, although it may appear that the last one was the most successful.

Even if this design tends to fall short of the experimenter's expectations, it is appealing to practitioners in the real world because intervention is often modified in practice, and different techniques are used in the course of therapy. If everyone is happy that the behavior has changed in the desired direction, and treatment success seems to be in the air, neither client nor practitioner may need greater "proof" that the interventions worked.

Multiple Baseline Designs

Single-system research designs known as **multiple baseline designs** may be used when you are working with several clients who have the same problem or an individual with multiple problems *and* the same intervention is applied. For instance, suppose you are employed as a social worker in a nursing home. The staff begins to complain about a problem of urinary incontinence with three wheelchair-bound residents who have organic brain disorders. You've recently read an article describing the use of an intervention involving praise and cookies for patients like this that resulted in a decrease in urinary accidents. The staff is eager to participate and soon begin collecting baseline data.

Multiple Baselines Across Subjects Design

Keeping true to the standards on which single-system research designs are based, the intervention starts first with Mr. Smith. Only when there is clear indication of improvement is the intervention applied to the second resident, Mrs. Wright. Only when she shows improvement can the intervention be applied to the third resident. When success is achieved with all three residents, this becomes the basis for inferring that the intervention caused the observed changes. The shorthand notation for a **multiple baselines across subjects design** is $A_1A_2A_3B$.

You can see in Figure 4.7 that multiple baseline designs have baselines of unequal length and that intervention does not begin in the second graph until change has been shown with the first student. The next graph doesn't start until change is shown with the second student—and so on. Why is that? The multiple baselines across subjects design stretches the concept of a single subject and still attempts to be as true as possible to its roots. That is why the intervention is not applied to multiple subjects simultaneously. This design is a series of simple, single-system research designs.

Multiple Baselines Across Behaviors Design

Unlike the previous design, which allowed for an intervention to be tested with a very small sample of clients with the same problem, a **multiple baselines across behaviors design** can be employed if a single client has two, three, or more problems that are likely to respond to the same intervention. If the client has three target problems, then the notation would reflect the three separate baselines and one intervention; the notation would still be written $A_1A_2A_3B$. Whether across subjects or behaviors, the notation for both multiple baseline designs (across subjects and behaviors) is the same.

For instance, suppose you are working with a 15-year-old boy in a residential treatment facility for youth. John has been abused by a stepfather, is not doing well in school, and has poor impulse control, which gets him into frequent fights. He defies authority, is uncooperative with staff, and boasts of his skills in shoplifting. John is bright and personable, capable of finishing college but currently doing poorly in school. Where would you start addressing his multiple problems?

Following the principles we learned earlier, baselines must be started on all of the behaviors that are problematic and of concern. Since he is living in a residential center, it is very important he be able to get along with other boys in the facility. Let's say that John and his social worker agree that it is critical to reduce the incidence of fighting with residents at the treatment center and to start with that behavior. When there is progress with that, another behavior like being less defiant of authority might be attempted, and then when there is progress with that one, perhaps John would be receptive to making a greater effort on his schoolwork.

Practitioners may want to consider the multiple baseline designs because of the inferences that can be made about the effectiveness of treatment. An intervention that produces strong rates of change across various behaviors or with different clients is showing generalizability, or **external validity**. In other words, these designs provide evidence that the intervention was responsible for the improvement. The assumption is that other social workers who employ this intervention could also expect to find the same beneficial effects with their clients.

However, it is also possible that a multiple baselines across behaviors design could seem too impractical or unwieldy to use. Often, social workers find it necessary to begin working on several of the client's problems at once. There simply is not the luxury of time to address problems sequentially with an adequate baseline

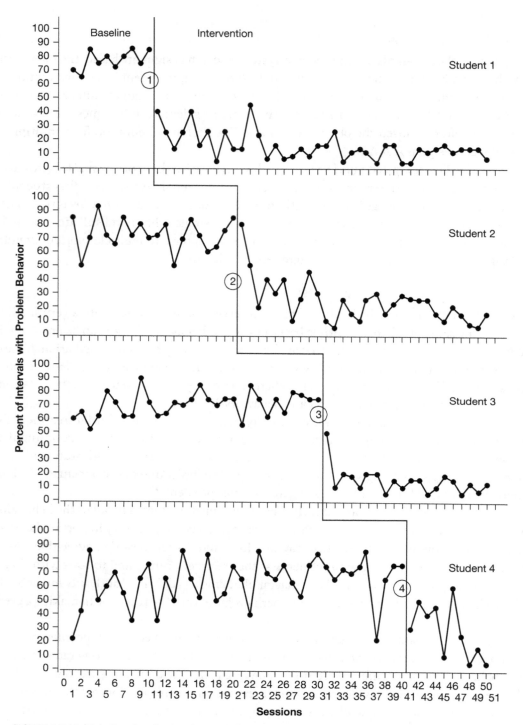

FIGURE 4.7 Multiple Baseline Design Across Subjects

for each that began with the monitoring of the first behavior. In real life, John could receive more than one intervention; for example, there could be individual therapy, group therapy for impulse control, and the center probably employs a token economy or other point system. Given the multiple interventions, it may make more sense to think of monitoring John's behavior with a series of AB designs. Teachers in the school program could probably keep their own graphs, as could John's probation officer, his social worker at the treatment center, and possibly the social worker managing his case for the state.

Validity and Reliability Considerations

Characteristics of the design chosen can affect what you as a practitioner conclude about the success or effectiveness of the intervention. Some SSRD designs are more rigorous than others and allow one to eliminate more of the alternative explanations and thus to come closer to concluding that it was the intervention that made the difference. **Internal validity** is concerned with whether the intervention was the cause of the observed change. When a study has good internal validity, then one can place more confidence in the finding that it really was the intervention and not some other extraneous variable (for example, nutritional supplements or an exercise program) that made the difference. Several common threats to the internal validity of single-system research designs are listed in Table 4.1. SSRDs generally have good internal validity because research participants serve as their own controls. However, always consider whether these threats might have contributed to any findings that an intervention was successful or not.

External validity in single-system research designs is concerned with whether the findings from the study can be generalized elsewhere—to clients with similar problems in other settings, to other practitioners who use the same intervention. In other words, is it reasonable to assume that the

TABLE 4.1 Threats to the Internal Validity of Single-System Research Designs

Threat	What the Investigator Must Question or Consider
1. History	Did anything happen during the study period beyond the investigator's control that might have had an effect or influence? (Could be an extremely positive or negative event.)
2. Maturation	Did the change occur because the individual grew older, matured, or became more experienced with the passing of time?
3. Instrumentation	Did the measurement process change during the course of the study?
4. Testing	Did simply having the individual complete tests or questionnaires, tally behavior, or reflect about it have an effect by sensitizing him or her to the occurrence of the behavior? Did behavior change occur because of self-recording or knowledge that the behavior was being monitored?
5. Mortality	Did some clients drop out of the study? Do those at the end resemble those at the beginning?
6. Statistical Regression	Were there extreme scores at the beginning of the study that might naturally be expected to be less extreme later—even if there had been no intervention?
7. Contamination/Diffusion	Was there a possibility that the clients being studied benefited from learning from clients enrolled in other programs or from other sources?

results would be reproduced in a similar, but different, population? This would be particularly import-ant, for instance, if you had developed a new intervention and wanted practitioners in other states or countries to consider it.

There are several ways in which the external validity of a study can be affected. Take the example of a supervisor who trains three or more staff in a new intervention. They try the intervention with clients having the same problem using an SSRD, but two months later vastly different results are obtained. At that point, the supervisor might want to consider whether the intervention might have been applied differently. The supervisor would likely suspect there was variation in the way key components of the intervention were stressed or emphasized. If the intervention is sensitive to differences in the practitioner's experience or training, then that variable might need to be examined—as well as differences in the clients themselves with regard to such variables as age, sex, education, and so on. The idea with external validity is that powerful interventions should produce the same type of result with similar clients. The trick, of course, is to make sure that the intervention is applied in the same way in each location. This is referred to as the **fidelity of the intervention**. Providing staff with training manuals describing the intervention protocol improves the fidelity of the intervention and can also increase the likelihood that an intervention's effectiveness can be replicated in other locations—that the results can be generalized.

External validity in the quantitative research tradition is generally sought by obtaining a representa-tive sample of the population through random sampling. However, with single-system research designs, there rarely is a random selection of clients for the study, and so the main threat to the external validity of these studies comes from the lack of representativeness in terms of the selection of clients or problems that is the study's focus. The issue is that without random selection and with very small samples involved in SSRD research (e.g., $n = 1$), it is difficult to know how well one client being evaluated resembles other clients with the same problem. SSRDs tend to have low external validity; however, with replication of the results in other studies, greater evidence of external validity is afforded.

Reliability concerns the ability to repeat or reproduce the measurements or observations that are made during a study. For instance, if you and Tamatha are observing Fernando during math class and you see that he was distracted 12 times, but Tamatha counts only 8 times, the measurement process does not have good reliability. Reliability might be improved if they can agree upon a definition of what it means to be distracted. Even better would be a printed list of the distracted behaviors (e.g., looking out the window, doodling, putting his head on the desk, etc.). The amount of agreement between two observers is referred to as **interrater reliability** and could be expressed as a percentage of agreement or a correlation. The higher the reliability, the better. Generally, one hopes to achieve agreement at least 75% to 80% of the time.

Statistical Analysis

The major selling point on single-system research designs is that practitioners find it useful that SSRD graphs can be interpreted visually—no knowledge of statistics is necessary. Indeed, most of the experts on single-system designs acknowledge that visual analysis is the main strategy for interpretation. Statis-tical analysis tools, however, have been developed and can be used to augment visual analysis. (For those who are interested in using statistical tools, readers may wish to consult Cohen, Feinstein, Masuda, and Vowles, 2013 and Kratochwill et al., 2013). For those who want to go just a bit further than "eyeballing" the graph, consider computing the means for the different phases in the SSRD graph.

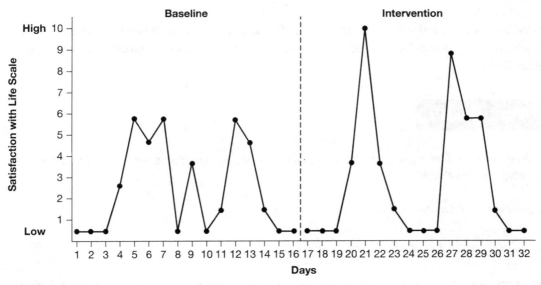

FIGURE 4.8 Example of an Ambiguous Graph

Comparing the means. Compute the mean for the baseline and each phase of the treatment. In an AB design, you would then have a mean score for the *A* phase and the *B* phase. If the goal is to reduce the behavior, the key question here is whether the mean of the behaviors is lower in the *B* phase. And if the goal is to increase the behavior, then the behaviors should be higher in the *B* phase. (Okay, if you are too embarrassed to ask: the mean score is computed by adding up all the scores in that phase and then dividing by the number of observations. For example, scores of 10, 12, 14, and 16 = 52. Dividing 52 by 4 observations = mean of 13.)

As a practitioner, you may sometimes encounter a situation where it is difficult to be sure whether intervention really made a difference by simply looking at the chart. An example of such a situation can be seen in Figure 4.8. This is the kind of situation where it might make perfect sense to compute the means for both halves of the SSRD chart and to see if the intervention side is higher or lower than the baseline. But be careful in what you conclude. As Figure 4.8 shows, this individual's satisfaction with life varies a great deal, even with 16 observations in the baseline; it is difficult to conclude there is a stable pattern or trend.

As a practitioner, it is important to understand the difference between clinical significance and statistical significance. It is easy to distinguish between the two if we take the case of a young man, a 16-year-old who is not performing at a high academic level in the tenth grade—actually failing most of his courses but wanting to improve his grades in order to play varsity football. After working with the school social worker for a whole grade reporting period, the student said that his attitude had changed and he was doing a better job of turning in his homework assignments. Even his GPA had improved! The school social worker, however, wasn't so sure that he had really turned the corner. She decided to look at his GPA. His GPA was 1.00 when he began meeting with her and improved to 1.75 in the next grading period. While this is an improvement (let's say that it was a statistically significant improvement), it doesn't really mean anything if the school required all athletes to have a *C* average in order to participate in spring practice or to participate on an athletic team. In this sense, one might argue there really wasn't clinical significance, since only minimal improvement was obtained. It also suggests that as practitioners, we might need to abandon "soft" assessments of improvement (like impressions that a student is working harder or has an improved attitude toward school). In terms of SSRD, it might have been better to assess the percentage of homework assignments being submitted or the number of hours the young man studied each night, as well as GPA.

Would you have recommended an ABCD SSRD for the young man discussed above with a low GPA who wanted to play football?

[Answer at the end of the book.]

Statistics are not normally needed with single-system research designs. Because these designs rely on graphs and visual inspection, eyeballing them usually is enough to determine if improvement occurred. Statistical tests at best only rule out a chance occurrence in the data and do not eliminate rival explanations or permit conclusive causal inferences. Occasionally, unusually high or low data points affect statistical techniques. Clearly, the ideal situation would be a single-system graph in which an intervention's success (or lack of it) was visually obvious.

Rubin and Knox (1996) caution us about ambiguity in single-system research designs. They found ambiguous outcomes in 7 of 23 graphs where male adolescent sex offenders were self-monitoring on pro-social behaviors and in 7 of 16 graphs where parents were reporting on their sons' antisocial behaviors. The point is this: You should be prepared for the possibility that some SSRDs will turn out to have unstable, indistinct baselines. These might be recognized by improvement that begins during the baseline and by cyclical periods of problematic and non-problematic behaviors during the intervention phase. An example is provided in Figure 4.8 of an ambiguous SSRD graph.

If you look closely at Figure 4.8, you'll note that although the spike for life satisfaction is higher during the intervention period, the client actually experiences only one more day than in baseline when his satisfaction with life was self-reported as either 6 or higher. Also, during the 16 days after baseline, the client experienced only one more day than baseline when he rated his satisfaction with life a 6 or higher. With this SSRD, it could be argued that something of an optical illusion creates the sense of successful treatment. When we compute the means for the baseline and the intervention, we discover the baseline mean of 2 and the intervention mean of 2.56. Again, this is a slight improvement, but is it enough for the social worker to be convinced that the program was working? What would you say?

Advantages and Disadvantages of the SSRD

Single-system research designs have a lot to offer social workers for several reasons. *First* of all, single-system research designs readily lend themselves to clinical practice situations. If a social worker wants to objectively evaluate his or her practice, single-system research designs do not require either control groups or large groups of clients to demonstrate that the intervention is working.

Second, single-system research designs are not disruptive to the treatment process. In fact, they support and complement practice nicely by focusing on specific treatment goals or problems. Often, they serve to clarify or confirm a worker's initial assessment of a client. Furthermore, these designs are constructive in that they provide continuous feedback to the practitioner as well as the client. There is no need to wait until the treatment has ended to determine progress. Many clients have "failure" identities and need to be reassured that they are progressing. Single-system research designs can visually demonstrate the progress that has been made. These designs do not take control away from the practitioner or involve denial of service to those in a control or comparison group.

Third, single-system research designs do not normally require computers, knowledge of statistics, or clerical help in compiling data. These designs do not require that you develop a hypothesis to test. In short, they are not burdensome to one's practice. They are easy to use and understand. *Last*, they are theory free and can be applied regardless of the worker's theoretical application. For social workers who are interested in some form of accountability but not able to undertake large-scale research projects, there is much to recommend in SSRDs.

On the other hand, these designs have some major limitations. A considerable one is the problem of generalization. Even though one uses a rigorous SSRD and clearly demonstrates that the intervention worked, there will still be those skeptics who say, "So? Maybe you worked well with this one client. Show me that your approach works with lots of clients." A practitioner could be very effective with a single client and yet ineffective with the rest of the caseload.

A number of practical problems sometimes emerge during the use of single-system research designs. Ideally, all phases should be of equal length, yet realistically, an intervention might be longer than the baseline or longer in one phase (the *B* phase) than another phase (the *C* phase). In actual practice, it is unlikely that all phases would be the same length. Other problems are encountered when we know the baseline behavior is not stable, but we must start intervention immediately, or when several interventions have to be applied simultaneously.

Another problem is that even experienced practitioners may be hard-pressed to think of situations in which they would deliberately withdraw or remove an intervention that is working just to show that it is the intervention that was responsible for the change in behavior. As a consequence, some of the more experimental single-system research designs (for example, ABAB) may not be viewed by practitioners with much interest.

BOX 4.4 PRACTICE NOTE: IMPEDIMENTS TO USING SINGLE-SYSTEM RESEARCH DESIGNS

Laura Epstein wrote this wonderfully evocative line: "Practitioners need research to put reason and order into the madness of practice" (1996, p. 113). For those students who have yet to experience full-time work in a social service agency, it is difficult to prepare you for the stress and urgency with which complex decisions must be made—sometimes with insufficient information. It would be terrific if every practitioner had enough time on the job to thoughtfully plan and reflect on every client's progress. Realistically, though, there is seldom enough time to do all that needs to be done. Even though SSRDs are not as labor intensive as the group research designs (discussed in Chapter 5), they still demand *some* time—and may always be a lower priority than addressing pressing client needs. In fact, having the time to do them might be considered a luxury in some practice settings. There are likely to be three barriers keeping you from using SSRDs as a clinical monitoring tool:

- Lack of time
- Inability to find a suitable measure or instrument when needed
- Settings that are not amenable to single-system research designs (e.g., acute care hospitals, jails, etc.)

Additionally, the multiproblem constellation of problems that clients bring to social service agencies do not always lend themselves to SSRDs. Clients' problems are often not discrete and well defined, but rather convoluted and intricately involved. Agencies that are attempting to show policy makers and funding sources that their services have an impact on the community are much more likely to use aggregate (group) data than single-case designs.

The Choice and Use of the SSRD

There are many more single-system research designs than can be practically presented in this chapter. One cannot employ the excuse "I can't find the right design for my client." Whether it is simple or complex, the right design is out there, waiting to be used.

The SSRD that is "best" to use depends on how much evidence you feel that you need to rule out alternative explanations for improvement; it is also dictated by the target behaviors or problems identified in the treatment plan. Knowledge of the client and his or her problems is an important consideration in the choice of a design. For instance, you may not want to attempt an ABAB design with a client who agrees to a maximum of three contacts. With another client, you may feel that it is important to monitor three or more target behaviors. With single-subject designs, you have a great deal of flexibility. As a general guideline, however, let your knowledge of the client dictate the design rather than choosing a design and attempting to find a client who conforms to it. If we were all to wait for the "ideal" client to come along before beginning to evaluate our practice, not much evaluation would get done.

It is important not to forget that the purpose and best use of single-system research designs is to identify whether a client is progressing. These designs cannot explain why an intervention isn't working. Their purpose is only to inform you about whether the intervention is succeeding.

It requires self-discipline to conduct research. One must be conscientious about keeping records and monitoring changes in behavior. For many practitioners whose agencies do not require formal evaluation, it is easier to use subjective determinations ("I think the client is doing better"; "The client is acting more appropriately"; "I feel that the couple is getting along better"). However, subjective judgments do not advance the profession or build practice knowledge. Single-system research designs can help you discover what works under which circumstances.

Single-system research designs have practical value and can benefit you and your clients. You may find that if you make use of them, you gain an appreciation for empirical research and are more willing to engage in it. As a practicing social worker, you will surely find that you are too busy to attempt an SSRD for every client. That's understood. However, unless you make an effort to evaluate some clients, you'll soon forget how to go about it. What do I recommend? Simply that you use an SSRD with your most difficult clients. That will help you keep your skills fresh and your supervisor happy, and you'll be able to determine objectively whether these clients are making progress.

Key Terms

target behavior

baseline

multiple baselines across
  behaviors design

AB design

ABA design

reliability

ABCD design

ABAB design

ABC design

successive interventions
design

multiple baseline designs

multiple baselines across

subjects design

experimental single-system

research design

external validity

internal validity

fidelity of the intervention

interrater reliability

$A_1A_2A_3B$

retrospective baseline

prospective baseline

stable pattern

x-axis, y-axis

SELF-REVIEW
(Answers at the end of the book.)

1. T or F. An SSRD *must* contain a baseline.
2. T or F. In an SSRD, time is recorded on the vertical axis.
3. How many baselines does the design ABA contain?
4. Which design is better for knowledge building, the ABCD or the ABAB?
5. If you were trying out a new intervention to manage incontinence problems with three nursing home residents, which SSRD would you use?

   a. ABA
   b. ABAB
   c. ABCD
   d. $A_1A_2A_3B$.

6. What makes for an ambiguous SSRD graph?
7. List the advantages of using an SSRD.
8. What is the major limitation of single-system research designs?
9. Besides the fact that it involves more than one client, how is the multiple baselines across subjects design different from the traditional AB design?

10. Why should social workers use single-system research designs?

11. What is perhaps the main thing that keeps social workers from using single-system research designs?

12. What do you think would be the most challenging as a practitioner: a) having a client with an unpredictable pattern of behavior in the baseline; or b) an unpredictable pattern of behavior during the B phase?

13. Name five threats to the internal validity of an SSRD.

14. External validity is concerned with what?

15. What is the largest threat to the external validity of an SSRD?

QUESTIONS FOR CLASS DISCUSSION

1. Think again about the discussion of the 12-year-old who had stomachaches. Why wouldn't you want to graph the behavior in terms of times per day? (*Hint:* Sketch a quick graph on the whiteboard showing the reduction at the end of the intervention.)

2. Is there more than one way graphs can show lack of improvement? Choose a target behavior and draw suggestions from the class that demonstrate lack of improvement.

3. Why is the ability to operationalize target behaviors important for single-subject designs? What happens if the target behavior is not operationalized well?

4. What would be a good argument for monitoring more than one target behavior with a client?

5. Think about how to set up a graph for a particular target behavior. Would there be advantages in graphing positive behaviors (for example, number of days on the job) rather than negative behaviors (for example, days of work missed)?

6. A coworker tells you that she has just completed an SSRD on a family that has received intervention for seven months. She is pleased with what she has done and brings a graph to show you.

   a. What would be your initial reactions about her competence?

   b. Can the single-subject research design "prove" that your coworker is an excellent social worker? Why or why not?

7. With a multiple baselines across subjects design, what is the reason for waiting for a change in the behavior of the first subject before beginning intervention on the second? Can you think of any reasons intervention shouldn't be started on all three subjects at the same time?

8. Susan is failing the ninth grade. At a conference with her mother, Susan's teachers said that she simply was not studying or turning in any homework. The family's social worker wants to develop a single-subject design to monitor the effect of requiring Susan to study two hours every afternoon before the television can be turned on. The social worker plans to have the vertical axis show "yes" or "no" regarding the completion of two hours of study time every afternoon. Could this design be improved? How?

9. Tim created an SSRD graph with a baseline and a dotted line indicating when the baseline was over and when the intervention started. He started his numbering of observation days on the horizontal line at the base of the dotted line. Is this correct? Why or why not?

10. Of the different SSRDs discussed in this chapter, which one do you see yourself using in the future? Why?

RESOURCES AND REFERENCES

Bloom, M., Fischer, J., & Orme, J. G. (2013). *Evaluating practice: Guidelines for the accountable professional.* Boston, MA: Allyn & Bacon.

Bloom, M., & Orme, J. (1993). Ethics and the single-system design. *Journal of Social Service Research, 19,* 161–180.

Cohen, L. L., Feinstein, A., Masuda, A., & Vowles, K. E. (2013). Single-case research design in pediatric psychology: Considerations regarding data analysis. *Journal of Pediatric Psychology,* 1–14.

Corcoran, K., & Fischer, J. (2013). *Measures for clinical practice.* New York, NY: Free Press.

Epstein, L. (1996). The trouble with the researcher-practitioner idea. *Social Work Research, 20*(2), 113–118.

Horner, R. H., Carr, E. G., Halle, J., McGee, G., Odom, S., & Wolery, M. (2005). The use of single-subject research to identify evidence-based practice in special education. *Exceptional Children, 71*(2), 165–179.

Horner, R. H., Swaminathan, H., Sugai, G., & Smolkowski, K. (2012). Considerations for the systematic analysis and use of single-case research. *Education and Treatment of Children, 35*(2), 269–290.

Janosky, J., Leininger, S. L., Hoergen, M. P., & Libkuman, T. M. (2009). *Single subject designs in biomedicine.* New York, NY: Springer Books.

Kratochwill, T. R., Hitchcock, J. H., Horner, R. H., Levin, J. R., Odom, S. L., Rindskopf, D. M., & Shadish, W. R. (2013). Single-case intervention research design standards. *Remedial and Special Education, 34*(1), 26–38.

Lee, E., Mishna, F., & Brennenstuhl, S. (2010). How to critically evaluate case studies in social work. *Research on Social Work Practice, 20*(6), 682–689.

Lenz, A. S. (2015). Using single-case research designs to demonstrate evidence for counseling practices. *Journal of Counseling & Development, 93,* 237–393.

Macgowan, M. J., & Wong, S. E. (2014). Single-case designs in group work: Past applications, future directions. *Group dynamics: Theory, Research, and Practice, 18*(2), 138–158.

Meany-Walen, K. K., Kottman, T., Bullis, Q., & Taylor, D. D. (2015). Effects of Adlerian play therapy on children's externalizing behavior. *Journal of Counseling & Development, 93,* 418–423.

Ray, D. C. (2015). Single-case research design and analysis: Counseling applications. *Journal of Counseling & Development, 93,* 394–402.

Rubin, A., & Knox, K. S. (1996). Data and analysis problems in single-case evaluation: Issues for research on social work practice. *Research on Social Work Practice, 6,* 40–65.

Rymer, R. (1993). *Genie: An abused child's flight from silence.* New York, NY: HarperCollins.

Wong, S. E. (2010). Single-case designs for practitioners. *Journal of Social Service Research, 36,* 248–259.

Yin, R. K. (2014). *Case study research: Design and methods.* Thousand Oaks, CA: Sage.

Xu, Y. (2013). Moral resources, political capital, and the development of social work in China: A case study of City J in Shandong Province. *British Journal of Social Work, 43*(8), 1589–1610.

Credit

ASSIGNMENT 4.1

Preparing a Single-System Research Design

Objective: *To learn how to operationalize a client's behavior for an SSRD.*

Think about a client; if you are not in a practicum, then reflect back to people you know who have some kind of problem that might lend itself to monitoring with an SSRD. Perhaps a client forgets to take his medicine on a regular basis. What about a teen who spends too much time watching television? You might want to create a fictitious client.

1. Briefly describe the client's problem.

2. Identify the context. What is the agency? What is your role as a social worker?

    The actual or likely agency:

    My role as social worker:

    The intervention is:

3. Operationalize a target behavior so that it can be easily measured. What will be counted on the vertical axis?

4. What unit of measurement will you use on the horizontal axis?

ASSIGNMENT 4.2

Identifying All the Components for an SSRD

Objective: *To learn all of the parts needed for an SSRD.*

Before constructing an SSRD, identify the following important components:

1. What are the units of measurement for the operationalized target behavior?

2. What units will be used to measure increments of time (that is, minutes, hours, days, weeks, months)?

3. How long will the baseline be?

4. What design will you be using?

5. Will your SSRD show that intervention on the client's problem was successful or unsuccessful? Who will be counting or measuring the target behavior?

6. Besides the effect of your intervention, what other factors might contribute to the client's success (or lack of it)?

ASSIGNMENT 4.3

Creating an SSRD

Objective: *To learn how to prepare the graph for a single-system research design.*

Construct a graph for an SSRD. Either use Excel or a straightedge to help you create a tidy and professional-looking graph. Be sure to label both the vertical and horizontal axes so that a reader who has not seen your responses to Assignments 4.1 and 4.2 will be able to understand your effort. Also, give your graph a caption or title, being careful to disguise any real names of clients. Show data both for the baseline and intervention phases. Your instructor may suggest you discuss the client's problem and the operationalized behavior on another sheet.

CHAPTER 5

Research Designs for Group Comparisons

B ILL'S EYES LIT up when he noticed the homemade cookies that Mrs. Simpson had brought to their meeting. "I love this placement!" he declared as he reached for two cookies.

Sophia studied the cookies in the round tin box and then selected the smallest that she could find.

"Have you two had much luck in finding literature to inform the intervention we want to create for our women offenders?"

Bill was eager to answer, but his mouth was full of cookie—he held up a finger to indicate he would answer shortly. Sophia opened a file folder and took out a sheet of paper.

"I can start," she said, "while Bill, um, chews his last cookie."

Looking relieved, Bill settled back into his chair then leaned forward and reached for another oatmeal-chocolate chip.

"I found an article that examined risks for AIDS and thinking myths regarding HIV risk behaviors—and the authors used a bunch of different measures like the HIV Knowledge Questionnaire and the Rosenberg Self-Esteem Scale in a randomized study conducted in four different state prisons."

"Very interesting," Mrs. Simpson said. "I think I will want to read that one."

Sophia beamed, then said, "And in a later article, the authors discuss their *Reducing Risky Relationships for HIV* intervention designed for women within correctional institutions."

"Did they use a group research design to evaluate their intervention?"

"Yes, they did and actually compare their results with four other studies. In two of them, the researchers did not collect post-release data; one study found no significant change in risk behaviors after a 4-session educational intervention, while in the fourth study, a much longer intervention with 16 sessions seemed to have good results." Sophia sat attentively on the edge of her seat, eager to take another question.

"Good work," Mrs. Simpson said. "I heard two important things just then: that it is important for us to follow our women after they are released from the facility and that we need to be thinking about a lengthier intervention—not just a handful of presentations to them."

Sophia nodded her agreement and handed Mrs. Simpson and Bill a sheet with these two citations:

✓ Leukefeld, C., Havens, J., Staton-Tindall, M., Oser, C. B., Mooney, J., Hall, M. T., & Knudsen, H. K. (2012). Risky relationships: Targeting HIV Prevention for women prisoners. *AIDS Education and Prevention, 24*(4), 339–349.

✓ Knudsen, H. K., Staton-Tindall, M., Oser, C. B., Havens, J. R., & Leukefeld, C. G. (2014). Reducing risky relationships: A multisite randomized trial of a prison-based intervention for reducing HIV sexual risk behaviors among women with a history of drug use. *AIDS Care, 26*(9), 1071–1079.

Bill took a drink of water to chase a cookie crumb from his throat and then handed Mrs. Simpson and Sophia a sheet listing the articles he had found.

Showing his sense of humor, he walked to a lectern in the corner of the room, turned it around and stood like he was making a formal presentation to the two women.

"The first reference provides the number of women in state and federal prisons and the proportion of those estimated to be HIV-positive or to have confirmed AIDS—thought we might need that if we write a grant for additional funds. And it talks briefly about some of the prevention studies in correctional facilities. The second article also provides some context and has a really nice set of references attached to it."

He paused for effect, then continued: "The next, most recent article discusses some of the challenges in trying to evaluate this type of intervention once inmates have been released and are residing in different communities. We want to go into our evaluation planning with our eyes wide open and anticipating that we will lose … be unable to find some of the study participants later on."

Mrs. Simpson said, "Excellent, Bill. Nice job."

Pretending to be a stodgy lecturer, Bill responded stiffly with, "Thank you. I shall continue. He cleared his throat and began again. The third article deals with an HIV risk reduction intervention for incarcerated youth. Yes, I realize it is not exactly our population, but thought there might be something there we could learn."

Both Sophia and Mrs. Simpson agreed, and he started again: "As we begin to think about explanations, theories, and so forth in planning our intervention, we need to keep in mind that traumatic events may play a role in some of our inmates becoming substance abusers. This last article talks about a trauma-informed treatment group approach. If we are able to incorporate some of that into our intervention, we may reduce substance abuse rates once inmates leave the prison, which could help them avoid becoming HIV positive."

"Thank you, Bill and Sophia." Mrs. Simpson pushed the cookie tin first toward Sophia and then to Bill. "You've found some wonderful articles to start us thinking about what should go into our psychoeducational intervention program and some ways to go about evaluating it. I'm so pleased! After we've all had time to digest these articles, let's put our heads together next week and see if we can begin to shape an intervention and evaluation plan. You might want to contact the principal investigator in each of the studies to get any additional information about their programs they are willing to share."

Both Bill and Sophia made notes as Mrs. Simpson asked, "Any questions before I go on to my next meeting?"

Single-system designs (SSRDs) are impractical on a large scale. If you are the director of a community agency that provided a recreational program to 750 young people last summer, you would not want to create or even quickly glance over several hundred SSRDs that might suggest the program's success. The staff's possible selection of diverse and wildly different target behaviors aside, single-subject designs in this instance would be the wrong research tool because the focus is no longer on a particular client but on the larger group. Did the *majority* of participants benefit from the program? That is the important issue to be decided.

The research designs contained in this chapter are the quantitative approaches commonly used for program evaluation and basic research in the social sciences. The results they report are concerned with group averages, not with an individual client's success. In the stronger group designs, one group is provided with an intervention, and these results are compared to a **control group** that does not receive any treatment. As you will see, most of these designs are based on the concept of *comparison*

BILL'S LIST OF REFERENCES

✓ Amaro, H., Dai, J., Arevalo, S., Acevedo, A., Matsumoto, A., Nieves, R., & Prado, G. (2007). Effects of integrated trauma treatment on outcomes in a racially/ethnically diverse sample of women in urban community-based substance abuse treatment. *Journal of Urban Health: Bulletin of the New York Academy of Medicine, 84*(4), 508–522.

✓ Fleming, E. B., LeBlanc, T. T., & Reid, L. C. (2013). The status of HIV prevention efforts for women in correctional facilities. *Journal of Women's Health, 22*(12), 1005–1008.

✓ Goldberg, E., Millson, P., Rivers, S., Manning, S. J., Leslie, K., Read, S., ... & Victor, J. C. (2009). A human immunodeficiency virus risk reduction intervention for incarcerated youth: A randomized controlled trial. *Journal of Adolescent Health, 44*(2), 136–145.

✓ Pettus-Davis, C., Howard, M. O., Dunnigan, A., Scheyett, A. M., & Roberts-Lewis, A. (2016). Using randomized controlled trials to evaluate interventions for releasing prisoners. *Research on Social Work Practice, 26*(1), 35–43.

✓ Rowell-Cunsolo, T. L., El-Bassel, N., & Hart, C. L. (2016). Black Americans and incarceration: A neglected public health opportunity for HIV risk reduction. *Journal of Health Care for the Poor and Underserved, 27,* 114–130.

and usually employ statistical analysis to understand change. They are not designs typically used by qualitative researchers.

Why do you have to learn them? Few of us would want to hire a carpenter who is skilled only with the use of a hammer. It is essential for carpenters to know how to use other tools as well. Similarly, single-system designs will not always be the right tool for every research occasion. Many times, you need to aggregate data to understand to what extent a group, program, or community improved as a result of your services. Group research designs are particularly appropriate for those who work with various services, agencies, and communities and are involved with administration of programs, community development, and social policy analysis. Direct service social workers often find that they need knowledge of group research designs to develop evaluation procedures when they apply for grants or wish to evaluate specific interventions used in their agencies.

Choosing the Right Design

Numerous research designs can be used to guide research projects, and choosing the right one is somewhat analogous to picking out a new car. The primary consideration with a car may be how much money you have or how big a monthly payment you can manage. Similarly, the researcher must also consider how much has been budgeted for the research. Design issues related to finances include: the use of staff time for collecting data (for example, making follow-up contacts with clients in person or by phone); postage, telephone, or travel expenses; purchase of copyrighted instruments or scales; computer processing of the data; the use of consultants; release time to write the report; and so on. These and other variables contribute to the cost of the project.

While the car buyer considers what optional equipment is really necessary, the researcher decides which facets of the study are essential. For instance, the researcher may believe that the success of the intervention should be determined by the more expensive methodology of personal interviews instead of mailed questionnaires.

Besides the issue of cost, car buyers and researchers must simultaneously consider other variables. Both car buyers and researchers are presented with decisions about no-frills, low-prestige models. The experimental designs that we will talk about are highly respected, but other, less rigorous designs are often adequate. We want our vehicles to be dependable; researchers desire instruments that produce reliable findings and high response rates. And while the car buyer may consider how long a particular vehicle might be expected to last, the researcher must give thought to the amount of time that the study should run. Often, collecting more data makes for a stronger study.

Various motives or considerations have a bearing on the choice of a research design. No one design will be applicable or correct in every situation. The design depends on the questions being asked, the nature of the problem being investigated, the availability of participants or other data, monetary and staff resources, the amount of time one has to complete the project, and what will be done with the research.

In terms of evidence-based practice, group research designs with randomized assignment to the treatment condition (experiments) or with time-series designs with a good comparison group provide the most credible evidence. Time-series designs without a comparison group provide a middle range of credibility. Before and after designs with no comparison group provide the least credible evidence of effectiveness—for reasons that will become clear as you read this chapter.

Social work researchers generally move from interest in a problem to the selection of a design—not vice versa.

Selecting Subjects

Even before choosing a research design, most researchers have to give some thought to the individuals who will be asked to participate in their research project. Sometimes it is not possible to draw a sample from a larger population of potential subjects or clients. That is, the question being investigated or intervention being tested may involve only the 30 most chronic abusers of the agency's 24-hour crisis line. Or the school social worker may be concerned with evaluating the progress of 18 children in two support groups who have bereavement issues. It is often the case that group research designs do not employ random assignment to treatment groups. Researchers can, and often do, however, randomly assign clients to either an experimental or control condition when a more rigorous study is planned. Even with 30 chronic hotline abusers, half (n = 15) could be randomly assigned to participate in a new intervention to address their frequent calling and the other half could constitute the control group (receiving no new intervention).

Sometimes, researchers have the good fortune to be able to plan months in advance and can build a process for future recruitment of eligible clients (**proactive research**). On occasion, current clients are the group of interest; they also may be compared to clients who previously completed a program or who have already dropped out in the past (**retroactive research**). In retroactive research, the investigator often draws on existing data in agency records. As a practitioner in a social service agency, sometimes your access to research subjects is limited to only your clients or those in the program where you are assigned; often, you must take what you can get because random selection opportunities may be limited.

Group research designs are classified as explanatory research (remember this discussion from Chapter 2?); more often than not, they involve small samples of research subjects as they look for cause-and-effect relationships (causal research).

Researchers conducting explanatory research are not as concerned with representativeness or generalizability in the same sense that survey researchers are. For survey researchers, if the sample doesn't represent the larger population, then there may be little or no generalizability, and the whole survey effort may fail to meet expectations. Investigators conducting explanatory research hope that their findings will be so solid that other researchers will want to come along and replicate the original study; and if the findings are repeated again, this begins to look like or approximate generalizability.

While the sample size relative to the larger population is not a huge concern for those conducting group research designs, what is terribly important is that the control and intervention groups be created by random assignment in experiments; this creates the condition of maximum comparability. In the quasi-experimental designs (those without random assignment), the more the control group resembles the experimental group, the better the study. Conversely, a weaker study results when the two groups are very dissimilar at the beginning of a study; this could come about quite easily, for example, if the students in two different schools (e.g., one in a rural area and one from the inner city) were compared.

Experimental Research

The classic experimental design is the ideal, the gold standard or model to which all other research designs are compared. Even though the opportunities to conduct true experiments may not often come your way, the experimental design remains the benchmark when it is important to be as scientific as possible. Other designs in this chapter are discussed in terms of how close they come to this ideal design.

For many social workers, the notion of experimentation involving human subjects brings to mind misconceptions about unethical, painful, or presumably painful stimuli being inflicted on unsuspecting persons in a climate-controlled laboratory. These notions are best forgotten. Today, there is much greater concern for and widespread protection of the rights of persons participating in research than in the past. The federal government requires institutional review boards (IRBs) to oversee research involving human beings—research funded by investigators associated with organizations receiving federal money.

What is an **experiment**? Simply stated, it is a controlled study where clients or subjects are randomly assigned to a group (sometimes called a condition) where they will receive a new (or different) intervention from those designated to be in the control group. Data collection in these studies typically involves the use of standardized quantitative instruments. Individuals in the control condition may receive the customary or usual treatment for comparison with the new one. The notion of random assignment is crucial—it prevents a number of **extraneous variables** or possibly confounding variables and biases from interfering with the researcher's ability to make a conclusion about the strength or weakness of the intervention. Notice that in the next section, three different experimental designs will be discussed: the classic experiment, the posttest-only control group, and the Solomon four-group, which combines both previous designs.

The Classic Experimental Research Design

True experiments are the most rigorous of research designs and the ones that best permit causal inferences to be made. These designs have two main features that distinguish them from other designs. *First*, clients (or subjects) who participate in the experiment are **randomly assigned**. That is, no favoritism or bias is shown in appointing them to one condition or the other. *Second*, besides the experimental group, some subjects must be assigned to a control (or comparison) group that does not get the new intervention.

The shorthand notation for the classic pretest-posttest control group design is often written as follows:

$$R \quad O_1 \quad X \quad O_2$$
$$R \quad O_1 \quad \quad O_2$$

The **R** in this notation scheme stands for the random assignment of clients to either the experimental or the control group; the **X** represents the intervention or stimulus. Observations, measurements, or assessments of each group are made twice. The first observation (O_1) is called the **pretest**, and the second observation (O_2) is called the **posttest**. This design provides information not only about changes in the group that receives the intervention, but also comparable information from the group that does not get the experimental intervention. What kinds of changes would the true experiment pick up? This result depends entirely on the dependent variable or variables the researcher has chosen and the way they have been operationalized. Random assignment *must* occur prior to the intervention. One should never begin a treatment—and if clients are not improving—subsequently assign them to the control group.

As an example of this design, suppose you are a medical social worker assigned to a dialysis clinic. Let's further assume that managing anxiety is a major problem for patients in the clinic. You decide to start a support group for anxious patients because you believe it will help alleviate some of their health concerns.

Because you are limited in the amount of time you can allocate for this project, you want to start small with about 25 patients. Since the facility is a large dialysis clinic with hundreds of patients, you have no problem finding willing participants. In keeping with the experimental **pretest-posttest control group design**, you randomly assign 25 dialysis patients to the support group and randomly assign approximately the same number to the control group.

Next, you use a standardized measure like the Clinical Anxiety Scale to determine the anxiety level of both groups prior to the start of the intervention. The support group begins and runs its normal course (six to eight weeks). Afterward, you administer the instrument a second time to both groups and make comparisons. Has the average level of anxiety in the experimental group decreased? Has the average amount of anxiety in the control group remained about the same or increased? Finally, is the level of anxiety in the experimental group less than in the control group at posttest? If so, then you have evidence that the intervention was effective.

This is a strong design because the group that receives no intervention provides a "control" for possible alternative explanations affecting the experimental group. (Random selection of subjects makes the groups roughly equivalent and minimizes bias that could result from a flawed method of selecting participants before the intervention begins.) For instance, if clients tend to make better decisions because they grow wiser with the passage of time (maturation) and not because of the intervention, then the control group would also show similar improvement or outcome. (There would be little reason to believe that the intervention was responsible for any changes if the same changes were also found in the control group.)

Researchers sometimes choose to strengthen their studies even more (particularly in medical and pharmaceutical research) by using a **double-blind procedure**. In double-blind experiments, neither the researcher nor the research subject knows whether participants are in the control or the experimental group. (Obviously, someone other than the experimenter has to know, but this information is not shared.) This procedure eliminates any experimental bias—for instance, in unintentionally giving those in the experimental group more attention or advantages because the experimenter wants the intervention to work.

The Posttest-Only Control Group Design

A second true experiment design, the posttest-only control group design, is handy for those situations where a pretest might affect the posttest results or when it is not possible to conduct a pretest. This design is also useful in situations where anonymity is paramount—so it would not be possible to compare an individual's pretest and posttest scores.

Campbell and Stanley (1963) note that there is a common misconception that pretests are always needed in an experimental design. Not so, they say. As with the previous design, random assignment of subjects establishes the initial equivalence between the experimental and control groups. Measurement of the control group (O_2) then serves as a pretest measure for comparison with the experimental group's posttest (O_1).

$$R \quad X \quad O_1$$
$$R \quad\quad\quad O_2$$

As an example of this design, consider the following problem. Counseling agencies often find that 30% or more of scheduled appointments result in no-shows or last-minute cancellations. Productive or billable time is lost, which can seriously affect the revenue needed to operate an agency. Suppose you have a hypothesis that the 30% no-show rate could be reduced by the agency's receptionist calling clients to remind them of their scheduled appointments. The group receiving the phone calls would constitute the experimental group. Those clients who do not receive a reminder constitute the control group. Membership in either the experimental or control group would be randomly determined. (For instance, the clients requesting an appointment during a month could be numbered and after tossing a coin to decide who goes first, the even-numbered ones could be assigned to the experimental group and would get a reminder phone call. Odd-numbered clients would be assigned to the control group, where they would be scheduled an appointment but receive no reminder.) At the end of the study period, the cancellation rates for the two groups could be compared.

The Solomon Four-Group Design

The third true experiment design is called the **Solomon four-group design**. As you can see from the following notation, it is composed of the basic experimental design plus the posttest-only control group design. This is an elaborate, sophisticated design that social workers may not often have the opportunity to use because of the logistics involved with the creation and maintaining of four different groups.

$$R \quad O_1 \quad X \quad O_2$$
$$R \quad O_1 \quad\quad\quad O_2$$
$$R \quad\quad\quad X \quad O_2$$
$$R \quad\quad\quad\quad\quad O_2$$

This design provides two opportunities (two treatment groups) for the treatment effect to be demonstrated. The design's strong point is that the investigator can maximally control for alternative explanations and thus increase the confidence that can be placed in the findings. While this is a rigorous design and provides greater confidence that the intervention produced any observed changes, the tradeoff for this certainty is greater difficulty in coordinating and implementing the design.

Bill walked out of their afternoon class with Sophia and said, "Remember how concerned you were yesterday when we talked about ways to continue to support our study participants once they are released and go back to their communities?"

"Of course," said Sophia. "We need to figure out a way to give them booster shots of intervention."

"What would you say if I told you that I had figured it out?"

Sophia stopped dead in her tracks. "How? What? What do you mean?"

"I found an article where the investigators sent their participants weekly text messages for three months … and it described the research design as a randomized control trial with a Solomon four-group."

"Remind me—what's a randomized control trial?"

"Just like its name suggests—an RCT is an experiment where participants are randomly assigned to one or another clinical interventions to see which one is the most effective. Here," he said, "I've already read it. You can give the article back to me on Monday."

This is the article using a Solomon four-group design that Bill handed to Sophia:

✓ Ishola, A. G., & Chipps, J. (2015). The use of mobile phones to deliver acceptance and commitment therapy in the prevention of mother-child transmission in Nigeria. *Journal of Telemedicine and Telecare, 21f*(8), 423–426.

ANXIETY CHECK 5.1

Bill was concerned that he didn't understand the difference between internal and external validity. Sophia told him that if the concern was simply on how well the study generalized to other populations, then it was external validity. Was she correct? Decide before you read the next section.

[Answer at the end of the book.]

Internal and External Validity

Campbell and Stanley (1963) and Cook and Campbell (1979) are prominent in social science research because of their conceptualization of research designs. Their books are classics on the topic, and research methodology books usually acknowledge their work. Besides identifying a host of experimental, quasi-experimental, and preexperimental research designs (more about these a little later), these authors contributed much to our understanding of **internal** and **external validity**.

The internal validity of a study (that is, whether the intervention was truly responsible for the observed differences in the dependent variable) can be threatened by extraneous variables (those not considered or purposely incorporated into the experiment). Studies with greater internal validity allow the researcher to rule out alternative explanations and rival hypotheses. Studies with less internal validity cannot control (account for) the effect of extraneous variables on the experimental group. As we learned in the single-system design chapter, unplanned and unexpected variables can affect the intervention's outcome. Group research designs also are susceptible to threats to their internal validity.

The following section will help you think about the way your study can be affected by variables that can make it difficult to determine if your intervention was effective. As you learn more about research, you will develop an appreciation for factors (not limited to those listed here) that can interfere with your study.

SIDEBAR: VALIDITY UNPACKED

Validity is a concept that can have many nuances. Here is a quick review of what we've learned thus far:

- Internal validity relates to minimizing extraneous variables that can sneak into a study and rob the investigator from concluding that the intervention was the cause of the client's improvement. Researchers must consider threats to the internal validity to help understand the results that were achieved. For instance, did the intervention appear less effective than it really was because clients who improved dropped out of the study before its conclusion? To assess whether the threat of mortality might have been undermining the findings, researchers can consider such information as the number of clients who began and finished the program.

- External validity is concerned with whether a study can generalize well to other populations, locations, and client groupings. Generally, random selection of individuals who compose the study sample is a good way to build external validity. Being able to demonstrate that a sample is, in fact, representative of a larger population adds to the credibility of a study and its external validity. Many studies are published each year that do not involve random sampling; the fact that they appear in print does not make their findings generalizable. If some wanted to make an argument that a study didn't generalize well, they would probably complain that the individuals in the study were somehow different, that the location was out of the ordinary, or that the timing of the study was unusual.

- Measurement validity is concerned with how well an assessment instrument measures the concept it was designed to capture. Investigators conduct studies to learn if the empirical measure they've created or adapted successfully operationalizes the abstract idea of it. In other words, they gather empirical data to assess the performance of the instrument. Various forms of this type of validity include criterion related, face, construct, and content validity. (More on these later.)

- Conversational uses of "validity" or "valid" when applied to a research project generally mean that a study was real, authentic, meaningful, relevant, or simply just a "good" study—probably meaning that it seemed to have used an appropriate methodology or that the findings support the speaker's ideas about the topic. However, this is an inexact and confusing way to refer to a study. A researcher will want to know more specifically if the speaker is talking about whether the study's instruments revealed strong measurement validity, whether the study's design anticipated threats to internal validity, and to what extent the study's design allowed for generalizability (external validity). In other words, be careful when you say a study is valid!

Major Threats to Internal Validity

1. ***Maturation.*** The aging of participants or different rates of physical growth or development within comparison groups are examples of influences that you should recognize and attempt to control as much as possible. Certainly, there is a lot of difference between kindergarten students at the beginning of the school year and at its end. Why? Because they have grown older and have been socialized into the culture of becoming "students." Similarly, anyone who has been hurt when a relationship breaks up knows that there is a lot of truth to the adage that "Time heals all wounds." The simple passage of time is an alternative explanation that should not be discounted when gauging the effects of an intervention that runs over several weeks or months. The longer the intervention, the more likely that (client) maturation (the passage of time) may play a role. Another example: Sometimes, our clients cease certain behaviors not because of any special intervention they received but because, for example, they become too old to engage in criminal behavior—they are not as fleet-footed and no longer have the athletic quickness to avoid arrest. Clients sometimes change for reasons independent of the intervention they've received because of maturity or life experiences that finally "click."

2. ***History.*** This refers to specific events (for example, national crises, tragedies, or on a local level, a large factory laying off hundreds of employees) that occur between the pretest and posttest that were not part of the researcher's design and that could influence the results. For instance, if you were trying to evaluate the impact of an HIV prevention program and a national celebrity made a public announcement about obtaining the disease (as television star Charlie Sheen did in November 2015), this could constitute a threat to the internal validity. That is, his admission and example could affect study participants who heard his announcement—complicating things for the researcher trying to understand if the intervention alone was responsible for any change in the outcome variable.

   Personal events in a client's life (for example, a "history of abusive relationships") are not generally considered to be threats to the internal validity of a study. However, significant events that occur in the world and within an agency or a group can become factors that influence the trajectory of an intervention. Consider a treatment group that is well established (there is a strong sense of "the group")—and one of the members commits suicide. This event may become a threat to the internal validity of the study. Group members may be adversely affected and lose the progress they have made. Or they might pull together in a way that was completely unexpected and make much greater strides than they would have without the suicide. History is a threat to validity because once an event occurs, the investigator doesn't know whether it was the intervention or the event that caused the improvement. If the group shows no improvement, was it because of the suicide or because the intervention was ineffective?

3. ***Testing.*** Taking a test on more than one occasion can affect later test results. Repeated testing provides practice and in itself can improve test scores. If clients' scores improve over time, but they were measured three times with the same scale, was the improvement because they figured out what you were measuring or because the intervention made a difference? The threat of testing is sometimes known as the ***practice effect***. The influence of testing can also be a factor when pretests sensitize subjects to issues or attitudes and cause some reflection so that subjects' responses change as a result of measurement and not intervention. Instruments can also be too difficult or too lengthy; subjects can get bored (**test fatigue**) and may not pay careful attention to how they

respond the second or third time they are asked to complete an instrument. If you anticipate that testing may be a problem, then you can choose designs to assess it (Solomon four-group) or eliminate the pretests altogether (that is, posttest-only control group design).

4. ***Instrumentation.*** This term refers to changes in (a) the use of the measuring instrument; (b) the way the instrument is scored; (c) procedures used during the study; or (d) the way the dependent variable is counted or measured. Suppose you administer a timed test to some students, and because you are not paying attention, you give them five fewer minutes at the posttest than they had at the pretest. You have created a situation where the intervention could appear less powerful than it really is. (Because they had fewer minutes to complete the test, double-check their answers, and so forth, their scores will be lower.) Conversely, if you accidentally give them too much time—maybe you were interrupted by a phone call—then you might conclude that the intervention was more effective than it actually is. Not administering the instruments the same way each time or not according to directions—and not training staff on how to collect the data—can result in inaccurate reporting. Another instrumentation problem would be to change instruments and use different ones at posttest than were used at pretest.

5. ***Selection of subjects.*** This threat to internal validity stems from any bias that causes the experimental and control groups to be different from each other or to be different from those individuals in the larger population that they should represent. For instance, suppose you have come up with a new intervention for parents who are having difficulty getting along with their teenagers. You purchase an advertisement in the local newspaper paper or on its website that says: "Having trouble communicating with your teenager? Call *321-7654* for information on a free parents' group at Shiloh Baptist Church on Wednesday evenings." How does the ad create a selection problem? First of all, some parents who are having trouble with their teens may not respond because they can't read or don't subscribe to the newspaper or look at its website. Other parents needing the intervention may not respond because they don't like the idea of discussing their problems in a group. So, who would be most likely to respond to the ad? Possibly better-educated individuals who may be somewhat comfortable in social situations and certainly, *motivated* parents who might be most concerned or worried about their adolescents. A researcher who uses such an ad has to remain cognizant that the parents in his or her study may not represent all parents who are having trouble communicating with their teens. If the intervention works well, then the researcher may want to find a group of less motivated or less educated parents to see if the intervention works equally well with them.

    Selection is nearly always a concern in studies because of self-selection that occurs when clients choose one agency over another (for example, a public or private agency) or possibly when one chooses one type of treatment modality over some other kind. This threat to the internal validity of a study is best handled by random sampling from the population of interest. However, this is not always possible, and researchers quite often have to admit that their studies have **limitations**—problems that may prevent the study from generalizing well to the larger population or other geographical areas—because of the way their subjects were chosen or selected.

6. ***Statistical regression.*** This refers to the selection of subjects who were chosen because of extreme scores. There is a tendency for extreme scores to move toward the group average on a second testing. For instance, think about a situation where you scored a perfect 100% on your first test in research methods. Even though you may be a very bright individual, it will be a lot easier for you

to do not as well on the second test than it will be to score 100 again. So, even if you obtain a 95 on the second test, your score will have regressed. Similarly, if you score 15 on the first test, it is quite possible that you will improve on the second test and your score will move more in the direction of the class average. Statistical regression as an internal threat to the validity of a study means this: Subjects who were chosen because of extreme scores (either low or high) at pretest can be expected to have either higher or lower scores at posttest simply because of statistical regression. As a researcher, you can't prevent this occurrence, but you can measure it when there is random assignment and a comparison group. (Any improvement that the control group shows could be due to statistical regression. To understand the impact of the intervention, this amount can then be subtracted from the improvement shown by the experimental group.)

7. **Mortality.** Also known as **attrition**, this threat to internal validity refers to the loss of research subjects (for example, they terminate services, move out of town, get sick, or simply drop out of the study). The loss of subjects may change the overall group makeup or composition and may produce differences in the data at the posttest that have nothing to do with the intervention.

   Think about a scenario where you are running a group for nine sixth-grade boys who have behavior problems in the classroom. The intervention is going well, but for one reason or another, the group dwindles to four participants by the end of the school year. While all four showed definite improvement, what about the five who dropped out or moved to other school districts? Had they been present at the posttest, would you still have been able to conclude the intervention was a success? A major loss of subjects from a study can undermine whatever conclusion the researcher is prepared to make regarding the effectiveness of the intervention. Social work researchers have to be aware that individuals in the control group are at risk for dropping out of the study or may be unavailable at posttest. Because they are less involved with the study by nature of the fact that they are receiving no intervention, participants may be less motivated to participate in posttesting. Especially when testing procedures are lengthy or demanding, **incentives** like coupons for a fast-food restaurant or small gifts may be necessary to keep subject mortality from being a problem. Here's another tip that might help for long-term studies: Some researchers have discovered that mailing out birthday and holiday cards is a useful way to stay in contact with study participants when attrition might be a problem. Because the post office will forward mail for only one year, mailing twice a year keeps addresses current for longitudinal studies.

8. **Interaction effects.** This occurs when any of the extraneous variables interact with one another. In a selection and maturation interaction, the subjects in one group may mature at a faster rate than those in the comparison group. In a selection and mortality interaction, there could be differences in motivational level or severity of psychiatric illness between the groups, with resulting differential dropout rates. By the study's end, the groups could look vastly different—and not because of the intervention. Another example could be that the demands on subjects at pretest could force many to reconsider their participation—forcing a selection and mortality interaction. Interactions with extraneous variables may complicate the investigator's ability to understand the true impact of the intervention.

Threats to the internal validity of a study are like viruses that can infect and weaken it. They sap the confidence that you as a researcher have in the finding that it was the intervention—and only the intervention—that was responsible for any improvement in the clients' lives.

The use of experimental designs will help you gauge the extent of any of these threats to the internal validity of your study. Randomization and a control group allow the investigator to determine if any extraneous variable has exerted an unexpected influence. For instance, if you notice an unexpected improvement in the control group, you might suspect that an extraneous variable (such as history, maturation, or testing) had an effect on the study.

When you have considered these eight threats and ruled them out as having produced an effect, then you have established that your study has internal validity. You can now conclude with some confidence that the intervention was likely responsible for the observed changes. Then, if you want to ensure that the findings from your study can be generalized to different subjects or settings, you should consider the threats to the external validity of the study.

Major Threats to External Validity

Campbell and Stanley (1963) must also be given credit for identifying several ways in which the external validity (the generalizability or representativeness of the study) can be threatened. External validity is important if you want to convince others that your study or experiment has produced a major scientific discovery.

Note first, though, that in those situations where you are evaluating a specific program in your agency, it might *not* be important to demonstrate external validity. In such instances, you are concerned only with whether treatment worked in a local program—you may not be interested in generalizing your results to their communities or subjects because your program is not like any others.

On the other hand, if you *are* concerned with generalization and obtaining maximum credibility, you'll want to use an experimental design and attempt to anticipate all the potential threats to the internal and external validity of your study. In particular, you will want to pay attention to these factors that could influence external validity:

1. *Reactive or interactive effect of testing.* This occurs when a pretest affects the respondent's sensitivity or awareness to important variables associated with the study. The pretest could make the subjects unrepresentative of the population from which they were drawn by raising their consciousness or by stimulating new learning, or simply because they realize that they are involved in a study. This threat should seem familiar to you because it is similar to the internal validity threat of testing.

2. *Interactive effects of selection biases and any research stimulus.* These occur when there are problems getting a random sample. If you are conducting a study that requires in-depth interviews of two or three hours' duration, the majority of persons you contact might turn you down and not participate. Those who agree to the interview may not be representative of the larger population—they have volunteered when most others have not. They may have some traits or characteristics (for example, they are lonely) that make them less representative and therefore affect the generalizability of the study. Selection bias is not a problem in experiments with random assignment; it is always a concern in quasi-experimental designs with nonequivalent comparison groups.

3. *Reactive effects of arrangements.* This concerns the experiment being conducted in a setting that is different from the subject's usual experience. Subjects' behavior may change because of the different environment. Subjects may be more productive or more wary and nervous. They may behave in a way not indicative of their normal style. (Would your behavior change if you knew that you were being videotaped or observed through a two-way mirror?)

4. ***Multiple-treatment interaction.*** This becomes a problem when there is more than one intervention. The researcher needs to be sure that the same timing, sequence, or order is followed for each subject. Multiple treatments may have a cumulative effect, which could make reaching conclusions about a specific intervention difficult.

Researchers who want to generalize their findings beyond the setting in which they conducted the study need to be concerned that: (a) subjects in the study are representative of other clients with the problem or the population to which they are being compared; (b) the intervention is not vague but well defined and structured; and (c) staff are qualified and trained, and that they uniformly deliver the intervention in the same way using the same approaches, theoretical orientations, and emphases.

Those colleagues who will read your research and want to implement the intervention must be given sufficient detail to replicate the study. Without critical information about the characteristics of your clients (for example, are they first-time or multi-offenders?), your staff (for example, are they MSWs with at least five years' experience or graduate students?), and the nature of your intervention (did the group meet twice a week for a total of three hours weekly or once a month?), those who attempt to replicate your study may not achieve the same results. This would be most unfortunate if you had a successful intervention, but because you failed to provide sufficient explanation about it, the staff, or the clients, assumptions were made that resulted in another researcher using a weaker or diluted version of the intervention or choosing a tougher client population and then encountering a lack of success.

In summary, there are always distinct threats to a study's internal and external validity. Experimental research designs use random assignment of subjects to comparison groups to help the researcher monitor and understand the threats to internal validity. As a rule, the more control you have over the situation or experiment, the greater the internal validity. However, there is a corresponding cost in terms of external validity.

As greater effort is made to control for possible influences on the subjects or in the experimental setting, the investigator runs the risk of creating a situation that is very different from the way most programs of a similar type would be run in real life. Sometimes, it is comforting to realize that all studies have some limitations or weaknesses. Research with actual clients and in real social service agencies often means that compromises have to be made.

I once learned of an evaluation being conducted of a family preservation program. Families in crisis were randomly assigned to the special intervention or to a control group that received the usual services provided by the agency. After the death of a child whose family was receiving the customary (not intensive) services, a decision was made to end the random assignment. Supervisors placed families with the most serious problems into the special intervention condition. The control group from that point on no longer resembled the new intervention (because their problems had been judged to be less serious). The evaluation of the intensive (new) intervention was seriously compromised due to differences between the two groups. These are the kinds of things that can happen when a research or evaluation project is conducted in an agency and the researcher doesn't have full control.

Preexperimental Designs

Suppose you are a counselor in an agency and are working with a group of tremendously shy individuals. You have developed an approach that, over the course of 10 meetings, significantly alleviates social anxiety.

You administer a social anxiety scale to the group on its first meeting, and the average score for the group is 35. From the scores and your clinical impressions, you know that this group qualifies for intervention. Your group meets 10 times, and you administer a posttest on the last session. You find that the group's average score has gone up to 62, which indicates major improvement.

This type of design does not have the complexity of an experiment. Because subjects are not randomly assigned to a treatment or a control group, **preexperimental designs** are pragmatic and often used in evaluations of social service programs. This design (which is similar to the AB design) is called the **one-group pretest-posttest design** and can be designated with the notation:

$$O_1 \quad X \quad O_2$$

Here, again, the O_1 represents the pretest measurement or observation and the O_2 the posttest.

Even though you, as a clinician, have seen major improvement in the individuals of the group, this design cannot rule out alternative explanations for the changes. It cannot rule out the internal validity threats of history, maturation, testing, instrumentation, statistical regression, or the interaction of selection and maturation. Any of these extraneous variables may have produced the changes in the shyness scores. Without a control group, it is impossible to say that these threats did not have an effect. You, however, may be able to rule out some of these threats because of the particular situation or context within which the study occurred. Although this is a weak design, it serves a purpose when no control group is available for comparison.

If there were no pretest data associated with the earlier study of shy individuals, the resulting design would be the **one-group posttest-only design**.

$$X \quad O$$

With this design, an intervention is delivered, and later, observations are recorded to determine the intervention's outcome. This design stipulates only that you make an observation after the intervention. If you were working with the group of shy individuals described previously, this design would require only a posttest after the intervention. Because there would have been no pretest for comparison, an average posttest score of 62 would not provide much information—certainly no objective information to show improvement. With no data available for comparison, any perceptions of a reduction in shyness are unsubstantiated. Instead of the intervention having an effect on shyness, extraneous variables such as selection, history, maturation, or mortality may have contributed to any perceived changes after treatment.

With the one-group posttest-only design, sometimes it is possible to know if there has been an effect depending on what is being measured. For instance, imagine you are conducting a study of a group of clients who are trying to quit drinking. If most group members reported after 10 weeks that they weren't drinking, you would be pleased and willing to take the credit. Indeed, your colleagues may have no difficulty attributing the cessation of drinking to the intervention. However, the "success" might have been due to spouses or mates threatening to leave if loved ones didn't stop drinking, bosses threatening to fire inebriated employees, court appearances for driving while intoxicated, or a combination of several factors. Again, without a control group, it is difficult to know the extent to which extraneous factors could be influencing the outcome.

The third and last preexperimental design is called the **posttest-only design with nonequivalent groups**. It is expressed:

$$X \quad O$$
$$O$$

This design is an improvement over the previous two in that the control group functions as a pretest condition and can be compared with the group that receives the intervention. While it may seem logical to infer that any observed differences are due to the intervention, this is debatable because we cannot assume that the two groups were similar prior to the intervention (there was no random assignment to the groups). As a consequence, differences between the two observations may be due to their nonequivalence in the beginning and not to the intervention.

By way of example, think of the population of women who have been battered by their partners. Assume we want to know if service programs connected with a shelter for battered women are instrumental in helping these women avoid returning to abusive situations. Of the battered women who contact the shelter, some request shelter services, while others request only information about child custody, jobs, and police protection and soon attempt to leave abusive situations on their own without spending time in the shelter. There are, then, two groups of women with the same basic problem: One group gets the intervention (the shelter) and its counseling services, while the other group does not. For the purpose of follow-up research to determine how many women were living in abusive situations one year later, would these two groups be equivalent? I think not. They may differ in the amount of financial resources at their disposal (those who don't stay at the shelter may have more money), in the extent of family or social support systems, and possibly with regard to the severity of the abuse experienced.

ANXIETY CHECK 5.2

If there are two shelters in the community for women who have domestically violent partners and if one shelter begins a new program designed to help these women, can a classical experimental design be used with women at the other shelter constituting the control group?

[Answer is at the back of the book.]

These two groups of women may be convenient groupings in terms of trying to determine the effect of a battered women's shelter, but if it were later found that a greater proportion of the women who used the shelter's services than of women who didn't were still in abusive situations, what does this say about the shelter's services? It would be risky to conclude that the shelter was in some way responsible for its clients returning to abusive situations. While it could appear that women who avoided the shelter were more successful in not returning to abusive situations, we must keep in mind that the two groups of women may not have been all that similar, even though they shared a common problem. In fact, we might expect differences in the two groups with this design even before looking at our data. Of course, the more similar (or **homogeneous**) the two groups are, the more comfortable everyone will be that the intervention did indeed have an effect. The absence of randomization makes this design weak; we are unable to rule out such internal validity threats as those of selection, mortality, and interaction among variables (such as selection and client maturation).

These three preexperimental designs provide minimal information and should not be used if stronger designs can be implemented. Fortunately, alternatives exist—they are known as quasi-experimental designs.

Quasi-Experimental Designs

Quasi-experimental designs are those that fall a little short of the ideal. Often, in agency settings, it is not acceptable or possible to randomly assign clients to one of several treatment modalities or to a control group receiving no intervention. When randomization cannot be achieved, the researcher should consider quasi-experimental designs. Note that in this section three different quasi-experimental designs will be discussed.

The **nonequivalent control group design** is one of the most commonly used quasi-experimental designs because it is the most internally valid design that can be implemented in applied settings where random assignment is not possible. The notation for the nonequivalent control group design is

$$O_1 \quad X \quad O_2$$
$$O_1 \qquad\quad O_2$$

In this design, a control group is used, just as with the experimental design. However, there is no randomization. Usually, a convenient natural group (for example, another class of fifth graders, another AA group, and another group of shy clients) is selected that is similar but may not be truly equivalent to the group receiving the intervention. The control group consists of clients who have been chosen because they possess certain similar characteristics; it can come from clients on a waiting list for service, clients receiving alternative services from the same agency or from another similar agency, or even from non-clients who agree to participate.

Researchers can attempt to match the two groups on important variables (such as age, socioeconomic status, diagnosis). As you can imagine, matching can be difficult because of the number of variables that could be involved. A major problem with matching is that dependent variable differences between the control and intervention groups at the end of the study may have been due to the influence of unmatched variables. Consequently, when you must match, the best advice is to match the groups on as many of the relevant variables as possible. Equivalence is not guaranteed with matching, but it does serve to approximate equivalency. When random assignment is not possible, matching is the next best thing.

With this design, it is usually plausible to assume that the treatment produced the effect. Like the experiment, this design does provide the investigator with the ability to monitor internal validity threats such as those from testing, maturation, instrumentation, history, and mortality. The main threat to this design's internal validity comes from interaction of selection with maturation, with history, or with testing, because random assignment wasn't used (so there was no guarantee of equivalence). Still, this design is better than the preexperimental designs because of the use of a control group. The more similar the control and the experimental groups at pretest, the more confidence you can have in your findings.

As an example of this design, consider the problem of relapse among individuals with chronic mental illness. You want to know whether those patients who are served by your state-run hospital stay as long in the community and without relapse as those in a similar institution in a different part of the state. With the cooperation of both hospital administrators, you make comparisons of such variables as staff-to-patient ratios, percentage of first-time admissions, diagnosis, and average age of patients to establish that the patients and the facilities are roughly equivalent.

Suppose you find that the patients from your hospital do seem to have longer stays in the community than patients of the other hospital. You might conclude that the programming or staff at your hospital is better. However, this design cannot unequivocally demonstrate this outcome. It could be that more of the clients in the other hospital return to rural areas, where there is not the same level of community support services (after-care) as are available to the patients from your hospital (who tend to remain in an urban area). There could be differences in staff experience or morale at the two hospitals (which might affect the treatment received by patients) or in the ease of readmission or screening procedures. Could differences in the physical facilities be a factor? So, while you can be bolstered by your patients' success, the dissimilarities in the hospitals prevent you from *conclusively* determining that the intervention obtained there is the main reason for the patients' longer stays in the community.

Another quasi-experimental design is called **time-series** or **interrupted time-series**. This design is one of the older designs used in the natural sciences. The time-series design is an extension of the one-group pretest-posttest design, where a series of measurements is taken before and after an intervention. This step allows the researcher to understand trends and patterns in the data before the intervention is applied and then provides for continued monitoring for major changes. Notation for a time-series design is:

$$O_1 \quad O_2 \quad O_3 \quad X \quad O_4 \quad O_5 \quad O_6$$

With this design, the researcher is able to see incremental changes (if any) in the study group's behavior prior to the intervention and then to determine if the change after intervention is greater. When possible, an equal number of measurements should be made before and after the intervention. However, you may see one baseline measure and then multiple posttests. Also, the period of time between the measurements should be comparable. The researcher determines the period of time between intervals; it is not imposed from the design. The amount of time between O_1, O_2, and the other observations could be two weeks or three months, for example. This design is particularly well suited for research in social policy when historical or archival data are available. Each observation could then represent a year's data. For instance, you might monitor the number of child fatalities before a new child abuse hotline is promoted publicly.

On a smaller scale, you might use the time-series design to look at staff productivity before and after the executive director implements a new four-day, 40-hour workweek. When using the time-series design in this way, it is important to watch for seasonal variations. Would it be all right to compare January (O_1), February (O_2), and March (O_3) with June (O_4), July (O_5), and August (O_6)? This wouldn't be a fair comparison if productivity were lower in the summer months. To protect against making a conclusion influenced by seasonal or other natural fluctuations in data, include enough observation periods to get a stable baseline.

When the data from time-series are graphed (recall the AB designs in the last chapter), the slope of the line is often helpful in understanding whether the observed effect was caused by the intervention. On a graph, you can readily determine if the frequency of a behavior is increasing prior to and after an intervention. Because the measurements are obtained over an extended period of time, history is the chief threat to the internal validity of this design. A threat from testing might also be apparent in some instances.

This time-series design provides even better information if a corresponding control group can be added:

$$O_1 \quad O_2 \quad O_3 \quad X \quad O_4 \quad O_5 \quad O_6$$
$$O_1 \quad O_2 \quad O_3 \quad \quad O_4 \quad O_5 \quad O_6$$

This new design with a control group is called the **multiple time-series design**. It resembles a stretched-out nonequivalent control group design. Campbell and Stanley (1963) recommend this design for research in school settings. It is a strong quasi-experimental design with no serious internal validity threats. The investigator can use the control group to check for the influence of history and to understand the effects of testing, maturation, mortality, and instrumentation.

Advanced Designs

As the questions the researcher is concerned with become more sophisticated, there is a need for more complex designs. This section will present two examples of sophisticated designs that can be used when the quality of the evidence for making decisions is of high importance.

Factorial Designs

Experimental **factorial designs** are often employed when Intervention A is being compared to Intervention B *and* both vary along some other dimension (for example, frequency, intensity, or duration). In the factorial design that follows, the researcher is able to determine not only whether Intervention A is more effective than Intervention B, but also whether the factor of meeting more frequently results in even greater improvement than the weekly sessions. Figure 5.1 shows two treatments and two levels of frequency, making this a 2 × 2 factorial design. If clients could also have been randomly assigned

Interventions

Frequency	Intervention A Once Weekly	Intervention B Once Weekly
	Intervention A Twice Weekly	Intervention B Twice Weekly

Factorial design (2 × 2)

FIGURE 5.1 Factorial Design (2 X 2)

to groups that met every day, five days a week, then this would have been a 2 × 3 design. Although it is not shown in Figure 5.1, random assignment is understood.

A major reason for using this design is so that the investigator can look at the combinations associated with frequency for the interventions of interest. Within the same study, the investigator can assess the effects of separate interventions under different conditions—resulting in a savings of time and effort (compared to doing two different studies).

Crossover Designs

Crossover designs can be used when investigators think that the order in which clients receive interventions may affect their success. This design allows for the testing of that hypothesis. Let's take a hypothetical example. In Figure 5.2, men who have been arrested for battering their partners are randomly assigned to participate in treatment—either Group 101 or Group 102 for the first month. Those in Group 101 receive praise and encouragement for every unsolicited comment, vocalization, or question they raise. In a sense, participation—not the content of their communications—is rewarded. After four weeks, their counselors start giving them verbal reinforcement only when they take responsibility for their actions, express remorse for their past behavior, or their questions or comments make an empathetic response regarding their victims of abuse. Facilitators in Group 102 start with rewarding only the empathetic and remorseful statements where participants take responsibility for their actions. After four weeks, these clients "cross over" and then begin verbal praise for participating with any comment, question, or vocalization. Assuming the goals were to help these men to take responsibility for their actions and keep them engaged in therapy, the investigator would be using a standardized instrument—perhaps examining any changes in empathy at two different points of time (after the first four weeks and after eight weeks). This design lets the researcher determine which sequence produces the best overall results.

You can see in Figure 5.2 that each group experiences three assessments. O_2 and O_5 do double duty, functioning both as posttests and as pretests at the beginning of the second treatment.

There are many other variations of group research designs (such as a Latin square for randomly ordering the sequence of multiple interventions) that you may want to use as a social work researcher. If you are feeling overwhelmed—that there are too many different designs to learn—it might be helpful to sort them into the three broad categories of preexperimental, quasi-experimental, and experimental designs. And if that doesn't help, remember this: Having many designs to choose from is certainly a better situation than having fewer models that don't fit your particular application. By analogy, you wouldn't want to set about baking a cake and have only a pizza pan to bake it on.

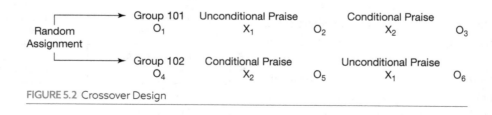

FIGURE 5.2 Crossover Design

Design and Validity Considerations

The main reason that researchers choose experimental over preexperimental or quasi-experimental designs is that the former make causal inference easier. Let's say that as a social work practitioner, you have a notion that an intervention employed by your agency is more effective with certain clients than others. To test this hypothesis, you would probably choose one of the experimental designs described in this chapter. Sometimes, however, social workers have questions like "Are parents of disabled children more likely to abuse their children than other parents?" or "What proportion of the homeless have a problem with substance abuse?" Questions such as these do not require experimental research designs. Rather, they are more likely to be explored using secondary data analysis or a survey research design—and we'll be examining these approaches a little later.

As previously discussed, preexperimental and quasi-experimental designs are susceptible to problems of internal validity. Yet, useful information and valuable studies can come from designs that are not truly experimental. For example, if you are hired as a school social worker in an alternative school providing group therapy and support groups for teens at risk, random assignment may not be possible. Consequently, if you were interested in evaluating the success of your groups, the best design remaining might be the nonequivalent control group design. Even though experimental designs are the most rigorous, quasi-experimental designs should not be summarily dismissed, particularly when you are engaged in what might be called "salvage" research (when you're trying to rescue data that otherwise might be lost). In such cases, even using the one-group pretest-posttest design is better than not examining the data at all. As we've previously stated, you have a responsibility as a social worker and evidence-based practitioner to evaluate your efforts.

To make your study as strong as possible, careful planning is required. Thinking about ways of preventing extraneous variables from influencing (or explaining away) the effect of your intervention will result in a stronger study. While the selection of a good research design is important, it is no substitute for good planning. Even a strong design can be poorly implemented and go awry when little attention is paid to details. If, for instance, you lose most of your participants through attrition, even an experimental design will be of little assistance in helping you infer that the intervention caused the observed changes in the treatment group.

BOX 5.1   MINIMIZING THREATS TO INTERNAL VALIDITY

1. Keep the time between the start and the end of the study short. This helps diminish the threat of *history*. (Note that this suggestion does not apply to time-series designs.) Also, keeping the study period short can help reduce the threat of maturation (especially a problem when studying children and youth), as well as any interaction of maturation with selection.
2. Test subjects only once or use different versions of the same test at posttest to minimize the threat of *testing*.
3. Train your assistants and administer the instrument the same way every time. (This helps minimize the threat of *instrumentation*.)

BOX 5.1   MINIMIZING THREATS TO INTERNAL VALIDITY (CONTINUED)

4. Use innocuous or placebo treatments, brief treatments, or mild incentives so that control group subjects do not drop out of the study. Keep in touch with those in the control group when there is a long period between observations. (This helps reduce the threat of *mortality*.)
5. Be careful with choosing subjects on the basis of one extreme test score. (This helps decrease the threat of *statistical regression*.)
6. Randomly assign where possible. If you must match, match on as many key variables as is practical. (This helps minimize the threat of *selection*.)

Source: Mitchell and Jolley (1988).

Research designs are only guides to the research process. They structure a problem-solving process and provide an outline for how data will be collected. Choosing the right design is a complex decision that often hinges on feasibility considerations. Should you need to choose a group research design sometime in the future, remember that numerous other designs (and multiple variations of the designs in this chapter) are available to you. Regardless of the design you choose, devote time to considering how extraneous variables may affect the internal and external validity of your study.

Selecting the "Right" Design

One might ask, how do I know I have selected the correct research design? The answer is, the design is correct if it answers the question you need to know with the degree of credibility and confidence you require. If you want a quick assessment and the stakes are very low (for instance, a student project or pilot study), then a preexperimental design could be sufficient for beginning first steps. If a little more is involved, but not big money or your or the agency's reputation, a quasi-experimental design might be a good choice. It would allow you to collect some credible information and might get you some recognition. When a lot is at stake within the agency or you aspire to publish your findings or present them at a prestigious conference, then go for the gold standard—one of the experimental designs.

Ethical Research and Group Designs

Before closing this chapter, it is important to address concerns that some social workers have about experimental designs. Like an urban myth, occasionally one may hear that group research designs are unethical because clients would be assigned to nontreatment control groups. Denying clients needed services would be unethical—no disagreement there. However, programs usually are evaluated by comparing them against another program—clients in an experimental group might be provided with a new or more intense intervention, but those in the control group would still receive the traditional treatment. The experimental intervention may not, in fact, be any better than the usual and customary treatment. In other words, there doesn't have to be a definite disadvantage to being in the control group.

Another way to think about acquiring a control group is that many agencies have waiting lists, and these form natural control groups. Those on the waiting lists can be administered pretests at the point of application for service and posttests later when they arrive for their first appointment. That posttest, by the way, is actually a second pretest. A third observation (the real posttest) would actually be taken toward the end of treatment to assess improvement. Clients on a waiting list might also be given some mild form of intervention (such as educational pamphlets or a video to watch) while they are waiting their turn for service.

Pre-Experimental Designs

One-group pretest-posttest design:$\quad\quad\quad O_1 \quad\quad X \quad\quad O_2$

One-group posttest-only design:

$$X \quad O$$

Posttest-only design with non- equivalent groups:

$$X \quad O$$
$$O$$

Quasi-Experimental Designs

Non-equivalent control group:

$$O_1 \quad X \quad O_2$$
$$O_1 \quad\quad\ O_2$$

Time-series or interrupted time-series:

$$O_1 \quad O_2 \quad O_3 \quad X \quad O_4 \quad O_5 \quad O_6$$

Multiple time-series design:

$$O_1 \quad O_2 \quad O_3 \quad X \quad O_4 \quad O_5 \quad O_6$$
$$O_1 \quad O_2 \quad O_3 \quad\quad O_4 \quad O_5 \quad O_6$$

Experimental Designs

Classic Experimental Design:

$$R \quad O_1 \quad X \quad O_2$$
$$R \quad O_1 \quad\quad O_2$$

Posttest-Only Control Group Design

$$R \quad X \quad O_1$$
$$R \quad O \quad O_2$$

Solomon Four-Group Design

$$R \quad O_1 \quad X \quad O_2$$
$$R \quad O_1 \quad\quad O_2$$
$$R \quad\quad X \quad O_2$$
$$R \quad\quad\quad O_2$$

FIGURE 5.3 The Basic Pre-Experimental, Quasi-Experimental, and Experimental Design Notations at a Glance

People normally form themselves into groups. Some men with anger management problems would rather go to jail than attend a psychoeducational treatment program. Other men may start treatment but drop out. Still others may be released with community service, fined, and put on probation. Even if random assignment is not possible, worthwhile information could come from examining the recidivism of individuals in each of these groups.

Social work researchers must be just as ethical as their colleagues who provide direct services. And, as you learned earlier, institutional review boards safeguard society in reviewing human subjects research. One of the key guidelines that all researchers must follow is to cause no harm to those participating.

Randomization is not always possible even in the most research-friendly agencies. And when it is not feasible, comparison groups from other agencies or populations can be useful. Even the lowly preexperimental designs have a role. As exploratory or pilot studies, they attempt to expand our knowledge about the interventions we use and their effects on our clients. They may not be great studies, but they have the potential for providing new knowledge that can be explored later in greater depth and precision with a more powerful and rigorous design. In some instances, preexperimental designs provide all the evidence necessary to convince a funding source to underwrite a more involved scientific study. In the same way, qualitative studies also may lead to the funding of a larger-scale group research design study.

If you are really eager to dig into and understand more about the use of experimental designs in social work, please go to Bruce Thyer's 2015 major contribution, "A bibliography of randomized controlled experiments in social work (1949–2013): Solvitur Ambulando." *Research on Social Work Practice*, 25(7), 753–793.

Key Terms

Attrition	Limitations
Control group	Measurement validity
Crossover design	Mortality
Double-blind procedure	Multiple time-series design
Extraneous variable	Nonequivalent control group design
Experiment/experimental design	One-group pretest-posttest design
External validity	One-group posttest only design
Factorial design	Preexperimental design
History	Pretest
Homogeneous	Pretest-posttest control group design
Incentive	Posttest
Instrumentation	Posttest-only control group design
Interaction effects	Posttest-only design with nonequivalent groups
Internal validity	Practice effect

Proactive research   Statistical regression

Quasi-experimental design   Test fatigue

Randomly assigned   Testing

Reactive/interactive effect   Time-series design

Retroactive research   interrupted time-series

Solomon four-group design

SELF-REVIEW

(Answers at the end of the book.)

1. Marsha has 80 clients meeting in grief counseling groups at a large hospice. At the end of each session, she wants to administer a depression inventory. She's planning to evaluate these participants with 80 single-system designs (AB). Is this an appropriate design?

2. What two features must a true experiment contain?

3. _____ variables are those that confound the researcher's ability to interpret the data.

4. T or F. A posttest-only design with random assignment meets the requirements for an experiment.

5. T or F. Maturation is a possible threat to the interval validity of any study where the passage of time between pretest and subsequent observations is one or more years.

6. T or F. Instrumentation is the name of the threat to internal validity where subjects are administered the same instrument on multiple occasions.

7. T or F. The use of volunteers, especially paid volunteers, should always suggest a possible threat to the internal validity of selection.

8. T or F. An example of statistical regression is where subjects were selected originally on the basis of their high pretest scores.

9. T or F. The following notation represents a true experiment:

$$O_1 \ X \ O_2$$
$$O_1 \quad O_2$$

10. What design in this chapter was said to be well suited for social policy research?

11. T or F. Both the factorial and crossover designs require randomization.

12. What would be the major problem with using an O X O design?

13. Noah is interested in planning a study of patients who have received services from his agency over the past five years. About 30% dropped out. Could this constitute a control group for comparing the percent of dropouts from the newest program?

14. T or F. Group research designs require an excessive number of clients or subjects.

15. T or F. With quasi-experimental designs, it is highly important that clients be randomly assigned to each group.

16. T or F. Measurement validity deals with how well the study approximates the size of the population being studied.

QUESTIONS FOR CLASS DISCUSSION

1. What are the different pretest-posttest comparisons that can be made with the Solomon four-group design?
2. What kinds of experiments would you like to conduct? Explain.
3. Consider the threats to internal validity as presented in this chapter and discuss how they also may pose threats to single-system designs.
4. Discuss how pragmatic considerations (the agency setting, its clientele) influence the choice of a research design. Could the possible implications or findings of the study affect the choice of a design?
5. Which two designs discussed in this chapter are identical except for the use of randomization?
6. How might the use of experimental designs in social service agencies involve ethical considerations? Are there still ethical issues you are concerned about?
7. Do you think practitioners who want to conduct research start with a specific research design they want to use or start with an intervention they want to evaluate and then seek a research design that fits the situation?
8. Discuss the arguments for choosing an experimental design over a quasi-experimental design to evaluate an intervention.
9. Why is replication for researchers conducting explanatory research important?

RESOURCES AND REFERENCES

Bamberger, M., Tarsilla M., & Hesse-Biber, S. (2016). Why so many "rigorous" evaluations fail to identify unintended consequences of developmental programs: How mixed methods can contribute. *Evaluation and Program Planning, 55*, 155–162.

Campbell, D. T., & Stanley, J. C. (1963). *Experimental and quasi-experimental designs for research*. Skokie, IL: Rand McNally.

Collins, L. M., Dziak, J. J., Kugler, K. C., & Trail, J. B. (2014). Factorial experiments. *American Journal of Preventive Medicine, 47*(4), 498–504.

Cook, T. D., & Campbell, D. T. (1979). Quasi-experimentaton: Design and analysis issues for field settings. Skokie, IL: Rand McNally.

Marsh, J. C. (2013). Think fast and slow about causality: Response to Palinkas. *Research on Social Work Practice, 24*(5), 548–551.

Mitchell, M., & Jolley, J. (1988). *Research design explained*. New York, NY: Holt, Rinehart and Winston.

Palinkas, L. A. (2014). Causality and causal inference in social work: Quantitative and qualitative perspectives. *Research on Social Work Practice, 24*(5), 540–547.

One-Group Pretest-Posttest

Galla, B., O'Reilly, G. A., & Kitil, M. (2015). Community-based mindfulness program for disease prevention and health promotion: Targeting stress reduction. *American Journal of Health Promotion, 30*(1), 36–41.

Patterson, D., & Resko, S. (2015). Is online learning a viable training option for teaching sexual assault forensic examiners? *Journal of Forensic Nursing, 11*(4), 181–189.

Quasi-Experimental

Coleman, D., & Del Quest, A. (2015). Science from evaluation: Testing hypotheses about differential effects of three youth-focused suicide prevention trainings. *Social Work in Public Health*, *30*(2), 117–128.

Fleming, P., Biggart, L., & Beckett, C. (2015). Effects of professional experience on child maltreatment risk assessment: A comparison of students and qualifying social workers. *British Journal of Social Work*, *45*(8), 2298–2316.

Smith-Osborne, A. (2015). An intensive continuing education initiative to train social workers for military social work practice. *Journal of Social Work Education*, *51*(1), S89–101.

Experimental

Choi, S. (2015). Improving service utilization with substance abuse problems: Experimenting with recovery coaches in child welfare. *Journal of Evidence-Informed Social Work*, *12*(6), 547–555.

Greeson, J. K. P., Garcia, A. R., Kim, M., & Courtney, M. E. (2015). Foster youth and social support: The first RCT of independent living services. *Research on Social Work Practice*, *25*(3), 349–357.

ASSIGNMENT 5.1

Creating a Group Research Design

Objective: *To gain firsthand experience in planning a group research design.*

Imagine that an agency director has asked you to come up with a research design to guide the evaluation of a pilot program that is scheduled to begin in a couple of months. You may be as creative as you wish, but you must build in a control group. The control group can receive the typical or standard treatment. Try to use an experimental design if possible. If you can't randomly assign, use the quasi-experimental nonequivalent control group design.

1. Describe the intervention you have in mind:

2. What is your hypothesis or research question?

3. How will you operationalize your dependent variable?

4. Based on the number of clients going through the program, how long will it take you to collect data? Will the posttest be immediately after the end of treatment or sometime later?

5. How will you recruit your subjects so that there is no dual relationship problems?

6. What research design will you be using?

7. How will you create a control group?

8. How will you randomly assign clients? What will your procedure be?

ASSIGNMENT 5.2

Analyzing My Research Design

Objective: *To identify areas where my study may be vulnerable to possible internal validity threats.*

Once Assignment 5.1 is complete, evaluate it in terms of the threats to internal validity. Briefly explain your decisions in each instance. Alternatively, your instructor may want you to exchange your work with another student and assess his or her Assignment 5.1.

1. **Maturity** is a possible threat to the internal validity of the study.   Yes_____ or No_____. Why?

2. **History** is a possible threat to the internal validity of the study.   Yes_____ or No_____. Why?

3. **Testing** is a possible threat to the internal validity of the study.   Yes_____ or No_____. Why?

4. **Instrumentation** is a possible threat to the internal validity of the study.   Yes_____ or No_____. Why?

5. **Selection** is a possible threat to the internal validity of the study.   Yes_____ or No_____. Why?

6. **Statistical regression** is a possible threat to the internal validity of the study.   Yes_____ or No_____. Why?

7. **Mortality** is a possible threat to the internal validity of the study.   Yes_____ or No_____. Why?

8. **Interaction** is a possible threat to the internal validity of the study.   Yes_____ or No_____. Why?

9. The number of "Yes" responses that I've checked in this assignment is _____.

10. What does your response to Question 9 tell you about the confidence you could place in the proposed study's findings?

11. What one modification could you make to the study that would improve it by eliminating at least one threat to internal validity?

ASSIGNMENT 5.3

A Case Scenario for Assessing Threats to Internal Validity

Objective: *To obtain additional experience in identifying threats to internal validity.*

Read the case scenario presented on this page and then use Assignment 5.2 to identify and discuss internal validity problems apparent in the vignette.

Hooked On Vowels

Susie has begun a new job in a residential facility for adolescents who have been in trouble with the law on numerous occasions. Because the state agency that supplies the majority of the facility's funding requires an evaluation, Susie is asked to conduct a study showing that their programs make a difference. Susie wants to start with helping the teens to read and spell better. When their success in school improves, she believes that the teens will stay out of trouble with the law. The intervention that she plans to employ is a computer software program called Hooked on Vowels. It comes highly recommended and is affordable. Here are some of the facts about the study:

There are about 150 boys who live in 10 different cottages; each cottage has three computer stations.

Boys can be randomly assigned to receive the Hooked on Vowels intervention.

About half of the boys will be designated to a control condition without the special intervention; about half will receive it.

Some boys stay in the facility three, four, or five years. Some boys spend less than six months.

Her director has already informed Susie that once the boys leave the facility, it will be hard to keep track of them. In a previous study, only 10% of the boys who had left the facility responded to a questionnaire.

Susie wants to employ these dependent variables: number of new arrests, GPA after leaving the facility, highest grade level attained before quitting school, attitudes toward school, current reading level.

None of these boys like to study history; all of the boys have a history with the law.

The instrument Susie was thinking of using to measure attitudes toward school is homemade. That is, she developed it herself and doesn't really know how well it will measure attitudes toward school. Susie has never developed an instrument before.

Susie was planning on learning about the boys' GPA by writing them and asking them to write her back with their grades after leaving the facility. That is, they would self-report their grades.

Susie's friend Callie recommends that instead of involving all the boys in the study, she test her intervention with a group of boys who volunteer to do the Hooked on Vowels program.

Six months into the study, the agency director—beloved by all the staff and residents and who was constantly advocating that the boys stay in school—was exposed by a newspaper article that revealed he had misrepresented information on his résumé at the time he was hired. In fact, he had never finished college.

Susie believed strongly that the intervention would make the boys so much more enthusiastic about school. Because of that, she proposed to measure their attitudes weekly over a six-month period.

The assistant to the director recommended that Susie not base her study on all the boys in the facility, but instead to target those who performed the worst on their last reading test.

CHAPTER 6

Understanding and Using Research Instruments

A S WE LEARNED in Chapter 2, quantitative social work researchers often use and sometimes design their own research instruments (scales) to measure concepts. Sophia and Bill are getting closer to thinking about what scales or instruments they might need for their research project.

After Sophia finished her salad and while Bill dug into a piece of pecan pie, she said, "I don't think we can just outline a program from Mrs. Simpson and then walk away in a couple of months when our internship is finished."

"Why not?" Bill asked, uncharacteristically putting down his fork while he waited for Sophia's reply.

"If we really want to make a difference with this population of incarcerated women, we have to consider not only the program as it is designed, but also *who* might be presenting it."

"Good point," said Bill, looking back from Sophia to his pie again. "But we won't have any control over that."

"We just might," she said, picking up her sweater and standing. "We've been focused all this time on the inmates. Yes, we can focus on their knowledge of HIV/AIDS and identify risky behaviors. But what about the presenters' attitudes toward these women?"

"Wait. You mean whether they like them or not?"

"No, more than that, Bill. Do they think of the inmates in stereotypes—you know, as criminals, addicts, thieves? Or do they view them more compassionately—as someone who could be a sister, daughter, or mother?"

"Hmmm. Would it make that much difference?" Bill picked up the last piece of crust and popped it into his mouth.

"I think it could. If they are judgmental and fearful of HIV, their prejudice might come through their presentations."

"That wouldn't be good," Bill said. He opened his wallet to look for money for a tip.

"No, it wouldn't," Sophia agreed. "We need to look into this and find a good instrument that will let us assess the providers' stigma toward persons with HIV/AIDS."

"I don't mind looking for an instrument," Bill said as Sophia slid out of the booth. "Although I don't have a clue how we would evaluate it. That will be your department."

"No problem," said Sophia, smiling. "I read ahead in the textbook. We just have to first make sure the instrument is a good fit for our research."

"And reliable and valid," added Bill. "I learned that much!"

Reliability

Reliability is an easy term to understand because its usage by researchers is close to its use in everyday conversation. When a watch keeps time accurately, it is said to be reliable. If, on the other hand, your watch gained a half hour in one week, lost 17 minutes the second week, and gained three hours at the end of the third week, you would suspect that something is wrong with it—that it is not reliable. Similarly, a scale or instrument that consistently measures some phenomenon with accuracy is said to be **reliable**. When an instrument is reliable, then administering it to similar groups under comparable conditions should yield similar measurements.

One of the ways we evaluate standardized instruments is by their reliability. Generally, this information resembles a correlation coefficient in that reliability coefficients must have a numeric value that falls between 0 and 1. In one of the "gold standards in psychometric theory," Nunnally (1994) says that in the early stages of research, one can work with instruments having modest reliability, by which he means .70 or higher; that .80 is needed for basic research; and that a reliability of .90 is the minimum when important decisions are going to be made with respect to specific test scores. If there is no reliability data on a scale, reliability cannot be assumed—the scale could have poor reliability. Data produced from a scale with poor or unknown reliability should always be suspect. When reading about scales or instruments in professional literature, always try to find the information regarding reliability and validity.

Researchers want their instruments to have a form of reliability known as **internal consistency**. This means that individual items correlate well with the full scale. If this doesn't happen, the items have little in common.

BOX 6.1   A NOTE ON CORRELATION

Correlation is a statistic that expresses the relationship between two variables. The strength of their association is a decimal between 0 and 1. When variables are correlated, it means as the values in one variable increase (for example, years of education), then generally the values in the other variable increase, too (for example, annual salary)—creating a positive correlation. An inverse or negative association could result when a variable like hours of watching television is correlated with Grade Point Average (GPA). (The more hours spent in front of the TV, the lower the GPA. For example, -.58 might summarize that relationship.) In any group, there will be individuals who do not conform to the pattern generally found with the others. When there is no clear pattern, the correlation coefficient will be closer to zero—e.g., r = 06.

For example, say you construct a scale to measure assertiveness, and you write the following items:

The Slap-Together Assertiveness Scale

	Agree	Disagree
1. I always speak my mind.		
2. I am frank about my feelings.		
3. I take care of myself.		

After creating these three items, you develop writer's block. As you try to think of additional items to include, you recall your friend Zack, who is the most assertive individual you have ever known. You ponder

Zack's distinctiveness and remember how fanatical he is about baseball. Maybe knowledge of baseball and assertiveness are somehow related, you think. So, you write a new item:

4. I believe professional baseball is superior to all other sports.

TABLE 6.1 Coefficient Alpha Info on Slap-Together Assertiveness Scale

	Item-Total Correlation	Alpha if Item Deleted
Item 1	.53	–.35
Item 2	.51	–.29
Item 3	.26	.12
Item 4	–.54	.72

These four items complete the scale, and you administer the Slap-Together Assertiveness Scale to a large cross-section of adults. One of the ways to obtain information about the scale is by running the Reliability procedure available through the Statistical Package for the Social Sciences (SPSS)—computer software available at most universities.

After you've entered the way each individual responded to the items on the scale, the computer program will produce a reliability coefficient and indicate those items that do not correlate well with the rest. By dropping these items, it is often possible to improve a scale's internal consistency. For example, a simplified printout might show something like this:

The software program shows how strong the items are individually and the contribution they make to the scale. In the first column, Item 1 has the highest correlation with the group of four items in the tentative scale, followed by Item 2. Item 3 has a weak correlation, and Item 4 has a negative correlation, suggesting that it is not measuring the same concept, but something different. The second column of information presents the **coefficient alpha** (the empirical representation of the concept of internal consistency). The "Alpha if Item Deleted" column shows the relative contribution of each item to the overall scale. The –.35 and –.29 alphas indicate that the scale's reliability suffers tremendously if either of these two items is deleted. In fact, the scale's internal consistency would be meager and the scale would have terrible reliability. If these two items were left in and Item 3 were deleted, the draft scale would have positive—but inconsequential (terrible)—reliability. What the second column shows is that all of the first three items are necessary for the scale to have acceptable reliability. We see this in the SPSS printout when it shows deleting Item 4 improves the overall scale's internal consistency to .72 (rounded). Dropping this item would be a good decision and would leave us with a three-item scale with an acceptable coefficient alpha of .72.

BOX 6.2   OTHER TERMS FOR INSTRUMENTS FOUND IN THE LITERATURE

- Scale: a collection of items that comprise a single concept
- Index: a set of items that produce a summated score—in effect, a scale
- Questionnaire: a group of questions or items used in survey research (internal consistency is not usually an issue for questionnaires)

- Checklist: a list of items related in some way to each other (for example, the Child Behavior Checklist)
- Self-Report: usually a brief instrument completed by the client or research participant
- Inventory: a collection of scales that are thematically related and used to assess different dimensions (e.g., of psychological well-being or dysfunction)
- Test: generic term for any measurement procedure
- Subscale: one of several smaller scales contained within a larger index or inventory; to be useful, each subscale must be reliable and valid

What if we wanted even higher reliability? Because internal consistency is based both on the number of items and the way they correlate together, it is reasonable to assume that writing a few more new items might increase our reliability. The Spearman-Brown Prophecy Formula (and you can find a calculator on the Internet) can be used to estimate the effect on the instrument's reliability when more items are added. For instance, by doubling the number of items in the previous example, we might increase our reliability to .83. Tripling the number of items would likely produce a reliability of .88. Also, when a true/false response format has been used, another strategy for improving reliability is to modify the format to a five-point Likert scale (*Strongly Agree, Agree, Undecided, Disagree, Strongly Disagree*) so that greater variability in responding is allowed. If you create an instrument with several scales, you will need to compute the internal consistency for each scale.

Researchers sometimes measure internal consistency by dividing their longer scales in half (either top versus bottom or even versus odd items) and examining how well the two halves correlate with each other. This method is known as the *split-half* technique. Another approach is to devise *parallel* or *alternate versions* of the scale and administer both forms to similar groups. The researcher hopes that both versions will correlate with each other—the higher the correlation coefficient, the stronger the reliability.

Once a scale has been shown to have internal consistency, another step is often to show that its capability is not impaired by differences in space and time. Would those individuals who were identified as being assertive on October 15 still be assertive two weeks later? What about in January? To determine temporal stability, researchers will commonly administer a scale to the same group on more than one occasion to see, for example, if persons with high test scores at the first administration maintain high scores at the second administration. This is called **test-retest reliability**.

Over short periods of time, scores (e.g., of attitudes, behavior, and knowledge) should remain fairly consistent when an instrument is reliable. While it is expected that some individuals will show increases or decreases, possibly as a result of an intervention or some personal event that happened only to them, there would be no logical explanation for why the majority of a large group should experience extreme changes in their scores. Should this happen—and if the researcher can find no other explanation—it is reasonable to assume that there is some problem with the instrument because it did not show temporal stability/test-retest reliability.

With the example of the Slap-Together Assertiveness Scale, there could be too few items to give it stability over time. Item #3 is a little vague and might mean different things to different people. It could have reliability problems if it showed internal consistency with subjects from one part of the United States but not from another geographical area. What good would such an instrument be?

Internal consistency cannot be computed on a single item. Remember the rule: fewer items usually equate to lower reliability. All else being equal, adding relevant items usually improves reliability, as does expanding the number of response choices—for example, going from two to five.

Reliability of Procedures

Even if you don't use an instrument but instead depend on observation of some behavior (such as how many times a special education child gets out of his seat during class), you must make every effort to standardize your procedures for counting the phenomenon of interest. Similarly, procedures should be uniform whenever instruments are used and scored.

An associate related an account illustrating the importance of standardized conditions. She had been going into homes of rural families on welfare during the summer months. Much of their housing was dilapidated with substandard fixtures. Many often had only one or two electrical outlets per room. In fact, sometimes she had to ask those she was interviewing to unplug the TV, fan, or air conditioner so that she could plug in her laptop. It stands to reason that if the interviewees are hot and uncomfortable, they may abbreviate their responses, become impatient, or even terminate the interview quicker than if they were not forced to sit in stifling heat. In short, the quality of the data could be affected.

When more than one person is involved in rating clients' behavior, it is desirable to compute **interrater reliability** to determine the percentage of time the raters are in agreement. For instance, two individuals were observing a child in a special education class for the number of times he got out of his desk during class, and let's say Bill and Sophia both independently counted 9 instances. Upon watching a video of the classroom, they both agree that the child actually got out of his desk a 10th time to pick up a dropped pencil, but neither one of them caught it. Thus, they correctly recorded 9 out of a total of 10 instances and agreed with each other 90% of the time. A correlation between their independent ratings may also be computed using the statistical software SPSS if the situation is more complicated and a correlation is desired. If the correlation is low, then the criteria may not be well defined (e.g., should legitimate reasons to leave one's desk—as when retrieving a pencil—get counted? Does it change the count if the child tossed the pencil on purpose?). If the obtained correlation is high (.70 or above), then the researcher has evidence that the rating scale has succeeded in providing a reliable measurement.

BOX 6.3 CROSS-CULTURAL AND MULTICULTURAL ASSESSMENT CONSIDERATIONS

Many of the older assessment instruments were largely tested and based on Euro-American populations and did not include persons of color. When you are examining an instrument for potential use with a cross-cultural or multicultural sample, it is important to try and determine if persons of color/minorities were included as deliberate samples. Saying this another way, the instrument should be developed from a sample of persons representative of a multicultural population.

Similarly, it is important to make sure that an instrument designed to use with persons of color is culturally relevant. Test items should have the same connotative and denotative meanings, for instance, with both African Americans and European Americans.

When instruments are determined to be reliable and valid on a cross-cultural and multicultural basis, they will measure the same construct dependably for all groups.

Practice-Focused Reliability Overview

Although there may seem to be too many types of reliability to keep track of, here are several key points you ought to remember about reliability:

- Internal consistency is also known as coefficient alpha or **Cronbach's alpha**. Most researchers compute it with statistical software, and it will always be less than 1. The closer it is to 1, the more reliable the scale, and the better all items work together to measure the same concept.

- The Spearman-Brown Prophecy Formula can be used if you want to develop your own scale and to improve its coefficient alpha. If you are not developing a scale or trying to improve an existing one, you may not need this formula. (Interactive calculators can be found on the Web.)

- The split-half method of computing internal consistency is an old, time-tested method but not seen much today because computer software like SPSS is so easy to use.

- Parallel or alternate versions of computing internal consistency is, again, an approach that you are not likely to use unless you are involved in creating standardized tests.

- Test-retest reliability is frequently reported in social science literature because the concern is that the measure should be stable over time—that the instrument should perform the same way. For instance, if one is inclined to be fatalistic about life in general, then a person with a high fatalistic score in January should also be on the high end of the fatalism measure in March, assuming no intervention or other major influences. Generally, the expectation is that two administrations of the same instrument within a short period of time (for example, two weeks or a month) should yield a strong correlation. This would suggest that the instrument was measuring *the same thing* at two different times. (The coefficient alpha does not, you'll remember, suggest what that concept is—that's a job for a validity study.)

- Standardization of the data collection procedures is something you need to be concerned with whenever you are doing research that involves collecting data with multiple personnel, with observers, or whenever instructions are provided to research participants. Anything that is unclear or confusing can affect the reliability of the data gathered.

Reliability—Qualitative Perspective

Reliability in qualitative research is understood a little differently than in quantitative research. It is not computed with statistics and does not derive from numbers. Instead, reliability is concerned with whether content derived from interviews and observations fits together in a pattern that is understandable and dependable. Reliability comes from the steps the qualitative researcher has taken to obtain the data and the process through which the investigator engages in data reduction and makes sense of the findings. Reliability, then, has to do with the plausibility of the data and the similarity of accounts from group members and informants. In contrast to the reliability of standardized instruments, reliability from the qualitative perspective depends on the researcher's own insight and ability to test suppositions about the data and sources of data by questioning and examining their credibility (Kreuger & Neuman, 2006). Reliability is, in some ways, inseparable from validity. Lincoln and Guba (1985) observe: "... there can be no validity without reliability"—so a demonstration of validity can establish reliability (p. 16).

Validity

An instrument is said to be **valid** when it measures the construct it was designed to measure. For instance, an intelligence test should measure intelligence. An instrument designed to measure anxiety should provide an accurate assessment of anxiety, but not social responsibility, dogmatism, or paranoia, or anything but anxiety.

Validity research demonstrates how a scale performs—identifying its limitations and its strengths. Because the same instrument may be valid in one situation but not in another, validity research seeks to gather evidence to document that the instrument does, in fact, do a good job of assessing the construct in question. Why would this be necessary?

Let's take an example. Suppose you develop a self-esteem scale for use with high school students. Unconsciously, the items you develop for the scale might be heavily influenced by what could be considered "academic self-esteem"—students' perceptions of their worth based on the grades they were making. Students who were having trouble with algebra or chemistry might score very low on such a scale. That instrument would be a rather narrow way of thinking about self-esteem, which doesn't include other dimensions in the student's life. How might he or she feel during the summer months when working and not in school? What other ways can students feel good about themselves other than excelling academically? And the use of your scale, even if it were valid for a high school population, might not be valid for assessing the self-esteem of a different group of subjects—incarcerated adults, for example.

These are the situations when a researcher should conduct validity research:

- When an instrument is new and unproven
- When an instrument designed for one age group is going to be used with another
- When an instrument designed for one culture is going to be used with another
- When an instrument is being adopted for a different use from what it was intended for
- Whenever a researcher wants to improve the instrument.

There are numerous ways to go about establishing the validity of an instrument. Demonstrating validity is more of an ongoing process than a single, one-time effort. We usually have the most information about an instrument's validity when it has been around for a while and different studies have been done with it. Efforts to confirm an instrument's validity are generally discussed in terms of three general categories, and each of these will be discussed in turn.

1. **Content validity**
2. **Criterion validity**
    a. concurrent approaches
    b. predictive approaches
3. **Construct validity**
    a. convergent
    b. discriminant
    c. factorial (structural)

To have **content validity**, an instrument needs to sample from the entire range of the concept that it was designed to measure. For instance, it could be difficult for a behavioral scale measuring anger in children under the age of eight to be valid if the scale did not consider pouting, hitting, or temper tantrums as manifestations of anger. Likewise, a scale measuring anxiety in adolescents might not have content validity if it did not include such behavior as nail biting, crying, stomachaches, and sleeplessness. To the extent that an instrument contains a representative sampling of the universe of behaviors, attitudes, or characteristics that are believed to be associated with the concept, then it is said to have content validity. Content validity is established when a panel of experts examines the scale and agrees that the items selected are representative of the range of items associated with the concept to be measured. However, there are no standardized procedures for assessing content validity, and no computed coefficient of validity is produced.

While the terms *content* and *face validity* are sometimes used interchangeably, they are not quite the same. An instrument is said to have **face validity** when it appears to measure the intended construct. Again, a panel of coworkers or persons familiar with the concept could look at the scale and consider the items on it, the way they are worded, and so forth. They then report their impression that the instrument has or does not have face validity. Note that face and content validity are beginning, minimal efforts and do not establish that an instrument is valid or that it will allow generalizability.

Once the researcher is reasonably confident that the scale has content validity, then the next step is to plan a strategy to demonstrate that the collection of items possesses other, more substantial, forms of validity. **Criterion validity**, the second major category of validity research activities, is based on the scale's ability to correlate positively with some external criterion assumed to be an indicator of the attitude, trait, or behavior being measured. Criterion validity can be established in several ways. We will quickly discuss two approaches or subtypes of this form of validity.

Concurrent validity is demonstrated by administering your scale simultaneously along with another scale that has documented validity to the same subjects. If the two scales correlate well in the direction expected, then your scale has demonstrated concurrent validity. As an example, suppose you had developed the Drug Attitude Questionnaire (See Appendix B). How would you go about showing that it had concurrent validity? One way would be to administer it along with another "proven" instrument that also measures attitudes about drugs. In fact, this is what we did. We correlated the Drug Attitude Questionnaire (DAQ) with a similar but shorter (14-item) instrument. This meant that students in that study had to complete both instruments.

We found that the DAQ correlated .76 with the shorter instrument at posttest using a sample of ninth-grade students, and correlated .79 using a sample of college students. These relatively high correlations show that low scores on one test correspond to low scores on the other, and vice versa. When strong correlations are obtained between two tests presumed to be measuring the same concept, then concurrent validity is demonstrated.

Predictive validity is another subtype of criterion validity and is demonstrated when scores on a test or scale predict future behavior or attitudes. The Drug Attitude Questionnaire would have predictive validity if, years later, you find that within your study group of ninth-grade students, those who had prodrug attitudes were suspended from school or arrested for drug possession before finishing high school, while those with antidrug attitudes were not suspended or arrested for drug possession.

The third major category in validity research is **construct validity**. Construct validity is an overarching or fundamental type of validity. It is not a specific procedure; rather, it is a collection of evidence that allows the researcher to see patterns in the way the instrument performs along expected theoretical lines. It is the ability of an instrument to distinguish among individuals who have a lot of, some of, or none of the characteristic being measured that makes the instrument useful. The theory that gives rise to the instrument allows for various hypotheses to be tested about relationships among constructs. This may involve group differences, factor analysis, or other methods as described later in this chapter.

Convergent validity is obtained when theoretically relevant variables demonstrate a relationship with the measure. For example, an instrument that you created to measure children's self-reported fear of bullies could, for instance, be correlated with teachers' or parents' rankings of children's fearfulness. If the different assessments yield scores that are strongly correlated, the researcher can rule out alternative explanations for the students' scores. This helps to establish validity because the adults independently were able to confirm any fear of bullies that any of the children might have had.

In **discriminant validity**, the researcher hopes to find no relationship between the instrument's measurements and variables that should not, in theory, be related to the construct. That is, self-report from children who are fearful of bullies should not correlate with other self-reports indicating that these same children are best friends with the bullies. To state this another way, an instrument should discriminate between those with and without a given trait or characteristic. Children who are most fearful of bullies may also be more anxious or depressed than other students who are not being bullied. Such findings would establish discriminant validity.

With **known groups validity** efforts, the researcher expects to find large differences in groups that are conceptualized as having high and low levels of the trait or variable. For instance, a new instrument designed to assess combat-related posttraumatic stress disorder (PTSD) should find much more of it in soldiers who have served in Iraq or Afghanistan than in a sample of college students who have never been in the military. Students who report bullying experiences should have different scores from students who have never been bullied.

Factor analysis is another way involving the use of statistical software to establish construct validity. When a large number of items have been created to compose a scale, factor analysis can be used to reduce the number of items to a smaller group that are correlated. Factor analysis also helps researchers to explore inner structure and reveals the number of subscales that instruments may contain.

To illustrate, let's go back to our earlier example of developing a self-esteem scale. Let's say that we write 85 different items that seem to have face and content validity. After administering the instrument to 150 students, we then enter the data into a statistical software program and run the factor analysis program. In this hypothetical example, the computer reveals that instead of one simple scale, we have items that group together in five different areas that we think form measures of: academic self-esteem, social competence, satisfaction with personal appearance, self-centeredness, and assertiveness. We might decide that these five factors are the "essence" of self-esteem and keep all of them, or perhaps we would pare out a factor or items that don't fit with our notion of the concept. For instance, we might throw out the group of items clustering together that seemed to measure self-centeredness.

Depending on what we want from our instrument, we might choose to combine the items associated with the remaining four subscales into a new instrument that provides a global measure of self-esteem. Many times, researchers hope that factor analysis will produce only a single, one-dimensional scale like the Rosenberg Self-Esteem Scale shown later in this chapter. However, factor analysis can reveal that what was considered a simple concept actually has various components or dimensions (the factors).

Factor analysis is a fascinating but somewhat sophisticated procedure and beyond the level of this introductory text. You may encounter the term as you read professional journal articles about the development or refinement of scales. The term *loads* is used to indicate that a scale item correlates well with the collection of items that cluster together to form a factor—as in "Item 3 loads higher on assertiveness than on social competence." Factor loadings are interpreted the same way as correlation coefficients.

Establishing validity is not a one-time or single-shot effort but rather an ongoing process. Different uses of the instrument become opportunities to show its ability to discriminate among different populations, which adds to the accumulated evidence of its validity. For example, even though the Drug Attitude Questionnaire was designed for ninth-grade students, it might be employed with inpatients or outpatients in drug treatment programs to determine if attitudes about drugs changed as a result of intervention. Instruments that have been around for a long time often have extensive bibliographies associated with them as various researchers report the results of their use of the instrument in different settings and with diverse populations.

BOX 6.4 EXAMPLES OF ARTICLES DESCRIBING THE DEVELOPMENT OF INSTRUMENTS

✓ Lopez, A., Yoder, J. R., Brisson, D., Lechuga-Pena, S., & Jenson, J. M. (2015). Development and validation of a positive development measure: The Bridge-Positive Youth Development. *Research on Social Work Practice, 25*(6), 726–736.

✓ Auerbach, C., Schudrich, W. Z., Lawrence, C. K., Claiborne, N., & McGowan, B. G. (2014). Predicting turnover: Validating the intent to leave child welfare scale. *Research on Social Work Practice, 24*(3), 349–355.

✓ Negi, N. J., & Iwamoto, D. K. (2014). Validation of the revised BSI-18 with Latino migrant day laborers. *Research on Social Work Practice, 24*(3), 364–371.

✓ White, E. B., & Montgomery, P. (2014). A review of "wandering" instruments for people with dementia who get lost. *Research on Social Work Practice, 24*(4), 400–413.

✓ Blair, K. D., Brown, M., Schoepflin, T., & Taylor, D. B. (2014). Validation of a tool to assess and track undergraduate attitudes toward those living in poverty. *Research on Social Work Practice, 24*(4), 448–461.

✓ Butcher, F., Kretschmar, J. M., Lin, Y., Flannery, D. J., & Singer, M. I. (2014). Analysis of the validity scales in the Trauma Checklist for Children. *Research on Social Work Practice, 24*(6), 695–704.

For the purpose of instruction, reliability and validity are usually presented as separate concepts. However, these two concepts are interrelated in a complex fashion. On the one hand, when we can empirically demonstrate that an instrument is valid, it can generally be assumed to have adequate reliability. On the other hand, a reliable instrument may not be valid. That is, an instrument may provide dependable measurements, but of some concept unrelated to what we thought we were measuring. Both reliability and validity must be demonstrated as evidence that an instrument's **psychometrics** are strong. Information about these two concepts informs researchers about the psychometrics (the objective measurement capacity and theory) associated with an instrument.

As you come across various instruments in practice or in your reading, it is important to realize that if you know nothing about the reliability and validity of a scale, then any results you obtain from its use may have little meaning. The scale may not provide consistent results (poor reliability), or it may measure something quite different from what you intended (poor validity). The importance of knowing a scale's reliability and validity cannot be emphasized enough.

Validity—The Qualitative Perspective

For the qualitative researcher, validity is not focused on the data collection instrument because the researcher *is*, for all practical purposes, the instrument. Instead, validity has to do with the extent to which data can be corroborated.

Triangulation involves the use of multiple sources or multiple approaches to see if the same pattern or conclusions would be drawn from the data. Thus, after interviewing high school dropouts, one might also want to interview teachers as well as the disciplinary principal or attendance officer to see if the stories dovetail and form a coherent whole. Using the example of incarcerated women, one might wish to talk to police officers, family members, even confirm events with court or public records. According to Neuman (2006), "A researcher's empirical claims gain validity when supported by numerous pieces of diverse empirical data ... Validity arises out of the cumulative impact of hundreds of small, diverse details that only together create a heavy weight of evidence" (p. 197).

Another approach is to employ **member checking** (or member validation), where the qualitative researcher provides preliminary results to some or all of the individuals the original data were collected from so that they have an opportunity to point out any inaccuracies or errors of interpretation.

Unlike the quantitative researcher who attempts to objectively measure or count, convincing others of the validity of the research by using a strong methodological design and instruments which yield precise and dependable results, the qualitative researcher is not always concerned when the data supplied by different informers provides a greater diversity of opinion or perspective than expected. What could trouble the qualitative researcher, for instance, would be little correspondence between her interpretations and the member checking. In quantitative research, the researcher bears all of the responsibility for establishing the validity of a study. In contrast, the qualitative researcher largely leaves it to the reader: "Readers can decide for themselves whether the descriptions justify the claims." Lillian Rubin (1976) referred to this as the "aha" standard of validity (Preissle & Grant, 2004, p. 178).

Locating Research Instruments

Research instruments can be found in journal articles, by searching in electronic databases, or consulting in printed reference books. A brief discussion of each of these approaches is provided below:

Print Resources and Reference Books

A good comprehensive collection of instruments is *Measures for Clinical Practice and Research: A Sourcebook for Couples, Families, and Children* by Corcoran and Fischer (2013). This two-volume set contains several hundred paper-and-pencil instruments. Each scale is shown, and a brief description is provided as well as contact information. These scales tend to be short, rapid assessment instruments, and the range of instruments is quite comprehensive. It is a valuable resource for practitioners. Personally, I keep a copy on my bookshelf and always start here first.

Other useful books are listed in the following box.

BOX 6.5   OTHER PRINTED RESOURCES CONTAINING INSTRUMENTS:

✓ Fisher, T. D., & Davis, C. M. (2010). *Handbook of sexuality-related measures*. New York, NY: Routledge.

✓ Fayers, P. M., & Machin, D. (2000). *Quality of life: Assessment, analysis, and reporting of patient-reported outcomes*. New York, NY: Wiley-Blackwell.

✓ Kelley, M. L., Reitman, D., & Noell, G. H. (2013). *Practitioner's guide to empirically based measures of school behavior*. New York, NY: Springer.

✓ McDowell, I. (2006). *Measuring health: A guide to rating scales and questionnaires*. New York, NY: Oxford University Press.

✓ Boyle, G. J., Saklofske, D. H., & Matthews, G. (2014). *Measures of personality and social psychological constructs*. Academic Press.

✓ Sajatovic, M., & Ramirez, L. F. (2012). *Rating scales in mental health*. Baltimore, MD: Johns Hopkins University Press.

Journal Articles

While complete scales are sometimes reproduced in journal articles, they don't appear all that often because of space limitations in the journals. It is not all that uncommon for journal articles to provide only examples of items from a scale along with information about its reliability and validity. This usually means that you will have to consult the article's reference list and may have to search through several other articles to see if any of them contain the actual scale, or perhaps you may have to email the author to request it.

Some instruments are protected by copyright. To use them, you will have to purchase copies of these instruments from a commercial source or acquire permission from the author. Entire instruments that you find in journal articles are not likely to be protected by copyright. However, good research etiquette dictates that you contact the author and request permission to use the instrument. In any case, it can be useful to make contact. Most authors want to keep informed of research conducted with their instruments. They'll be interested in yours. They may be able to help in ways that you didn't expect. Sometimes they have prepared shorter or newer versions of old instruments or may share a bibliography of recent articles that have used the instrument.

Electronic Databases

Finding an appropriate instrument without immersing yourself completely in the literature can be a bit like chasing a rainbow. However, several good electronic sources for scales may help you find just the instrument you require. One place to start is with the Test Link, which is a computerized database accessible from the Internet **(ets.org/testcoll/)**. Enter the topic or the name of the test you are trying to locate in the search engine, and it will return a list of instruments. (If there are too many, try again with the Advanced Search feature.) When you find one or several possible instruments, you can read the brief abstract about the corresponding scales. If ETS is authorized to distribute these, you can obtain an electronic copy for $25. For those instruments found in the literature, the website also provides the reference. Sometimes, the instrument can only be obtained by contacting its author, and contact information is supplied.

The Cumulative Index to Nursing and Allied Health (CINAHL) is a powerful search engine. When you enter a topic (e.g., anger), it will then return a long list of references on the subject, but more importantly, will give you the ability to select those articles that specifically describe an instrument or way to measure the concept (look to the box on the lower left).

The Buros Center for Testing's website allows you to locate tests and purchase reviews of them. (These tend to be well-developed, standardized tests used in educational settings for the most part.) The center also publishes a reference volume which may be housed in your university library that contains "information about tests to test users including test purpose, intended test population, administration times, scores generated, price, test publisher ... publication date(s), and test author(s)," as well as "candid test reviews written by testing experts."

You can also go to Google or Google Scholar and type in the concept you are seeking (for example, assertiveness) and then *scale, questionnaire,* or *instrument.* You'll be amazed at the great variety of instruments already developed and also at the number of different approaches the developers have taken in creating them.

When You Can't Find the Instrument You Want

Idea 1: *Narrow your topic.* Most often, when students complain that they can't find an instrument they need, they've had a problem narrowing down exactly what they want to measure. A student once told me she had spent hours in the library without finding the kind of instrument she was looking for. As we talked more, she revealed that she'd been searching under *children* and *families,* when it would have been more profitable for her to look for literature on *parenting programs.* A great deal of time can be lost if your search terms are too broad. Talk with the reference librarian if you need assistance.

Idea 2: *Try the Web of Science.* Occasionally, starting with one instrument that you know about can lead you to others. The Web of Science is an electronic database available at many universities that allows one to enter an author of an article and/or the journal name, and then it can inform you of other authors who have cited that particular study in their own articles. At a minimum, you'll find researchers writing on the same topic. You may find that they have developed a new instrument or have revised or provided important information about the original instrument.

Idea 3: *Consult with knowledgeable experts*. Don't overlook the obvious resource people you may know; for example, faculty who conduct a lot of research and particularly those who have a specialty in a related area.

Idea 4: *Modify an existing instrument.* If you conduct an exhaustive literature search and even consult with knowledgeable people and still can't find the instrument you want, two avenues still lie before you. First, you can take an existing instrument and modify it to meet your needs. It is reasonable to take such drastic action if, for instance, you've found a potentially useful scale developed for teens that is too long to use with younger children.

You may want to write to the author of the original instrument to ask if any newer versions of the form have been developed or if you can use portions of the instrument you plan to revise. Most authors, particularly if their scales have appeared in professional journals and are not copyrighted, will likely be interested in your research and grant you permission. The only caution here is that any time you modify an existing instrument, the burden is on you to prove that the resulting instrument is reliable and valid. Just because the longer instrument was psychometrically sound does not guarantee that a shorter version will be.

It is not at all unusual for researchers to take a scale developed by someone else and to adapt it for a different purpose. Here is an example: The Social Distance Scale was created by E. S. Bogardus in 1925 to measure acceptance of different nationalities or races. Bogardus asked respondents if they would admit someone *different from themselves* into such situations as:

Kinship by marriage
Club membership
Neighbors
Employment in one's occupation
Citizenship in one's country
Visitors to one's country

Years ago, when AIDS was not understood by most of the public, a colleague and I used some of these same items in order to understand acceptance of persons living with AIDS. This is what we came up with using *Strongly Agree, Agree, Undecided, Disagree,* and *Strongly Disagree* as the response choices:

SA A U D SD

I would be opposed to persons with AIDS living on the same street as me.

SA A U D SD

I would exclude persons with AIDS from visiting my country.

SA A U D SD

I would be uncomfortable if I had to work in the same department or office as persons with AIDS.

SA A U D SD

I would allow persons with AIDS to become citizens of the U.S.

Even with just these four items, the reliability was quite strong (.82). Because this was an exploratory study, we didn't attempt to establish the validity of the instrument, but we did find that our Social Distance Scale (the one you see above) correlated .67 with our Fear of AIDS Scale and −.68 with our Empathy for Persons with AIDS Scale.

ANXIETY CHECK 6.1

Interpret the last sentence above: "the Social Distance Scale correlated .67 with Fear of AIDS and –.68 with Empathy for Persons with AIDS Scale."

[Answer at the back of the book.]

Idea 5: *Create your own scale.* If you find no instruments you like, another option is to create your own scale. Once again, it will be your responsibility to establish that the instrument measures what you intended and does so reliably. Just because you think it has content or face validity does not make it a good instrument. Take, for example, Questions 7 through 15 of the Attitudes about Research Courses Questionnaire (from Appendix A):

7. **T** or **F.**
I dread speaking before a large group of people more than taking a research course.

8. **T** or **F.**
I would rather take a research course than ask a server to return an improperly cooked meal to the chef.

9. **T** or **F.**
My fear of snakes is greater than my fear of taking a research course.

10. **T** or **F.**
My fear of spiders is less than my fear of taking a research course.

11. **T** or **F.**
I would rather take a research course than ask a total stranger to do a favor for me.

12. **T** or **F.**
My fear of research is such that I would rather the university require an additional two courses of my choosing than require one research course.

13. **T** or **F.**
I dread going to the dentist more than taking a research course.

14. **T** or **F.**
I fear a statistics course more than a research methodology course.

15. **T** or **F.**   I have always "hated math."

Can you guess what I was trying to measure with this scale? Although I thought it might have face validity, the scale's reliability was so poor after a pilot study that I've never attempted any further research with it. What struck me as a clever way to measure fear of research simply did not work. I suspect that individual responses to such things as spiders and dentists interfered with rather than facilitated the concept I was trying to measure. This is the way research moves forward. Sometimes our best efforts fail.

How do you go about constructing a scale? Normally, you begin by creating a pool of items that you think will measure different dimensions or degrees of the behavior, knowledge, or attitude that you have in mind. Sometimes, experts in the field are invited to contribute items. Then, one begins to weed out some items and prepare a first draft of the instrument. This version is then administered to a large group. From the data the group supplies, one uses computer software to identify which items correlate together to form a scale. Factor analysis may be computed. Items may be thrown out.

Depending on the results obtained, one might decide that the refined list of items is adequate. Or if the reliability coefficient is lower than desired, one could add new items and administer the second version to another set of people, dropping and adding new items until satisfied with the internal consistency of the instrument.

When would it be important to establish that a scale has validity? This would be something you would want to do if you were planning further research with the instrument or were thinking about publishing an article about it. Perhaps the scale you are developing could help social service employers screen out applicants who have no empathy for clients or those who would be too fearful to work with HIV/AIDS patients. Or if your responsibility with an organization is to provide in-service training, you might want a valid scale to help you evaluate what the participants acquired from the in-service training.

BOX 6.6 EVALUATING INSTRUMENTS FOR USE IN PRACTICE

Before adopting an assessment instrument for use in practice, social workers should consider several important questions:

PRACTICALITY—IS THE INSTRUMENT:
- Affordable?
- Easy for clients to read and understand?
- Easy to administer?
- Easy to score and interpret?
- Not too long?

PSYCHOMETRICS—DOES THE INSTRUMENT HAVE:
- Good reliability (.70 for research and at least .90 for clinical decision making)?
- The necessary sensitivity to detect small increments of improvement?
- Validity established through multiple studies and usages?

THEORETICAL APPLICATION—WILL THE INSTRUMENT:
- Measure the concept that is the best indicator of client improvement in the particular population? Is the concept understandable to clients? Policy makers? Funding sources?
- Allow you to make predictions consistent with the theory underlying your intervention?
- Allow you to compare your findings with other practitioners working with similar populations?
- Provide useful information to service providers?

Especially if you have several instruments to choose from, comparing them using the criteria above can help you or a committee make better decisions about the instruments you are considering.

BOX 6.7   PRACTICE NOTE: ETHNICITY AND MEASUREMENT ISSUES

Researchers have not always been sensitive to persons of color and other minorities during key phases of the research process. Listed below are illustrations of ways that ethnicity and cultural issues should be on the researcher's radar.

- Many, if not most, of the measurement tools currently in existence have been developed by European Americans, and these instruments have been most often interpreted based on scores obtained primarily from white subjects.
- The terms *race* and *ethnicity* are frequently confused and misleading. Many Hispanics, for instance, may identify their race as white. Persons who are biracial may not always be classified accurately.
- Socioeconomic status (SES) can be a confounding variable when investigators are looking at differences in their dependent variables by ethnicity.
- Instruments designed for one cultural group may contain substantial measurement bias when applied to another ethnic group. The ethnicity of the rater may affect those being rated.
- There has not been a great deal of study of bias (or lack of it) in cross-cultural studies pertaining to validity issues and psychological assessment.
- Instruments translated from one language into another then need to be back-translated by another independent party to make sure that the translation is accurate. In some cases, a literal translation is not as accurate as an idiomatic or conceptual equivalence. For a good description of the process required in making a cultural adaptation for Latino children, please review Chavez, L. M., Matías-Carrelo, L., Barrio, C., & Canino, G. (2007). The cultural adaptation of the Youth Quality of Life Instrument, research version for Latino children and adolescents. *Journal of Child and Family Studies, 16*, 75–89.
- A relevant but brief discussion about cultural adaptation can be found in Sampson, M., & Torres, L. R. (2015). What tension between fidelity and cultural adaptation? A reaction to Marsiglia and Booth. *Research on Social Work Practice, 25*(7), 828–831.

Sources: Foster, S. L., & Martinez, C. R. (1995). Ethnicity: Conceptual and methodological issues in child clinical research. *Journal of Clinical Child Psychology, 24,* 214–226; Malgady, R. G. (1996). The question of cultural bias in assessment and diagnosis of ethnic minority clients: Let's reject the null hypothesis. *Professional Psychology, Research and Practice, 27,* 73–77; Land, H., & Hudson, S. (1997). Methodological considerations in surveying Latina AIDS caregivers: Issues in sampling and measurement. *Social Work Research, 21,* 233–246.

A Sampling of Instruments

This chapter has discussed instruments and scales from a technical standpoint. Now that you know how to evaluate them, it is useful to examine several examples more in-depth. In the section that follows, you'll see how different authors have approached the problem depending upon their perspective.

Sophia could tell that Bill was excited about something from the way he practically jumped out of his chair to meet her when he saw her in the doorway.

"Look what I found!" He said, pulling an article off the table where they worked. "It is an HIV Stigma Instrument! Just what we need to determine if our presenters have any stigma toward persons living with

HIV/AIDS! I was on the computer almost all night. I found a knowledge scale by Carey and Schroder (2002) that was too much about transmission of HIV and a brief nine-item scale by Kalichman and colleagues (2005) that was designed for use in Africa, but then I found this one—with real potential."

"Okay, slow down a bit. Let me take my coat off and try to digest all of this. So you have found at least two scales that don't fit our needs and one that might work?"

"That's right," Bill said, taking the scale he had typed from the Emlet article and handing it to Sophia.

HIV Stigma Scale

Sophia stared at the scale for the longest time and didn't say anything.

	Key: **Not at all** = 1 **Rarely** = 2 **Sometimes** = 3 **Often** = 4
1. I felt blamed by others for my illness.	————
2. I felt ashamed of my illness.	————
3. I thought my illness was a punishment for things I've done in the past.	————
4. I feared that I might lose my job if someone found out about my illness.	————
5. I felt compelled to change my residence because of my illness.	————
6. I avoided getting treatment because someone might find out about my illness.	————
7. I feared that people would hurt my family if they learned about my illness.	————
8. I thought other people were uncomfortable being with me.	————
9. I felt people avoid me because of my illness.	————
10. I feared I would lose my friends if they learned about my illness.	————
11. I feared my family would reject me if they learned about my illness.	————
12. I felt I wouldn't get as good health care if people knew about my illness.	————
13. People who know I am HIV positive treat me with kid gloves.	————

Source: Emlet, C. A. (2005). Measuring stigma in older and younger adults with HIV/AIDS: An Analysis of an HIV stigma scale and initial exploration of subscales. *Research On Social Work Practice*, 5 (4), 291-300. Originally developed by Sowell et al. (1997).

FIGURE 6.1 HIV Stigma Scale

After what seemed like minutes, Bill couldn't take it any longer. He blurted out, "It has three subscales: Distancing, Blaming, and Discrimination. What do you think? Will it work?"

"Hmmm. It is interesting. But Bill, this scale measures stigma felt by individuals who are HIV positive. We can't use it to assess whether our presenters are prejudiced against persons living with HIV/AIDS."

"I know," said Bill triumphantly. "That is why I started with that scale and have modified it so that we could get a handle on any biased attitudes or tendency to discriminate again our population. Here's my revision we could use with the presenters."

He grabbed another sheet of paper from his side of the table and presented it to Sophia with a big smile.

Bill's Provider HIV Empathy Scale

"Well, what do you think?" Bill asked, looking over Sophia's shoulder as she continued to read. "Could it work?"

Key: **Not at all** = 1   **Rarely** = 2   **Sometimes** = 3   **Often** = 4

1. I blame others for their HIV illness. _____
2. I am ashamed of those with HIV. _____
3. Their illness is a punishment for things they've done in the past. _____
4. They should fear losing their job if someone found out about their illness. _____
5. I would feel compelled to change my residence because of HIV next door. _____
6. If I had HIV, I might avoid getting treatment because someone might find out about my illness. _____
7. I would fear that people would hurt my family if they learned I had HIV. _____
8. I am uncomfortable being around people with HIV. _____
9. I purposely avoid being around people with HIV. _____
10. I fear losing my friends if they learned I had HIV. _____
11. I fear my family would reject me if they learned I had HIV. _____
12. I wouldn't get as good health care if people knew I had HIV. _____
13. People who knew I was HIV positive would treat me with kid gloves. _____

(Revision by Bill S.)

FIGURE 6.2 Bill's Provider HIV Empathy Scale

"Maybe," said Sophia. "It's a great start, but I'd rather not have to go to the trouble of convincing everyone that it's a good instrument if we don't have to. Let's compare it to an instrument I found by Froman and Owen (1997) for nurses. Like you, I made some modifications. We can see which one we like better."

ANXIETY CHECK 6.2

What is your reaction to Bill's revised instrument? What would you have to do to convince skeptics that it was psychometrically strong?

[Answer is at the back of the book.]

"Here's what it looks like." Sophia pulled a sheet out of a folder and handed it to Bill.

Sophia's Provider Empathy Scale for PLHA

Note that the two drafts of instruments are quite different. Bill's effort comes across as examining one's fear of acquiring HIV/AIDS and its ramifications. We could assume that persons who are more fearful would project their lack of acceptance of persons living with HIV/AIDS (PLHA) and come across as prejudiced.

Sophia's effort, on the other hand, allows respondents to blame the PLHA for their situation with three items, but the rest of the scale focuses on respondents' attitudes toward PLHA. Which of the two efforts do you like better? Which scale do you think would work best?

Key=Strongly Agree=5, Agree=4, Undecided=3, Disagree=2, Strong Disagree=1

1. I think people who are IV drug users deserve to get HIV/AIDS. 5 4 3 2 1
2. I have little sympathy for people who get AIDS by trading sex for drugs or selling themselves. 5 4 3 2 1
3. Most people who become HIV+ have only themselves to blame. 5 4 3 2 1
4. Persons with HIV/AIDS should be treated with the same respect as any other person. 5 4 3 2 1
5. It is especially important to work with persons with HIV/AIDS in a caring manner. 5 4 3 2 1
6. I am sympathetic to the misery that people with HIV/AIDS experience. 5 4 3 2 1
7. I would like to do something to make life easier for people with HIV/AIDS. 5 4 3 2 1

(Sophia R.'s revision)

Note:[1] PLHA = persons living with HIV/AIDS

FIGURE 6.3 Sophia's Provider Empathy Scale for PLHA[1]

Sophia knew that she might have a hard time convincing Bill to reject his draft scale and to accept hers. She could tell that he was quite happy with his scale. As she pondered how to discuss the merits of his effort in a way that could help him see that its approach wasn't the only, or best, way to conceptualize the presenter's attitudes toward PLHA, Mrs. Simpson pulled up a chair and sat down.

"Guess what? I went to a conference yesterday and they were all talking about this instrument Rutledge and colleagues (2011) designed called the HIV/AIDS Provider Stigma Inventory. I really like it. Let me read several of the items to you."

Mrs. Simpson began, "If I know or suspect a PLHA is gay, an injection drug user, or has many sex partners, I am more likely to keep quiet when others say hurtful or mean things about PLHA. If I am concerned that others in my life will think of or treat me differently because I work with PLHA, I am more likely to blame them for bringing problems on themselves. If I think of or use unpleasant names (e.g., queer, junkie, hooker, etc.) to describe my patients or clients, I am more likely to think of them as a "case" rather than a unique human being." She looked up and observed that both Bill and Sophia were following her and then added, "And just one other item—'If I always try to act in ways that meet PLHA's needs rather than reacting to negative feelings I have about their behaviors, I am more likely to work to maximize services and referrals for each individual PLHA.'"

"Interesting," Sophia said.

"Hey, you said that about my scale!" Bill laughed.

"Just another one for consideration. The published article doesn't provide all 81 items in the instrument. I'll have to e-mail the lead author to get it. Then, I think we should ask Marta and Ron to join us in a discussion about which of these instruments might help us to review any conscious or unconscious bias toward PLHA some of our staff might have—particularly those who might be involved with the intervention we are planning."

"When are you thinking about meeting?" Bill asked. "I might want to continue to revise and refine my scale before we show it to the other committee members."

"How about a week from today?" Mrs. Simpson asked.

As Sophia nodded her okay, Bill said, "I'm fine with that."

ANXIETY CHECK 6.3

Although you haven't seen all 81 items of the instrument Mrs. Simpson obtained, what are your thoughts about using it? You may want to read the full article describing it: Rutledge, S. E., Whyte, J., Abell, N., Brown, K. M., & Cesnales, N. I. (2011). Measuring stigma among health care and social service providers: The HIV/AIDS Provider Stigma Inventory. *AIDS Patient Care and STDS, 25*(11), 673–682.

[Answers at the end of the book.]

"Before we break up," Mrs. Simpson said, standing and stretching her back, "I've been giving some thought to other ways to measure the success of the intervention with our inmates. I'm wondering if their self-esteem might improve. And if they were depressed—and who wouldn't be in prison—maybe they will be a little less depressed? Anyway, why don't you look at the CES-D Scale and the Rosenberg Self-Esteem Scale to see if you think they might be useful."

CESD Scale

Description Developed by the staff at the Center for Epidemiologic Studies, National Institute of Mental Health, the CESD is a brief self-report scale designed to measure depressive symptomatology in the general population (Radloff, 1977). It was developed from previously existing scales and was designed not to distinguish primary depressive disorders from secondary depression or subtypes of depression but to identify the presence and severity of depressive symptomatology for epidemiologic research, needs assessment, and screening (Radloff & Locke, 1986). See Figure 6.4 for an example of the slightly revised CESD Scale which is in the public domain and can be used by students without special permission.

Psychometric Data This depression scale has been found to have high internal consistency (.85 in the general population and .90 in the patient sample) and acceptable test-retest stability. The CESD scores discriminate well between psychiatric inpatient and general population samples and moderately well among patient groups with varying levels of severity. The scale has excellent concurrent validity, and substantial evidence exists of its construct validity (Radloff, 1977).

Availability The CES-D Scale has been used in hundreds, if not thousands, of studies. It may be used without copyright permission. The Epidemiology and Psychopathology Research Branch of the National Institute of Mental Health is interested, however, in receiving copies of research reports that have used the instrument.

Below is a list of some of the ways you may have felt or behaved. Please indicate how often you have felt this way during the past week by checking the appropriate box for each question.

Items	Rarely or none of the time (less than 1 day)	Some or a little of the time (1-2 days)	Occasionally or a moderate amount of time (3-4 days)	Most or all of the time (5-7 days)
1. I was bothered by things that usually don't bother me.				
2. I did not feel like eating; my appetite was poor.				
3. I felt that I could not shake off the blues even with the help from my family or friends				
4. I felt that I was just as good as other people.				
5. I had trouble keeping my mind on what I was doing.				
6. I felt depressed.				
7. I felt that everything I did was an effort.				
8. I felt hopeful about the future.				
9. I felt my life had been a failure.				
10. I felt fearful.				
11. My sleep was restless.				
12. I was happy.				
13. I talked less than usual.				
14. I felt lonely.				
15. People were unfriendly.				
16. I enjoyed life.				
17. I had crying spells.				
18. I felt sad.				
19. I felt that people disliked me.				
20. I could not "get going."				

FIGURE 6.4 Center for Epidemiologic Studies Short Depression Scale (CES-D 20)

Scoring Because the CES-D is a 20-item scale, it is easily scored. Responses are weighted 0 for *rarely or none* to 3 *for most or all*. Items 4, 8, 12, and 16 are reverse scored (given a 3 for *not at all* and 0 for *nearly every day*). The range of possible scores is 0 to 60. High scores indicate high levels of depression symptomatology, with scores of less than 16 indicating "no clinical significance."

Recent Uses of the Instrument: Illangasekare, S. L., Burke, J. G., McDonnell, K. A., & Gielen, A. C. (2013). The impact of intimate partner violence, substance use, and HIV on depressive symptoms among abused low-income urban women. *Journal of Interpersonal Violence, 28* (4), 2831–2848.

Dass-Brailsford, P., Eckman, A. K., & Kwasnik, D. L. (2014). The complexity of women's lives: Decision-making about maternal HIV Disclosure. *Current Psychology, 33,* 557–577.

Rosenberg Self-Esteem Scale

Description The Rosenberg Self-Esteem Scale was originally developed on a sample of over 5,000 high school juniors and seniors from 10 randomly selected schools in New York State. Since it was published in 1965, hundreds of studies have employed this simple instrument, possibly the most popular measure of global self-esteem. Others have used it to check for concurrent validity while developing their own self-esteem measures. See Figure 6.5 for the Rosenberg Self-Esteem Scale.

Instructions: Below is a list of statements dealing with your general feelings about yourself. If you Agree with the statement, Circle A. If you strongly agree, Circle SA. If you disagree, circle D. If you Strongly Disagree, circle SD.

	Strongly Agree	Agree	Disagree	Strongly Disagree
1. On the whole, I am satisfied with myself.	SA	A	D	SD
2. At times, I think I am no good at all.	SA	A	D	SD
3. I feel that I have a number of good qualities.	SA	A	D	SD
4. I am able to do things as well as most other people	SA	A	D	SD
5. I feel I do not have much to be proud of.	SA	A	D	SD
6. I certainly feel useless at times.	SA	A	D	SD
7. I feel that I am a person of worth, at least on an equal plane with others.	SA	A	D	SD
8. I wish I could have more respect for myself.	SA	A	D	SD
9. All in all, I am inclined to feel that I am a failure.	SA	A	D	SD
10. I take a positive attitude toward myself.	SA	A	D	SD

FIGURE 6.5 Rosenberg Self-Esteem Scale

Psychometric Data Fleming and Courtney (1984) report a Cronbach's alpha of .8 and test-retest correlations of .82 with a one-week interval. Rosenberg (1965) presents a great deal of data on the construct validity of this measure.

Availability This scale is in the public domain and may be used without securing permission.

Scoring Using the Likert procedure, responses are assigned a score ranging from 1 to 4. Items 1, 3, 4, 7, and 10 are reverse scored. (For example, item 1, "On the whole I am satisfied with myself," the *strongly agree* response is assigned a score of 4 and *strongly disagree* is assigned a score of 1.) This procedure yields possible total scores ranging from 10 to 40. The higher the score, the higher the self-esteem.

Recent Use of the Instrument: Edmondson, D., Arndt, J., Alcantara, C., Chaplin, W., & Schwartz, J. E. (2015). Self-esteem and the acute effect of anxiety on ambulatory blood pressure. *Psychosomatic Medicine, 77*, 833–841.

Final Chapter Notes

Students occasionally ask about handling clients who deliberately misrepresent the truth on assessment instruments—especially when they may know of an actual incident (for example, a beating by a partner that required medical attention) that the client did not acknowledge on the scale. All self-report scales are based on the assumption that some error is involved and most respondents are honest. It is good to remember that an inaccurate response to any one item on a scale generally does not create a measurement problem. Thus, people who live with abusive partners would still likely have higher scores on a scale measuring intimate violence than those who don't have hurtful partners—even if they are dishonest on a few items. Of course, clients may be motivated to lie, and this might not always be detected—particularly in shorter instruments that don't allow the researcher to check for inconsistencies. Our human nature is normally to minimize our extreme behavior when discussing or reporting it to others—especially when it would be frowned on in polite society. We'll discuss this more in the next chapter.

BOX 6.8   RESPONSE BIAS: WAYS THAT RESEARCH PARTICIPANTS CAN BIAS THE RESEARCH

- Social desirability—putting the "best foot forward," not reporting behavior or attitudes that might meet with disapproval from one's friends or peers
- Faking good—creating a false positive impression
- Faking bad—creating a false negative impression
- End-aversion—avoiding extreme categories like "never" and "always" and consistently choosing a middle response on a scale
- Acquiescence—tending to agree with or give positive responses regardless of what is being asked

---

Researchers can also introduce bias unknowingly into a study. Because of previously formed impressions about someone (for example, knowledge that a client has been dishonest in the past or a coworker who is thought to have been unethical), individuals who are rating the behavior or performance of others may find it difficult to assess everyone *objectively*. Thus, there may be a tendency to rate a client who is friendly and personable as higher functioning than he or she really is, and, conversely, a client who has caused trouble or complained a great deal may be viewed as having made less progress. This is known as the **halo effect.** The use of behaviorally anchored scales may help to reduce this expectancy effect. How hard do you think it is when you are asked to rate another individual? Can you always separate your subjective feelings, values, or beliefs from the objective facts?

Key Terms

reliable

internal consistency

interrater reliability

valid

content validity

face validity

criterion validity

concurrent validity

predictive validity

known groups validity

discriminant validity

Cronbach's alpha

construct validity

factor analysis

triangulation

member checking

halo effect

social desirability

acquiescence

psychometrics

coefficient alpha

test-retest reliability

convergent validity

SELF-REVIEW
(Answers at the end of the book.)

1. Pam has created a scale and administered it to the same group of her chronically mentally ill clients on two occasions, a week apart. It is likely she is trying to determine:
    a. construct validity
    b. test-retest reliability
    c. a correlation coefficient with all the extraneous variables
    d. content validity.

2. If an item correlates strongly with the other items on a scale, would Pam want to throw it out or keep it because it would add to the scale's internal consistency?

3. If you and another school social worker were independently observing children with suspected attention deficit disorder and each of you is using the same rating scale for each child, what would you call the effort to determine the correlation between your two ratings that would indicate how often you were in agreement?

4. _____ is when an instrument measures the concept it was designed to measure.

5. T or F. Pam shares her newly created instrument with several coworkers, and they agree it appears to possess face validity. Pam doesn't need to conduct any other validity studies before using her scale in a large project involving 300 clients over a two-year study period since her colleagues are suggesting it should be published in a professional journal.

6. T or F. Factor analysis is the approved way of establishing concurrent validity.

7. T or F. Predictive validity is when the researcher finds no relationship between the scale's measurements and variables that should not be correlated with the construct.

8. T or F. A scale with an internal validity of .60 could be said to be "quite strong."

9. T or F. Once a scale is determined to be valid, say, with a group of clients with chronic mental illness, no additional validity studies would be needed if the scale was then used with a group of high school underachievers.

10. T or F. The problem with designing a new instrument each time you need one is that it always has unknown psychometrics until studies establish its reliability and validity.

11. Marcy has developed a scale to measure fear of statistics. With seven items, she obtained a coefficient alpha of .83 and wants to publish her results. Is that reliability level too low for her to be able go forward with her plans? Should she add more items to get the reliability over 150%?

QUESTIONS FOR CLASS DISCUSSION

1. Why would a researcher prefer to measure a concept like depression or self-esteem with an instrument rather than just by observation?
2. Does it make sense to debate whether reliability is more important than validity? Why or why not?
3. Do you think it is important to disguise from research participants the title of the scale they are completing? Under what circumstances might it make sense to cloak the title or purpose of a study?
4. The term *discrimination* usually has a negative connotation, such as when it is associated with sexism or racism. However, does the term have a positive or negative connotation when we think about a scale with construct validity as being able to discriminate well among different populations?
5. Discuss the decision that Sophia, Bill, and Mrs. Simpson have to make in choosing among the scales that will help them find the best presenters for their intervention. Would you throw them all out and start from scratch? Are there items that you would want to include that aren't there now? If so, what are they?

RESOURCES AND REFERENCES

Abell, N., Springer, D. W., & Kamata, A. (2009). *Developing and validating rapid assessment instruments*. New York, NY: Oxford University Press.

Boyle, G. J., Saklofske, D. H., & Matthews, G. (2014). Measures of personality and social psychological constructs. Cambridge, MA: Academic Press.

Carey, M. P., & Schroder, K. E. E. (2002). Development and psychometric evaluation of the brief HIV Knowledge Questionnaire. *AIDS Education and Prevention, 14*(2), 172–182.

DeVellis, R. F. (2011). *Scale development: Theory and applications*. Newbury Park, CA: Sage.

Emlet, C. A. (2005). Measuring stigma in older and younger adults with HIV/AIDS: An analysis of an HIV Stigma Scale and initial exploration of subscales. *Research on Social Work Practice, 15*(4), 291–300.

Fleming, J. S., & Courtney, B. E. (1984). The dimensionality of self-esteem. Hierarchical facet model for revised measurement scales. *Journal of Personality and Social Psychology, 46*, 404–421.

Fowler, F. (2013). *Survey research methods*. Thousand Oaks, CA: Sage.

Froman, R. D., & Owen, S. V. (1997). Further validation of the AIDS Attitude Scale. *Research in Nursing & Health, 20*, 161–167.

Kalichman, S. C., Simbayi, L. C., Jooste, S., Toefy, Y., Cain, D., Cherry, C., & Kagee, A. (2005). Development of a brief scale to measure AIDS-related stigma in South Africa. *AIDS and Behavior, 9*(2), 135–143.

Kreuger, L., & Neuman, W. L. (2006). *Social work research methods: Qualitative and quantitative approaches*. Boston, MA: Allyn & Bacon.

Lincoln, Y. S., & Guba, E. G. (1985). *Naturalistic inquiry*. Beverly Hills, CA: Sage.

Neuman, W. L. (2006). *Social research methods: Qualitative and quantitative approaches.* Boston, MA: Pearson Education.

Nunnally, J. C. (1994). *Psychometric theory*. New York, NY: McGraw-Hill.

Preissle, J., & Grant, L. (2004). Fieldwork traditions: Ethnography and participant observation. In Kathleen DeMarrais and Stephen Lapan (Eds.), *Foundations for research: Methods of inquiry in education and the social sciences*. Mahwah, NJ: Lawrence Erlbaum Associates.

Radloff, L. S. (1977). The CES-D Scale: A self-report depression scale for research in the general population. *Applied Psychological Measurement, 3*, 385–401.

Radloff, L. S., & Locke, B. Z. (1986). The Community Mental Health Assessment Survey and the CES-D Scale. In Myra M. Weissman, Jerome K. Myers, & Catherine E. Ross (Eds.), *Community surveys of psychiatric disorders*. New Brunswick, NJ: Rutgers University Press.

Research on Social Work Practice, 12(1). (2002, January). Special issue on scale development and validation.

Ringenberg, M., Funk, V., Mullen, K., Wilford, A., & Kramer, J. (2005). The test-retest reliability of the Parent and School Survey (PASS). *School Community Journal, 15*(2), 121–134.

Rosenberg, M. (1965). Society and the adolescent self-image. Princeton, NJ: Princeton University Press.

Rubin, L. B. (1976). *Worlds of pain: Life in the working-class family*. New York, NY: Basic Books.

Rutledge, S. E., Whyte, J., Abell, N., Brown, K. M., & Cesnales, N. I. (2011). Measuring stigma among health care and social service providers: The HIV/AIDS Stigma Inventory. *AIDS Patient Care and STDS, 25*(11), 673–682.

Sowell, R. L., Lowenstein, A., Moneyham, L., Demi, A., Mizuno, Y., & Seals, B. F. (1997). Resources, stigma, and patterns of disclosure in rural women with HIV infection. *Public Health Nursing, 14, 5*, 302–312.

Springer, D., Abell, N., & Hudson, W. W. (2002). Creating and validating rapid assessment instruments for practice and research: Part I. *Research on Social Work Practice, 12*(3), 408–439.

Springer, D., Abell, N., & Nugent, W. (2002). Creating and validating rapid assessment instruments for practice and research: Part II. *Research on Social Work Practice, 12*(3), 805–832.

Credits

ASSIGNMENT 6.1

Creating a Scale

Objective: *To obtain practice in developing an instrument to be used to measure a single concept.*

We use many concepts every day in conversation and assume that others share our same definitions. In the following space, identify a single concept (for example: honesty, impulse control, altruism, stress, depression, self-esteem), then attempt to develop at least 10 items that would measure that concept. Show the *response set* as well as the individual items. You may want to create your rough drafts on other sheets and then transfer your effort to this page. (*Note:* Since depression and self-esteem scales are provided as examples in this chapter, it will be your challenge to try to come up with different items than those shown.)

The concept I want to measure is:

The response set would consist of:

My scale is composed of the following 10 items:

ASSIGNMENT 6.2

The Psychometric Properties of a Scale

Objective: *To learn about the various evidence needed for reliability and validity and ways to document it.*

The concept being measured in Assignment 6.1 is:

1. **Reliability:** To show that my scale is reliable, I would need to:

2. **Known Groups Validity**

To find persons who would likely have high levels of this concept, I would need to collect data from:

I anticipate finding low levels of this concept in the following persons:

3. **Concurrent Validity:** A good indication of concurrent validity would be if my scale correlated well with:

4. **Predictive Validity:** I would know my scale had predictive validity if it:

ASSIGNMENT 6.3

Finding a Measurement Instrument

Objective: *To become familiar with the literature and the resources that aid in locating research instruments.*

This chapter gives several suggestions for finding a measurement instrument that could be the primary dependent variable for a study that you design. For this assignment, try to find a scale that measures some concept of interest to you (or perhaps one that your instructor assigns). (*Note:* Commercial instruments will not likely be as available to you as those from the academic sector.)

Step 1. Attach a copy of the instrument that you have located.

Step 2. How did you find the instrument?

Step 3. Summarize what you have learned about the instrument's reliability.

Step 4. Summarize what you have learned about the instrument's validity.

Step 5. Conclusion: After having read at least one journal article about this instrument, what do you conclude about it? Is this a psychometrically strong instrument? Why or why not?

ASSIGNMENT 6.4

Critiquing a Measurement Instrument

Objective: *To develop skills analyzing research instruments.*

One additional instrument that could have been mentioned in this chapter is entitled the Health Care Provider HIV/AIDS Stigma Scale. It can be found in an article by Wagner, A. C., Hart, T. A., McShane, K. E., Margolese, S., & Girard, T. A. (2014). Health care provider attitudes and beliefs about people living with HIV. Initial validation of the Health Care Provider HIV/AIDS Stigma Scale (HPASS). *AIDS and Behavior, 18*, 2397–2408.

Step 1.   Read the article.

Step 2.   What did you learn about its reliability?

Step 3.   Summarize what you have learned about the instrument's validity.

Step 4. As you review the items constituting the scale, what are your thoughts about using it for Bill and Sophia's project?

CHAPTER 7

Developing Data Collection Instruments

Scales, Questionnaires, and Interview Schedules

IN THE PREVIOUS chapter, we examined ways to evaluate our measurement instruments for reliability and validity. Researchers often want to locate instruments that have already been designed and used in previous studies—we can consider them tried and tested. If an instrument works consistently and dependably in another study, adopting it can give you a fast start on your study. Otherwise, you lose valuable time developing a new one and testing its psychometric properties. However, sometimes no instrument can be found exactly like what you need—or the ones you find have problems or flaws that make them unattractive. They might be too long, too short, too sophisticated, or too simple for your population. Or perhaps they just don't seem to fit the concept in the way you think it should. Sometimes it is necessary to create a new scale or questionnaire. To prepare for such situations and equip you to develop your own questionnaires, this chapter will examine some of the details that go into the construction of data collection items and instruments.

Social workers become very familiar with the use of questionnaires. In almost every social service agency, initial data collection is conducted before new clients are admitted for services. This process is called intake, screening, completing the face sheet, or taking the client's history. Although most agencies' admission forms may not have been designed for research purposes, they have enough in common with research questionnaires that we can use them to increase our knowledge about designing our own instruments.

Think for a moment about an agency's admission form (or any other questionnaire with which you are familiar). Someone (or perhaps a committee) may have spent considerable time deciding which questions were important to ask and which ones were not. One of the purposes of the questionnaire is to standardize the information gathering process so that the *same* set of questions is asked the *same* way each time. The prepared questionnaire also guarantees that no questions will be forgotten.

From the agency's perspective, this standard set of questions provides the minimal level of information needed from each client. The social worker does not have to guess or anticipate what information the agency wants, because it has already been predetermined on the printed form. The social worker is also freed from worrying about wording the question the same way each time. If the social worker had to decide with each new client how to phrase the questions, these items might not generate the same type of information each time. With a standard set of pretested questions in a carefully designed admission form, problems are minimized.

Similarly, research questionnaires collect data in a uniform way to produce the information desired. Carefully considered questions structure the respondents' answers (for example, instead of asking the respondent to state his or her age, the questionnaire may ask for year of birth). Through exact wording and attention to such matters as the sequence and order of questions, researchers attempt to minimize the collection of erroneous data.

Questionnaire design requires greater precision than in the words we use and the questions we ask in ordinary conversation. In casual conversation, Bill might say to Sophia, "Do you think Chanita has low self-esteem?" It would be a little unusual for the other party to respond, "How are you operationalizing self-esteem?" (However, you might expect Sophia to reply that way.) To conduct research, we must clearly operationalize our terms—especially in our data collection forms and instruments. Unlike conversation and personal interviews when there can be opportunities to follow up and clarify, ambiguities and vague terms in questionnaires can cause problems for respondent and researcher alike. As we'll see, poorly worded items create GIGO—garbage in, garbage out. Many times, problems can be discovered and eliminated during pretests of the questionnaire.

De Vaus (1986) illustrates the importance of specificity in developing useful items for questionnaires:

> It is not enough to say, "I'm interested in getting some answers about inequality." What answers to what questions? Do you want to know the extent of inequality, its distribution, its causes, its effects, or what? What sort of inequality are you interested in? Over what period? (p. 27)

Designing clear and concise research questions that result in data that can be used by the researcher is not an easy task. Questions that seem straightforward to college-educated agency staff may be confusing to clients who didn't finish high school. In an effort to become precise, it is possible to become too wordy and the question is transformed into a puzzle. Our first draft of questions may inadvertently omit important response choices or contain overlapping response choices. And we can unconsciously bias responses simply by the way questions are phrased.

Even professionals can slip. After the movie *Schindler's List* was released, a Roper poll seemed to suggest that 34% of Americans were uncertain about whether the Holocaust actually occurred. However, the Roper question contained a double negative construction. It asked, "Does it seem possible or does it seem impossible to you that the Nazi extermination of the Jews never happened?" How many times do you have to read that question to understand it?

A subsequent Gallup poll used this wording: "In your opinion did the Holocaust definitely happen, probably happen, probably not happen, or definitely not happen?" When asked this way, 79% said it definitely happened and another 17% said it probably happened—for a total of 96% of Americans expressing the belief that the Holocaust did occur (Moore & Gallup, 1994). This example shows how seriously we must take item construction for our survey questionnaires, needs assessments, and scales.

Importance of Appearance

The vast majority of this chapter discusses phrasing of items in the construction of questionnaires and scales. However, before moving to that discussion, here are a few thoughts about the appearance of the instruments you prepare.

In real estate, there is an expression about the three most important considerations when buying or selling a house. They are: location, location, location. In the preparation of data-gathering instruments, a similar aphorism might guide us: appearance, appearance, appearance. Saying that the success of our research rests solely on the physical attractiveness of questionnaires and scales is, of course, putting it much too strongly. But remember, more times than not, our research subjects are *voluntarily* providing

---

WHAT IS YOUR OPINION???

DO YOU AGREE OR DISAGREE WITH THESE COMMENTS!!!

1. People who ask for help should do as they told and not complain.

   /_/ Strongly Agree   /_/ Somewhat disagree

   /_/ Somewhat agree   /_/ Strongly disagree

   /_/ Don't know

2. The social workee always knows what's best for the client.

   /_/ Strongly Agree   /_/ Somewhat disagree

   /_/ Somewhat agree   /_/ Strongly disagree

   /_/ Don't know

3. Most workers don't know what it really like to need help.

   /_/ Strongly Agree   /_/ Somewhat disagree

   /_/ Somewhat agree   /_/ Strongly disagree

   /_/ Don't know

4. When she comes to an agency for help, a person usually knows what he needs.

   /_/ Strongly Agree   /_/ Somewhat disagree

   /_/ Somewhat agree   /_/ Strongly disagree

   /_/ Don't know

5. Most people can choose their own services good if they know.

   /_/ Strongly Agree   /_/ Somewhat disagree

   /_/ Somewhat agree   /_/ Strongly disagree

   /_/ Don't know

6. Most people who come to an agency don't really know what they needy.

   /_/ Strongly Agree   /_/ Somewhat disagree

   /_/ Somewhat agree   /_/ Strongly disagree

   /_/ Don't know

FIGURE 7.1 Illustration of a Crude Questionnaire

---

us with data they may not be eager to share. *They don't have to cooperate!* When you conduct research in the community, your respondents are doing you a favor. We need to make our instruments look as if professionals prepared them—easy to understand and complete.

As a social work researcher, you are more likely to get a higher rate of completed forms if they are visually appealing—when they don't appear too long or appear to be too difficult. They also should not look amateurish, as do the two examples provided in Figure 7.1 and Figure 7.2. Questionnaires that look like they were quickly thrown together with misspelled words or poor grammar will not entice most people to respond unless the topic is one that they are passionate about. So, always revise several times, looking carefully for any potential ways that an item can be misinterpreted, and eliminate any spelling or grammar problems. Having others to read or pilot-test your items is always informative. You will want

Recently You Went To _____

They sent you to another agency. We want to know your feelings about what happened to you. But first,

1. How much money do you make a week?_____

2. Do you have insurance?_____

3. What do you do when not working?_____

4. Why did you go to _____ (agency)?

_____Wanted to obtain food or clothing

_____Wanted better housing

_____Wanted to talk about money (Social Security, unemployment, emergency aid, etc.

_____Wanted a job.

_____Wanted to know about going to school.

_____Wanted to know about medical or dental services.

_____Wanted to talk about family problems.

_____Wanted to know about day care or child care.

_____Wanted transportation.

_____Wanted to talk about legal matters.

_____Wanted to know about budgeting or credit.

_____Wanted to work on personal problems.

_____Wanted medication.

_____Wanted to complain about neighbors.

_____Other_____

FIGURE 7.2 Illustration of an Uninviting Questionnaire

to make sure your small sample in the pilot test understands the questions and responds, more or less, as you had intended.

What problems do you see with the example in Figure 7.1? What would be your reaction if you were asked to complete the questions?

In Figure 7.2, there are too many choices. If there is no other way around that, then some verbiage could be eliminated by just listing the problem (such as housing, transportation, child care). That would result in a set of responses that could be read faster and require less effort. How important is a clear, easy-to-read font?

Before Starting

First and foremost, you must have a clear idea of what data are needed. What is it that you want to find out? What are the specific content areas to be covered? If you are designing a questionnaire for a survey, then you must concurrently decide which survey modality will be used to present the questions to the respondents. Some formats (for example, questions requiring many response options) work better in mail surveys than in telephone surveys. In mail surveys, respondents can simultaneously view all of the response categories (such as *Strongly Agree, Agree, Undecided, Disagree, Strongly Disagree*) before choosing one. In telephone surveys, respondents may find it difficult to keep the question, as well as all of the response options in mind—particularly if the response categories keep changing. Even five categories can stretch a respondent's ability to keep a whole scale in mind at once if they aren't regular or standardized. Consequently, respondents may remember some but not all of the responses, and their responses may have a narrower range of variation (*Agree* or *Disagree*). When the questions are sensitive or very detailed, personal interviews may be the best approach.

The nature of the content, the intended survey approach, the targeted respondents, and their reading level affect the final form that the questionnaire takes. Only after consideration has been given to these areas should further conceptualizing of the questionnaire begin.

A review of the literature can provide questions or examples of ways that researchers have approached the topic of interest. It is not unethical, but rather good research practice, to use questions that have worked well for other researchers (Bradburn & Sudman, 1982). Do not, however, "borrow" items that are protected by copyright without the author's permission. Customarily, one would contact the author of the items or instrument for permission to use it and request any additional information that the author may have on the instrument.

On occasion, the author can refer you to other researchers who have recently modified or used the instrument with interesting results. Besides the possibility of saving time in questionnaire design, a *big* advantage of using questions that have already been employed by other researchers is that you can then compare your findings to those from existing studies.

As you begin selecting and composing questions for the first draft of a questionnaire, you will have to give some thought to whether your research topic requires **closed-ended questions** (multiple-choice type responses) or **open-ended questions** (unstructured responses).

Closed-Ended Questions

Closed-ended questions are those that have their own predetermined response set. The major advantage of closed-ended questions is that a great deal of time is saved in tabulating the data and coding it for analysis. Because the response choices are supplied (for example, *Yes, No,* or *Strongly Agree, Agree,* and so on), the person who is organizing the data does not have the problem of deciphering lengthy phrases, sentences, or illegible responses. Virtually no interpretation is required of what a respondent intended. Another advantage is that closed-ended questions with their response options communicate the same frame of reference to all respondents.

Writing good items for a survey questionnaire or measurement instrument requires that you consider your audience. Will they be ninth-grade students? Physicians? Child abuse investigators? Participants at a senior citizens' center? What vocabulary items might they use or not use? Could each group's view of the world be slightly different from another group? And what if your survey would involve participants from each of these groups and others? Could it be important to standardize and explain concepts used in the survey—to not assume that everyone has the same understanding or view?

Closed-ended questions are used when you can easily anticipate how respondents might reply. If you really want to learn more about *why* they think a certain way, open-ended questions allow for exploration of ideas and behaviors. A small pilot study may inform you about what words or special terms respondents tend to use in responding. Once you have identified frequent or common responses as well as the range of responses to open-ended questions, you could then create closed-ended questions for use with a hundred or more respondents.

Closed-ended questions can be used effectively in practically all areas of social work practice. For example, perhaps you are interested in residents' adjustment to nursing homes. One area that you feel is important is how the residents evaluate the food prepared by the nursing home. You might construct a closed-ended question that allows for their ratings of meals as *Excellent, Good, Fair,* or *Poor.* However, a fair rating does not provide a wealth of information about the food. It doesn't tell you, for instance, whether oatmeal is served every day for breakfast, whether it arrives cold or warm, or if a variety of breakfast foods are available. This is why sometimes the best solution is to use both closed-ended and open-ended questions in the same study.

Open-Ended Questions

Open-ended questions do not contain prepared response choices. This form of question allows respondents to communicate without having to choose from a set of prepared response categories. Open-ended questions are best suited for those occasions when the researcher intends for direct interviewing to be employed. Few respondents take the time to elaborate on their thoughts or feelings when they must write them out on paper; as a result, mailed questionnaires that rely heavily on open-ended questions have a poorer response rate than those that use closed-ended questions. With the ease of electronic communication, it may be that respondents type out longer responses than they write in longhand.

Some evidence suggests open-ended questions, when asked by an interviewer, result in greater reporting of sensitive or socially disapproved behavior than closed-ended questions on a self-reporting questionnaire. One possible explanation is that respondents will avoid placing themselves in categories that indicate high levels of socially unacceptable behavior when they can choose from categories that suggest a more acceptable level of behavior.

At times, you may want greater detail than closed-ended questions typically provide. For example, if you wanted to know more about the quality of life in a nursing home the residents experience, closed-ended questions are not likely to provide you with much insight into their personal reflections. Open-ended questions can supply you with quotations from residents—their experiences in their own words. Because open-ended questions produce greater detail and depth, they are greatly favored by qualitative researchers.

One disadvantage to open-ended questions is that a respondent can ramble; it can require a skillful interviewer to bring a talkative respondent back on topic. Another disadvantage is that if the respondents are especially interested in the topic and use a lot of words and sentences to explain themselves, this creates a *lot* of pages of data to be digested.

BOX 7.1   BRIEF EXAMPLE OF A STRUCTURED INDIVIDUAL INTERVIEW

Structured interview questions have the advantage of presenting the same questions asked in the same way in the same order. Interviewers simply ask the questions on their interview schedule and don't have to get creative in rewording or asking them in a different way. In other words, use of a structured interview schedule standardizes the question-asking process. Respondents, however, are free to answer any way they choose. See the example of open-ended questions in the following structured interview schedule:

1. The Appalachian Cancer Survivors Network has been in existence about four years. What changes have you seen over that period of time?
2. How would you describe your level of involvement as a board member of the Network?
3. If you had a magic wand that could grant you any wish, what three wishes would you make regarding the Network?
4. How do you think health care professionals in the community view the Network?
5. The director of ASCN is stepping down next year. What kinds of skills do you think the next director should have?
6. What difficulties do you think the next director might experience?

BOX 7.2   QUALITATIVE RESEARCHERS AND OPEN-ENDED QUESTIONS

Qualitative researchers may use open-ended questions in a number of ways. They might, for instance, conduct a focus group discussion or a group interview. Group discussions tend to allow the group members maximum freedom to range freely all over a topic. In group interviews, the researcher is more active, if necessary, in keeping the group focused on a specific set of questions. Open-ended questions are also asked during structured individual interviews. During these interviews, the qualitative researcher might use a technique called free listing, which uses open-ended questions like this: "If you were the director of the Women's Clinic, what three changes do you think you would make right away?"

In any given survey, it is possible to combine both closed- and open-ended questions. In the example of an evaluation of a nursing home, you could rely chiefly on closed-ended questions for rating various facets of the nursing home (for example, courteousness of the staff, noise level, social and recreational opportunities) and still employ an open-ended question such as: "Is there anything else you would like to tell us about how it feels to live in this skilled nursing facility?" Alternatively, you could use these open-ended questions: "What is the *best* thing about living in this skilled nursing facility?" and "What is the worst thing about living in this skilled nursing facility?"

Your use of open- or closed-ended questions depends on the goals of your research and the type of information you require. Keep in mind that open-ended questions are easier to develop than closed-ended ones, but they are harder to analyze. For instance, suppose you ask a group of volunteers this question: "What kinds of things did you do as a Big Brother or Big Sister?" You might get back a list of such activities as:

Went out to eat	Played Monopoly and other board games
Played basketball	Worked on my car
Went to movies	Went fishing
Tutored	Watched television
Visited the mall	Went bicycling
Visited the zoo	Went to the library
Went shopping	Baked cookies
Built model planes	Took a walk
Talked on the phone	Visited friends

Now, suppose you want to analyze the data you obtained. How would you summarize these responses into a few categories to understand what kinds of activities Big Brothers and Big Sisters favored? Would you use categories of athletic and nonathletic activity? If so, is fishing athletic? Would you create categories for those activities that require spending money (such as going to a movie or to a restaurant) versus those that don't (such as watching television)? But then, couldn't making cookies involve an expense (if you had to buy chocolate chips and sugar)? Does fishing involve an expense? A visit to the mall doesn't have to be expensive, but it could be if the Big Brother bought soft drinks and tacos or ice cream later.

Take my word for it, closed-ended questions are a great deal easier to analyze. The only problem is that if you use something other than the Likert scale, you have to anticipate in advance how the respondents might answer. However, a small pilot test can often suggest the categories or response set that you need for the item.

Whether you adopt questions that have been used by other researchers or write your own, be sure to circulate a rough draft of the proposed questionnaire among your colleagues for their comments and suggestions. Use their responses to revise the questionnaire before it goes out for a pilot test. After the pilot test, scrutinize the questionnaire again for questions that might have been misunderstood, biased items that suggest responses, insufficient response categories, typographical errors, and similar problems. Only after several revisions should the questionnaire be finalized and distributed.

BOX 7.3 PRACTICE NOTE: OPEN-ENDED QUESTIONS

The best argument for why open-ended questions should be included in most questionnaires comes from a student who was interning in a state social service agency. Foster children were routinely given questionnaires on which they could evaluate their placement.

On one particular form completed by a female adolescent, the girl indicated that the placement was satisfactory on all the criteria used by the agency. The last question on the back of the form asked simply, "Is there anything about this placement you don't like?" The teen wrote in response, "One thing I didn't like was that Jim [the foster father] came into my bedroom every night about the time I started getting ready for bed."

Obviously, the foster father's behavior was inappropriate. He had no business trying to make conversation in the foster child's bedroom when she was changing into pajamas. As a result, this foster home was viewed as not being acceptable for future placements.

To assist you in developing good questionnaires, the next section will elaborate some important guidelines. These guides will help you recognize the ways in which item construction can affect the data you obtain. Poorly phrased or constructed questions appear in this chapter; consider each of the examples, and try to decide why it is flawed before reading the discussion accompanying it.

Pitfalls in Writing Good Questions

Writing crisp, clear questionnaire items is not always easy. Researchers may load up their questions with too many considerations, making the items overly complex. Also, they may overlook the fact that not everyone is as interested in the topic as the researchers. Questionnaires can't waste potential respondents' time and must be easy to understand and respond to. In this section, you will find a few tips for how to write your questionnaire items so that you get useful data for your study. In this section you will find tips for how to write questionnaire items so that you get useful data as well as see examples of flawed items that produce worthless information.

Double-Barreled Questions

The following example of a **double-barreled question** asks about two different behaviors but is structured so that only one response is expected. A response of "Yes" could mean that the respondent had donated blood and been to the dentist. It is also possible that some respondents might respond "Yes" when they had visited the dentist but not donated blood, and vice versa. Some respondents will indicate "No" when they have done one but not the other, while other "No" responses will mean that the respondent has neither donated blood nor gone to the dentist. If it is impossible to interpret just what any response means, then the item is not a good one.

> **Have you donated blood or gone to the dentist this month?**
> ( ) Yes   ( ) No   ( ) Don't know

As a rule, a question should ask about *one* issue, thought, or event at a time. If more information is desired, additional questions should be asked. In this example, two separate questions should be constructed—each one focusing on a single issue.

However, sometimes a single question might be used when there are two similar things to consider. For instance, if we were interviewing abuse victims to see if they were threatened with a weapon, it could be acceptable to ask, "Were you threatened with a gun or a knife?"

On the other hand, a questionnaire item like "Have you ever been called names or threatened with harm?" is poorly constructed because being called names is a fairly common occurrence and doesn't imply the same order of danger as being threatened with harm.

ANXIETY CHECK 7.1

Is this a good item? "Some people are dissatisfied with their jobs. Are you unhappy with your present position because of the workload and salary?"

[Answer at the end of the book.]

Leading Questions

Leading questions guide the respondent into thinking along certain lines. Most of us want to be agreeable and get along with others. And most of us believe it is important to be respectful by agreeing and avoiding confrontation when possible. The following example is a leading question that Bill suggested. Does it suggest a desired response?

> **Don't you agree with our senator, who has stated that the federal government should spend $100 billion in new money to support a manned mission to Mars?**
>
> ( ) Agree　　　　　　( ) Disagree　　　　　　( ) Don't know

Here's another question for you to consider: "Don't you agree that the federal government should spend more on social services and less on the manned mission to Mars?" This item is both leading and double-barreled. Besides begging for an *Agree* response, it also asks for information about two different things. First, it wants to know if the government should spend more money on social services. Second, it wants to know if the respondent thinks the government should spend less on sending humans to Mars. Again, the respondent could agree with one of these two thoughts and disagree with the other and be confused about how to respond. (What might a *Disagree* response mean?)

Inadvertently, sometimes we create a leading question by suggesting a characteristic. To ask, "How tall was President Lincoln?" just might provide a hint that he was tall or taller than average. It could be better to ask, "What was President Lincoln's height?"

Unavailable Information

Respondents should not be asked for information that would not normally be available to them. For instance, because most of us do not keep records regarding how much time we spend watching television—and it may vary by day—any response that we might give to a question like this could be no more than a wild estimate. A much better way to get at this kind of information would be to ask the respondent to estimate the average number of hours of television watched daily or weekly. Or better yet, the researcher could provide the respondent with a calendar or electronic drop-down menu for recording the number of hours watched per day over a period like a week or two weeks. Here's an example of a question attempting to gather information so unavailable that its accuracy is immediately suspect.

> **How many hours of television did you watch last year?**

Sophia remembered a perfect example of a question asking for information likely to be unavailable to most people. The item was in a questionnaire used by an agency that once offered her a job. The item asked of all clients: "Describe your mother's pregnancy with you; for example, were there complications?" While it is true that a few individuals may have acquired this information because they were born prematurely, would the vast majority of Americans have information about their mother's health status during pregnancy and delivery?

The recall of distant events is always problematic, and increased error is associated with the passage of time. As a rule, it is better to ask about events and activities that have happened recently, say, within the past 30 days. However, sometimes it is necessary to ask what are known as lifetime questions, such as, "Have you ever been arrested?" or "How many times have you been in any kind of treatment program for alcohol or drug problems?"

Asking for information that might not be available to all respondents can present another problem. Consider the following question: "Do you agree or disagree with the philosophy of the state's Commission on Literacy?" This question is a poor one if the philosophy of the state's Commission on Literacy is not well known. If, on the other hand, the commission has recently been in the news because of some unusual or controversial philosophy, then it would be reasonable to ask this question. However, it might be better to ask in one question, "Is there a commission on literacy in this state?" Then, one might want to ask those respondents who answer "Yes" to describe the commission's philosophy. A third question in this series might ask if they agree or disagree with the commission's philosophy. This approach involves the use of **contingency questions** (branching questions that can also be thought of as filter or screening questions). Those respondents who answer "Yes" to the first question are directed to the second and third subquestions. Those who respond "No" to the first question are guided to another set of questions. See Figure 7.3 for an example of a **contingency question.** Contingency questions can also be called **filter questions** because the investigator may want to study a certain subgroup of subjects with particular characteristics.

BOX 7.4   PRACTICE NOTE: HUMAN MEMORY

Human memory is far from perfect. This has implications for social workers in everyday practice and research. Lalande and Bonanno (2011), for example, conducted a study of potentially traumatic events (PTE) over a four-year period in a weekly Web-based study. They found a relationship between the amount of distress felt and the recalled number of PTEs—no surprise there. However, almost a quarter of all participants (23%) *overestimated* the number of PTEs they had experienced, but higher distress was not associated with over-remembering. And individuals who were "self-enhancers" tended to under-remember PTEs—even if they were distressed.

Use of Jargon and Technical Terms

Do you feel that Freud's structural hypothesis is an improvement over his topographic hypothesis?

Even those who are familiar with psychoanalytic theory may not know how to respond to this question. It is too technical, using jargon not known to most Americans. Your goal as a designer of questionnaire or scale items is to use familiar, rather than unfamiliar, language. Being cognizant of the reading level and vocabularies of your possible subjects, you would not want to use terms that might not be understood by

We have discussed several self help groups found in our area. Now we would like to examine some additional services that may be available statewide.

1. Can you tell me if the state funds a Commission on Literacy?

( ) Yes, it does

( ) No, it doesn't

( ) Don't know

GO TO QUESTION 12

10.a Can you describe the Commission's philosophy?

__ Takes an aggressive approach in promoting literacy

__ Takes a laid-back approach to promoting literacy

__ Don't know its philosophy

10.b Does the Commission on Literacy deserve more funding?

__ Deserves more funding

__ Does not deserve more funding

__ Don't know

FIGURE 7.3 Illustration of a Contingency Question

everyone. For example, if you were surveying teens about their use of birth control methods, would you want to use the word "prophylactic?" Probably not. Would high school dropouts understand "narcissism?" Even terms that you think everyone should understand can be too sophisticated. A study of health literacy involving six items from the nutritional information placed on all food packages found that 21% of participants had a "high likelihood of limited literacy"; 27% had the "possibility of limited literacy"; and only about half (52%) had "adequate literacy" (McCune, Lee, & Pohl, 2016).

Use the simplest terms and vocabulary possible—in other words, the language that we use in everyday speech (sometimes called **Standard English**). Avoid colloquialisms (that is, slang) or informal conversation such as "guys" when both men and women are present, abbreviations (for example, t.i.d., TIA), and foreign phrases. The general rule is to aim for a seventh- or eighth-grade comprehension level—unless, of course, you are dealing with younger children. Keep sentences short and simple. Avoid compound sentences if possible.

Insensitive Language

How do you people really feel about President Obama's accomplishments? Do you Hispanics go to Starbucks often?

Insensitive items make some people uneasy because they suggest "you people" may be different from "my people" and may imply a racial or class bias. They accentuate differences among respondents by suggesting, in effect, that the respondent is not a member of an "in-group." Instead of asking questions in the format of "How do *you blacks* [or *you Hispanics*] feel about …?" simply ask "How do you feel about …?" Or present a statement and ask the respondent to choose a response that reflects his or her feelings about the subject. Later, when analyzing the data, you can determine if racial groups differ in their attitudes or opinions—if you have included an item on the respondents' racial/ethnic identity as part of your questionnaire. Avoid using any **insensitive language** in a questionnaire.

Inflammatory or "Loaded" Terms

> *Are you a religious fanatic?*
> *Are you a Bible thumper?*
> *Do you live in the redneck part of the state?*
> *What do you gun nuts think about ...?*

As we learned earlier, **social desirability** is a term used to describe the tendency of people to want their behavior to be perceived as socially acceptable. Our human nature leads us to avoid categories or labels that are stigmatizing—creating a possible response bias. Few of us want to be labeled a fanatic, zealot, or any other term that has socially undesirable connotations. Even though a respondent may have strong convictions, he or she would likely deny having tendencies toward fanaticism.

Just as the word *fanatic* is loaded, few people would want to be labeled a drunk or alcoholic. Questions that get the desired information without labeling or stigmatizing should be employed. A better way to explore the extent of problem drinking is to ask respondents about specific behaviors; for example, "Do you try to avoid family members when you are drinking?" or "Are you in a hurry to get your first drink in the morning?"

ANXIETY CHECK 7.2

Is this a loaded question: "What is your favorite way of cheating on exams?

[Answer is at the end of the book.]

You want to provide a series of items that gives a respondent an opportunity to describe his or her drinking or other behavior as objectively as possible. Similarly, avoid **loaded terms** such as *crisis*, *innocent*, *victim*, *forced*, and *coerced*. No one wants to be forced, and most of us want to help innocent victims and avoid crises.

Response Choices That Are Not Mutually Exclusive

How often do you drink?
a. I rarely drink.
b. I'm a social drinker.
c. I occasionally drink to excess.
d. I frequently drink to excess.

In our quest to avoid socially unacceptable labels, we might create another problem. Are the choices of *social drinker* and *occasionally drink to excess* **mutually exclusive response choices**? That is, could they overlap? Would it be possible to think of oneself as a social drinker *and* to occasionally drink to excess? If you agree, then this response set will not provide clear data. Being a social drinker is a more attractive response to some individuals than revealing they drink to excess. More accurate data might be obtained by asking about the number of times a person drinks in an average week. That approach eliminates confusion over what constitutes the social drinker category or how often *occasionally* is and provides a more precise way of separating light drinkers from moderate or heavy drinkers. Behavioral measures generally give researchers more objective data.

The problems of overlapping response categories and finding good behavioral measures are obvious examples of why you need to refer to the literature as part of the research process. It is likely that other researchers have struggled with these problems and have developed response sets or categories (if not whole questionnaires) that you could use in your research.

We're not always aware of overlapping response choices. Can you detect any problems with the responses in the following items?

Examples of Overlapping Response Sets

How often do you date?

a. almost every night

b. once or twice a week

c. a few times a month

d. three to four times a week

e. once every two weeks

f. a few times a year

What category best describes your income?

1. 0–$5,000

2. $5,000–10,000

3. $10,000–15,000

4. $15,000 or higher

What is your grade point average?

1. Below 2.00

2. 2.00 to 2.50

3. 2.50 to 3.00

4. 3.00 to 3.50

5. 3.50 to 4.00

Vague and Ambiguous Terms

> **How many times in the past year have you seen a social worker?**
> **Do you attend Alcoholics Anonymous regularly?**

The problem with both of these questions is that they are vague. "Seeing" a social worker can be interpreted at least two different ways (to see or observe and, in informal conversational language, to have a meeting or appointment with). Is the intent of this question to find out how many social workers are observed (seen)? Or is it to learn the number of appointments or sessions the respondent had with a social worker last year? To rephrase the question to "How many times in the past year have you talked with a social worker?" is not a great improvement, because one can talk informally or socially with social workers. Would it be better to ask "How many appointments have you made with your social worker in the past 30 days?" Or, because it is possible to make appointments but not keep them, "How many sessions have you had with your social worker in the last 30 days?"

The problem with the second example is that "regularly" is one of those terms that means different things to different individuals. Some respondents may attend Alcoholics Anonymous (AA) regularly once a week or regularly once a month. Other respondents may attend regularly the first Wednesday of the month. Some respondents may attend every day. A better way to ask for information of this type would be: "How many times a month do you attend Alcoholics Anonymous meetings?"

Another example of the use of vague terms is this question: "What is your income?" This question is problematic because the respondent must figure out whether the information sought has a yearly, monthly, or weekly referent. It also is unclear whether the respondent should report annual salary (gross income) or the amount after all the deductions have been made (take-home pay, or net income). A further problem is that the question does not indicate whether combined family income is expected or whether the respondent should report only his or her personal income (even though others in the household may be working).

Similarly, "Are you employed?" may be difficult to answer because there are several responses that can be made in addition to "Yes" or "No." The status of being employed usually includes full-time and part-time workers. Also, respondents could be employed seasonally (for example, college students who work full time in the summer or at Christmas but not at all when school is in session). Finally, there are those who help with a family business (such as a spouse who keeps the books) but who do not receive a paycheck.

Vague and ambiguous terms do not convey the same frame of reference to all respondents. For instance, some respondents will read "Has your child missed a lot of school?" and think in terms of the whole school year. Other parents may think only about absences in the past month or week. Parents may also respond to this question in terms of their own experience in missing school or compare one child to another, so that even though Hugh has missed 14 days of school in the first grading period—that's not "a lot" compared to his sister Evie, who missed six weeks due to illness. It is better practice to provide the same frame of reference for everyone—for example, by asking, "How many days of school did your child miss during the first grading period?"

Even when we think an item is not vague, pretesting may show that respondents have different impressions of what it is asking. Do you think the item "I have difficulty getting up in the morning" may have different meanings and therefore be ambiguous?

All-Inclusive Terms

> **Are you always in bed by 11:00 p.m.?**

The use of such words as *always* and *never* creates problems for the respondent and for the researcher attempting to interpret the data. Does *always* allow for exceptions? For instance, what if you are in bed by 11:00 P.M. every night of the year except for New Year's Eve, when you stay up until 12:01 A.M.? Does that mean you should respond with a "No" to the preceding question? *Always* and *never* imply that there are no exceptions. Researchers are more concerned with general patterns. A better way to ask the question might be, "On most weeknights, what time do you usually go to bed?"

Negatively Constructed Items

> **My friends believe marijuana should not be decriminalized.**

The statement in the box is a good example of how the word *not* can confuse the meaning of a statement. In this instance, it reverses the meaning of *decriminalized*, so that a person agreeing to the statement is saying in effect that marijuana usage should be illegal. A respondent disagreeing with the statement is saying that marijuana use should be made legal. It is much clearer and more straightforward to ask, "Should the private use of marijuana be made legal?" Where possible, the term *not* should be avoided in questionnaires.

Sequencing Items

The first questions in a questionnaire or interview should be of interest to the respondent. Respondents need to "warm up" to the survey process and get a feel for how it will be presented. Respondents may need a little time to establish a sense of trust or rapport with the researcher in an effort to grasp how much they should reveal—or even to decide if they want to participate. You've got to remember that possible participants probably do not know you and may not be familiar with how researchers treat the data (especially sensitive data) that may be asked of them. Accordingly, the first several questions should be interesting but easy to answer and applicable to all respondents. It is often a good idea to start with closed-ended items on survey questionnaires. In personal interviews, open-ended questions can work well. Information about potentially sensitive areas such as age and income should occur at the end of the questionnaire. Such information, if asked at the beginning of the interview or questionnaire, may result in early refusals to participate and a lower response rate. (This applies more to a cross-sectional type of study in the community than to groups like college students where most respondents are close to the same age.)

More important questions should be asked earlier than less important ones in case the respondent decides to terminate the interview or stop working on the questionnaire before all questions have been completed. Respondents can tire after answering complicated or tedious questions. **Respondent fatigue** can especially be expected with very long questionnaires. Experts agree that topically related questions should follow one another in some sort of recognizable sequence, as opposed to being randomly spread throughout the questionnaire. Usually, some sort of "funnel sequence" is used, in which general questions are followed by more narrowly focused questions.

	Strongly Agree	Agree	Undecided	Disagree	Strongly Disagree
1. As a child I felt unwanted.	_____	_____	_____	_____	_____
2. My parents called me hurtful names.	_____	_____	_____	_____	_____
3. I wanted to leave my family—to run away.	_____	_____	_____	_____	_____
4. My parents were happy with me.	_____	_____	_____	_____	_____

FIGURE 7.4 Phrasing Items to Avoid Acquiescence

Researchers must also be alert to potential **question order effects**. That is, a prior item may affect the way respondents answer subsequent questions. For instance, Van de Walle & Van Ryzin (2011) divided a community survey into two samples. One group was asked to evaluate their satisfaction with public services where a general question about all the services was asked first. The other sample was asked to evaluate specific services first, and then the general question was asked. The authors found when the general question was asked first, respondents rated their overall satisfaction with local government services statistically higher than when the general question was asked after rating their satisfaction with specific services. In other words, question location impacted reported satisfaction levels.

Acquiescence, a tendency where some respondents tend to agree with items regardless of their content, can be countered by constructing items that must be read because they could be either positive or negative. With a little creativity, items can be prepared so that the respondent does not know which response is the one desired by the researcher. Figure 7.4 provides an example of wording questions so that a respondent indicating child abuse in his or her life could not respond either *Strongly Agree* or *Agree* to all four questions. In any listing of choices (or scales you build), you might consider creating at least one check for acquiescence. This could tell you if respondents are actually reading all the questions. For example, if asking high school students about books they have read, you might include a nonexistent book as a check.

Thinking About Guidelines

The problem with guidelines is that sometimes it makes sense to violate them. At times, you might use a loaded question to try to determine the extent of some socially undesirable behavior. For instance, the implication that "everyone does it" may be useful in reducing the respondents' concern about reporting some behaviors. This approach is illustrated in the following examples. Which one do you think is the better approach?

a. "How many times in the past month did you scream at your children?"
b. "All parents get angry when their children misbehave. About how many times in the past month did you scream at your children?"

Besides the guidelines previously identified in this chapter, the researcher must keep other things in mind, too. Crowded, cluttered, or text-heavy questionnaires result in lower response rates than those that appear interesting, inviting, or simple to complete. Questionnaires should be visually attractive. Blank or white space should be used to full advantage. The responses should appear in the same area of the questionnaire so that the respondent can easily locate them. Instructions, questions, and response categories must be brief, and diagrams should be used when necessary to visually direct the respondent. Numbering the questions is useful to both respondents and those processing the data. If you have multiple components or parts to the study, use a sentence or two to smooth the transition between parts (for example, "Now we would like to change the subject just a bit and ask some health-related questions").

In Appendix B, you'll find a shortened version of the Drug Attitude Questionnaire, an instrument designed to measure the effects of a drug education program implemented in a high school. A longer version than I've shown here had excellent reliability (.93 to .97). You might want to examine the Drug Attitude Questionnaire to review some of the items. If you look closely, you'll note that this reliability came despite some items that I would change if I were to write them again. For instance, what about Items 8, 9, and 17? Do they violate any guidelines that we have learned in this chapter?

Self-Anchored Scales

Another option available to you when developing a research instrument is to generate **self-anchored scales** (behaviorally anchored single-item scales for measuring clients' problems). These types of scales are especially valuable when you need to estimate quickly the magnitude or severity of a problem. A chief advantage is that they can be used to assess a client's thoughts and feelings (such as anger or security in a relationship) when you don't have a standardized measurement tool nearby.

While many self-anchored scales are based on 10 equal intervals, it is not unusual to find scales based on 5, 7, 9, or even 100 points. The only thing tricky about designing these scales is keeping in mind that only one dimension of a concept should be presented. For instance, Angry and Not Angry would be logical to place at opposite ends of a continuum. However, using Angry at one end and Happy at the other involves two concepts instead of one and may make the scale less accurate because of different feelings associated with anger and happiness.

Self-anchored scales can also be used in single-subject designs as a repeated measure to keep track of progress resulting from intervention. When self-anchored scales are designed for specific clients, their

The Amount of Anger I Felt Today

```
    0    1    2    3      4    5    6    7    8    9    10
   None                       Moderate              Extreme
 Had a pleasant            Slammed the door      Shouted obscenities,
 Conversation             and walked away         punched the wall
```

How Satisfied I am with My Life

```
    0    1    2    3      4    5    6    7    8    9    10
 No Satisfaction              Average             Very Satisfied
```

Involvement in My Community

```
    0    1    2    3      4    5    6    7    8    9    10
 Not Involved                 Medium              Very Involved
```

Emotional Intimacy with My Partner

```
    0    1    2    3      4    5    6    7    8    9    10
 Not At All Close                                 Very Close
 (Unhappy; no real                                (Happy; lots
   of sharing)                                      sharing)
```

FIGURE 7.5 Examples of Self-Anchored Scales

actions and feelings—described in their own words—can be used to anchor the ends of the continuum. To demonstrate what self-anchored scales look like, several examples are shown in Figure 7.5.

One problem with the use of single-item scales—and even single questions—when used in a large survey or in an interview is that ordinarily it is not possible to compute their reliability or validity in the same way that is possible for a well-developed scale. However, certain facts can sometimes be checked. For example, imagine you give a questionnaire to a class of high school students in a health class. You know ahead of time from the teacher that 20 are sophomores, 5 are juniors, and 3 are seniors. If you ask on the questionnaire for students to report their classification, and if you then examine that item on the 28 surveys and find 20 sophomores, 5 juniors, and 3 seniors, then you know that at least that item captured reliable data.

ANXIETY CHECK 7.3

What kinds of questions do you think high school students may not answer so reliably if you planned a survey?

[Answer is at the end of the book.]

Generalizing Results

Even if you have a strong sampling design that would ordinarily allow for generalizing your results, a poorly constructed questionnaire or scale can ruin your study. The old expression "garbage in, garbage out" applies here. Minimize the inclusion of worthless items by ensuring that your target respondents can understand each and every item as you intended it. Don't be afraid to circulate your draft among colleagues whose opinion you respect and pilot-test the instrument. Good questionnaires do not result from a single draft.

The items you develop for your study are the foundation for any knowledge that will be acquired. If you do a good job with the design of your questionnaire, respondents will not find it burdensome. In fact, it just might be possible to make it so interesting that respondents *enjoy* participating; when they are cooperative and honest, you will have much better data. Poorly designed questionnaires generate worthless data when interviewers or raters get confused and enter data on the wrong line or in the wrong box. A well-designed questionnaire will not only be easy to complete, but it will allow the investigator to easily interpret responses and process data.

Although this chapter has emphasized the wording and phrasing of individual items, other elements can influence the responses you obtain. For instance, research subjects may need a line or two of simple directions. The survey may require a brief introduction explaining why the study is being conducted, who is involved, how the respondent was chosen, and the extent to which confidentiality is afforded. It is also good practice to inform potential participants how much of their time the survey will take.

BOX 7.5   SURVEY QUESTIONNAIRE CHECKLIST

☐   Do you have a cover letter or introduction that explains and invites participation?
☐   If printed, is it on professional letterhead and in color?
☐   Does the survey have the support of a well-recognized organization or person?
☐   Is the questionnaire visually attractive?
☐   Does the questionnaire look like it can be easily completed? (Is it of reasonable length?)
☐   Are the questions easily distinguished by a larger or different font than the response set?
☐   Are the directions simple?
☐   Is there plenty of room for responses to be recorded?
☐   If mailed, is a postage-paid, self-addressed return envelope included?
☐   Is the mailing list accurate and free of duplication?

Finally, review each question to make sure it gives you essential information; all of the questions taken together should help you conclude something worthwhile about the topic of your investigation.

Perhaps my relating an actual experience will show the importance of linking the survey questions to the topic of investigation. A group of local citizens once asked for my assistance in conducting a mental health needs assessment of their community. "Okay," I said, "tell me more." Their spokesperson indicated that they had found a book about needs assessment that included, in its appendix, a complete set of questions that could be photocopied and used with little modification. As I looked at the needs assessment instrument, I saw a question that asked the respondents to list three problems in their neighborhood and another that asked for a ranking of the most serious problems in the community. I anticipated that some respondents would be concerned with streetlights and potholes, police protection, and other community concerns. That particular questionnaire didn't appear to produce much usable information about the mental health needs of the community. I asked the spokesperson, "What do you hope to learn from the community needs assessment?" "Well," she said, "we want to know about all the mental health needs in the community." Somehow she hadn't made the connection to the needs they wanted to learn about and the questionnaire they had found.

After taking a big breath, I tactfully asked the group to meet together to determine what, exactly, they wanted to know about the mental health needs in the community. I'm not sure the group ever conducted a community needs assessment. I strongly suspect that there was no agreement among them on what was important to learn about their community's mental health needs—or how the information could be used. As you can see, the point is not just to develop a set of questions—the questions we ask must have a clear focus and purpose. Each question should add another increment to that sum of information we require. The well-designed questionnaire asks no less and no more than is needed for our research. Anyone can develop a questionnaire or conduct a survey, but the test of a good survey is whether it produces useful data. Genuinely useful information seldom comes about just because someone happens to find a set of already prepared questions.

Key Terms

closed-ended questions

open-ended questions

contingency questions

filter questions

social desirability

acquiescence

vague and ambiguous terms

negatively constructed items

loaded terms

respondent fatigue

mutually exclusive response choices

structured interview schedule

double-barreled questions

Standard English

leading questions

insensitive language

all-inclusive terms

question order effects

self-anchored scales

SELF-REVIEW
(Answers at the end of the book.)

1. T or F. Ideally, closed-ended questions should communicate the same frame of reference to all persons.

2. T or F. With large samples, it is easier to analyze the data obtained from open-ended questions than from closed-ended questions.

3. T or F. Double-barreled questions are useful to researchers because they allow the respondent to supply twice as much information in a single answer.

4. What is wrong with asking a child this question: "When did you last see the principal?"

    a. insensitive, inflammatory
    b. prevents contingency mock-up
    c. uses jargon
    d. vague item

5. What is wrong with this question: "Do you agree or disagree that EMDR contributes to resiliency among victims of PTSD?"

    a. implies social desirability
    b. uses jargon
    c. is negatively constructed
    d. creates acquiescence

6. What is wrong with this question: "How many times did you argue with your mother in 2015?"

    a. implies social desirability
    b. insensitive language
    c. unavailable information
    d. creates acquiescence

7. What is wrong with this question for teens: "When you are punished by your parents, do you act like a jerk?"

    a. leading question
    b. insensitive language
    c. unavailable information
    d. uses loaded terms

8. What is wrong with this question: "Would you say as a parent, you are a totally dominating tyrant?"

    a. vague
    b. insensitive language
    c. leading question
    d. uses loaded terms

9. What is wrong with this question: "Do you always get your phone privileges revoked when you don't clean up your room?"

   a.   negatively constructed
   b.   is all-inclusive
   c.   leading question
   d.   uses loaded terms

10. What is wrong with this question: "Do you regularly disagree with your parents' judgment on important issues?"

   a.   uses loaded terms
   b.   unavailable information
   c.   leading question
   d.   vague

11. What is wrong with this question: "Don't you think the city council should change the teen curfew to midnight on weekends?"

   a.   uses loaded terms
   b.   unavailable information
   c.   leading question
   d.   vague

12. Another name for a branching-type question would be a _____ question.

13. Jack is interested in how adults in their twenties and thirties adjust in the first year after becoming divorced. He's particularly interested in identifying the range of coping strategies that these adults might use. In your opinion, would he be better advised to use open-ended or closed-ended questions?

QUESTIONS FOR CLASS DISCUSSION

1. What is a frame of reference, and why is it important that the questionnaire communicate the same one to all respondents?

2. What would be a good way to check questionnaire and scale items to make sure that they do not contain jargon or some other problem?

3. To what extent do the items we construct reflect our view of the world and our values?

4. From a research perspective, what is the advantage of self-anchored scales over single-item scales that do not contain anchors?

5. What bothers you most when you are asked to complete a questionnaire?

6. Why is it important to decide on the survey methodology before designing the questionnaire to be used?

7. Do the advantages of open-ended questions outweigh their disadvantages?

8. What are the disadvantages of closed-ended questions?

9. IDEA FOR SMALL-GROUP PROJECTS: Break the class up into groups. The assignment is to construct a 10-item instrument designed to determine if parents of children under the age of 21 are in favor of having their children vaccinated for human papillomavirus (HPV). Alternatively, other groups can design a questionnaire to learn whether college students (nonparents) favor having all children vaccinated for this virus. Groups can discuss how their projects differ in terms of assumptions and wording. Groups can also swap their scales and critique the items developed by other groups.

RESOURCES AND REFERENCES

Abell, N., Springer, D. W., & Kamata, A. (2009). *Developing and validating rapid assessment instruments*. New York, NY: Oxford University Press.

Bradburn, N. M., & Sudman, S. (2004). Asking questions: The definitive guide to questionnaire design—for market research, political polls and social and health questionnaires. San Francisco, CA: Jossey-Bass.

Croyle, R. T., Loftus, E. F., Barger, S. D., Sun, Y.-C., Hart, M., & Gettig, J. (2006). How well do people recall risk factor test results? Accuracy and bias among cholesterol screening participants. *Health Psychology, 25*(3), 425–432.

De Vaus, D. A. (1986). *Surveys in social research*. London, UK: George Allen and Unwin.

DeVellis, R. F. (2011). *Scale development: Theory and applications*. Thousand Oaks, CA: Sage.

Lalande, K. M., & Bonanno, G. A. (2011). Retrospective memory bias for the frequency of potentially traumatic events: A prospective study. *Psychological Trauma: Theory, Research, Practice, and Policy, 3*(2), 165–170.

McCune, R. L., Lee, H., & Pohl, J. M. (2016). Assessing health literacy in safety net primary care practices. *Applied Nursing Research, 29*, 188–194.

Moore, D. W., & Gallup, A. (1994). The Holocaust: It happened. *Gallup Poll Monthly, 340*, 25–27.

Saris, W. E., & Gallhofer, I. (2014). *Design, evaluation, and analysis of questionnaires for survey research*. Hoboken, NJ: Wiley.

Springer, D., Abell, N., & Hudson, W. W. (2002). Creating and validating rapid assessment instruments for practice and research: Part I. *Research on Social Work Practice, 12*(3), 408–439.

Springer, D., Abell, N., & Nugent, W. Creating and validating rapid assessment instruments for practice and research: Part II. *Research on Social Work Practice, 12*(3), 805–832.

Van de Walle, S., & Van Ryzin, G. G. (2011). The order of questions in a survey on citizen satisfaction with public services: Lessons from a split-ballot experiment. *Public Administration, 89*(4), 1436–1450.

ASSIGNMENT 7.1

Developing a Questionnaire

Objective: *To develop skills in designing questionnaires for survey research.*

Develop a set of questions to use in interviewing nursing home residents about the quality of their lives. Use a mixture of open- and closed-ended questions. It is assumed that sociodemographic information (that is, age, sex, marital status, education, income, etc.) will be made available to you—it won't be necessary to ask about those items.

1. List your five open-ended questions.

2. List your five closed-ended questions along with their response set (in parentheses).

ASSIGNMENT 7.2

Critiquing a Peer's Questionnaire

Objective: *To obtain practice in evaluating items in a questionnaire.*

Take the questions that you developed in Assignment 7.1 and swap with another student in your class. Read that student's questions carefully and check to see if you find any of the problems discussed in this chapter (that is, double-barreled questions, jargon, insensitive language, etc.). Lastly, what is your subjective reaction to these questions? Are you confident that they will give you good insight into nursing home life? Write the name of the student whose questionnaire you are reviewing here:

PROBLEMS DETECTED

Open-ended Q1:
Open-ended Q2:
Open-ended Q3:
Open-ended Q4:
Open-ended Q5:

PROBLEMS DETECTED

Closed-ended Q1:
Closed-ended Q2:
Closed-ended Q3:
Closed-ended Q4:
Closed-ended Q5:

SUMMARY COMMENTS:

ASSIGNMENT 7.3

Critiquing a Questionnaire

Objective: *To obtain practice in objectively evaluating items making up a questionnaire.*

Critically review the draft of a set of questions (below) designed for a client group of men charged with domestic violence. How many mistakes can you find? Some problems are major, while others merely require that the item be revised to yield more useful information.

	Question	**Problem**
Example:	Are you presently employed?	Can't determine if respondent is working part time or full time
Q1	Have you received any counseling since you left the program?	
Q2	Have you talked with anyone since you left the program?	
Q3	Are you getting along better with your spouse?	
Q4	Are you using more drugs than are good for you?	
Q5	Would you say that your behavior was motivated by feelings of anger and powerlessness?	
Q6	How many times have you hit, kicked, or otherwise injured a female partner?	

Q7   Could both overt and covert forms of narcissism be risk factors in the prediction of your interpersonal violence (IPV)?

Q8   Wouldn't you agree that your IPV has improved since you've been with the agency?

Q9   Do you tend to be friends with scum like yourself—people with rage problems?

Q10   Are you always easy-going?

CHAPTER 8

Sampling

Sampling Theory

SAMPLING METHODOLOGY IS of paramount concern in quantitative research. Researchers must wrestle with issues such as:

- **Sample size**—how big a sample do I need?
- **Sampling method**—how do I best access the population of interest?
- **Representativeness**—will my sample adequately represent the larger population?
- **Generalization**—can I generalize my findings beyond my sample?

Whether you are conducting a survey of clients' satisfaction with services, a community needs assessment, or a statewide survey, you will have to make decisions about how to obtain your sample and what a particular sampling method will allow you to infer about the larger population.

The concept of sampling is one you are already familiar with. Virtually every day, you are involved in sampling. On cold winter days, you may stick your foot out from under the covers and decide that it is too cold to get up right then. Later on, you test your bath or shower water to see if the temperature is right before jumping in. You might take a sip of coffee and decide it is too strong. Sometimes, you walk into a clothing store, glance at a few price tags, and decide the store's items are more expensive than you can afford. When you have a physical, a tiny amount of your blood is tested.

In each of these instances, sufficient information came from sampling. It was not necessary to experience the *whole* of the phenomenon. You didn't have to drink the whole cup of coffee to realize it was too strong. One sip served as a sample of the whole cup. You didn't have to examine every article of apparel in the clothing store to know that the store catered to an exclusive clientele. The phlebotomist at the medical center didn't have to draw a sample from every part of your body because your blood is pretty much the same regardless of whether it is in your arm or foot or ear.

The notion behind sampling theory is that a small set of **observations (sampling units)** can tell you something about the larger population. In social work research, we can define a **population** as all of the individuals you want to learn about. It could be the adult population of a city, the older adults in the state's nursing homes, the children from a given county who have been in foster care for the past 10 years. Populations vary greatly in size and depend on the researcher's interest or research questions. A **sample** is a subset of a population.

Let's say that you have been elected to a school board in a town with 50,000 registered voters. If there is a movement to raise taxes to build a new high school, you wouldn't have to talk to all 50,000 registered voters to get an accurate notion of whether the majority of adults in the community were in favor of this tax. A telephone poll of several hundred randomly selected registered voters could provide you with an accurate assessment of support for a new tax. Polling 50,000 individuals is both impractical and unnecessary.

Sampling works because trends or tendencies within a large population can be discovered from a smaller number of individuals if the sample is well chosen. For instance, if 90% of the registered voters in the community were in favor of building the new high school and increasing their taxes, support for the tax issue should be apparent whether you sample 100, or 300, or 500 of the registered voters (if these voters are randomly selected). The larger sample merely allows for greater confidence and precision in estimating the "true" level of support or nonsupport for the tax issue. It is possible that if you sample only a handful of individuals, these few may not feel, act, or believe as the majority of the larger population. But if the sample is large enough, and there is no bias in the selection of the individual sampling units, then the pattern or characteristics found in the sample should match what you would find if you could contact everyone in the total population. This is great news for quantitative social scientists. Can you imagine how difficult it would be to conduct surveys in large cities like New York or Chicago if you couldn't sample? As you might guess, sampling saves money and time.

ANXIETY CHECK 8.1

If 90% of voters favor building a new high school, how many voters would be supportive in a sample of 200? In a sample of 500?

[Answer at the back of the book.]

You can get a rough idea of how sampling works by imagining that a friend has a bowl with 10 marbles in it. She holds it where you can't see into it and asks you to guess the colors of the marbles in the bowl. You may change your opinion each time, if you wish, after you have drawn a marble out. On your first draw, you retrieve a blue marble, so you might think that most of the marbles are blue. On the second draw, you obtain a red marble, so your best guess at this point is that there are five red and five blue marbles. The third draw produces another blue marble, so you revise your estimate to two-thirds blue and one-third red. The fourth draw is a blue marble, as are the fifth, sixth, and seventh draws. At that point, it is clear that the majority of marbles are blue. In fact, over 80% of those marbles selected have been blue. However, the remaining 3 could all be red, and so the most conservative estimate would be that 60% of the marbles are blue (because six blue ones have already been selected). Alternatively, you might take a bit of a risk and guess that 70%, 80%, or 90% of the marbles will be blue when all 10 are examined.

What this brief example shows is that at some point in drawing a sample, it becomes clear if one viewpoint, opinion, candidate, or color of marble is represented more often than some other viewpoint, opinion, candidate, or color. The proportion found in the sample gives the researcher a "window" into the larger population and a good basis for estimating the actual occurrence in a larger population. If, that is—and this is a very important point—the sample derives from a random selection process.

Imagine your friend's bowl held 200 marbles instead of 10. Let's say that she carefully placed 190 red marbles in the bottom of the bowl and 10 blue ones on top of the red. If you chose a marble off the top each time without stirring the marbles up or moving them around, it would be clear why a sample of

6 blue marbles was obtained. If the marbles had been shaken up or stirred before you selected your first 6 or 7, might you have made a different guess as to the true proportion of red and blue marbles?

Researchers employing scientifically selected samples (known as **probability samples**) are meticulous about how their respondents are selected. Their attention to random selection and sample size gives these surveys a great deal of accuracy in their findings.

Probability Samples

Depending on how you draw them, samples can be extremely accurate—or next to worthless. Of all the samples that can be created, probability samples are the most accurate and are also known as scientific samples. Nonprobability samples (their name is a dead giveaway) are the least accurate. How accurate is accurate? Organizations which poll the public regarding who they will vote for in the next election develop samples from the whole nation and state that their results will be accurate within plus or minus 3 percentage points. Accuracy rates depend on several factors such as how the respondents were chosen, the number of the respondents, and so forth. Surveys (polls) can be as accurate as ±1 percentage point all the way up to plus or minus 10 percent; however, ±5 percent is fairly common. When was the last time you were able to predict anything within ±3 percent?

When talking to some of the inmates last week, Bill and Sophia heard stories from them that often were very critical of the police. The inmates, having been arrested by the police might, understandably, not be completely objective. That's how Bill and Sophia explained the mean jokes and critical comments they had been hearing.

At the end of the day on Thursday, Bill was on his tablet waiting for Sophia to finish her practicum log. Just last night in class, Dr. Griffiths discussed some of the national polling firms, and the Gallup Organization was one that Bill remembered. Checking out their website (gallup.com), Bill found a report entitled "In U.S., Confidence in Police Lowest in 22 Years."

"Hey, Sophia. Look. This report says that only 52% of Americans have expressed 'a great deal' or 'quite a lot' of confidence in the police—that's the lowest since 1993. It reached a high of 64% in 2004 but has been averaging about 57%."

"Dr. Griffiths said it was important to look at the level of confidence and margin of error. What was the sample size? And was it a nonprobability sample?"

"Nope. The last poll involved 1,527 adults from all 50 states and the District of Columbia, interviewed by phone. And it had a 95% confidence level and sampling error of plus or minus 3%," Bill said.

"Sounds like a good study. Did they say if all of the respondents were reached on land lines?"

"Let's see," said Bill scrolling. "They had a mixture of 50% land lines and 50% cell phones and used random-digit dial methods for both."

"You know," said Sophia, "we could do a quick survey of the female inmates here to see what proportion of them would have 'a great deal' or 'quite a lot' of confidence in the police."

"Nice," said Bill. That would just about sew up an *A* in Dr. Griffiths's class."

"Would that be your only motivation?" Sophia gave Bill a hard look.

Eyes downcast, Bill scrolled a bit more on his tablet before answering. "I'd like to have an *A*." He looked up at Sophia. "But I'd also like to know if the women here would have a completely different view of the police than a cross-section of Americans. I mean, we would understand if 90% of them said they had no confidence in the police. But what if 57% of them were in agreement with the national surveys—would that mean they thought about the question objectively and perhaps had insight into their behavior and its consequences?"

"Bill," said Sophia. "Sometimes you amaze me."

With probability sampling, the investigator must have a good idea of both the number of people or units in the target population and their characteristics. With knowledge of these parameters, the researcher can determine if a sample is representative. For instance, if the population is 48% female, then the sample ought to come close to that parameter. If the sample turns out to be 75% female, for example, then it is likely the sampling procedure was flawed. That is, it is not a good fit with the known population characteristic (or parameter) of 48%.

Design Types

The term ***cross-sectional survey design*** refers to probability sampling designs. The term indicates that a survey was conducted with a randomly selected sample. The cross-sectional design allows a broad representation of the population and thus involves persons of all ages, incomes, and education levels. (This term will make more sense when you later read about purposive samples, which do not provide a cross-sectional view.)

There are several probability cross-sectional sampling designs to consider. The first one we will examine is the **simple random sampling design**, where each sampling unit in the population has the same probability (an equal chance) of being chosen.

Suppose the president of your university is retiring, and the board of trustees is interested in selecting a former governor for the new president. You think it is a good idea, but you want to know what the rest of the student body thinks. You find out from the registrar that 19,787 students are enrolled in the university. Knowing the population of university students, you can begin to make some decisions about how many to contact and which survey approach to use.

Assume the registrar provides you with a listing of all the enrolled students as well as their contact information. With this list, you could use a table of random numbers to find a starting place and begin randomly selecting a sample of students to contact. This listing would be known as the **sampling frame**. Let's say you decide to contact a sample of 100 students. If you have a good list and you randomly select from it, the names you draw for your sample should be representative of the population enrolled at the university. Your sample should be a microcosm of the population of university students. The proportion of males and females in the sample should reflect their proportion at the university, as should the proportion of freshmen, sophomores, juniors, and seniors. (For example, if you find that 42% of your sample are seniors, and yet seniors make up only 18% of the student body as a whole, then you should suspect something is wrong with either your sampling procedure or your list of students.)

Sometimes, researchers talk about **systematic sampling**. What they mean by this is best explained by way of example. Let's say that you plan to take a 10% sample of the 19,787 university students. However, a quick calculation shows that this would require almost 2,000 interviews (1,978.7, to be exact). Because you plan to conduct the telephone survey in a week's time, you decide that this would be too many students to contact. As you think about the realistic constraints on your time, you decide that 200 interviews is much more feasible. Dividing the proposed sample size of 200 by the university's population of 19,787, you get a **sampling ratio** of .01, which means that your sample will draw one name for every hundred students enrolled in the university.

In this example of systematic sampling, the next thing you need to do is number all of the students on the listing you received from the registrar—or, at least, have the ability to quickly determine where, say, Student #425 or #3433 is located. Then, you use a random number generator from the Internet (e.g., **www.random.org**) to get a random starting place (any number between 1 and 19,787). Excel can also produce random numbers.

Why is it important to get a random starting place? Because lists are often organized in a logical manner. The list you get from the registrar might place seniors first and then juniors, or it might be organized by grade point average or by whether students are undergraduates or working on a graduate degree. Starting with the first one or the last one in a list that is organized by some category and choosing every 1/100th name might mean your sample would be composed only of undergraduates or only those with the lowest or highest GPA.

While probability sampling is the best insurance against a sample being unrepresentative, sometimes chance or some form of unexpected bias will produce a random sample that is not representative. For example, 48% of the university population may be female, but 54% of those drawn for your sample could be female. If you play cards, you understand how this could happen. Even though the deck is shuffled many times, luck plays a role in which cards you are dealt; it is possible to get all hearts or four aces. Similarly, any sample from a population is by definition only an approximation of the total population. Numerically large samples are the best guarantee against obtaining unrepresentative samples.

Some researchers try to guard against a freak or fluke sample by using the more precise **stratified random sampling design**. When certain important characteristics of the population (for example, the percentage of men and women) are known, exact proportions are obtained by dividing the study population into subgroups or subsets called **strata** and sampling the appropriate proportion from each stratum.

For instance, suppose that instead of sampling from the whole student body, you want to interview only seniors and first-year students about the reasons they chose the university. You already know that there are twice as many first-year students as seniors and that you could interview 300 students. You again approach the registrar and this time ask for two listings: one for the first-year students and another for seniors. Once again, you number each of the first-year students and seniors, choose a random starting place for each stratum, and begin selecting from them. Because there are twice as many first-year students as seniors, you decide to select 100 seniors to interview and 200 first-year students. This keeps the proportion of seniors to first-year students in your sample the same as it is in the university, and you have retained the sample size that you think is manageable. This is not simple random sampling because sampling was done within each stratum.

At this point, it would be good to note that while single random, systematic random, and stratified random sampling techniques are often used in community surveys, you can still use the same techniques in other research projects. For example, if you were asked to evaluate a program in your agency and needed to randomly assign 60 clients to either the control condition (where they would receive the usual intervention) or to the experimental condition (where they would get the new, hopefully improved intervention), you could decide which random sampling procedure would work best for selecting clients for possible participation.

When it is not possible to obtain or feasible to construct a sample frame of all the individuals who make up a population (for example, the names and addresses of all social work majors in the United States), researchers sometimes employ a **cluster sampling design**.

Used primarily for convenience and economy, cluster sampling randomly selects individuals from natural groupings, or clusters. Because human beings are social creatures, we tend to belong to groups like universities and schools, civic organizations, clubs, fraternities, sororities, churches, etc.

For example, if you want to know locally how the parents of children with emotional, mental, or learning problems view social workers, you might go to your local mental health center and ask for their cooperation to obtain a sample. But if you wanted a more geographically diverse sample, you might want to contact such national organizations as the National Alliance for Mental Illness (NAMI), the Attention Deficit Disorder Association (ADDA), or the Learning Disabilities Association of America (LAD), or possibly other organizations. Once you obtain a list of their chapters, you could then call, write, or e-mail selected chapters to ask for permission to survey their membership. Such organizations may be supportive of your research and eager to assist.

An example of **one-stage cluster sampling** would be dividing the population of a town into households (households would be the clusters because they usually contain more than one individual) and then taking a sample of households and obtaining information from all the members of the household. **Two-stage cluster sampling** would involve dividing the population into households or clusters and then taking a sample of members from each selected household.

A **multistage cluster sampling design** consists of several steps that must be taken prior to sampling the population of interest. Suppose you want to conduct a survey of hospital social workers who regularly are involved with mothers giving birth to opiate-addicted babies. You might start by identifying which states have the highest birth rates of these babies. From that cluster of states, you could identify those with cities having hospitals with large neonatal care units. Depending on the size of that list (because large cities can have many hospitals), you could randomly select hospitals or take all of them. The last stage could involve writing the directors of the hospitals' departments of social work and asking them to identify social workers who had worked with mothers who gave birth to an opiate-addicted baby in the past year. From this listing, you could send questionnaires to the social workers with this experience.

ANXIETY CHECK 8.2

Using the multistage sampling design described above, what group of babies and their mothers would likely not be represented?

[Answers are at the end of the book.]

Professional survey organizations often use multistage cluster samples simply because there is no sample frame of all American citizens. Typically, they randomly draw from large geographic tracts. The next stage would involve drawing from cities, towns, and even smaller units such as census tracts or blocks—and from those, clusters of dwellings from which respondents would be selected.

> **BOX 8.1   EXAMPLE OF A PURPOSIVE SAMPLING STRATEGY WITH FOCUS GROUPS**
>
> African Americans participate less frequently than whites in practically all federally funded research, including clinical treatment trials investigating new interventions for cancer, stroke, and cardiovascular disease. No less than 10 studies have found distrust of academic and research institutions is the greatest attitudinal barrier that African Americans report (Scharff et al., 2010). And the Tuskegee Syphilis Study seems to figure prominently as a reason for their mistrust of medical research. But other studies have also found attitudes linked to racial disparities in health care and limited access to health care, as well as negative encounters with health care providers and a lack of culture competence. Scharff and his colleagues undertook an exploratory qualitative study to understand barriers keeping African Americans from participation in research studies. Eleven focus groups were created involving 70 individuals who either had participated in research or had not. Perhaps not surprisingly, they found that the participants' knowledge of the Tuskegee study negatively impacted their level of trust. Participants "stressed that disrespect and discrimination towards African-Americans continues to occur" (p. 890).

One of my students used a multistage cluster sampling design in connection with a research project. She had been reading about transracial adoption and found little information about the black community's attitudes toward this topic. Because she was not interested in white people's attitudes, a random community survey would have been inefficient. Instead, she selected a multistage cluster sampling design.

She (with assistance from another colleague and me) first identified the 9 census tracts in one city containing the highest concentrations of blacks. From these 9 tracts, 3 were randomly selected (because she was doing the interviewing all by herself, there was no need to walk her legs off). From these 3 tracts, 40 city blocks were randomly chosen. Finally, every sixth household was selected from these blocks (after getting a random starting place) until 150 interviews had been completed.

Because the individuals within a cluster tend to be more homogeneous than individuals in different clusters, the researcher typically maximizes the number of clusters for greater representativeness. Sampling error is reduced when researchers take fewer individuals from more clusters rather than more individuals from fewer clusters. This may mean that few individuals are selected from any one cluster. However, there is no obligation to sample from each cluster.

Determining Sample Size

How big a sample is necessary for a good survey? This is a major question that confronts us and must always be answered. Unfortunately, there is no simple response to this question. Sample size is related to the researcher's objectives, monetary and personnel resources, and the amount of time available in which to conduct the research. A precise sample size cannot be determined until you are able to state your expectations in terms of the accuracy you need and the confidence that you would like to have in the data. The accuracy of your survey is much more dependent on the size of the sample than on the population size.

Let's acquaint ourselves with several terms useful for discussing statistical probability statements associated with surveys. **Margin of error** refers to the precision needed by the researcher; that is, the amount of sampling error that can be tolerated. A margin of error of 5% means that the actual findings could vary by as much as 5 points either positively or negatively. A consumer satisfaction survey, for instance, with a 5% margin of error associated with a finding of 65% of clients being "highly satisfied" with services would mean that the true value in the population could be as low as 60% (65 − 5 = 60) or as high as 70% (65 + 5 = 70). If you believe that greater precision is needed (for example, plus or minus 2 points), then you must plan on obtaining a larger sample to support that precision. This can be seen in Table 8.1 if you compare the sample sizes in the .05 column with those in the .02 column. For instance, if you were planning a survey of all 400 current clients in your agency (the population size column), you would need to receive responses from 196 of them (the .05 column) to be able to discuss your findings plus or minus 5 percentage points. If greater accuracy were desired, then you would need to obtain responses from 343 clients to have plus or minus 2 points of accuracy or 384 clients if you wanted accuracy within 1 percentage point (the .01 column).

The other term that is important to understand is **confidence level**. A confidence level (or level of confidence) is a statement of how often you could expect to find similar results if the survey were to be repeated. Because every sample varies slightly, the confidence level informs about how often the findings will fall outside the margin of error. For example, in a sample developed to have a 95% confidence level with a 5% margin of error, the findings would be expected to miss the actual values in the population by more than 5% only 5 times in 100 surveys. (Similarly, in the previous example, findings of less than 60% or more than 70% of the clients were "highly satisfied" would also be expected to occur no more than 5 times in 100 surveys.) The use of a 95% confidence level and a 5% margin of error is a common standard in the social sciences.

There are three ways to determine sample size in a probability-type survey once you know the size of the population.

1. Consult a prepared table.
2. Consult the Internet.
3. Manually compute sample size with a formula.

We'll start first with consulting a prepared table. Examine Table 8.1 to decide how large a sample might be needed for a survey you want to conduct. This table is used when you don't have any idea about how those surveyed will respond, but you want to be reasonably confident in the findings (95%). The table assumes that at least 50% of the respondents will respond one way. (If, say, a prior survey had already been conducted and a larger percentage of respondents were found to be in favor of or opposed to something, then a different table would be needed because a smaller sample could be used.)

While the samples in Table 8.1 are based on a fixed 95% level of confidence, researchers can set both the level of confidence and margin of error independently of each other. These can be adjusted up or down in the planning stages of your survey as you consider cost, time, etc. Each adjustment has implications for sample size. Look now at the table to see that to be 95% confident, the same findings would have occurred in 95 surveys out of 100; to be accurate to within plus or minus 5 percentage points, you would need to interview 79 persons in a population of 100. However, in a population of 1 million, you would have to interview only 384 persons. The greater precision you require, the larger your sample must be. However, once you reach a certain critical mass, the sample size is not proportional to the population in an easy-to-figure way. Note that for a permissible error of 1% with the same population of 1 million, you would need a sample of 9,513.

TABLE 8.1 Appropriate Sizes of Simple Random Samples for Specific Permissible Errors Expressed as Absolute Proportions when the True Proportion in the Population Is 0.50 and the Confidence Level Is 95%.

Population Size	Sample Size for Permissible Error (Proportion)				
	0.05	0.04	0.03	0.02	0.01
100	79	86	91	96	99
200	132	150	168	185	196
300	168	200	234	267	291
400	196	240	291	343	384
500	217	273	340	414	475
600	234	300	384	480	565
700	248	323	423	542	652
800	260	343	457	600	738
900	269	360	488	655	823
1,000	278	375	516	706	906
2,000	322	462	696	1,091	1,655
3,000	341	500	787	1,334	2,286
4,000	350	522	842	1,500	2,824
5,000	357	536	879	1,622	3,288
6,000	361	546	906	1,715	3,693
7,000	364	553	926	1,788	4,049
8,000	367	558	942	1,847	4,364
9,000	368	563	954	1,895	4,646
10,000	370	566	964	1,936	4,899
15,000	375	577	996	2,070	5,855
20,000	377	583	1,013	2,144	6,488
25,000	378	586	1,023	2,191	6,938
30,000	379	588	1,030	2,223	7,275
40,000	381	591	1,039	2,265	7,745
50,000	381	593	1,045	2,291	8,056
75,000	382	595	1,052	2,327	8,514
100,000	383	597	1,056	2,345	8,762
500,000	384	600	1,065	2,390	9,423
1,000,000	384	600	1,066	2,395	9,513
2,000,000	384	600	1,067	2,398	9,558

Source: McCall, C. R. (1980). Sampling and statistics handbook for research in education. (1980). Washington, DC: National Education Association. Courtesy of Chester McCall. Reprinted with permission.

If you had conducted prior studies and had a good idea of what proportions the survey would likely reveal (for example, 90% opposed to a tax increase), then other tables will allow you to get by with smaller samples. In the example of a 90/10 split in a community with 100,000 adults, then a sample of approximately 138 individuals would provide a 95% level of confidence and 5% margin of error. With an expected 80/20 split, a sample of 245 would be needed for a 95% level of confidence and 5% margin of error. Because a pattern is more easily detected as the proportions move away from a 50/50 mix, smaller samples can be used.

If you want to use a different confidence level or expect that the presumed 50% proportion in the population doesn't fit and there are no prepared tables available, another approach is to go to the Internet and insert the necessary data into an interactive sample size calculator. For instance, **www.surveysystem. com** is one of many sample size calculators found on the Internet. Go there to set the confidence level at 99% or 95%, and by stating your population size and margin of error (which this site calls the confidence interval), a sample size will be calculated. It also will allow you to work backward—it will calculate your margin of error/confidence interval if you enter the population size, the sample that you obtained, and the confidence level and proportion found.

The importance of selecting the correct sample size can be seen by consulting the illustration below in Figure 8.1. Let's pretend that the 12 figures represent a population of college students. If we were to obtain a random sample that involved selecting a single figure, would that one figure be a good representation of the population? What if we enlarge our sample to two randomly selected individuals? (You can try this yourself by using a random number generator and requesting numbers between 1 and 12.) You may find that it will take you several tries to get a 50/50 split of men and women. And using a 95% level of confidence and 5% margin of error, you may find that the computer is telling you that your sample must be the same size as your population. You won't find this problem when the population is larger—say, in the hundreds.

FIGURE 8.1

A third approach to finding the right sample size is to manually calculate it using a formula. However, because of the convenience and easy availability of the Internet, most students prefer to *not* hand-calculate sample size.

Sample size will always be a concern if you are planning a probability sample; it is much less of a concern if you'll be using a sample of convenience. (More about this later.) Besides the margin of error and level of confidence considerations, *the researcher must also anticipate how many respondents might respond*. When the sample size needed is, say, 196 for a 5% margin of error and 95% confidence level, one cannot simply send or hand survey forms to 196 individuals and feel that you have reached the precision needed—especially if only 30% to 40% of the 196 take the time to respond. You may have to remind nonresponders and contact them on multiple occasions. This also means that you may have to initially begin with a larger sample so that you end up with 196.

The quantitatively oriented researcher must also give thought to analysis of the data—will there be subgroup analysis by gender, ethnicity, age group, and so forth? If the beginning sample is too small, then it may not produce a sufficient number of respondents in the subgroups for analysis. So, for the quantitatively minded, more subjects are almost always better.

ANXIETY CHECK 8.3

Imagine a scenario where an agency has 1,000 active clients, and you are asked to design a survey regarding their opinions about services. After consulting Table 8.1, you randomly select 250 clients to receive the survey. Have you now guaranteed that your survey results will provide a margin of error of ± 5% margin of error with 95% confidence?

[Answer at the end of the book.]

The View from the Qualitative Perspective

Thus far in the chapter, sampling from the qualitative perspective has not been discussed. It wasn't that you dozed off or missed it accidentally—it is just that qualitative researchers aren't nearly as concerned about sample size as the quantitatively oriented researchers. For qualitative investigators, sample size is a matter of judgment or intuition; there is not a set rule or pattern to which they must conform. Mark Mason (2010) conducted a study of PhD theses (usually called dissertations in the United States) conducted in Britain and Ireland that used qualitative interviews. He has reported that 80% of them had at least 15 participants, 49% had a range of 20 to 30 participants, and the median number was 28. However, these dissertation writers (most likely hoping to become faculty members and researchers) probably used larger qualitative samples than needed because they must be able to successfully defend their study's methodology before a faculty committee. And thus they may have had larger samples than the typical qualitative study "just to be on the safe side" (Mason, 2010, p. e-11). It is not unusual for qualitative studies to have fewer than 15 participants—some may have as few as 5 or 6.

For qualitative researchers, **saturation** is more important than any given sample size. Saturation is when the data begin to be repetitious, when the new data confirm existing findings, and when adding more data doesn't provide new insights, improved or better information than what you already have. To say this another way, data saturation means that others should be able to replicate the study's findings (Fusch & Ness, 2015). These authors speak to the question of how many interviews are enough and state, "There is no one-size-fits all method to reach data saturation ... If one has reached the point of no new data, one has also most likely reached the point of no new themes; therefore, one has reached data saturation" (Fusch & Ness, 2015, p. 1409).

Since in-depth interviewing is very labor intensive (and therefore expensive), small samples may yield sufficient information—especially if the participants are relatively similar. To make up for a small sample, qualitative interviewers may interview participants on multiple occasions. As Deborah Padgett (2008) notes, "The smaller the sample, the more intense and deep are the data being collected" (p. 56). Most qualitative researchers do not "play the numbers game" and would not concern themselves with confidence levels, margins of error, and probability samples.

One way to understand the difference in these two research orientations is to think about quantitatively oriented researchers focusing on *breadth* of data (for example, a wide exposure to people and their different experiences as represented in the larger population), while qualitatively oriented researchers are concerned about the *depth* of their data. Padgett (2008) says that the two views are represented in the expressions "a mile wide and an inch deep" and "an inch wide and a mile deep" (p. 56). Thus, researchers must make a decision about whether they would prefer to contact fewer individuals—but in greater depth—or to contact a larger number of people in less depth.

This is not to say that qualitative researchers care nothing at all about sample sizes; it is just that their approach is different. Instead of following the rule that "more research subjects is better," the qualitative researcher is more likely to sample until they aren't learning anything new about the problem or issue. When they begin to encounter redundancy in responses, then they know that their sample is large enough (saturation has been obtained). In other words, size of the sample doesn't matter. What's important is feeling that one has a good understanding of the issue at hand because of the responses obtained.

Some quantitative researchers view the qualitative approach to sampling as less rigorous because there is no ability to state margin of error and level of confidence, and they don't know how representative the sample is. However, it is not uncommon for even these researchers to occasionally conduct a mixed-method study with a small number of qualitative interviews.

My guess is that practicing social workers employ more qualitative and nonprobability designs than probability ones because these designs are generally cheaper, faster, and more easily conducted. Both qualitative and quantitative researchers make use of nonprobability sampling designs, which we'll discuss next.

Nonprobability Sampling Designs

Nonprobability sampling designs are often used when a master list of potential respondents doesn't exist or can't be constructed ahead of time. These designs *do not allow* the researcher to make a probability statement or to assert that each individual in the population had an equal chance of being chosen. Nonetheless, they can provide useful information about problems for social workers. Assume you are concerned about some issue—maybe it is the number of homeless women on the streets in your city—and it appears to you that the community leaders are ignoring this problem. You want to see if others agree with you, that it isn't your imagination, so you decide to poll 10 friends. That would be easier to do than randomly selecting a sample from the 50,000 registered voters in your town. Your nonprobability approach is called taking a **sample of convenience**.

When you draw a convenience sample, you do so because it is easy or quick, and you want *some* information—you're willing to settle for less than the best data to take the pulse or get a quick reading. But this type of sampling can be prone to error. Your friends, for example, knowing how strongly you feel about an issue such as the homeless may not be completely honest in telling you how they would vote. Furthermore, the reasons they are your friends (common interests and values; perhaps they are also social workers) will likely influence how they would vote. In other words, your 10 friends may not be representative of the other 49,990 voters in your town.

Accidental/Available/Convenience Samples

There is a good reason that samples of convenience are also known as **accidental** and **available samples**. I once watched different individuals approach a television camera crew for "person-in-the-street" interviews. What interested me was the number (perhaps the majority) of individuals who, seeing the camera, crossed to the other side of the street to avoid it. While the process of indiscriminately asking people for their opinions may seem random, there was actually a noticeable bias in those who constituted the sample. Did the individuals who wanted to be on camera represent the views of the community better than the shy ones? This cannot be determined in a sample of convenience. Unlike a random sample, which provides a cross-section of the whole community, the convenience sample involves "whomever" and may come with serious selection problems (due to self-selection or avoidance).

With nonprobability convenience samples, the consumer of the information is often left to figure out if the group of persons who were interviewed or surveyed is a fair representation of the larger population. What may appear to be a random process (for example, choosing every other shopper going into the grocery store) may, in fact, contain a bias due to the time of day and location of the store (e.g., upscale or inner-city neighborhood?).

ANXIETY CHECK 8.4

Here's the scenario: You stand outside of a supermarket to obtain a convenience sample of shoppers. On Friday, you arrive at 10:00 A.M. the second day, you begin interviewing at 11:30 P.M. The third day, you arrive a t 11:00 A.M. on Sunday. Using this strategy, what persons are likely to be in the majority of persons who are shopping then, who might you miss during scheduled times?

[Answer provided at the back of the book.]

If you were to skim a wide variety of professional journals, you would find that many surveys of college students are conducted each year. Why do you think that is? Could it have anything to do with the ease with which researchers might access them? And as a convenience sample, how well do college students represent the other adults in our population? Could they be younger, more educated, and more liberal in their views? Although college students may not be representative of the adult population, researchers may pilot-test with a convenience sample of students before committing to a larger-scale investigation.

Although some Asian Americans live in areas known by such names as Chinatown and Little Saigon, most do not. Because of their geographical dispersal, it is not easy to obtain a representative sample of Asian Americans by using random methodologies such as random-digit dialing. As a result, much of the research from this population has come from convenience samples. For instance, doctoral student Stephanie Rhee was interested in the acculturative stress and depressive symptoms among Korean immigrant elders who resided in non-Korean ethnic enclaves.

To obtain her sample, she began with a 2008 Korean directory of Cincinnati. She also found a Korean American Association of Kentuckiana (2009–2010) directory and then used whitepages.com to search for Korean surnames (e.g., Park, Kim, Pang) in the Lexington, Kentucky, area. She also contacted the pastors of Korean ethnic churches in Cincinnati, Columbus, and Louisville and employed snowball sampling in order to obtain her convenience sample of 111 participants (29% response rate from 382 questionnaires sent out). Twenty-one percent of the sample reported depressive symptoms.

Nonprobability sampling is often done when the extent of the population is not known or cannot be easily calculated.

Purposive Sampling

One type of nonprobability sampling is known as **purposive sampling** because the respondents had to have certain characteristics in common to be selected. For instance, you might wish to interview college students who are veterans, or those who have children under the age of six, or those who are working full-time jobs and enrolled in classes. Qualitative researcher Deborah Padgett has made this observation: "As a general rule, qualitative researchers use purposive sampling—a deliberate process of selecting respondents based on their ability to provide the needed information ... [It] is done for conceptual and theoretical reasons, not to represent a larger universe" (p. 53).

There are many types of purposive samples. Here is a selected listing of those to be discussed in this chapter:

- Extreme/deviant cases
- Maximum variation
- Homogeneous
- Typical case sampling
- Snowball sampling

A purposive sample where only **extreme or deviant cases** are examined would be appropriate when trying to understand a problem where answers are not immediately obvious. For example, why do *some* children remain a long time in foster care? In this instance, a representative sample of foster children isn't needed; the researcher might want to learn more about those children who have had, for instance, 10 or more foster home placements.

A variation of extreme case sampling would be to identify those cases or clients that are widely or vastly different. **Maximum variation sampling** might involve not only the children who were in foster care the longest, but also those who were in foster care the shortest period of time. This allows the qualitative research to look for themes or characteristics that distinguish the two groups, as well as those that might be shared in spite of the wide variation.

On the other end of the spectrum, in **homogeneous sampling**, the researcher looks for a particular characteristic. For instance, instead of interviewing all homeless persons, the researcher might be interested in collecting a series of interviews from those women who would be similar by being over the age of 50, originally from a rural area, and not having any history of substance abuse or mental illness.

Typical case sampling is just what it sounds like—the researcher chooses cases or clients to review or interview who are not remarkable; they are ordinary or thought to be similar to the "average" case or client. **Critical case sampling** involves cases or clients who have had a major incident such as those in outpatient treatment who attempted or committed suicide.

When one respondent leads you to another, and that one refers you to another, the approach is known as **snowball sampling**. Suppose as a school social worker you encounter a high school student who, for all practical purposes, is homeless. He stays first with this friend and then that one, sometimes sleeping in his car or in an abandoned building. When you talk with him, he indicates that he has several friends in the same predicament. If he leads you to them and they lead you to others, then you have created a snowball sampling design. This type of nonprobability sampling design grows by referrals to other potential responders. Remember, just because you don't know the respondents does not mean that you are selecting them randomly—you are not. They are all linked, in some way, to the small number of individuals you started your study with. This approach can be used when it is difficult to locate respondents by any other means.

ANXIETY CHECK 8.5

Would you expect a snowball sample to be more or less homogeneous than a random sample of individuals? Why or why not?

[Answer at the end of the book.]

Quota Samples

Quota sampling is an attempt to make sure that subgroups of a population are represented in a nonprobability design that specifies a number or percentage of respondents with a certain characteristic. Thus, if one had time enough to interview only 100 undergraduate college students, the sampling design might stipulate interviewing 25 First-Year Students, 25 Sophomores, 25 Juniors, and 25 Seniors. Although this approach may look like a stratified random sample, it is not. Quota samplers might take the first 25 sophomores they find in the student center or walking across campus. The resulting sample could be highly unrepresentative of the total population of sophomores because they were not drawn randomly from all of the enrolled sophomores. In quota samples, researchers have a great deal of freedom in finding respondents.

To take a different example, one could easily obtain a quota of 25 persons between 65 and 74 and 25 individuals over the age of 75 by going to the nearest nursing home or respite care center for senior citizens.

If the survey were to report later that all of those 65 and older were impaired in some way, that finding could be entirely true but not be representative of the population of persons 65 and older who lived on their own in the community. Quota samples are convenience samples with specifications regarding a certain number or proportion of respondents.

The problem with all nonprobability sampling designs is not knowing how representative the sample is or how closely it resembles the "true" population. Quantitatively oriented researchers and qualitatively oriented researchers view this issue somewhat differently. While the quantitative researcher tends to think of the non-probability sample as less rigorous because it is difficult for the investigator to know how well it estimates the attitudes or behaviors found within the larger population, the qualitative researcher views the nonprobability approach as a way to learn more detail about a problem or issue. The qualitative researcher is less concerned with generalization from any survey—more emphasis is placed on better understanding the problem or topic.

Dunlop, Dretler, Badal, and Logue (2013) used a quota sample in their study of mothers in a WIC program. You may want to see how they presented their survey findings.

Bias and Errors in Surveys

Whether you are planning a probability or a nonprobability sampling design, be alert to any limitations that could result in your sampling frame being less inclusive than you had planned. Be particularly alert to **sample selection bias** that could occur because of the order or organization in which the sample units are presented. For instance, a list of students' names from the university registrar might come already arrayed by hours completed or by GPA. It might contain residential students only. If you were to select the first 100 names on such a list, it is likely that you would not have a full representation of all the students at the university. In other words, you could have a biased sample. One always must be alert for incomplete listings (for example, part-time students or graduate students might not be in the listing provided by the registrar unless you were clear about what students the sample frame should contain).

Another possible problem occurs when respondents self-select. Ideally, every person asked to complete an interview or survey form would comply. People make decisions based on how much time they have, the topic, what their children or pets are doing, and the presentation made by the interviewer. Many people don't want to be stopped on the street and interviewed, even if it is presumably for a reputable organization because they fear there is some catch such as being asked to donate money.

Other factors that can affect your samples (and ultimately the findings of your surveys) include:

- **Interviewer bias**—An often unconscious bias that leads individuals to approach people like themselves, to avoid those they fear or dislike, and to attribute positive or negative attributes based on such traits as gender, race, or age—is a serious concern when interviewers and telephone callers have few guidelines regarding whom to include or exclude for a survey.
- **Interviewer error**—To minimize mistakes, inconsistencies, and interviewer bias when interviews are being employed, one needs to train interviewers to prevent careless errors in the field or in the recording of responses. Sometimes, with telephone surveys, a small portion of respondents are contacted again to validate their answers. Knowing this might help to keep the interviewers more honest and accurate. Of course, that shouldn't be a problem, but a sociologist once told me that as a student, he sat in a coffee shop and made up information for a community directory when he should have been going door-to-door to obtain the data.

- **Respondent error**—Clients of an agency may distort their satisfaction with agency services because they might fear losing the services they currently have. They may also not respond honestly out of concern about being recognized.
- **Instrument error**—Questionnaires that are difficult to read or comprehend can result in flawed, unreliable data. Instruments that look like they will take a long time to complete will produce samples that may have fewer respondents and a lower response rate. Also, persons with lower levels of education may be less likely to complete complicated mailed surveys than persons with higher levels of education. As mentioned in the last chapter, the sequence and order of questions can also affect responses.

For the quantitatively oriented researcher, a low **response rate** is just as problematic as too small a sample. If less than a majority of the respondents reply (for example, 40%), you are left wondering about the attitudes or characteristics of the 60% who chose not to respond. Might a different set of findings emerge if the response rate was 80%? There is no way of knowing. A very low response rate (such as 20%) brings to mind the old story of three blind men who encounter an elephant for the first time. One fellow standing beside a massive leg says, "An elephant is like a tree trunk."

"No," the second one says, feeling the elephant's trunk, "it is more like a boa constrictor."

The third man touches the elephant's tail and says, "It has a tail like a pig."

Low response rates don't allow you to get the whole picture—you may hear from the most satisfied or the most dissatisfied clients, the most compulsive or educated, but you can't be sure of what you've got until you have a majority of the responses. The more you have, the better you can understand your "elephant."

Whenever you conduct a survey, allow sufficient time to follow up on nonrespondents. Sending reminder postcards and mailing second and third questionnaires to nonrespondents greatly increases response rates. In telephone and face-to-face interviewing, unless you follow up on those who are not home when you call, you run the risk of having a bias against those who work during the hours that you attempt to reach them.

BOX 8.3   PRACTICE NOTE: RATES OF SEXUAL MINORITY WOMEN (SMW)

As we've discussed, nonprobablility sampling does not provide the accuracy of probability sampling. However, at times, probability sampling is almost impossible to achieve. For a good applied example of how researchers in health care have tackled a difficult, but real, issue, read the article "Comparing Sexual Minority Status Across Sampling Methods and Populations" by D. J. Bowen, J. Bradford, and D. Powers in *Women & Health* (2006), *44*(2), pp. 121–134. The authors point out that few probability samples have been conducted with sexual minority women (lesbians, bisexuals and transgendered women). The studies that have been conducted show so much variability in the data as to make them difficult to interpret. For instance, mammography screening rates among these women have been reported to vary from 40% to 70%, depending on the study. Do these women have higher health risks than heterosexual women? To answer the question, researchers need to find a way of identifying the population.

In this article, the authors provide the results of four different surveys designed to better understand how different sampling strategies provide different estimates of the SMW population.

Key Terms

observations (sampling units)	sample
probability samples	population
cross-sectional survey design	sampling frame
simple random sampling design	systematic sampling
sampling ratio	strata
stratified random sampling	one-stage cluster sampling
cluster sampling design	two-stage cluster sampling
multistage cluster sampling design	confidence level
margin of error	sample of convenience
nonprobability sampling design	maximum variation sampling
purposive sampling	snowball sampling
accidental and available samples	saturation
quota sampling	sample selection bias
response rate	interviewer bias
interviewer error	respondent error
instrument error	homogeneous sampling
typical case sampling	critical case sampling
extreme or deviant cases	

SELF-REVIEW

(Answers are at the end of the book.)

1. T or F. Sampling is based on the concept that a much smaller randomly selected group can yield approximately the same findings as one would obtain with interviewing every person in that population.

2. _____ surveys are not noted for their generalizability.

3. _____ is the list of every person or unit eligible to be contacted in a survey.

4. T or F. Systematic random sampling is recognized by the ratio of the sample to the population—as in contacting every fourth client.

5. If you were implementing a probability sampling design and wanted to make sure that the exact proportions of BSWs, MSWs, and PhD social workers were represented in the sample, the type of design would be_____.

6. T or F. Margin of error and confidence interval are independent. One could select, for example, a 90% confidence level and a 3% margin of error.

7. T or F. The relation of sample size to population is this: generally, greater accuracy requires larger samples.
8. T or F. Sample size is more of a consideration with samples of convenience than with probability surveys.
9. Other terms for convenience samples are _____ and _____ samples.
10. T or F. A quota sample is a type of probability sampling.
11. T or F. Once one has a randomly selected sample of about 385 persons, that sample can adequately represent a population of 100,000 or 1 million—assuming a 95% level of confidence, a 5% margin of error, and a 50/50 split in response proportions.
12. The type of sampling where one respondent leads the researcher to another possible participant is called _____ sampling.
13. _____ bias is the tendency of an interviewer to shy away from people who do not resemble the interviewer.
14. T or F. When it comes to sample size, both qualitative and quantitative researchers take the position that "more is better."
15. William is drawing a random sample of 100 from a population of 850 clients. What is the first random number he will begin with, and how does he choose it?

QUESTIONS FOR CLASS DISCUSSION

1. You want to conduct a national survey of social workers. What are three ways in which you might stratify the sample? Why might you want to stratify the sample?
2. Give an example of a topic that could best be explored with the following:
   a. snowball sampling
   b. cluster sampling
   c. a stratified random design
3. Your agency has asked you to conduct a random sampling of clients to determine how satisfied they are with the agency's services. After some discussion, it is decided that a telephone survey is the most sensible approach. If the agency closed approximately 3,000 cases last year, how big a sample would be needed to have 95% confidence in the findings, plus or minus 5%? If the agency decides to use a mail approach, how many persons would you have to contact to get the same level of confidence and accuracy? (Keep in mind that about 30% of the respondents in a mail survey respond on the first mailing.)
4. Let's pretend that *Money* magazine prints a questionnaire in a recent issue mailed to subscribers. One of the questions asked is "What do you think about most—money or sex?" Can the findings from this study be considered to represent the thinking of most American adults? What bias is suggested from this survey approach? If you wanted to investigate that question, what would be a better way to do it?
5. Several years ago, a book was published where the author distributed approximately 100,000 questionnaires through women's organizations and got back approximately 3%. Further, she instructed respondents that they didn't have to answer every single question but only those that interested

them. And the author didn't standardize her questionnaire, but used multiple versions. Could she claim a representative sample? Did her methodology deserve criticism?

6. Nelson Flake constructs a sample of students: 200 African American, 200 Hispanic, 200 Asian American, and 200 white students at a large state university. What type of sample design is this? After Nelson Flake conducts his study, can he generalize his findings to all college students in America? Why or why not?

7. IDEA FOR SMALL GROUP PROJECTS: Divide the class into small groups. The task is to estimate the number of homeless within the state. Each group should consider a methodology which would attempt to provide representative data and solid information for service providers about the numbers of the homeless population. Each group will have a budget of about $40,000 and three months to gather data and write the report.

RESOURCES AND REFERENCES

Dillman, D. A., Smyth, J. D., & Christian, L. M. (2014). *Internet, phone, mail, and mixed mode surveys*: The *tailored design method*. New York, NY: Wiley.

Dunlop, A. L., Dretler, A. W., Badal, H. J., & Logue, K. M. (2013). Acceptability and potential impact of brief preconception health risk assessment and counseling in the WIC setting. *American Journal of Health Promotion, 27*(3), S58–65.

Fusch, P. I., & Ness, L. R. (2015). Are we there yet? Data saturation in qualitative research. *Qualitative Report, 20*(9), 1408–1416.

Mason, M. (2010). Sample size and saturation in PhD studies using qualitative interviews. *Forum: Qualitative Social Research, 11*(3), e1–14.

Padgett, D. K. (2008). *Qualitative methods in social work research*. Thousand Oaks, CA: Sage.

Rhee, S. (2013). Acculturative stress and depressive symptoms among Korean immigrant elders residing in non-Korean ethnic enclaves. (Unpublished doctoral dissertation.) Lexington, KY: University of Kentucky, Lexington.

Scharff, D. P., Mathews, K. J., Jackson, P., Hoffsuemmer, J., Martin, E., & Edwards, D. (2010). More than Tuskegee: Understanding mistrust about research participation. *Journal of Health Care for the Poor and Underserved, 21*, 879–897.

Credits

ASSIGNMENT 8.1

Locating and Critically Reading a Survey Study

Objective: *To be able to identify studies involving surveys and to be able discuss the strengths and weaknesses of survey efforts.*

For this assignment, you should browse one of the social work journals and locate a research article where the methodology involves the use of a survey. Print a copy of the article and attach it to your responses on this page.

1. Give the full APA citation of the article that you read.

2. Was a probability or nonprobability sampling design employed? Was a margin of error reported? What was it? Give the more specific name for the sampling design.

3. What was the sample size?

4. Does the sample appear to be adequate? Does its size and construction give you a sense of confidence in the study's findings? Explain.

5. Did the author devise a questionnaire or scale just for this study, or did he or she use one already developed?

6. List three major findings of the study.

ASSIGNMENT 8.2

Creating a Random Sample

Objective: *To obtain practice in producing random numbers and creating a random sample.*

Assume that you are a social worker in an agency that closed 750 cases last year. Your supervisor asks you to draw a random sample of 50 clients for a utilization chart review that she wants done.

Go to the website **www.random.org** for a random number generator. Enter the highest and lowest numbers that will be in the sample (for example, 1 and 750). Then, answer the following questions:

1. How do you go about selecting a sample of 50 from the list produced? List the steps that you would need to take.

2. Would you get a random sample if you chose the first 25 numbers (1 to 25) and the last 25 (725–726) to form your sample?

3. If you asked for a second set of 50 random numbers from the random number generator, would you expect to get the same numbers a second time? Why or why not? Would something be wrong with the generator if you got one or two of the same numbers both times?

4. If you wanted to do a systematic random sample by taking every fifth client from the pool of 750, how many clients would be in your sample? And what would be your first three steps in drawing the sample?

ASSIGNMENT 8.3

Agency Surveys

Objective: *To be able to identify studies involving surveys and to be able discuss the strengths and weaknesses of survey efforts.*

1. If you are interning in an agency, see if you can find any reports or studies the agency has conducted that involved a survey. These may involve client satisfaction or feedback studies, community needs assessments, etc. Alternatively, you may want to see what surveys have been conducted by your local city government or by some agency where you might want to intern or be employed someday.

2. Describe the context of the survey: a) when it was conducted; b) who conducted the survey; c) what survey methodology was used; d) whether it was a probability or nonprobability design; and e) how large the sample was.

3. Critique the methodology used. Does the sample size seem large enough? Are there any obvious sources of bias or limitations to what was learned? What would you have done differently if you had been conducting the survey?

CHAPTER 9

Survey Research Methods

I F THE TOPIC of experimental design in an earlier chapter seemed foreign to you, survey research should be more familiar. We hear or read about the results of surveys almost every day. Social work literature abounds with surveys, and they are frequently conducted and used by social workers. Surveys have been conducted to explore such issues as job burnout, values and ethical dilemmas, client satisfaction with services, and the African American community's image of the social work profession. Pick up any social work journal, and you are likely to find some type of survey. Surveys have been called "the single most important information gathering invention of the social sciences" (Adams, Smelser, & Treiman, 1982), and it is essential that social workers—both as consumers and producers of research—understand them well.

Surveys (sometimes called **polls**) can be thought of as snapshots of attitudes, beliefs, or behaviors at one point in time. Using a predetermined set of questions or issues, surveys reveal what a group of respondents is thinking, feeling, or doing. Social workers might use surveys to uncover particular needs within their communities or within groups of clients. To put this into a practice context, social workers use surveys of clients to learn what they think of the services they have received and to learn what the community knows about the services that are available. Specialized surveys, called **needs assessments**, might try to determine the prenatal care needs of low-income clients, understand transportation barriers, or help agencies plan how to improve services. These surveys provide information about what the targeted population knows or perceives about the acceptability, availability and/or accessibility of services and can also identify unmet needs or gaps in services. Needs assessments may consist of prepared questionnaires or personal interviews and may solicit information from clients, their caseworkers, other professionals such as parole officers or physicians, or citizens randomly selected from the community. Even physicians and other professionals may not know about new programs available in the community.

Social service agencies can also use these surveys internally to identify areas where staff members feel they need additional training or continuing education. Following a situation where a client fought with another family member in the agency, the administration might conduct a needs assessment of staff to identify ideas about how to provide greater security. In short, there are many social work practice applications for surveys.

Types of Needs Assessment

Needs assessments may involve surveys of **key informants**—individuals in the community who are likely to know about special needs as a result of their positions. They may be principals and guidance counselors, social service providers, clergy, public officials, and so on.

Another type of needs assessment involves **community forums**—public meetings or hearings where members of a community state their preferences or present their concerns. These meetings can be poorly attended or, when hot topics are involved, loud and boisterous. For the most part, clients typically seen by social workers seldom attend such meetings. A conceptual weakness with this approach is that those who attend and express their views may not be representative of the community or familiar with resources available or evidence-based approaches to the problem.

Possibly the most popular form of needs assessment involves some sort of **community survey**. These surveys can range from those hastily conceived and executed to those carefully prepared, providing researchers with a good deal of confidence in the findings. Surveys of clients are also quite common and often conducted in conjunction with program evaluation efforts. In short, there are many, many uses for surveys.

The Appeal of Surveys

Surveys are rooted in the grassroots process of asking people their opinions. We all like to be asked for our input. Surveys invite participation. Designing a questionnaire can be great fun, almost like a game. If a committee is designing a survey, practically everyone can contribute, either by suggesting items or by pointing out ways specific items could be improved. Other reasons for the popularity of surveys are that they are quickly implemented and convenient to administer. Once the survey instrument has been designed and a sampling plan is in place, the survey can often be handled by an office worker—freeing the researcher to attend to other matters until a sufficient number of survey questionnaires have come in for analysis. Sometimes, the investigator coordinates the collection of data from personal or telephone interviews. Each of these approaches has its own set of advantages and disadvantages that we'll discuss in the chapter.

Types of Surveys

Surveys come in many different varieties. It is common in social work literature for authors to note that they have conducted an **exploratory survey**. These surveys are generally recognized by their small samples. Exploratory, or pilot, studies are sometimes conducted prior to applying for federal grant dollars, and they allow investigators to gather initial data to form hypotheses or to develop and test interventions and instruments on a small scale. Because science is built by incremental steps, exploratory surveys are legitimate, even though the knowledge they produce is often limited.

When investigators are ready to test hypotheses, they must increase their sample sizes and address the problems of acquiring representative samples. An exploratory survey of teens dropping out of high school may consist only of 20 or fewer individuals.

A **descriptive survey** can be based on a very large sample. For instance, Taylor and Mumford (2016) have reported on adolescent relationship abuse with national data among over 1,800 adolescents aged 12 to 18. To give another example, a descriptive survey of the homeless in Ohio might involve having every shelter in the state collect data on a given night during a winter month in order to estimate the number of individuals sheltered statewide. Descriptive surveys often have a focus on the characteristics of a given group but generally do not try to explain phenomena like why individuals are homeless and living in shelters.

ANXIETY CHECK 9.1

How accurate do you think a census of homeless persons would be using the methodology that involved only counting those persons residing in a shelter on a specified night during a winter month? What part of the homeless population might not be included?

[Answer at the end of the book.]

During their weekly meeting, Mrs. Simpson asked Bill and Sophia to pull together a survey that they could use to obtain feedback from social workers in prisons for women. She wanted the students to ask what the other prisons were doing in the way of HIV prevention programming for their inmates close to release, what resources they knew about along that line, and what the other social workers would want if they were adopting a new program for their prison.

Bill's eyes grew wide as he began to imagine all of the work that the survey could entail. Sophia saw his concern and said, "This week in class we'll be discussing different modalities for conducting surveys. Do you have a particular preference, Mrs. Simpson?"

"Hmmm," she said. "I don't think so. Might not get a great response rate with a mail survey—they tend to be so busy. Personal interviews are problematic because of the cost of traveling. So, either a phone survey or electronic, e-mail one might be best."

"You're not thinking about a national survey, are you?" Bill asked.

"Heavens no, Bill. I think you two should just try to contact 10 to 12 other prisons. We'll see if we discover anything new, anything we can use for the program we're planning," Mrs. Simpson said. "Don't worry, I know you two have a lot to do. I just want to make sure that we aren't too insular in our focus."

As Bill looked confused, Sophia clarified things for both of them. "You mean in our planning, we shouldn't assume that the program we create will fit every setting because we know everything that's important to know and our resident population is just like those women in every other prison?"

"Right," said Mrs. Simpson. "We want to incorporate ideas from other professionals—as well as from our residents."

"Makes perfect sense," said Bill. I'll get on the Internet and begin looking for a list of the prisons for women."

MODALITIES FOR SURVEYS

- US Postal Service (Mail)
- E-mail
- Telephone
- Personal interview

Each of these approaches has both strengths and weaknesses. No single approach will work in every circumstance. Because of the changes in society brought about by widespread use of computers and smartphones, there is now no one mode of surveying that dominates or is more important than the others (Stern, Bilgen, & Dillman, 2014). In fact, one of the most recognizable names in survey research, Don Dillman, now advocates the use of "mixed-mode surveys" (Dillman, Smyth, & Christian, 2014). That approach will be discussed after we review each of the other modes in turn. First, though, we need to have a good understanding of response rate and what it tells us about our surveys.

The Response Rate

The number of persons who respond to a survey by completing a questionnaire or personal interview divided by the total number of persons contacted creates the **response rate**. If Bill was planning a party to celebrate the end of the fall semester and e-mailed an invitation to 60 of his classmates and received a 50% response rate, that would mean that 30 of his friends indicated they would be attending. A 10% response rate would suggest only 6 of his classmates planned to attend.

There are definitely challenges to obtaining high response rates in the social sciences. Keeter, Christian, Dimock, and Gewurz (2012) report that with fewer landlines and more available technologies to screen unknown callers, response rates in telephone surveys have declined from 28% in 2000 to 9% in 2012.

However, Dillman, Smyth, and Christian (2014) indicate that carefully planned mail surveys can achieve response rates of 50% or more. In five studies where a mail questionnaire was sent first, the response rate from the paper survey ranged from 49% to 70%. In four surveys where only mail questionnaires were employed, response rates ranged from 38% to 68%. When Web questionnaires were sent first in the five studies, the response rates from those who responded back via the Web ranged from 8% to 41% (pp. 429–431). Other research shows that when respondents are given a choice of answering by mail or another mode, "they most commonly choose mail, at least when the paper questionnaire is included in the mailing" (p. 351).

The Mail Questionnaire

There are numerous *advantages* to the mail questionnaire: (1) relatively inexpensive compared to telephone and personal interviews (but more expensive than Internet approaches); (2) large numbers of respondents can be surveyed in a relatively short period; (3) respondents can look up information if they need to; (4) privacy is maximized; (5) visual presentation of items can be used; (6) can be completed when convenient for the respondent; (7) respondents can see the context of a series of questions; (8) insulates respondents from the expectations of the researcher.

A final advantage of the mail questionnaire is that it reduces errors that might occur in the process of interviewing. Not all interviewers are equally skilled, and some may have traits that annoy, offend, or cause those being interviewed to be less than honest.

On the other hand, there are a number of specific *disadvantages* to the mail questionnaire. First, unlike with personal or telephone interviews, researchers experience some loss of control over the survey process once the questionnaire is mailed. Although the questionnaire may be delivered to the proper address, there is no guarantee that the intended recipient will be the one who completes the questionnaire. An 11-year-old child could respond for his or her mother or father, even though the researcher intended the survey to be completed by adults. A related problem is that the survey could be attempted under less-than-optimal conditions (for example, when the respondent is ill or intoxicated, or when the television is blaring or a party is going on in the next room).

Second, investigators cannot assume that all recipients of the survey will be literate or familiar with survey approaches. While college students are accustomed to questionnaires and multiple-choice response sets, individuals with lower levels of educational attainment may perceive structured response sets (such as *Strongly Agree, Agree, Undecided, Disagree, Strongly Disagree*) as irrelevant or too confining for the responses they want to give. A potential response bias exists if questionnaires are mailed to individuals who lack good reading skills. In such a situation, it would be likely that those who couldn't read wouldn't respond. Further, some client groups are frequent movers who don't always leave forwarding addresses or don't have addresses at all (e.g., the homeless).

Third, mail questionnaires tend to be tightly arranged and relatively short. These questionnaires may not provide the detail that could emerge from face-to-face contact. In personal interview situations, the interviewer is able to ask for additional information (to **probe**) if the respondent says something exceptionally interesting, or if the interviewer is not sure of the response or thinks the respondent did not understand the question. It is difficult to probe in mail surveys. Even if asked to explain a response, participants usually don't like to write long comments. And in mail surveys, respondents tend to skip or not complete items they don't understand or want to provide information on—so the nonresponse to specific items can be higher than in other approaches (Stern, Bilgen, & Dillman, 2014).

Fourth, it usually takes longer to gather data from this approach, as one might allow two weeks initially for responses to be obtained and then another possible two weeks if a second reminder or questionnaire is sent to nonresponders.

Mail questionnaires have become a popular gimmick with some businesses. (An official-looking survey form may arrive asking for information about how much you travel or take vacations, but its real purpose is to sell real estate or vacation time-sharing plans). Consequently, some Americans see surveys as a form of solicitation or junk mail. Even if a survey form arrives in an envelope carrying first-class postage, it can be experienced as an invasion of privacy and thrown away. Even individuals with good intentions can put the survey form aside until "later," with the result that questionnaires get lost, thrown out, or recycled.

Another problem is that Americans are a highly mobile population and are constantly changing addresses, last names, and places of employment. Your survey will be seriously disadvantaged if your mailing list is inaccurate or out of date. Take the time to ensure that the mailing list is current and as accurate as possible.

All these factors have a direct effect on the number of people who complete and return survey questionnaires. Commonly, only 25% to 35% of those who are mailed a questionnaire return it. The response rates for mail surveys are often as low as 5% to 10%, and response rates around 25% to 30% are common. Of course, if your addresses are recent and the topic is one that interests the respondents, response rates will improve. Rates are lower for those who receive one mailing. However, with a reminder postcard and the mailing of a second questionnaire to those who did not initially respond, these rates can be improved quite a bit—up to 50% or more. This is discussed in the next section. But first, what are the problems created when there is a low response rate?

- Less precision
- Potential bias
- A less credible study overall

Does it make sense that a low response rate is sometimes known as a **non-response error**?

Getting a Good Response Rate

Designing a mail questionnaire is not as simple as it may first appear. Extensive research exists on all aspects of the mail survey. (It is known, for instance, that using first-class postage results in better response rates than meter or bulk-rate mail). Similarly, increasing the personalization of each letter with handwritten addresses, personalized notes, and real signatures may improve the response rate. Other successful tactics include prenotifying the potential participants that they will be asked to participate in a survey, having a university or "official" sponsorship, and sending reminder postcards or making phone call follow-ups to those who have forgotten to return their surveys.

Dillman, Smyth, and Christian (2014) have outlined a view of survey design they call the Tailored Design Method. They suggest that the questionnaires must build positive social exchange and minimize cost to the responder (for example, by being short and not requiring too much time). They also recommend that a recognizable sponsor be obtained (e.g., a university, agency, or prominent organization), that a small token of appreciation might be provided in advance, that the importance of the task be made clear, and that respondents know that their confidentiality will be protected. Without going into a lot of detail, Dillman and colleagues say that every part of the survey's procedures must be examined. That means that cover letters ask for the respondent's help or advice, that questionnaires are visually attractive and not overly lengthy, and that the most interesting questions appear first. The whole questionnaire should be designed so that lowercase letters are used for all questions/items and uppercase letters for the response categories. Visual clues (arrows, indentations, and spacing) are used to their fullest advantage to help respondents answer in a straight vertical line rather than going back and forth across the page to indicate a response.

Incentives are sometimes necessary to increase response rates. The good news, however, is that ballpoint pens, key rings, phone cards, refrigerator magnets, bookmarks—and yes, even teabags—mailed with the questionnaire and even monetary inducements don't have to be very expensive. Wilk (1993) reports a systematic random survey of 400 names chosen from the NASW *Register of Clinical Social Workers* and found that a $1 incentive improved her response rate from 43% to 63%. Millar and Dillman (2011) found that a $2 bill sent in a letter to undergraduates requesting a response on the Internet improved the response rate from 21% to 38% compared to a letter with no incentive or an e-mail.

Interested in increasing participation in online research, Busby and Yoshida (2015) conducted an experiment and provided either a $20 incentive or one chance in a $100 lottery for either every 50 participants, 100 participants, 200, or 300 participants. They found that the $100 lottery for every 50 participants resulted in a 14% response rate, while the $20 incentive produced an 8.7% response rate. However, note that the average response rate in the four lottery incentive groups was slightly over 10 percent—clearly the incentive to participate wasn't all that strong!

Gendall and Healey (2008) report that postage stamps as an incentive yielded better results with people 55 and older, while chocolate squares worked better with those under 35. Garner (2005) even observes that in four American surveys, a handwritten Post-It® resulted in a 20% to 40% increase in response rates. Clearly, the use of incentives should be thoughtfully tailored to the group being surveyed. Remember, respondents don't *have* to cooperate; each one who does so is doing you a favor!

No matter which approach you select to conduct your survey, it is important to **pilot-test** (pretest) your procedures and instrument. Generally, pilot-testing is informal and can involve giving the survey instrument to a few friends or coworkers to see if they understand the questions and respond in the ways you anticipate. Even better, administer the survey instrument to a group of persons as similar as possible to the population that you will be surveying. The major purpose of the pilot test is to determine if the type of information you want is supplied by the respondents. Pilot-testing need not involve more than 20 persons if the respondents have no problems understanding the questions or recording their responses. Pilot-testing also provides estimates of the time required for completing the questionnaire and, in the case of telephone and face-to-face interviews, provides useful data for estimating the cost of the survey.

When designing a survey questionnaire, follow these steps:

- Make it interesting and easy to read, visually attractive, and professional looking.
- Keep the questionnaire as short as possible (response rates and length of questionnaires are inversely related).
- Pilot-test it to make sure the questions provide you with the information you seek.

Also, plan on sending at least one reminder letter and questionnaire to all nonrespondents. You may want to include a toll-free number for respondents to use if they have questions about the survey, how they were selected, that sort of thing. Some institutional review boards require that researchers routinely provide such a phone number for potential respondents to inquire about their rights as research subjects. (Clients of an agency, for instance, might worry that they could be in jeopardy of losing their services if they refuse to participate.)

Unless a new scale is being developed, designers of surveys don't often worry about calculating the internal consistency of their questionnaires. But they do worry about response rates because response rates are good indicators of how much faith can be put in the resulting data. With less than 50% responding, you have to estimate the size of the iceberg based on what you see sticking above the water rather than what's below.

ANXIETY CHECK 9.3

Why might the use of Post-It notes improve a survey's response rate? Explain.

[Answer at the back of the book.]

E-Mail and Web-Based Surveys

The popularity of the Internet and e-mail have made it possible for researchers to gather information at much less cost than mailed surveys and with less obtrusiveness than a telephone call or personal interview. Researchers have the option of sending out surveys attached to e-mails—if there is a way to obtain possible participants' contact information. Software companies such as SurveyMonkey.com and Qualtrics keep the electronic returns from cluttering up the researcher's inbox one at a time and respondents can remain anonymous. (Lack of anonymity to an e-mailed survey may affect response rates.) The commercial survey sites are secure and, unlike completed paper surveys that could sit around on someone's desk and possibly be read by an unauthorized person, only those people with the correct password are allowed to view the responses collected on the commercial software sites.

Online survey software makes it easy for the researcher to create questionnaires without needing to have a high level of computer skills. Those being surveyed can be directed to an electronic link or Web page from either electronic or printed media. Advantages are that there are no bulky envelopes or return postage to deal with, electronic questions can be presented one question at a time, and respondents can be automatically directed to different sections of the questionnaire, depending on their responses, or gender or age. Unlike a telephone interview, the software can present a range of possible responses from drop-down boxes that can be viewed. In contrast to mailed questionnaires, respondents cannot see how long or lengthy an online questionnaire is. This may work to the advantage of the researcher if the questionnaire is long, but on the other hand, some respondents may be hesitant to open an attachment or begin responding to an electronic survey if the researcher or host site is not known to them because they may fear acquiring a virus.

Although computers are standard equipment at most places of business, they are not found in every home across the country. The US Census estimated in 2013 that 78.5% of all US households own a desktop or laptop computer and 74% have Internet capability (File & Ryan, 2014). Thus, the generalizability of findings from Web-based surveys may be problematic if one is attempting to reach individuals who have lower levels of computer ownership. However, there is much less of a problem if the population to be sampled can be assumed to have easy access to computers (for example, university students). In fact, Parks, Pardi, and Bradizza (2006) surveyed 700 freshmen women at a large university in New York State on their alcohol use and the negative consequences of alcohol use. They found that 60% of those contacted by e-mail completed their survey, but only 45.7% of those contacted by telephone completed it. In addition, the costs for the telephone interviewer approach were more than six times higher ($26.19) per completed participant than the Web survey ($4.23).

These are the advantages of electronic mail surveys: (1) speed of delivery; (2) minimal cost; (3) greater control over who may read the e-mail; (4) convenience of sending and receiving responses; (5) ability to reach large numbers of people through e-mail blasts, social media, and blogs for recruitment; (6) ability to present graphic and other material visually.

Depending upon the type of information that you want to obtain, you may find that e-mail respondents write more comments than mail respondents and that the best response rate is obtained when you mail an invitation letter along with a small incentive.

Sending out long, unsolicited e-mail surveys may result in complaints from those who view them as spam. Given the higher response rates that can be obtained by using prenotification of the impending survey, it makes good sense to give potential respondents some information about the questionnaire (such as the topic, the number of items, how long it might take to complete it, and, if possible, the benefit or value of the study). Electronic surveys work best when the populations to be surveyed are discrete and easily identified (for example, university students, government office workers) and individuals are proficient on computers.

Busby and Yoshida (2015) found 45% of those contacted did not have a deliverable e-mail address. However, their participants came from individuals who completed an online survey called RELATE one to two years earlier. Did some of these individuals give false e-mail addresses to keep from being contacted? Or did a large proportion of them change their e-mail addresses? It is hard to know. (But wouldn't that make an interesting research question?) At any rate, it may be important to check or verify contact information before launching an electronic survey. One disadvantage of electronic surveys is that there is no way to obtain e-mail addresses for the general population.

The Telephone Survey

More expensive than mail and e-mail surveys—but less expensive than face-to-face interviews—is the telephone survey. Telephone surveys avoid the expenses associated with traveling to the respondent; they allow the interviewer to have control over the choice of respondent and give the interviewer the ability to probe when questions or responses are not understood.

Telephone surveys also allow interviewers access to individuals who will not open their doors to strangers and those who are not ambulatory. Another advantage is that when timeliness is important, special issues can be explored and data gathered almost overnight. A final advantage is that telephone interviewers can be closely monitored (either by a supervisor listening in or by a second interviewer calling and double-checking a respondent's information.) Telephone interviewers must ask questions correctly and code responses satisfactorily or they may get additional training or be fired.

A disadvantage of the telephone survey is that the interviewer cannot see the respondent. This means that some items such as the person's race or the condition of the house cannot be observed. When the phone is used, the interviewer misses facial expressions, which can indicate a participant's confusion or the beginning of an emotion like anger or sadness. Not everyone can be a successful telephone interviewer; he or she must be articulate, personable, and a good conversationalist. The quality of the interviewer's voice is also important. An interviewer must quickly establish rapport and enthusiastically interest the potential respondent in cooperating before the respondent loses interest. If open-ended questions are used, the interviewer must be able to record the responses speedily and accurately.

Another disadvantage of telephone surveys is that they must be kept short. Telephone interviews should be under 20 minutes, and the shorter the better. There are exceptions—much longer surveys have been successfully completed by phone, but respondent fatigue can cause hang-ups and incompletions. As a general rule, the more interesting the topic is for the respondent, the greater the probability that the respondent will complete the interview, even if it is lengthy.

Some believe that interviewing by telephone is unacceptable because of built-in bias associated with the inability to interview persons who do not have telephones. While it is true that telephone surveys will underrepresent the poorest of the poor, it is now estimated that 96% of Americans own cellphones (**https://www.pewinternet.org/fact-sheet/mobile/**).

Except when the most economically disadvantaged are being targeted, telephone surveys are generally thought to be adequate and representative of "most" Americans. However, professional market survey and polling organizations do not simply accept the responses of just anyone who answers the phone; rather, they often go to great lengths to find individuals who fit a specific category (for example, African American males who vote Republican). They may reject some households that represent categories in which they already have too many respondents (for example, white females over 65) in their quest to make their samples representative of the larger population.

Although it might seem like a good way to obtain a sample, the use of a telephone directory to produce a sample frame for surveys creates biased data. First of all, wireless phones aren't included. And many people do not want their landline numbers listed—police officers, celebrities, single and divorced women, mental health professionals, and public officials often do not have listed numbers. And the number of unlisted phones varies markedly by geographical area. To compensate for unlisted numbers, most large-scale telephone surveys use **random-digit** or **added-digit dialing procedures**. With random-digit dialing, the researcher intentionally selects the first three digits for the desired local exchanges, and a computer randomly generates the last four digits. In added-digit dialing, a legitimate "seed number" is provided for those local exchanges from which the samples are to be drawn, and then consecutive digits are added to the last digit or to the last two or three digits. While these procedures result in some phone calls to businesses or others who are not target respondents, it provides a good way of accessing households with unlisted numbers and thus getting a representative sample of all households with phones.

Another issue is that individuals who move from another state may choose to keep numbers after their move. Further, the government prohibits automatic or robocall random-digit dialing of cell phone numbers. Researchers must manually dial cell phones, and that makes it much more expensive and time consuming than when surveying families with landlines. Surveys of cell phone owners often produce a younger respondent pool than surveys of landline owners—which suggests the importance of trying to access respondents from each age group.

The use of computers in telephone solicitation in what is called **interactive voice response (IVR)** has resulted in what many Americans regard as "nuisance" calls. As a defensive measure, households often have resorted to screening their calls with voice mail—making it more difficult for legitimate researchers to conduct their telephone surveys.

Getting the Most from Telephone Surveys

Interviewers need to be trained in the conduct of the survey. This training should include role-play and practice interviewing other trainees to ensure that the purpose of each question is well understood. All interviewers should be given standardized introductory statements that move quickly to the survey questions. A brief introduction might go something like this:

> Hello. My name is _____. I'm calling from Friendly University's Survey Research Center. We're conducting a survey this month of people randomly selected from across the state. The survey will take 15 minutes. We have only a phone number and not any names, so all of your responses will be anonymous. If I have your permission, let me begin by asking how many years you have lived in this state ...

It is strongly recommended that the questionnaire and interview procedures be pilot-tested with a small sample ahead of time to determine if there are any unforeseen problems.

BOX 9.1   PRACTICE NOTE: THE RELIABILITY OF HIV RISK BEHAVIOR REPORTING

Students and investigators may worry about the honesty of respondents when asked sensitive questions about risky and illegal behaviors. Research subjects could be motivated to minimize stigmatizing behavior and fear that information could be shared with legal authorities. However, the literature suggests that the data reported from high-risk populations tend to be reliable. (This does not mean that 100% of individuals always tell the truth or that a client will never distort the truth.).

For instance, Napper, Fisher, Reynolds, and Johnson (2010) conducted a meta-analysis of 28 studies, where respondents answered the same questions (test-retest reliability) at different lengths of time (one, three, and six months later). Across all the items asking about drug use (involving drugs such as marijuana, heroin, cocaine, amphetamines, injection drug use, etc.), the Pearson correlation coefficient was .90 for 30 days and .84 at three months. There was no statistical difference in recall of use between three months and six months. In terms of sexual behavior (number of partners, condom use, type of sex, etc.), the self-report of these events combined was reliable at .95 (three months) compared to .82 at 30 days and six months. These data suggest that there is acceptable reliability in the recall of HIV risk-related behaviors, but the reliability depends somewhat on the particular behavior and length of recall.

Personal Interviews

The personal interview provides the interviewer with more control than either mail or telephone surveys. The interviewer can read facial expressions and moods, monitor environmental distractions, and determine if the interview should move to a quieter room or be continued at a later date.

I love this example from an interviewer:

> It was a three-ring circus—the respondent had five children ranging from 1 to 8 years and they all had a great time climbing all over the furniture. One child stood on her head on the couch next to me. I managed to hang onto my pencil, the questionnaire, my purse—but it wasn't easy! (Converse & Schuman, 1974, p. 3)

Observational data (for example, the respondent's affect, interest in the topic) can be determined from the personal interview without requiring questions to be asked of the person. Further, visual aids can be used to help a respondent. This is particularly advantageous if there is a need for a complex response set. In such situations, the respondent can be handed a card from which to choose a response. Another advantage is that the personal interview usually achieves a higher response rate than either mail or telephone surveys.

The prime disadvantage of the interview is that it is much more expensive than the two other approaches. While interviewers can be paid either by the hour or by the number of interviews completed, expenses include travel time to the respondents' homes. Occasionally, multiple trips must be made when appointments are broken (because they have been forgotten or emergencies arise). Interviewers can get lost, find it difficult to locate the respondent's residence, or be snarled in traffic. Comments hurriedly scrawled in the margin of the questionnaire can become difficult to discern hours later in the office. The safety of interviewers can also be a major concern, and sometimes interviewers must be assigned in teams of two. Supervision and quality control of the interview process can be more difficult to ensure than with the telephone survey.

BOX 9.2   PRACTICE NOTE: INTERVIEWING CHILDREN

Interviewing young children presents special problems for practitioners and researchers alike. Fortunately, the literature has been growing in this area. Saywitz, Camparo, and Romanoff (2010) offer a number of good practice recommendations for interviewing children in custody cases of divorce and dissolution.

- Children can be influenced by others in the same room. Interviewers may want to make sure the room is private, age appropriate, and that "intriguing objects" are removed. The interviewer should outline the process of the interview ("sitting in this room ... just the two of us talking." An adult support person may be necessary to sit behind the child—it may be possible for this person to leave once the child becomes more comfortable.
- The interviewer will usually have to educate the child about the legal system and explain the judge's role ("to make sure everything is fair and everyone stays safe") and will need to explain his or her own role in learning what the child believes is "important in his or her life and family."
- A nonjudgmental atmosphere is important, and children's opinions are valued; they are the experts. Children are asked what they think, feel, or remember, but are not forced or pressured to side with one parent or the other. One can summarize what the child said using their own words to show understanding.
- Children have to decide to trust the interviewer. Verbal interactions other than on the subject of the interview could be helpful. If silence is encountered to a question, wait 20–30 seconds; don't pressure. Consider asking, "What is making it hard to talk right now?"
- Provide social support of eye contact, smiling, warm intonation, and relaxed body posture, but monitor yourself so that you are not reinforcing only the answers you want to hear. Be cautious with yes/no questions; it is better to hear the child's own words to avoid a lack of objectivity in the interview process. Avoid this construction: "Did your Mom hit you?" Ask instead, "What happened next?" Or, "What did she do with her hands?" Although not all yes/no questions can be avoided (e.g., "Has that happened before?"), you can follow that question with one such as: "Tell me about another time."
- Don't suggest responses ("He hurt you, didn't he?") or use multiple-choice questions.
- Use short, simple sentences and words the child understands. "Tell me more." "What happened next?" Questions should be open-ended and not leading. Ask about who, where, when, why, and how to capture important details.
- Inform the child that honesty, accuracy, and completeness are important. Children need to talk about what really happened and not make things up. Even little details are important. You may want to consider asking the child to promise to tell the truth.
- Tell the child it is okay to say, "I don't know," and this can be practiced before asking the substantive questions. Children are reluctant to admit that they don't know something.
- Tell the child to ask if they don't understand a question. Practicing on a few incomprehensible questions may have positive effects. Rephrase instead of repeating a question they don't understand.
- Tell children you can't help them answer the questions because you don't know what happened.

An approach that is used as a "quick-and-dirty" survey when it not possible to obtain a random sample is called **intercept surveying**. Typically, surveyors position themselves in malls or on busy streets and attempt to interview those who are willing to stop and talk to them.

Intercept surveys are convenience samples (remember the "person-in-the-street" interviews from the last chapter?), where surveyors seek to capture information from a variety of persons or may select those with certain apparent characteristics (women pushing strollers). Even if they strive to reach a cross-section of persons, there's always a problem with self-selection (some people don't like to be stopped on the street). Also, these surveys are limited by the geographical location and times chosen to do the interviewing.

Because they draw nonprobability samples, there is no way to tell whether the data they obtain is representative of the larger population. On the other hand, interviewing convenience samples can be accomplished a lot faster and cheaper than going door to door.

BOX 9.3 PRACTICE NOTE: INTERVIEWING IN HIGH-CRIME NEIGHBORHOODS

Gwiasda, Taluc, and Popkin (1997) reported on their experiences in surveying for the Chicago Housing Authority's antidrug and crime prevention program. Although their report is a little old, it still provides good advice.

Among the steps they took to ensure their safety was to hire residents of the projects as interviewers because they had familiarity with other residents and the neighborhood. They avoided interviewing during evenings and weekends. Similarly, they interviewed during months when school was in session and worked in teams of two. Interviewers were instructed to complete the interviews in hallways and to never enter an apartment or building alone.

Surveyors going into risky neighborhoods need to inform residents by letter or newsletters, or even by TV or radio announcements; in other words, by using existing formal and informal networks so that residents can "be on the lookout" for surveyors and reduce possible perils. Advising the police of the surveyors' presence in the neighborhood is important, and it may be necessary to request additional patrols or to postpone the survey altogether when conditions are too threatening (such as the presence of warring gangs). Giving each interviewer a cell phone can also afford a measure of safety.

More recently, Pashea and Kochel (2016) describe the use of student interviewers in 71 "hot spots" in St. Louis County, MO. They mention that potential respondents initially thought that the interviewers were associated with the police because of their dress and wouldn't participate. Interviewers then changed the "dress code" and began wearing jeans, shorts, and T-shirts with sneakers, and respondents were more accepting. They also began telling respondents at the beginning that "We are not selling anything." Instead of knocking or banging on apartment doors, they were more successful when they knocked on windows—something the police didn't do.

This is a good article discussing matching interviewers to potential respondents, the attributes of successful interviewers (experience, mood, energy level, positive messages), the needed persistence, as well as the burden on the respondents and conditions affecting their participation. They write that "the potential respondent weighs the benefits to participation (e.g. gaining favor from an interviewer who is liked ...) vs. the consequences of participation (e.g. the time it takes to complete the survey, discomfort in answering questions, uncomfortable environmental conditions as one stands in a cold doorway letting heat escape from the home)," p. 97.

Getting the Most from Personal Interviews

Anyone planning on conducting a large number of personal interviews for research purposes should anticipate the questions that respondents might ask such as "How did you pick me?" and "What good will all this do?" Training for the interviewers is a necessity, as they must learn to ask questions exactly as they are worded and in the order in which they appear on the questionnaire. Interviewers cannot assume they know how the respondent will respond. Every question should be asked, even if a preface is needed ("I know that we have already touched on this, but ..."). Training should cover situations such as when the respondent doesn't understand a question or the interviewer doesn't understand the response. (You can probe by repeating the question, by being silent for a few seconds and giving the respondent time to expand on his or her thoughts, by repeating the respondent's reply, by making a neutral comment such as "Can you tell me a little more?" or "Anything else?" or by simply stating that you do not understand.)

It is critical that interviewers understand the intent of each question and the overall survey. Interviewers should achieve comfort and knowledge of the procedures in training and identify possible problems with the recording of responses. You also don't want interviewers to stumble over words or questions. How to dress should also be covered—interviewers should not dress in a way that calls attention to themselves.

Most large-scale survey operations employ a system of spot checking and validating the interviews by visiting the respondent a second time or calling to verify that they participated in an interview. The quality of the interview is kept at a high level when there is some monitoring of the interviewers. If you are a supervisor of interviewers, it is a good idea to review closely the first several completed interviews and then randomly sample the interviews later to ensure that all interviewers are capturing the same type of information.

Comparison of the Approaches

All of the approaches discussed in this chapter have something to recommend them. Lengthy surveys and complicated questions are sometimes more easily handled by a personal interview. Mailed responses allow the respondent to feel anonymity is protected. E-mail and telephone surveys can be implemented quickly when results are needed fast. Which is the best method? Researchers have to weigh such variables as costs, response rates, the types of questions being asked, the need for confidentiality, the length of the questionnaire, the characteristics of the targeted population, how fast the data are needed, and whom the technique includes or excludes. There is evidence that younger people prefer responding via the Web or mobile device, and thus it is important to know the characteristics of the target population. However, Dillman, Smyth, and Christian (2014) discuss a large statewide study in Nebraska showing 80% of responses coming back by mail and 20% by the Internet and then state that it "is consistent with findings from other research. It suggests a clear preference for mail when mail contact offers both a web or mail response" (p. 426). They favor offering multiple modes (Web plus mail) for responding.

Mixed-Mode Surveys

While Dillman, Smyth, and Christian (2014) recognize that at times it makes the most sense to conduct a survey with only one mode, they make a strong case for not relying upon a single mode, but instead using at least two modes to obtain higher response rates and to improve the speed of response. They point out that mixed modes lower cost (e.g., in the US Census, questionnaires are mailed and then only those who don't respond are contacted in person) and reduce nonresponse error.

The approach used by Dillman and colleagues employs a mailed letter with a small incentive. The sponsor of the study is emphasized, and the message contains a request for help with the project, which is clearly explained. There is a blue signature and a red font for the URL that respondents can use if they prefer. That URL is a meaningful word (e.g., **www.environmentstudy**).

Their book contains many guidelines; for instance, they recommend using the same question format and wording across modes so that they have the same visual layout whether paper or electronic.

Here are the steps in a very successful (77% response rate) mixed-mode survey reported in Dillman, Smyth, and Christianson, 2014. They report that in five separate experiments "offering a mail question-naire in follow-up to an initial web questionnaire increases response rates substantially" (p. 429).

1. Letter to sample requesting a response to survey back on the Web. A $2 incentive is enclosed. (Day 1)
2. E-mail sent to sample following up with electronic link to questionnaire. (Day 4)
3. Second e-mail request sent. (Day 10)
4. Letter sent offering the option of responding via US Postal Service. Questionnaire and addressed, stamped return envelope is enclosed. (Day 18)
5. Final e-mail follow-up. (Day 22)

These steps may not always produce the same high response rate as achieved by Dillman and his colleagues, but applying this model would very likely improve upon "the 20% to 30% range that student surveys" (p. 23) typically achieved at the University of Washington.

BOX 9.4 SURVEY CREDIBILITY CHECKLIST

☐ How was the sample drawn?

(It has more credibility if it employed a probability design and even more if the margin of error and lev-el of confidence are reported. It will also have more credibility if the sample appears to be reasonable and to have been constructed without bias.)

☐ *Sample size:*

(It has more credibility if the sample is adequate for the level of generalization the authors want to make.)

☐ *Response rate:*

(It has more credibility if the response rate is greater than or close to 50%.)

☐ *Recency:*

(It has more credibility if it is not outdated and when it is not confounded with recent developments that could affect its findings—e.g., possibly influential events occurring during the time when the sur-vey was being conducted.)

☐ *Item construction:*

(It has more credibility if you can read the questions and they are balanced and fair, not vague, lead-ing, and so on.)

Interpreting Surveys: Points to Remember

Surveys are versatile and powerful sources of information about the world. However, they can also be flawed—that is to say, in error—even though there was no intent to deceive. In this chapter, as well as in the previous chapter on sampling, we have discussed ways that surveys might mislead if important design elements are ignored. Whenever you are reading the results of a survey or preparing to conduct one, certain characteristics will help you to evaluate its worth. Knowledge of these characteristics can help you understand how seemingly similar survey efforts can produce dissimilar conclusions. Here's a checklist to review when evaluating surveys:

Surveys, particularly political polls, may appear to be at odds with one another, when in fact they were conducted at different times or used different questions or sampling procedures. Attitudes can and do change over time—sometimes on a national level almost overnight when a president or other important person does something decisive or unpopular. Another point made by Dillman et al. (2009) is that different response modes can produce different answers to the same questions. For instance, researchers found that telephone and IVR responders tended to use extremely positive categories more often than mail responders.

Also, you should not necessarily be persuaded by a large sample size. A faculty member in another discipline was responsible for mailing a survey to 5,000 families within the state. "Interesting," I thought to myself, as I read the newspaper report of the findings. "I wonder how they arrived at that number. Don't they know about random sampling?" A bit further into the article, I became convinced that the researchers didn't know much at all about survey methodology. What were the clues? Here are two: 78% of the respondents were women (what happened to the men?), and they used telephone books to construct their sample frame (we already know what bias that interjects into a study). Similarly, don't assume that large numbers of responders to a poll on a website make for a credible survey.

The survey designer also has to worry about how attitudes are measured. Questions can be too complex or too long, resulting in respondents forgetting response choices available or prematurely terminating the survey. The way we phrase a question—perhaps even the very act of raising a question—can influence a respondent.

While survey designers don't always obtain the results they expect, they usually have a good idea of what the survey would likely show. For instance, if you were thinking about homeless youth, would you anticipate many of these youth would have experience in foster care? What do you think? Golinelli, Tucker, Ryan, and Wenzel (2015) conducted a survey in four regions of Los Angeles County and found that an average of almost 35% of these youth had previously been in foster care. Almost 50% had been physically abused. Is that about what you would expect?

Key Terms

needs assessment	descriptive survey
community forum	probe
exploratory survey	pilot-test

intercept surveying	surveys
response rate	random-digit dialing procedure
community survey	added-digit dialing procedure
key informants	interactive voice response
incentive	nonresponse error
polls	

SELF-REVIEW

(Answers at the end of the book.)

1. Which approach of the following would be the most labor intensive?
    a.   telephone interview
    b.   personal interview
    c.   e-mail survey
    d.   mail survey

2. T or F. Incentives seem to increase response rates.
3. T or F. It is not uncommon for mail surveys to have response rates of less than 30%.
4. T or F. The use of a telephone directory produces biased samples.
5. A national poll on volunteerism in America had a good response rate. Which answer below indicates that?
    a.   10%
    b.   15%
    c.   35%
    d.   52%

6. One major advantage of a personal interview over a mailed survey is _____.
7. Exploratory surveys are generally noted by their _____.
8. List three advantages to using the mail questionnaire.
9. T or F. With mail questionnaires, a researcher can expect about a 65% response rate.
10. _____ is a pretest of a survey instrument to make sure that potential respondents understand the questions as intended.
11. T or F. Those who send and receive e-mail from home are a cross-section of all Americans.
12. T or F. It is estimated that less than 75% of Americans have phones.
13. Lengthy surveys and complicated questions are most easily handled by which method?
    a.   telephone
    b.   mail
    c.   personal interview
    d.   e-mail

QUESTIONS FOR CLASS DISCUSSION

1. Assume that you have a budget of $3,500 (exclusive of your own time) with which to conduct a national survey of social workers. What survey approach would you use? Why?

2. How have surveys advanced your understanding of human nature or society? Cite an example if you can.

3. Cite examples of surveys in which you have participated or experiences you have personally had with surveys.

4. Without referring to the book, list the advantages and disadvantages of the various survey methods discussed in this chapter.

5. Should an incentive be provided at the initial mailing of the questionnaire, or should it come only after the questionnaire has been completed and returned? What would you prefer as a research participant?

6. What are the advantages and disadvantages of using an interactive voice response (IVR) survey approach?

7. **IDEA FOR GROUP PROJECT:** Using SurveyMonkey or Qualtrics, have the class divide into groups of three to design an electronic needs assessment for the college student residents of the neighborhood(s) around the university. Alternatively, design a questionnaire that could be mailed to non–college student residents asking about problems or needs in the neighborhood.

RESOURCES AND REFERENCES

Adams, R. M., Smelser, N. J., & Treiman, D. (Eds.). (1982). Behavioral and social science research: A national resource, Part I. Washington, DC: National Academy Press. In S. E. Fienberg, S. E., Loftus, E. F., & Tanur, J. M. (1985). Cognitive aspects of health survey methodology: An overview. *Milbank Memorial Fund Quarterly/Health and Society, 63*(3), 547–564.

Busby, D. M., & Yoshida, K. (2015). Challenges with online research for couples and families: Evaluating nonrespondents and the differential impact of incentives. *Journal of Children and Family, 24*, 595–513.

Converse, J. M., & Schuman, H. (1974). *Conversations at random: Survey research as interviewers see it.* New York, NY: John Wiley & Sons.

Dillman, D. A., Phelps, G., Tortora, R., Swift, K., Kohrell, J., Berck, J., & Messer, B. L. (2009). Response rate and measurement differences in mixed mode surveys using mail, telephone, interactive voice response (IVR), and the Internet. *Social Science Research, 38*(1), 1–18.

Dillman, D. A., Smyth, J. D., & Christian, L. M. (2014). *Internet, mail, and mixed-mode surveys: The tailored design method.* Hoboken, NJ: John Wiley & Sons.

File, T., & Ryan, C. (2014). Computer and Internet Use in the United States: 2013: American Community Survey Reports, ACS-28. Washington, DC: U.S. Census Bureau.

Fink, A. (2016). *How to conduct surveys: A step-by-step guide.* Beverly Hills, CA: Sage.

Fowler, F. J. (2013). *Survey Research Methods.* Thousand Oaks, CA: Sage.

Garner, R. (2005). Post-It® note persuasion: A sticky influence. *Journal of Consumer Psychology, 15*(3), 230–237.

Gendall, P., & Healey, B. (2008). Alternatives to prepaid monetary incentives in mail surveys. *International Journal of Public Opinion Research, 20*(4), 517–527.

Golinelli, D., Tucker, J. S., Ryan, G. W., & Wenzel, S. L. (2015). Strategies for obtaining probability samples of homeless youth. *Field Methods, 27*(2), 131–143.

Gwiasda, V., Taluc, N., & Popkin, S. J. (1997). Data collection in dangerous neighborhoods: Lessons from a survey of public housing residents in Chicago. *Evaluation Review, 21*, 77–93.

Keeter, S., Christian, L. M., Dimock, M., & Gewurz, D. (2012). *Assessing the representativeness of public opinion surveys.* Cited in Dillman, Smyth, & Christianson, 2014, pp. 259–260.

Lyon, T. D. (2014). Interviewing children. *Annual Review of Law and Social Science, 10*, 73–89.

Millar, M. M., & Dillman, D. A. (2011). Improving response to web and mixed-mode surveys. *Public Opinion Quarterly, 75*(2), 249–269.

Napper, L. E., Fisher, D. G., Reynolds, G. L., & Johnson, M. E. (2010). HIV risk behavior self-report reliability at different recall periods. *AIDS Behavior, 14*, 152–161.

Parks, K. A., Pardi, A. M., & Bradizza, C. M. (2006). Collecting data on alcohol use and alcohol-related victimization: A comparison of telephone and Web-based survey methods. *Journal of Studies on Alcohol, 67*(3), 318–323.

Pashea, J. J., & Kochel, T. R. (2016). Face-to-face surveys in high crime areas: Balancing respondent cooperation and interviewer safety. *Journal of Criminal Justice Education, 27*(1), 95–120.

Royse, D., & Badger, K. (2015). Needs assessment planning: Starting where you are. *Australian Social Work, 68*(3), 364–374.

Royse, D., Staton-Tindall, M., Badger, K., & Webster, J. M. (2009). *Needs assessment.* New York, NY: Oxford University Press.

Saywitz, K., Camparo, L. B., & Romanoff, A. (2010). Interviewing children in custody cases: Implications of research and policy for practice. *Behavioral Sciences and the Law, 28*, 542–562.

Stern, M. J., Bilgen, I., & Dillman, D. A. (2014). The state of survey methodology: Challenges, dilemmas, and new frontiers in the era of the tailored design. *Field Methods, 26*(3), 284–301.

Taylor, B. G., & Mumford, E. A. (2016). A national descriptive portrait of adolescent relationship abuse: Results from the National Survey on Teen Relationships and Intimate Violence. *Journal of Interpersonal Violence, 31*(6), 963–988.

Wilk, R. (1993). Research note: The use of monetary incentives to increase survey response rates. *Social Work Research and Abstracts, 29*(1), 33–34.

ASSIGNMENT 9.1

Locating and Critically Reading a Survey Study

Objective: *To be able to identify studies involving surveys and to be able discuss the strengths and weaknesses of survey efforts.*

For this assignment, you should browse one of the social work journals and locate a research article where the methodology involves the use of a survey.

1. Give the full APA citation of the article that you read:

2. Was a probability or nonprobability sampling design employed?

    a. Was a margin of error reported? What was it?

    b. Give the more specific name for the sampling design:

3. What was the sample size?

4. Does the sample appear to be adequate? That is, does its size and construction give you a sense of confidence in the study's findings? Explain.

5. Did the author devise a questionnaire or scale just for this study or use one already developed? (*Note:* Your instructor may want you to append a copy of the article you read to this assignment.)

6. List three major findings of the study:

ASSIGNMENT 9.2

Creating a Survey

Objective: *To obtain practice in constructing a sampling design.*

In this assignment, think about a community issue or question that could be answered by a random survey of residents. You may use any of the probability designs. Your population might consist of clients of a single agency, students in a university, members of an organization, or citizens in a given community.

1. List at least five questions that you would like answered:

   a.

   b.

   c.

   d.

   e.

2. What is your population?

3. What is your sampling frame, and how would you acquire it?

4. What is the name of your sampling design?

5. What is your margin of error and confidence interval?

6. What sample size would you need?

7. Describe your methodology for obtaining the data you desire.

CHAPTER 10

Unobtrusive Approaches to Data Collection

What Is This Topic, and Why Study It?

Remember the discussion in the last chapter about needing to be careful when interviewing children because of their suggestibility? Whenever we interact with others to collect data, there is the potential for unintentionally influencing them in some way—because of our status, our gender, our appearance, the questions we ask, or the way we ask them. Let's look at several examples to demonstrate this.

Example 1: Imagine that you will be presenting a workshop to your coworkers on the avoidance of sexist language. A week before the workshop, you send each participant a small questionnaire pretest that asks if he or she uses certain terms or phrases in conversation. Suppose Bob reads the questionnaire, briefly considers how he will respond, and then indicates on the form that he does not use any of those terms in his normal conversation. However, driving home from work that night, he reflects back on the questionnaire and realizes that there are several other ways in which his choice of words or phrasing might be considered sexist. As a result of thinking about the pretest, he resolves to eliminate these terms and phrases from his speech and writing.

Your workshop is conducted as scheduled, and afterward you administer the posttest. An examination of the data reveals a decrease in the use of sexist language at the time of the posttest. But if others in the agency had the same experience as Bob, how would you know which had the most impact—the workshop or the pretest? Could the reduction in sexist language have been due to the influence of the questionnaire and not an outcome of the workshop? It is conceivable that as mild an interaction as attempting to measure attitudes, behavior, or knowledge could bring about changes.

In physics there is a principle known as the **Heisenberg's uncertainty principle**, which states it is impossible to measure with a great deal of precision both the position and velocity of an electron in motion; the very act of measuring its position may change its velocity. This principle applies to measurement in the social sciences as well. In fact, a study has shown that merely asking about intentions to eat healthy foods resulted in a greater tendency to choose a healthy snack (Wood, Conner, Sandberg, Godin, & Sheeran, 2014) and asking questions about blood donation (Godin, Germain, Conner, Delage, & Sheeran, 2014) affects subsequent donations in a positive way. Researchers need to be alert to the fact that what is called the question-behavior effect could influence the phenomena we are trying to understand.

*Example 2: A famous example of an unanticipated effect on research subjects has come to be known as the **Hawthorne effect**. Prior to World War II, researchers at a Western Electric plant in Chicago found that employees in the study raised their production output possibly because they realized they were being studied. Productivity increased, no matter what physical changes were made in their work environment (for example, the lighting was both increased and decreased). What researchers learned is that subjects are influenced by the knowledge that* *they are taking part in a research study. In fact, knowing that they were chosen to participate in a research project had more influence on them than other independent variables.*

Example 3: Some of the work of the prominent anthropologist Margaret Mead came under attack after her death. Perhaps best known for her work Coming of Age in Samoa, *Mead's thesis was that adolescence was much less difficult for teens in Samoa than in America. One of her "findings" was that Samoans had few "hang-ups" about sex and that teens had the opportunity to have casual sex almost for the asking—quite a contrast to American teens in the 1920s. The primary critic of Mead's Samoan work, Derek Freeman, suggested that the two teenage Samoan girls that she relied on for translation and interpretation were often uncomfortable with her questions about sexual activity. Consequently, they didn't ask the questions Mead intended and made up false answers. Were they giving Mead the answers they thought she wanted to hear? In a sense, every time we as researchers create a measurement instrument or conduct an interview, we hope that it translates well and that we don't imply the answers that we want to hear. As you've undoubtedly noticed by now, studying research methods involves designing research procedures and instruments that do not unduly influence or bias a study's findings. However, if Heisenberg's uncertainty principle applies to the social sciences (and I believe it does), then we can't totally prevent contaminating the research data we collect. At best, all we can do is to try to minimize our influence.*

A recent article really captures the spirit of unobtrusive research. Earl, Crause, Vaid, and Albarracin (2016) acknowledge the problem of providing information to prevent illness in target populations, since potentially at-risk individuals—indeed, most of us—selectively attend to the information available all around us. The researchers placed unobtrusive observers in a health clinic waiting room while a health video was playing to code alertness and amount of attention given to the video (either on flu prevention or HIV prevention). The research assistants didn't interview or hand questionnaires to those in the waiting room. They simply sat where they could see how much attention others were paying to the videos. (How's that for being unobtrusive?) The authors of the study reported that while there was no difference in attention with the flu-prevention video, African Americans were significantly less likely to attend to the HIV-prevention video. Was this because they had already been exposed to this information and it was less interesting? Because the information was scary and frightening? What other explanations might there be?

Unobtrusive Research: Secondary Data

One way to avoid problems with measurements affecting our studies is to use data that already exist instead of collecting new data. The use of existing data that does not involve interaction with research subjects fits into the category called **unobtrusive research**. The classic work in this area is that of Webb, Campbell, Schwartz, and Sechrest (1966), *Unobtrusive Measures: Nonreactive Research in the Social Sciences*. There are two primary ways that social work researchers conduct unobtrusive research. The first of these involves the use of **secondary data analysis**.

Whether or not we are aware of it, in performing routine tasks each day, social workers create mountains of data each year. Most of these data come from the ordinary processing of clients in and out of service delivery systems. Each use of an admission form, evaluation form, progress note, or social history generates valuable information. While these data are not usually collected with research purposes in mind, collections of such data represent a wealth of research opportunities for interested social workers.

Researchers who rely on public documents, reports, historical data, and even data from previous studies are said to be engaged in a type of unobtrusive research called **archival research**, or **secondary data analysis**. This type of research involves the analysis of an existing data set that results in knowledge, interpretations, and conclusions beyond those stated in the original study. The intent is not to find fault with another's study, but rather to test new hypotheses or explore questions not examined in the original report. For instance, the original study may have collected data on the attitudes of a cross-section of Americans; a secondary analysis of the same data set might examine only the attitudes of a minority subgroup. Secondary analysis extends or goes beyond what the initial investigators reported. An advantage of secondary data analysis is that new hypotheses can be tested without collecting new data. Investigators are not limited to a single data set or source document and may use several data sets from different agencies or studies.

The Importance of an Adequate Baseline

A good use of secondary data is to identify trends. For example, a student once approached me with some concern because she had heard from a relative that her home county had the highest suicide rate in the state. I was somewhat skeptical about this, but when I had the opportunity, I examined several of the Department of Health's Vital Statistics annual reports and found that in the most recent year, the county in question, with a population of slightly more than 12,000, had 7 suicides. This gave it a rate of 52.5 suicides per 100,000 population. (This is a standard basis of comparison; it is used so that urban counties can be compared with rural counties.) This was, in fact, one of the highest suicide rates in the state, as the overall average for the state was 14.3 suicides per 100,000 population that particular year.

This is the information the student had originally obtained for her specific county—it is easy to see why she was concerned:

Number of Suicides	County Suicide Rate	State Suicide Rate
7	52.5	14.3

Had the student gone to the library and looked at the previous year's data, this is what she would have found:

	Number of Suicides	County Suicide Rate	State Suicide Rate
Previous Year	0	0	13.2
Current Year	7	52.5	14.3

Thus, in the span of two years, the county had among the lowest and one of the highest rates in the state. Fluctuation like this is not uncommon when the actual number of events (such as suicides) is relatively small. This example shows the inherent danger in selectively drawing a single year's statistic instead of examining a longer span of time. Depending on the year she chose for representing the county's problem with suicide, she might have come away with completely different impressions about the need for a suicide prevention program there.

When secondary data are available, the competent researcher wants to examine trends to have confidence that there is a real pattern one way or the other. For example, if you looked at the same county for a period of 20 years, you would discover that Tobacco County's suicide rate exceeded the state's average in 17 of 20 years, or about 85% of the time. That's an indication this rural county possesses a noticeable tendency to have higher suicide rates than expected. Despite four years of no suicides, in the 20 years studied, its average rate was 19.28 per 100,000 population compared to the state average of 13.3. If you were associated with a suicide prevention program, would you be concerned about this county?

Here's an example of an article exploring a related topic with secondary data analysis:

- Bridge et al. (2015). Suicide trends among elementary school-aged children in the United States from 1993 to 2012. *JAMA Pediatrics, 169*(7), 673–677.

Advantages and Disadvantages of Unobtrusive Approaches

- Right away, some exciting advantages of unobtrusive research are apparent. First, if you discover that someone else has already collected data that you can use for a study, you can save considerable time and effort in your data collection phase. Once you identify an interesting database, it is often possible to move rapidly into data analysis. Secondary data sources may already be held in a depository at a university or a governmental agency. Data from federally funded studies are usually available to legitimate students and researchers.
- Second, any bias associated with the collection of the data may be known and accepted. It may be known, for instance, that the data tend to underestimate the true incidence of a social problem (as in the case of suicide data). Other data sets may overestimate the incidence of a problem. For example, data on psychiatric hospital admissions that didn't differentiate new patients from those patients with previous admissions could overestimate incidence of the most severe form of mental illness. The term *incidence* refers to the number of *new* cases or events during a given period, while *prevalence* is the total number of cases already present in a population at a given time. Because all studies have some limitations, the secondary data analyst may choose to use a data set, even though it has several known problems. Problems with the data set are not a reflection on the researcher using secondary data analysis. After all, the secondary data researcher is only borrowing the data set.
- Third, because you are not interviewing clients or patients or interacting with them in any way, you need not worry that your inquiries will put them at risk or have any harmful effects.
- The final, but best, reason for conducting secondary data analysis is that it both provides an opportunity to study social problems in terms of long-term change and enables comparative study. Secondary data studies can make comparisons across localities, states, and nations (presuming, of course, that the data are available).

On the other hand, some disadvantages are associated with relying on secondary or archival data, and these chiefly involve gaps or changes to the data set. Occasionally, historical records you need have been misplaced, shredded, thrown out, destroyed by accident, etc. Researchers well into their projects may find incomplete or missing records in the data because of changes in procedures or policies that affected the data collection. With the passage of time, it is quite possible for variables to change; categories can become more or less inclusive. Finally, time lags between their creation and the researcher's discovery of the data sets could mean that the data are not as current as would be desired.

I once discovered that a set of state child abuse archival data I wanted to explore was compartmentalized. The data were recorded in two different mainframe computers in two very different software formats because the data collection forms had been redesigned. There was no way to combine the data sets into one large file without going to the expense of hiring computer programmers. Consequently, I did no research with that data.

Sometimes, if data are reported more or less voluntarily, there may be more gaps than if 100% of the units were required to report. Several years ago, I was examining one state's outpatient admissions to community mental health centers and found that not all centers were fully cooperating in returning their monthly reports. While the vast majority of these centers did, perhaps 5% didn't. These tended to be small, rural centers without a lot of staff. While their failure to report on a timely basis didn't have a huge effect in terms of the total number of admissions in the state, it did raise questions about the reliability of the data set. Could there have been other, larger agencies that failed to report their admissions? Did anyone monitor the data to make sure there were 12 reports from each agency at the end of each year? Researchers using secondary data have to be concerned about the reliability of the data they intend to analyze. Depending on the source of the data, the researcher may want to check it against other information to better understand if confidence can be placed in the numbers reported.

Finally, recent data may not be available as soon as the researcher may desire it. It is not unusual for some agencies or departments to take six to 12 months (or longer) to produce their most current annual report of the previous year's data.

In summary, while many advantages are associated with secondary data analysis, you should be alert to changes in data items in terms of completeness, accuracy, or definition.

State-Maintained Data Sets and Secondary Analysis

Secondary analyses can be conducted in both private and public agencies. However, private agencies tend to be more protective of their data. Even though researchers agree not to divulge personal data, private agencies often feel that any research within their agencies may endanger the privacy of individual clients. These agencies may also feel that the proposed research will require too much clerical support for locating archival records or selected cases. Unlike private agencies, the data from public agencies and departments are often viewed as public information and available to all. While not all public agencies are as cooperative as many researchers would like, they generally do have some form of aggregated data each year that they make available to the public.

Table 10.1 contains examples of variables or **social indicators** (data that inform us about the extent and trends within social problems) that are commonly collected by all states. Generally, these data are reported by county. Public and university libraries often are designated as state depositories and receive reports from governmental agencies.

Applications of Secondary Data Analysis

If information is power (Francis Bacon noted that "knowledge itself is power"), then the possibilities of being able to effect change are enormous when one has access to secondary data.

TABLE 10.1 Examples of Variables for Secondary Research

Indicator	Typical Source
Marriages	Department of Health
Divorces	Department of Health
Suicides	Department of Health
Live births	Department of Health
Infant deaths	Department of Health
Deaths (all ages)	Department of Health
Deaths from cirrhosis of the liver	Department of Health
Inpatient admissions	Department of Mental Health
Outpatient admissions	Department of Mental Health
Temporary Assistance for Needy Families cases	Department of Public Welfare
Motor vehicle injury accidents	Department of Highway Safety
Motor vehicle deaths	Department of Highway Safety
Motor vehicle accidents	Department of Highway Safety
Abuse and neglect cases	Department of Child Welfare
Delinquency cases	Juvenile Court Statistics
Arraignments	Supreme Court Statistics
School dropouts	Department of Education
School enrollment	Department of Education
Unemployment	Bureau of Employment
Average weekly earnings	Bureau of Employment
Retail alcohol sales	Department of Liquor Control

Example 1: Suppose you are a school social worker, and a number of children have been injured because there is no traffic light at a busy intersection they cross to get to school. Let's further suppose that officials are dragging their feet, saying that a traffic light is not needed. You obtain a list of all the locations where vehicular and pedestrian-injury accidents have occurred in your city in the past year. What if the intersection that you feel needs a light was the site of more injury accidents than any other location in the city for the past three years? Isn't that powerful information that you could use to help advocate for a traffic light?

Example 2: You are a supervisor of a child abuse investigation team and painfully aware that your unit is understaffed. In talking with others, you sense that your unit may investigate more reported cases of abuse and neglect than any other unit. Yet, when you talk to the agency director about this problem, she is not sympathetic about your need for additional staff. The director indicates that cases of abuse are increasing everywhere.

However, because you occasionally have the opportunity to talk to other social workers, you learn that some investigation units are adding staff, while your unit has added no new staff in three years. A research question forms in your mind. Which county has the highest incidence of child abuse/neglect cases in the state? When you look at the data, you discover that while the more populous counties have significantly more cases of abuse and neglect, your county has more cases of child abuse and neglect *per thousand population* than any other county in the state. Would this information be enough to use for leverage to get some additional staff? If not, a next step might be to gather data on how many staff the other investigation units have and which units have the highest ratio of cases to staff. If your county has the highest ratio of cases to staff (the total number of cases divided by the number of caseworkers), this would be compelling information that could influence the agency director to allocate additional staff to your unit.

This example could be carried further. What if you were to examine the ratio of cases to child protective services staff in your state to those of surrounding states? This type of information might be used to influence your legislators to increase appropriations at the state level. You could also compare salaries of child protective workers in your state with those in other states. If workers in your state are paid below the average, this information could be used for lobbying for increased pay. Might high rates of employee turnover be linked to low salaries—still another study?

Example 3: You become concerned about the use of illegal drugs by adolescents in your community. You suspect that a new street drug is the cause of a rash of fatal overdoses, but you have no "hard" data to support this assumption. Because you want to conduct a drug education campaign for adolescents, you feel that local data are needed. You learn that while the police department has no data, the hospital emergency room keeps this data.

BOX 10.1   DATABASES AND STATISTICS ON THE INTERNET

One of the first places to start a search is **www.data.gov**, which can link you to literally thousands of data sets federal government agencies produce in the way of statistics, documents, and reports. A few of these agencies are: Bureau of Labor Statistics (even contains international data country by country, including data on such things as child labor and forced labor in other countries), Bureau of Justice Statistics (includes "Indian Country Justice Statistics"), Bureau of the Census, National Center for Health Statistics, Administration for Children and Families, Administration on Aging, Centers for Disease Control, National Institute on Drug Abuse, Federal Bureau of Prisons, and Indian Health Service. The website **www.usa.gov/statistics** can direct you to census information, demographics on the United States, and much more. In terms of criminal justice data, **www.fbi.gov/stats-services/crimestats** provides data from the Uniform Crime Reports and Hate Crime Statistics. Along this line, you may want to look at the National Archive of Criminal Justice Data (**https://www.icpsr.umich.edu/icpsrweb/NACJD/**).

In terms of child welfare, there is the Child Welfare Information Gateway (**www.childwelfare.gov/**) and in the private sector, the Annie E. Casey Foundation is a good source of child welfare and related variables. Their annual report, *Kids Count*, contains data on each state and breaks the data down by county. See **http://www.aecf.org/work/kids-count/**.

The United Nations supplies social indicators on the various countries around the world in such areas as childbearing, education, health, housing, literacy, unemployment, and youth and elderly populations at **http://unstats.un.org/unsd/databases.htm**.

Monitoring the Future contains scads of publications and survey results on the behaviors, attitudes, and values of American high school students, college students, and young adults. Each year, a total of approximately 50,000 eighth, tenth and 12th grade students are surveyed (12th graders since 1975, and eighth and tenth graders since 1991). Additionally, annual follow-up questionnaires are mailed to a sample of each graduating class for several years after their initial participation. View this website at **www.monitoringthefuture.org/**.

In sum, there is a great wealth of data sets available for secondary data analysis and general information.

Secondary data can be used in many ways. You could investigate whether the high school dropout rate has decreased within your community over the past five years. Has the dropout prevention program had an impact? With the right data, it would be relatively easy to determine if the dropout rate has changed. Other uses of social indicators include examining how your county or state compares with other states in terms of unemployment, Temporary Assistance for Needy Families (TANF) cash benefits, or some other social problem. Secondary data can also be used for needs assessments.

Additionally, you might want to formally test hypotheses. You might want to conduct correlational studies to see if increases in unemployment are associated with increases in mental hospital admissions or if high school dropout rates are associated with juvenile delinquency rates. You could be interested in examining the state-by-state data on child support enforcement to understand how well your state is doing.

Social indicators can also be used to make national comparisons. How does the United States compare with other industrialized countries on such indicators as infant deaths or literacy rates? Have we made advances recently, or have these indicators remained at about the same level?

There is virtually no end to social indicators that may be gleaned from state and federal departments, bureaus, agencies, and offices. And thousands of organizations collect information on their membership and the services provided. Most social service agencies across this nation very likely have questions they would like explored—if only someone with the right combination of research skills and interest would come along.

Secondary data analysis is versatile and can be used to find information on a wide range of problems. One of the main strengths of secondary data analysis is that there are generally multiple sources of data relevant to the topic in which you are interested.

Secondary Analysis of Survey Data

With the advent of computer processing has come a proliferation of large-scale surveys. These surveys—often with thousands of respondents—are generally available to students and researchers. They differ in several ways from the surveys social work practitioners conduct.

First, these surveys are designed so that they can be easily manipulated by computer processing. This greatly facilitates their use by researchers other than the original investigators. In fact, some of the surveys, like the General Social Survey, were designed particularly for secondary analysis. The General Social Survey, with thousands of variables, is described this way on their website, **www.gss.norc.org**:

> Since 1972, the General Social Survey (GSS) has been monitoring societal change and studying the growing complexity of American society. The GSS aims to gather data on contemporary American society in order to monitor and explain trends and constants in attitudes, behaviors, and attributes; to examine the structure and functioning of society in general as well as the role played by relevant subgroups; to compare the United States to other societies in order to place American society in comparative perspective and develop cross-national models of human society; and to make high-quality data easily accessible to scholars, students, policy makers, and others, with minimal cost and waiting.

The GSS is NORC's longest running project and one of its most influential. Except for US Census data, the GSS is the most frequently analyzed source of information in the social sciences. GSS data are used in numerous newspaper, magazine, and journal articles, by legislators, policy makers, and educators. The GSS is also a major teaching tool in colleges and universities: more than 26,000 journal articles, books, and PhD dissertations are based on the GSS; and about 400,000 students use the GSS in their classes each year.

RECENT STUDIES INVOLVING THE GENERAL SOCIAL SURVEY

✓ Campbell, C., & Horowitz, J. (2016). Does college influence sociopolitical attitudes? *Sociology of Education, 89*(1), 40–58).

✓ Donnelly, K., Twenge, J. M., Clark, M. A., Shaikh, S. K., Beiler-May, A., & Carter, N. T. (2016). Attitudes toward women's work and family roles in the United States 1976–2013. *Psychology of Women Quarterly, 40*(1), 41–54.

✓ Hout, M. (2016). Money and morale: Growing inequality affects how Americans view themselves and others. *Annals of the American Academy of Political and Social Sciences, 663*(1), 204–228.

✓ Lee, Y., Muennig, P., Kawachi, I., & Hatzenbuehler, M. L. (2015). Effects of racial prejudice on the health of communities: A multilevel survival analysis. *American Journal of Public Health, 105*(1), 2349–2355.

Second, these surveys tend to use large, national, cross-sectional samples. Some of these surveys have questions that are repeated at regular intervals so that trends can be observed over time. What trends do you see in the box *Public Opinion on Regulating Guns?*

Third, these surveys are usually indexed so that specific variables can be found easily. *Fourth*, usually even the entire data set can be purchased at nominal cost. Through the Internet, researchers can get a good idea of the data that is available before purchasing it.

The federal government funds hundreds of surveys every year. Perhaps the best known of these is the decennial Census of Population and Housing, but the various agencies of the government also provide

BOX 10.2   PUBLIC OPINION ON REGULATING GUNS

The public has been polled by the Gallup organization on numerous topics since the1950s. The survey data in Table 10.2 show how polling organizations track important social issues. Also, this example furnishes a quick glance at the kind of data that already exist from randomly selected national samples of adults, data that could be used with a secondary survey analysis to test hypotheses or research questions. What events or factors do you think might affect the public's attitudes either for or against regulating guns?

for special-purpose surveys that supply statistical information on different facets of our national character. In addition to those surveys, for-profit polling companies also conduct surveys and make results available. See the box below.

BOX 10.3   ADDITIONAL INTERNET RESOURCES

Many depositories and large databases exist. It just takes a little bit of sleuthing to find them. For instance, The Inter-University Consortium for Political and Social Research (**www.icpsr.umich.edu/index.html**) contains data collections on health and medical care, aging, criminal justice, and substance abuse/mental health and others where the user can perform statistical procedures on the data and create custom subsets without downloading the whole collection and importing the data into a statistical software package.

The National Data Archive on Child Abuse and Neglect is available at **www.ndacan.cornell.edu/**. Another collection of surveys on political topics and trends in American public opinion can be found at **www.pollingreport.com**.

Unobtrusive Data: Content Analysis

Content analysis is another unobtrusive research process that is often used to examine our communications with each other. Accordingly, content analysis conducted quantitatively involves searching for and counting key words, phrases, or concepts in communications such as newspapers, magazines, journals, books, television programs, audio- and videotapes, speeches, minutes from agency board meetings, congressional records, presidential addresses, and historical documents such as letters, diaries, and so on.

Key words and phrases may be counted for the frequency with which they occur or the amount of coverage given to a topic might be measured in terms of how much space is provided in a newspaper article or the amount of time allocated on national television or radio. Content analysis can be used either as **retrospective research** (to examine materials already in existence) or as **prospective research** (to analyze future, impending events or narratives). The major use of content analysis is to provide a framework so that a quantitative approach can be used to analyze communications after they have been spoken or printed.

TABLE 10.2 Question: In general, do you feel that the laws covering the sale of firearms should be made more strict, less strict, or kept as they are now?

Year Survey Conducted*	More Strict	Less Strict	Kept as Now	No Opinion
		%	%	%
Oct '15	55	11	33	*
Oct '13	49	13	37	1
Dec '12	58	6	34	2
Oct '11	43	11	44	2
Oct '10	44	12	42	2
Oct '08	49	8	41	2
Oct '07	51	8	39	2
Oct '06	56	9	33	2
Oct '05	57	7	35	1
Jan '04	60	6	34	—
May '00	62	5	31	2
Aug '99	66	6	27	1
Mar '93	70	4	24	2
Sep '90	78	2	17	3

Source: www.gallup.com/poll/1645/guns.aspx (Retrieval date 4/25/16)
*Partial listing of years from article

While the first dictionary definition of content analysis appeared in 1961, its intellectual roots go back considerably further. In 1910, Max Weber proposed a large-scale content analysis of newspapers at the first meeting of the German Sociological Society. Also, about the same time in this country, quantitative newspaper analyses (measuring the column inches devoted to specific subjects) were conducted because of concern that newspapers were not providing as much factual content as they were gossip, sports, and scandals (Krippendorff, 1980).

During World War II, content analysis was used to analyze propaganda. After the war, the value of content analysis as a research tool was widely recognized, and interest in it spread beyond the field of communications to other disciplines in the social sciences.

Content analyses may be either quantitative or qualitative in focus. The quantitative efforts are often concerned with counting how often certain key words, terms, or concepts are communicated, while the qualitative efforts attempt to identify patterns and themes in communications. For instance, a new governor might give public speeches which, in an overall context, criticize the former administration and its past policies instead of proposing new policies. Or the governor may indicate his or her budget priorities as building highways and bridges and never mention improving state funding for education or child welfare.

Marini, Bhakta, and Graf (2009) wanted to know more about the concerns of persons with disabilities. They reviewed over 160 letters written to the editors of two physical disability–related magazines. They found that despite the Americans with Disabilities Act, the most frequent issue addressed in the letters was about accessibility. This was followed by concerns about adaptive aid equipment and then health issues (for example, secondary conditions for persons with physical disabilities). The findings of such projects can be used to advocate for the population being studied.

Advantages and Disadvantages of Content Analysis

For many quantitative researchers, content analysis involves counting how many times individual words, expressions, or events occur in a communication. This is commonly known as the **manifest content**. However, as you know, often the actual choice of words we use is less important than how we say something. For instance, Bill might ask Sophia if she likes her new apartment, and Sophia responds sarcastically, "I *love* it. The tiny kitchen, too small to turn around in, is especially appealing." Bill then realizes his friend is really *not* impressed with the apartment. As we read this dialogue, we could count the words *love* and *appealing* and conclude that *twice* something good was said about the apartment. Not being there, we miss Sophia's wry smile, the way she rolls her eyes to the ceiling. The context in which something is said or done is often very important. In one study of TV violence, supposedly more than 70% of the time the perpetrators of the violence went unpunished. However, critics quickly argued that counting incidents of violence without looking at the context means very little. For instance, a police officer could save a family held hostage by shooting a bad guy. Does he become one of the "perpetrators" of violence who goes unpunished? Specific acts (e.g., deadly violence in a movie) as manifest content are easy enough to count.

Researchers concerned with less obvious content must develop techniques and categories that allow for interpretative analysis of the **latent content**. While manifest content is comparable to the surface structure in a message, latent content refers to the deep structural meaning. Qualitative content analysis examines the meanings, explanations, interpretations, or subtle messages that are contained in conversations, stories, speeches, etc. Suppose you are asked to read a set of essays from applicants to a PhD program. As you begin to look over them, you recognize right away that some writers want to enter the program because they want to teach and become educators. Others speak primarily about their passion for research. While you could code each paragraph in terms of which of these themes are predominant, you might also be comfortable with *not* counting the number of terms or sentences or paragraphs focusing on teaching or researching but instead looking for statements or quotations that represent the participant's interests, goals, experience, or views about earning a PhD. Like archival research or secondary analysis, content analysis relies on material that already exists.

Although it is a very old article, a content analysis that shows how simple the technique is to conduct and also how it might be and should be used more often by social workers is one by Mahon and Allen-Meares (1992): Is social work racist? A content analysis of recent literature, *Social Work, 37*(6), 533–539. It is one that I often suggest to students and one that provides a good starting point for discussion—both in terms of what it may suggest about those who published in social work journals during the specified time frame (and those who didn't) as well as possible limitations of the methodology. Give it a read and see if you agree!

BOX 10.4   INTERESTING APPLICATIONS OF CONTENT ANALYSIS

Like secondary data analysis, content analysis has five advantages:

1. It is unobtrusive.
2. It is generally inexpensive to conduct.
3. It allows the investigator to "mine" existing agency documents and databases.
4. It can deal with large volumes of data and over a long period of time.
5. No special training or expertise is required to conduct a content analysis—all that is needed is a research question or hypothesis and a set of communications or a database of source documents.

✓ Collins, S. E., Jones, C. B., Hoffmann, G., Nelson, L. A., Hawes, S. M., Grazioli, V. S., ... & Clifasefi, S. (2016). In their own words: Content analysis of pathways to recovery among individuals with the lived experience of homelessness and alcohol use disorders. *International Journal of Drug Policy, 27*, 89–96.

✓ Danzl, M. M., Harrison, A., Hunter, E. G., Kuperstein, J., Sylvia, V., Maddy, K., & Campbell, S. (2016). "A lot of things passed me by": Rural stroke survivors' and caregivers' experience of receiving education from health care providers. *Journal of Rural Health, 32*, 13–24.

✓ Feeley, T. H., O'Mally, A. K., & Covert, J. M. (2016). A content analysis of organ donation stories printed in U.S. newspapers: Application of newsworthiness. *Health Communication, 31*(4), 495–503.

✓ So, J., Prestin, A., Lee, L., Wang, Y., Yen, J., & Chou, W.-Y. S. (2016). What do people like to "share" about obesity? A content analysis of frequent retweets about obesity on Twitter. *Health Communications, 31*, 193–206.

✓ Holosko, M. J., Winkel, M., Crandall, C. A., & Briggs, H. E. (2015). A content analysis of mission statements of our top 50 schools of social work. *Journal of Social Work Education, 51*(2), 222–236.

✓ Lee, J. L., DeCamp, M., Dredze, M., Chisolm, M. S., & Buller, Z. D. (2014). What are health-related users tweeting? A qualitative content analysis of health-related users and their messages on Twitter. *Journal of Medical Internet Research, 16*(10), e237.

✓ Bushman, B. J., Jamieson, P. E., Weitz, I., & Romer, D. (2013). Gun violence trends in movies. *Pediatrics, 132*(6), 1014–1018.

✓ Badger, K., Royse, D., & Moore, K. (2011). What's in a story? A text analysis of burn survivors' web-posted narratives. *Social Work in Health Care, 50*(8), 577–594.

✓ Corley, N. A., & Young, S. M. (2018). Is social work still racist? A content analysis of recent literature. *Social Work, 63*, 317–326.

These are just a few examples of content analyses that can be found in the literature. Content analysis is a flexible methodology, and countless topics can be explored with it.

ANXIETY CHECK 10.1

Anxiety Check 10.1: Is content analysis similar to an experiment in that cause and effect can be demonstrated?

[Answer found at the end of the book.]

Steps in Conducting Content Analysis

Like secondary data analysis, content analysis has five steps.

Step 1: Framing a Research Question

Content analysis starts with a research question or hypothesis. Perhaps you have a notion that the news source you most frequently read has a negative opinion of social workers or some other definite bias that you want to document. Or you may want to test the hypothesis that fewer articles on community development have been written in social work journals during the past five years than on the topic of managed care. Whatever your interest, some question or assumption that can be tested through an examination of written or spoken communications must be stated.

Step 2: Deciding on Source Materials

After framing a research question, you begin to think about what materials would provide the best source of communications for the content analysis. Will you use a local newspaper, the *New York Times*, or some combination of professional journals? Naturally, you have pragmatic decisions to make. The materials should be relatively easy to obtain. You need familiarity with the source materials; some journals or newsletters may be less relevant to your topic than you originally thought.

Step 3: Deciding on Units of Analysis

You will need to decide what will constitute the **units of analysis**, or the recording units. You may choose to examine certain words or terms, behaviors, entire paragraphs, or the whole item itself (for example, an entire article or speech)—depending on whether you are looking for manifest or latent content.

With a quantitative approach, the most common units of analysis are individual words or terms. However, if you search for selected key words, you may miss other terms that could also refer to the concept you are studying. Thus, if you instruct reviewers to search for the number of times "clinical social worker" is used in job ads, they might overlook references to "family services worker" or "mental health therapist" or "counselors"—which might include those with clinical social work degrees. This problem is more likely to occur if the investigator doesn't pretest categories on a sample of source materials. Thinking about what you intend to count or quantify generally leads to conceptualizing what categories will be needed. These categories should not be developed apart from the material being reviewed; your familiarity with the material will assist you in devising definitions and categories. As with questionnaire development, the use of a pilot-test will help in refining the operational definitions of categories.

Written rules, especially if more than one person will be involved in the content analysis, improves the **coding** of the data process (classifying and categorizing). For instance, in analyzing employment ads, the researcher will have to decide whether an ad for a social worker I position should be counted in the same category as a social worker II position. If one wants to know about the various levels of positions in social work being advertised, it would make sense to code for multiple social work categories. However, if one simply wants to know if there were more social work positions than physical therapist or psychologist or other related positions, then one will code accordingly. It is important that codes for categories be exhaustive and mutually exclusive.

The examination of themes from whole items can involve some complex decision rules. Take, for instance, a situation where you want to determine what newspaper editorials reveal about a president's performance. Searching for a set of specific words or phrases (such as "the president is doing a good job in office") may not be of much help because there are so many ways to characterize the president's actions positively or negatively. Then there's the issue of balance—the editorial writers might like some of the president's policies but not others. Coding can get a little tricky.

BOX 10.5   CODING SCHEMES IN CONTENT ANALYSIS

Manifest Coding

- Counting the *number* (*frequency*) of words, behaviors, pictures (for example, persons of color appearing in ads)
- Measuring the amount of space allocated to a topic (for example, in a magazine, the size of graphics or pictures) or the amount of *time* dedicated to a topic (for example, on national news or in a speech)

Latent Coding

- Experiences, opinions, views, or positions (for example, positive or negative, supportive or nonsupportive, conservative or liberal)

Step 4: Deciding on Sampling Design

You also need to decide how much of the source material you can review practically. This is not a problem when the universe of materials is small enough that it is feasible to review all of it. However, if there are hundreds or thousands of items to be examined, then sampling is a logical decision. As discussed in the chapter on survey research, there are several ways to draw a sample. With regard to content analysis, it makes the most sense to think of a random or systematic random design. Convenience samples yield less valuable data.

Step 5: Conducting Reliability Checks

As with other methods discussed in this book, you will need to make sure your results meet the test of replication, especially with regard to reliability in the classification of content categories. Of chief concern is **intercoder or inter-rater reliability** (a desired high rate of agreement or similarity in the way they code). If those who code the content don't agree with each other very often, the coding system will not be reliable. Particularly if multiple coders work on the project, it is important to compute the reliability (consistency) of the categorization process. Reliability is strengthened when there is practice session training for the raters and clear coding instructions and rules. If one person is doing all of the coding, reliability can still be tested by giving an independent rater the criteria and a sample of the source materials already reviewed. A simple approach would be to select 10 samples and then see what percentage of the time Rater A agreed with Rater B.

A Practical Application of Content Analysis

A potential problem for mental health and social service agencies is poor public image. Bad publicity may affect agency admissions or the community's perception of the quality of care provided by an agency. What follows is an account of how content analysis was used as a research tool to bring about needed change.

Early in my career, I was employed by a mental health system that was too often in the local news (so the administrators thought). A newspaper reporter covered every board meeting, and much of the coverage had a negative slant to it. For instance, one editorial stated that the mental health system had "axed practically all hope of renewing the [mental health] levy with the construction of a $2.2 million building." Because the vote on the mental health levy was more than two years away, such a statement by the newspaper suggested a stance that was not supportive of the community mental health system's need for the county's property tax levy.

Our fear was that the newspaper could influence citizens in the community to vote against the mental health levy. Because more than half of the revenue to operate the mental health system came from the tax levy, it became clear that effort should begin right away to counter negative perceptions held by the newspaper staff. Our strategy was to demonstrate objectively how the content of their articles and headlines was not balanced and could have a detrimental effect on public opinion.

Every morning, the agency director's secretary clipped articles from the local newspapers that referred to the mental health system. These clippings were kept in a historical file. Clippings had been kept for about 10 years and constituted an obvious source of material for a content analysis. Because reading 10 years of newspaper clippings was a sizable task, we decided that reading headlines was much more manageable. All of the headlines and captions above the news articles were then listed, and this constituted our units of analysis.

While our interest was in identifying the amount of negative coverage by the newspaper, this quickly became problematic. It was not difficult to identify those headlines we regarded as negative ("Hostility Erupts at Mental Health Board Meeting," "Mental Health Board in Dispute," "Mental Health Officials Squabble"). However, some headlines were difficult to interpret ("Crisis Center May Resume Services" or "Judge Promises Fast Ruling") without reading the whole article. Consequently, we decided to conduct the content analysis on selected key words.

It was not possible to anticipate every term or key word that indicated a negative reflection on the mental health system. Even clusters of negative words or phrases would have been difficult to specify. Therefore, we decided to search for those key words that had something to do with the delivery of services or administrative issues.

Among our findings were 37 headlines that, over the 10-year period, contained the key word "facility" relative to the proposed new building. This number of appearances was larger than that of any problem-specific key words such as *divorce, alcohol, stress, depression, addiction, domestic violence, incest, runaways, death*, and so on. It also occurred more times than population-specific terms such as *aging, elderly, step-parent, families, teenagers, juveniles, children*, and *students*. Clearly, the newspaper was much more focused on the proposal to build a new facility than criticism of service delivery.

Since we had the clippings, it was easy to measure the number of square inches of newspaper coverage associated with each headline and so that information was also included in the study. We found that over 40% of all the clippings dealt with the mental health system's administrative board. The balance of the coverage was spread over the five local mental health agencies that delivered services to consumers. We also found that of the three local newspapers, the one perceived to be the most negative was providing about a third more coverage on the mental health system in terms of square inches than either of the two other local papers.

When the study was finished, it was nicely typed and presented to the publisher of the most negative newspaper. After reading the study and seeing examples of how the public could be interpreting their coverage, the paper began to soften their negative comments about the mental health system. Subsequent coverage was much more balanced and presented no opposition to the renewal of the mental health levy.

Final Thoughts on Unobtrusive Approaches

This chapter provides only a few examples of secondary data sources and content analyses and illustrations of how they might be used. Unobtrusive methods provide a needed alternative for those situations where resources are lacking for conducting large-scale surveys or other more rigorous forms of investigation. No need to reinvent the wheel if someone else has already collected the data for us!

Given the considerable wealth of information available in this society just for the asking, practitioners ought to look first to see what's available before planning a whole new original research project. Because unobtrusive methods do not require a lot of research expertise, even social worker practitioners who don't think of themselves as researchers can apply them. As a social worker, it is important to become familiar with the social indicators in your field so that it will be easier to find secondary data and monitor trends when needed.

Key Terms

Hawthorne effect

retrospective research

unobtrusive research

archival research

incidence

social indicators

manifest content

unit of analysis

secondary data

Heisenberg's uncertainty principle

prospective research

coding

secondary data analysis

prevalence

content analysis

latent content

intercoder or interrater reliability

SELF-REVIEW

(Answers are at the end of the book.)

1. T or F. Mailed surveys can be considered unobtrusive research.
2. How is a researcher who wants to conduct only secondary data analysis limited?
3. T or F. The identification of trends is often an important focus of secondary data analysis.

262 | Research Methods in Social Work

4. Comparing social service expenditures in Sweden, Ireland, and South Africa with the United States and Canada would be an example of:

   a. content analysis
   b. deconstructionism
   c. secondary data analysis
   d. systematic random sampling.

5. T or F. To conduct a secondary data analysis, the existing data set you examine must have been developed for a purpose identical to your own research interest.

6. T or F. Content analysis can be used with any set of communications, whether they are written, spoken, or performed.

7. Besides being unobtrusive, what is another major advantage common to both secondary data analysis and content analysis?

8. What is a disadvantage common to both secondary data analysis and content analysis?

9. What is the term associated with content analysis that describes context, subtle meanings, or nuances?

10. T or F. Course syllabi from major universities could be content analyzed to determine if term papers are more common than exams or tests for evaluating students' performance.

QUESTIONS FOR CLASS DISCUSSION

1. List the social service agencies where students have worked or been placed in a practicum. In a separate column, list the types of social problems these agencies deal with. Next, make a list of the social indicators that social workers could use to determine if their programs are having an impact on the social problems.

2. Using the social indicators listed in Table 10.2, discuss potential bias in terms of how each might under- or overestimate the extent of a social problem.

3. Among the social service agencies with which you are familiar, what local information do you think they might be required to report to the state capital each year?

4. Identify a local issue or controversy in your community or on your campus. Discuss how content analysis might be used to provide some insight into how important this issue is compared to others.

5. Discuss ways that secondary data or content analyses could be used to advocate for clients or for the profession of social work. Suggest studies that need to be conducted.

RESOURCES AND REFERENCES

Dunn, S. L., Arslanian-Engoren, C., DeKoekkoek, T., Jadack, R., & Scott, L. D. (2015). Secondary data analysis as an efficient and effective approach to nursing research. *Western Journal of Nursing Research, 37*(10), 1295–1307.

Earl, A., Crause, C., Vaid, A., & Albarracin, D. (2016). Disparities in attention to HIV-prevention information. *AIDS Care, 28*(1), 79–86.

Godin, G., Germain, M., Conner, M., Delage, G., & Sheeran, P. (2014). Promoting the return of lapsed blood donors: A seven-arm randomized control trial of the question-behavior effect. *Health Psychology, 33*(7), 646–655.

Habel, M. A., Liddon, N., & Stryker, J. E. (2009). The HPV vaccine: A content analysis of online news stories. *Journal of Women's Health, 18*(3), 401–407.

Krippendorff, K. (2012). *Content analysis: An introduction to its methodology.* Beverly Hills, CA: Sage.

Marini, I., Bhakta, M. V., & Graf, N. (2009). A content analysis of common concerns of persons with physical disabilities. *Journal of Applied Counseling, 40*(1), 44–49.

Neuendorf, K. A. (2016). *The content analysis guidebook.* Thousand Oaks, CA: Sage.

Webb, E., Campbell, D. T., Schwartz, R., & Sechrest, L. (1966). *Unobtrusive measures: Nonreactive research in the social sciences.* Chicago, IL: Rand McNally.

Wood, C., Conner, M., Sandberg, T., Godin, G., & Sheeran, P. (2014). Why does asking questions change health behaviors? The mediating role of attitude accessibility. *Psychology & Health, 29*(4), 390–404.

Credit

ASSIGNMENT 10.1

Conducting a Content Analysis

Objective: *To identify the key decisions required for a content analysis and to provide experience in conducting one.*

Three different ideas are presented for content analyses. These can be done individually, with a partner, or in a small group. On a continuum that has scientific merit on the right end of the spectrum, the first two projects would be way to the left. These two will yield results that are more fun than academically rigorous. The third idea, however, provides the basis for a project that could, if properly conducted, conceivably result in publication in one or more professional journals. Your instructor will tell you which project to choose and advise you how to post or forward your responses using the following boldfaced terms for the headings in your paper.

Idea 1: Select a popular magazine generally available in drugstores and supermarkets. Select two different issues of the same magazine and skim through them, paying particular attention to the advertisements.

1. State a **hypothesis** that you could test using the advertisements as the source material. (For instance, are there more products being marketed for men than for women? Do the ads appear to target certain income or age groups?)

2. Define your **units of analysis**. (Will you be looking at only ads with pictures or graphics? Do they have to be a certain size? Do personal or classified ads qualify?)

3. Because any one issue (for example, the December issue) may not be representative of typical issues, state a **sampling design**. How many issues should you review to be confident of your findings?

4. How will you conduct a **reliability check** of your findings?

5. Conduct your content analysis. What were your **results**? State the evidence that supports or does not support your hypothesis.

Idea 2: Before watching a movie, identify several behaviors that would *not* be examples of healthy role modeling for adolescents (for example, smoking, cursing, violence, etc.).

1. State a **hypothesis** that you could test using the movie as the source material.

2. Define your **units of analysis** (for example: What behaviors constitute an act of violence? Is kissing or hand-holding a sexual act?). Write down your definitions before watching the movie.

3. For a **reliability check**, get at least one other person (two others would be great) to count the behaviors that you have identified as the units of analysis to be tallied. Each of you should keep notes independent of the others. (No fair calling out, "There's one!")

4. Compare the findings from the different observers. What were the **results**? Does the evidence support your hypothesis?

Idea 3: Choose a social problem (for example, poverty, homelessness, drug abuse, mental illness, elder abuse) or a topic that you are passionate about. The purpose of this exercise is to see how much coverage it is receiving in one or more of the major social work journals.

1. Identify the **source materials** (the professional journal or journals that are appropriate for your investigation and the time frame covered).

2. State a **hypothesis** or research question that you could test using the journal as the source material.

3. For this exercise, the **units of analysis** can either be the number of articles on a particular topic or the number of pages devoted to a particular subject. Both of these can be easily determined from reviewing the journal's table of contents.

4. Because many social work journals have been in existence for decades, what **sampling design** will you use? How many tables of content will you review? How many years will you survey?

5. What would be a good plan for a **reliability check**?

6. Conduct your content analysis. What were your **results**? State the evidence that supports or does not support your hypothesis.

Conducting a Secondary Data Analysis

Objective: *To identify the key decisions required for a secondary data analysis and to provide experience in conducting one.*

Three different ideas are presented for content analyses. These can be done individually, with a partner, or in a small group. Your instructor may allow you to choose from the three or may direct you to a particular one. Be sure to describe your project clearly, and then use the following boldfaced terms for headings in your paper.

Idea 1: County Comparisons within a State. This chapter contains a table listing social indicators (for example, births, deaths, suicides, school dropouts) that generally can be found in state-maintained data sets. You may want to go back and skim that table. Then, choose one of the indicators and go to the Internet. Try to find relevant data from your state for the past five to 10 years. Once you are sure the data are easily accessible, follow the steps presented here. Before getting started, though, you might want to think about other variables that might help you to interpret your findings. For instance, would you want to consider the population of each county in terms of children under 18 if you are examining school dropout rates? Some databases may provide only raw numbers; others may provide only rates or ratios. Rather than compare raw numbers county by county, it would make sense to look at rates (for example, dropout rate per 1,000 students enrolled, suicide rate per 100,000 population).

1. State a **hypothesis**. For example, might urban counties have proportionately more of this problem than rural counties? Might a different problem (for example, suicides) be more of a problem for older adults than younger adults?

2. Identify your **source materials** (for example, the department that maintains the data) and the number of years you intend to survey (go back five years unless your instructor tells you differently).

3. Identify your **social indicator**. Is it a number, ratio, or rate?

4. Define **other key variables**. For instance, what is a rural county? An urban county?

5. What are your **findings**?

6. **Why** do you think you found the results that you did?

Idea 2: State Comparisons. This chapter contains several suggestions for Internet resources that provide data sets that allow for state-by-state comparisons. Explore a few websites until you find an interesting variable. Then, choose one of the indicators and compare your state with one that is similar to it in population (for example, Montana and Idaho, or Nevada and New Mexico). Once you are sure the data are easily accessible, follow the steps presented here. Before getting started, though, you might want to think about other variables that will help you to interpret your findings. If the database supplies only raw numbers, you might want to convert those numbers to rates or ratios based on population or some other variable.

1. State a **hypothesis**. Do you expect both states to have similar rates of the indicator?

2. Identify your **source materials** (for example, the agency that maintains the data) and the number of years you intend to survey (go back five years unless your instructor tells you differently).

3. Identify your **social indicator**. Is it a number, a ratio, or rate?

4. Define any **other key variables**.

5. What are your **findings**?

6. **Why** do you think you found the results that you did?

Idea 3: National Comparisons. Choose a social problem like infant mortality or illiteracy and find a database from the United Nations (**unstats.un.org/unsd/**) that will allow you to compare one nation with another. You might want to examine the social indicator in terms of other variables; for example, the amount of money spent on military expenditures. You might want to compare countries that are similar geographically—for instance, choose two countries in Africa or two in South America.

1.   State a **hypothesis**. Do you expect both nations to have similar rates of the indicator?

2.   Identify your **source materials** (for example, the agency that maintains the data) and the number of years you intend to survey (go back five years unless your instructor tells you differently).

3.   Identify your **social indicator**. Is it a number, a ratio, or rate?

4.   Define any **other key variables**.

5.   What are your **findings**?

6.   **Why** do you think you found the results that you did?

CHAPTER 11

Qualitative Research

SOCIAL WORKERS ENCOUNTER a wide range of people with problems that are both unique and, on some level, commonplace. While we sometimes think that life will be a straight line from one place or achieved goal to another, often there are setbacks, hardships, and barriers that can affect our happiness and enjoyment of life. Consider the pilot flying on vacation with his family. Inexplicably, the plane crashes. The pilot wakes up in the hospital discovering that the accident killed his wife and children. It is easy to understand the grief that he might feel, perhaps harder to know how to help him with the guilt and self-blame that he may always carry with him. What does he tell himself in the lonely hours when he can't sleep? What has helped him deal with his loss and guilt? Was he involved in counseling? A support group?

Take the situation of an attractive young woman whose car was involved in a six-vehicle pile-up traffic accident that resulted in the amputation of her right foot. Again, on some level, we can understand the depression and grief that she might feel as a result of the accident, but how did she recover? What does she tell herself about her appearance? Her future with someone? What gives her that can-do buoyant and optimistic outlook?

Maxine's half brother committed suicide when he was a teenager. She's always felt guilty—even 40 years later—believing that she should have recognized the signs, should have been able to get him help. As a teenager, she didn't have any training, wouldn't have known how to assess for suicidal intent. What does she tell herself about losing a brother? Why does she feel that her pain is worse than if Rob had died in combat or a traffic accident? As a mother, did she fear suicide could run in her family? Did she constantly monitor her children for signs of depression? Did she feel she was a better mother than her mother?

While life will always have surprises in store for us (for example, divorce, unemployment, illness), some people are able to overcome their trials and tribulations, while others seem to be forever scarred by them. What makes certain individuals resilient? (As I write these words, I'm thinking of the powerful movie *Unbroken* (2014), based on the life of Louis Zamperini. If you are not familiar with his story, you might want to see the movie or read the book with the same name by Laura Hillenbrand to get an idea of the obstacles he overcame—including 47 days in a life raft with no food or water and being starved and sadistically tortured in a Japanese prisoner of war camp for over two years. An earlier movie called *Mask* (1985) also describes a unique life and is based on the true story of Roy L. "Rocky" Dennis. Rocky had a stigmatizing facial deformity from a rare disease called craniodiaphyseal dysplasia, or lionitis. He couldn't go anywhere without people staring at him; Rocky died from the disease at age 17.)

How do certain life experiences shape a person—perhaps making some of them resilient? If you find yourself reading these vignettes and thinking that you would like to have the opportunity to interview these or other individuals and ask them questions about recovering from life's major setbacks, then you may be thinking like a qualitative researcher.

Why Conduct Qualitative Research?

There are several reasons that an investigator might choose to examine a problem or phenomenon qualitatively rather than quantitatively. For instance, you might select a qualitative approach if you are interested in the life stories of a small number of individuals, if you want to ask mostly open-ended questions, or if you want to investigate a group that is not often visible—one that is hard to reach or hard to find, possibly due to illegal activities.

Padgett (2008) suggests these reasons for conducting qualitative research:

1. When little or no literature or previous studies are available on the phenomenon—especially from the "inside" perspective. ("Inside" means from someone involved in that culture/world.)
2. When the topic requires great sensitivity to explore it—especially when a particular behavior is illegal, stigmatized, or taboo.
3. When the investigator wishes to obtain the perspective of participants in their own words and actions and wishes to obtain a "deep understanding" and to write a "rich description" of it.
4. When the focus is on the process and not the outcome of a program or activity (for example, what works well or poorly in an intervention program).
5. When the quantitative findings need more explanation, when an "impasse in understanding or explaining" has been reached.
6. When one wants to merge research with advocacy.

A qualitative approach might be chosen any time detailed, in-depth information is desired. It is *not* the appropriate approach if one wants answers to factual questions involving quantifiable variables. A *quantitative* approach would be needed to answer such questions as: What percent of my clients are over the age of 25? How many have been previously diagnosed with an anxiety disorder? and What is the proportion of female to male clients?

However, if you are interested in what life is like for college students with bipolar disorder, or how do the spouses of combat veterans with posttraumatic stress disorder describe their best and worst days, then you would probably want to approach your topic qualitatively.

Qualitative researchers can begin their investigations and examine the phenomenon or problem of interest through a variety of methodological approaches—there is not a single qualitative approach. "Qualitative research" is more a generic term than a precise description of a methodology. The characteristics that qualitative designs tend to have in common is that the researcher is, foremost and above all, *personally involved* with the collection and analysis of data from individuals. This normally requires *sustained contact* with the study participants in their natural settings (their neighborhoods or communities or where they normally congregate)—as opposed to the brief or minimal exchange of a survey. The focus is usually on the individuals' *experiences* living in their worlds. And last, qualitative research is characterized by *a narrative or descriptive report* of the findings. That is, qualitative research often uses the participant's own words to describe events, attitudes, knowledge, etc.

The steps that one would follow in a qualitative study depend on which methodology the researcher thinks would best provide the information that he or she desires. There are numerous methods that qualitative researchers use—too many, really, to be covered in this chapter. One effort at listing them might include these methodologies:

Action research	Analysis (IPA)	Life-world analysis
Analytic induction	Field research	Mixed methods
Biographical research	Ethnography	Narrative analysis
Conversation analysis	Grounded theory	Objective hermeneutics
Constructionism	Hermeneutics	Phenomenological
Comparative analysis	Symbolic interactionism	Discourse analysis
Ethnomethodology	Life history	

A description of each of these and other methodologies can be found along with suggested readings and related links at **onlineqda.hud.ac.uk/resources.php**.

Despite the array of approaches listed above, all the qualitative methods share common characteristics. The purpose of this chapter is *not* to provide you with in-depth information about each of these methods, but to provide a general overview to introduce you to qualitative research.

We'll start with the qualitative approach known as the case study.

The Case Study

A **case study** is an in-depth examination of a single client, family, adverse event, group, organization, or phenomenon. Any of the three individual situations mentioned at the beginning of the chapter lend themselves to a case study. In fact, a biography like Hillenbrand's *Unbroken* could be considered a case study. Case studies are detailed examinations of an individual or situation to better understand it. For instance, a local Veterans Affairs hospital conducts a case study they call a "psychological autopsy" whenever one of its patients commits suicide. Even though no two cases will ever be exactly alike, there are things that can be learned from a thorough assessment of a single case that might help social workers, doctors, nurses, and rehabilitation specialists in their work. Here are a couple of clinical examples of case studies found in the literature:

✓ Kukla, M., Whitesel, F., Lysaker, P. H. (2016). An integrative psychotherapy approach to foster community engagement and rehabilitation in schizophrenia: A case study illustration. *Journal of Clinical Psychology, 72*(2), 152–163.

✓ Bragin, M., Taaka, J., Adolphs, K., Gray, H., & Eibs, T. (2015). Measuring difficult-to-measure concepts in clinical social work practice operationalizing psychosocial well-being among war-affected women: A case study in Northern Uganda. *Clinical Social Work Journal, 43*(4), 348–361.

For those without a clinical interest, there are a surprising number of macro-level case studies in the literature as well. It is usually the uniqueness of the case that makes it worthy of study; for the qualitative researcher, there is no interest in generalizability. Whether having a micro or macro focus, qualitative studies are primarily descriptive in nature.

Here's an example from the book *Housing First: Ending Homelessness, Transforming Systems, and Changing Lives* by Deborah Padgett, Benjamin Henwood, and Sam Tsemberis (2016). In the chapter entitled "In Their Own Words: Consumers Share Their Stories," the resident called "Alfred" explains what having his own place means to him. You might want to contrast it with what you might say if someone were to ask you the same question.

> *And you know, after sleeping in shelters and halfway houses, it's amazing how just to be able to wake up in the middle of the night and smoke a cigarette without somebody yelling at you. You know, little things, being able to take a bath, things that people take for granted, are just so much. I truly enjoy these things. I don't share this with people, but I enjoy taking bubble baths. You know, just something I never was able to do. You know, so to be able to smoke a cigarette in my own bedroom, take a bath, or cook, you know, it's mine. And it's been almost nine years, and I still have that feeling every time I stick my key in the door. (p. 81)*

The back story is that Alfred was a drug user or abuser for over 20 years and had been delusional and violent. He finally accepted help when he was 40 and in prison.

Examples of macro case studies in the literature:

- ✓ Capp, G. (2015). Our community, our schools: A case study of program design for school-based mental health services. *Children & Schools, 37*(4), 241–248.
- ✓ Block, S. R., Wheeland, L., & Rosenberg, S. (2014). Improving human services effectiveness through the deconstruction of case management: A case study on the emergence of a team-based model of service coordination. *Human Service Organizations: Management, Leadership & Governance, 38*, 16–28.
- ✓ Mallett, C. A. (2014). The "Learning Disabilities to Juvenile Detention" pipeline: A case study. *Children & Schools, 36*(3), 147–154.
- ✓ Howells, B., McGuire, J., & Nakashima, J. (2008). Co-location of health care services for homeless veterans: A case study of innovation in program implementation. *Social Work in Health Care, 47*(3), 219–231.
- ✓ Chow, J. C. C., & Austin, M. J. (2008). The culturally responsive social service agency: The application of an evolving definition to a case study. *Administration in Social Work, 32*(4), 39–64.

A qualitative researcher conducting a case study would likely use as many sources of information as is feasible and the strength of that approach is that the same patterns or themes should emerge from different informants, a review of documents, and so on. However, the qualitative researcher may devise a study that involves only interviewing.

Social problems framed by large numbers (e.g., nationally, more than 400,000 children are in foster care). The magnitude of the problem does not help us to understand what an individual child's life might be in foster care. The value of a case study and qualitative research in general is its ability to illuminate some of their life experiences by closely examining the lives of a few.

BOX 11.1   TYPICAL STEPS FOLLOWED IN A CASE STUDY

BOX 11.1   TYPICAL STEPS FOLLOWED IN A CASE STUDY

1. Selecting the case: Will the unit of analysis be an individual, a social service program, a neighborhood, a school, a community, an incident (for example, a plane crash) or an organization of some sort (for example, a social service agency or even a street gang?).
2. Determining the issues and questions to be focused on.
3. Selecting the sources of data to draw upon. For example:
   - Interviews with neighbors, family, friends, etc.
   - Available documents and records.
   - Visits with and direct observation of the individual, organization, etc.
4. Collecting the data. Gaining entry to and the trust of those capable of providing useful information about the case.
5. Interpreting and analyzing the data.
6. Writing the report.

The Qualitative Interview

The qualitative interview is like a conversation that starts with a set of initial or guiding questions. Typically, these are broad, open-ended questions meant to elicit a narrative from the individual being interviewed. The researcher's role is to probe and seek more information. Details may emerge by saying something like, "Tell me more about that" or "What were your friends doing while you were doing this?"

From the responses received, interviewers frame new questions that may not have been planned and may actually lead into new areas of inquiry. Qualitative interviewers have much more flexibility and are less structured than survey interviewers. The emphasis for qualitative interviewers is on exploring the phenomenon at a deep level. Qualitative interviewers must be good listeners and not fill up the interview with their own chatter. However, they are free to share personal experiences as a way of building trust and rapport.

Because it is difficult to write down everything, and because the researcher doesn't want to lose important material, key interviews might be recorded so they can be listened to again and transcribed. Stories, jokes, and even digressions can be important for what they may reveal about the worldview or culture of the informant being interviewed. The interviewer often takes the position of one who is a learner and ignorant of the informant's daily life, which frees the informant to become a teacher who can explain the nuances or details that might otherwise not be explained or mentioned.

The qualitative interviewer needs to avoid:

- Long, complicated questions
- Questions that can be answered yes/no
- Vague questions that don't bring out specific details
- Leading questions based on the researcher's pet theories or assumptions
- Talking too much and not paying close enough attention to subtle signs that the individual might have more information to share if asked

As we discussed in a previous chapter, qualitative interviewers do not prepare detailed question-naires as a quantitative investigator might. However, they may use structured or standardized interview schedules—which are particularly useful if more than one interviewer is involved.

The person being interviewed is acknowledged as the insider, the expert concerning his or her world, and the qualitative researcher seeks to enter into that subjective reality, to discover that unique world. Unlike assessment or investigatory interviews that social workers may conduct, the qualitative interviewer does not try to maintain a formal distance or "objective" stance. The interview is conversational, and the goal is to form a dialogue to facilitate the investigator's understanding of the participant's life.

Early in their internship, even before they had the opportunity to interview any of the inmates at the prison, Mrs. Simpson had challenged Sophia and Bill to find some qualitative studies to read that would prepare them and help them understand some of the issues that the women prisoners faced.

Sophia immediately began searching and found the following articles that employed qualitative interviewing:

- ✓ Herbeck, D.M., Brecht, M.-L., Christou, D., & Lovinger, K. (2014). A qualitative study of meth-amphetamine users' perspectives on barriers and facilitators of drug abstinence. *Journal of Psychoactive Drugs, 46*(3), 215–225.
- ✓ Swan, H. (2016). A qualitative examination of stigma among formerly incarcerated adults living with HIV. *Sage Open, 6*(1), 1–9.

Bill must have been in the wrong database because he didn't find either of the two articles Sophia located. After 45 minutes of searching, he found one qualitative article that employed interviewing: Power, T., Jackson, D., Carter, B., & Weaver, R. (2014). Misunderstood as mothers: Women's stories of being hos-pitalized for illness in the postpartum period. *Journal of Advanced Nursing, 71*(2), 370–380.

Bill printed a copy and a little sheepishly handed a copy to Sophia. She looked at it and said, "But Bill, this doesn't have anything to do with the prison population."

"I know," he said. "But at least it is about women. And it used interviews. Don't I get some credit for that?"

"Are you asking me as a friend or to think about how our field instructor might respond?"

"Both," said Bill.

"In that case," said Sophia, handing the article back to Bill, "you'd better look some more."

Participant Observation

A researcher in the qualitative tradition might observe only, like spectators at a rodeo, but on occasion could become a **participant observer**—meaning that the investigator would try, as much as possible, to become fully immersed in that culture. To continue with the rodeo analogy, he or she might consider being a bronc rider or rodeo clown for a short time. Even though we will discuss participant observation and observation separately in this section, qualitative studies can be thought of as being on a continuum with studies involving observation only at one end, others involving the observer as a participant (perhaps even surreptitiously), and even others that might involve observation, interviewing, and participation.

Although the research is quite dated now, some of the best (and most fascinating) participant obser-vation was conducted by Rosenhan (1973). Eight sane pseudo-patients sought admission at a variety of psychiatric hospitals. All were admitted when they complained of hearing voices and were kept an average of 19 days (the range was from 7 to 52 days), although they ceased simulating any symptoms once they were admitted. None of them were detected as being sane, and most were discharged with a diagnosis of schizophrenia "in remission." Try to find the time to read his article, "Being Sane in Insane Places."

Other classic examples of participant-observer research might interest you as well. See, for example, Caudill, Redlich, Gilmore, and Brody (1952); Deane (1961); Ishiyama, Batman, and Hewitt (1967); Goldman, Bohr, and Steinberg (1970); and Estroff (1981) for their accounts.

For an extra-credit assignment one semester, an MSW student at my university attempted to find out how the public would view her if she were morbidly obese. She went to a thrift store and bought the largest sweater and the largest pants she could find and then used foam stuffing to make herself appear to weigh about 400 pounds. Once her disguise was in place, she went to a local mall and visited a lingerie store. She said she was surprised that no clerks even asked if they could be of help when she was "fat," but they were eager to assist her when she went back without the padding.

Contrast that participant-observer study with an observational study where a social work student goes into a classroom of second graders where three or more pupils are known to have attention deficit hyperactivity disorder (ADHD). As a quantitative researcher, the social work student might have constructed hypotheses to test and might have prepared a standardized observational form that could count, for instance, the number of times that the ADHD kids walked away from their desks during instruction, or recorded the duration of specific activities (like not paying attention). However, qualitative researchers don't go into a study with hypotheses as a rule, and would be unlikely to use standardized forms in their observations. What might you learn about ADHD by simply observing in a classroom?

Observation for the qualitative researcher involves capturing full visual details as well as auditory and sensory aspects of a classroom or other environment. Qualitative researchers could note that the wall between two second-grade classes was thin and that it was distracting to hear the students from the other class talking loudly with their teacher while having to sit in a different classroom with a soft-spoken teacher. The qualitative researcher would *definitely* note the hamster in the blue plastic ball rolling about the classroom and colliding with students' desks, and the street noise from trucks and traffic coming in the open window. Quantitative researchers may not pay a great deal of attention to the context from which their data are drawn, while good qualitative researchers record as many details as possible.

What exactly does one observe during an observation? Here are some suggestions:

Possible Observational Facets in a Qualitative Study

- The physical environment and context. (Where is the observation taking place, and what is the occasion?)
- The participants. (Who is in the setting?)
- Interactions/behaviors. (What are the participants doing? What behaviors are allowed, discouraged, punished, encouraged? What activities are planned? Are the activities planned or spontaneous? Are there routines?)
- Nonverbal communication. (How do participants communicate nonverbally?)
- Appearance. (Is there a special way of dressing to indicate rank or status?)
- Organization. (How are the participants organized? Is there a hierarchy?)
- Speech patterns. (Is there a special vocabulary or way of speaking?)

In addition to these elements, the qualitative researcher usually records his or her own interpretations (the meanings the researcher perceived) and may note any of the participants' reactions to the observer, as well as how any behaviors affected the observer. (For instance, a qualitative researcher might grow so frustrated with a second-grade teacher who talks too softly that the researcher finds herself tuning out the teacher and watching the hamster instead.)

Observation may be either overt, where it is clear to the participants that they are being observed, or covert when it is conducted surreptitiously. When observation is overt, it is important that the observer's presence not change the nature of the activities normally occurring. Good qualitative researchers take the time to allow the participants to get to know the investigator and establish rapport and trust.

As an example of a participant observation study, you may remember the Earl, Crause, Vaid, and Albarracin (2016) study in the last chapter, where research assistants sat in a public health clinic waiting room and observed how many patients were paying attention to two videos with prevention themes.

When Has Enough Data Been Collected?

There are several different indicators that can be helpful to the qualitative investigator for identifying when enough data have been collected.

- When the investigator has interviewed or collected data from all of the available key informants
- When there are no new findings or discoveries
- When there is enough consistency in the data that the investigator reaches **theoretical saturation**—the point at which new data replicate earlier findings.

Padgett (1998b) suggests that there is no good answer to the question of how many participants are needed in a qualitative study: "Because the emphasis is on quality rather than quantity, qualitative researchers sample not to maximize numbers, but to become 'saturated' with information about a specific topic" (p. 52).

What Does Qualitative Data Analysis Involve?

Unlike quantitative data analysis, which involves statistical analysis, qualitative data analysis entails coding data into constructs and looking for themes or patterns that can describe the phenomenon. Qualitative investigators often have many pages of text from their field notes, observations, and/or from transcribed interviews. While the search for themes and patterns can be done manually if the data set is small, qualitative investigators frequently employ computer software to manage the data and organize the findings. There are many qualitative software products available for turning documents into searchable databases.

In addition to written text, some allow the user to index and retrieve images as well as audio and video material. A list of qualitative software programs can be located on the Internet. Some programs are free, and others might be downloaded free from your university. The exact type of software one needs depends on the type of qualitative research one is doing.

Note that the qualitative software does not "process" or "analyze" the data. Instead, the software simply facilitates the sorting and ordering of passages that the investigator identifies. Documents are imported into the computer software, and a database is created. These data are unstructured ("free text")—unlike the variables in quantitative research. In quantitative data analysis, the researcher knows before data collection begins which variables will be examined and even what statistical procedures will be used. In qualitative data analysis, the researcher doesn't know what themes or patterns might emerge from the data and seldom are statistical procedures used.

Once the data are entered into the database, the qualitative investigator reads the text and identifies meaningful units of information. This step can be thought of as breaking the data into digestible chunks. When an observation or quotation is found that might be illustrative, it can be highlighted or coded so that it can be found later and grouped into a category or theme. These chunks can be a phrase or sentence, or one or more paragraphs—the researcher is not limited in length. Another way of thinking about this process is that the investigator is identifying *meaningful* units of information from the data. These units, or decontexualized segments, are grouped into constructs or categories. This coding process is known as **open coding**; that is, the categories are not predetermined but emerge from the data.

Identifying units of information that may reveal something about the phenomenon being studied relies entirely on the researcher's reading of the material and his or her construction of what might make sense to group into categories. A frustrating thing for quantitative investigators is that two different qualitative researchers can read the same passages but then develop different categories or themes, depending on their life experiences, knowledge, intuition about the data, and so on. It would be wrong to think that there is only one set of "true" themes or categories that exist within a data set just waiting to be discovered by the "right" qualitative researcher. Most qualitative investigators develop their own categories—allowing them to emerge from the data collected, rather than drawing them from other studies or theories. This is known as **grounded theory** because the themes are "grounded" in the original data collected by the investigator and his or her careful line-by-line reading of the material. This is an inductive approach because theory may arise from the data.

The qualitative researcher will usually read all of the collected material many times over to ensure that all the meaningful segments are identified and coded. As a next step, all of the segments composing each of the categories will be read or printed out so that the investigator can check to make sure that they have meaning within each category, as well as that the categories are unique and not overlapping. During this step, the investigator may read the passages composing each of the categories or themes multiple times. This is called **constant comparative analysis** and is an iterative process that involves checking for the best fit for coded passages.

Farber (2006) provides a good example for understanding this process using a closet full of clothes. Imagine on your first look into the closet, you notice all of the jeans that are folded on a top shelf. This might represent a category by itself, or they might be included in a category that included pants and slacks. After you have identified all of those items, you might turn your attention to shirts. Shirts might be coded as a single category initially and then on a subsequent visit might be conceptualized as those that are short-sleeved and those that are long-sleeved. You might even choose to develop separate categories for dress shirts or blouses and casual shirts. There may be skirts or uniforms in your closet that deserve a separate category, as would shoes, and so on. As you think about the items in each category, different facets might emerge. For instance, you might decide to code the items by color. Or by whether they have sentimental value, or by whether they were worn only on "special" occasions, or by their quality. This illustration explains why qualitative researchers may not agree upon or identify the same themes. What do you think a qualitative researcher would learn by looking at the closets of college and university students?

To take another example, consider this passage from an interview with a gang member: "I couldn't live without my gun. It's like the main thing. No respect without a gun." This excerpt might be coded to show that the gun is needed (1) for self-protection; or (2) because it places a gang member a rung higher in the gang's pecking order because it forces respect. There's also the possibility that it could be coded in some other way (for example, as part of the standard "uniform" that conveys membership in a particular group).

Qualitative research must present the best illustrations from the lives of others and convey these perspectives in a convincing way. Drisko (2005) cautions against using a single, brief quotation to illustrate an entire category or class of findings—what he calls the "sound bite" approach. Instead, he says, "[The] key is to provide the reader with ample raw data—the words and views of participants in their own voices. Use lots of direct quotes ... let participants' views come alive to the reader" (p. 592).

Here's an example of how Swanberg and Logan (2005) used the stories of women who were trying to remain employed even with abusive partners. They write,

Among respondents who suffered beatings prior to work, the majority of them attempted to go to work. One participant reported:

> [H]alf the time I wouldn't even want to go [to work] ... I feared what he'd do [to me] before I went to work. One time he had beat me so bad I had to walk to work and I don't even know how I made it. Since then I'm cautious before leaving for work. (p. 7)

BOX 11.2 CHARACTERISTICS OF QUALITATIVE RESEARCH

No experimental studies: There is no control group or experimental design or manipulation of the variables associated with the phenomenon under study. However, there can be qualitative evaluations of programs (using the perspectives of program participants).

Naturalistic: Unlike quantitative research, qualitative research (sometimes called field research because of its emphasis on conducting the study in the subjects' natural environment) is not as structured in the sense of knowing exactly what questions will be asked of whom and in what order. Before going into the field, they may not have identified all of the persons they hope to interview or even all the questions they want to ask. Many rely on a snowball methodology, where one informant may lead them to another and so on.

Participant observation: Researchers in the qualitative tradition rely primarily on in-depth interviewing and observations. They try as much as possible to "walk in the shoes" of the participant, to seek to understand the meanings associated with the participant's world.

Small sample size: Qualitative researchers do not worry about obtaining large, representative sample sizes. For example, Davidson (1997) conducted a qualitative needs assessment of relatives providing care for children who might otherwise have gone into foster care. Although she randomly drew names from a list of 420 relative caregivers, Davidson's goal was to obtain 10 interviews. She actually completed 9.

Little use of measurements: Unlike quantitative research, which deals with measurements and numerical values almost exclusively, qualitative research may use scales or questionnaires, but most don't. The investigator is the research tool; all data are filtered through his or her eyes and ears.

Journalistic narrative: The analyses produced by qualitative researchers most often are narratives and are based on the words used by informants to describe their life experiences. Jill Berrick (1995), for instance, learned enough as a participant observer of five impoverished families to write a book entitled *Faces of*

BOX 11.2 CHARACTERISTICS OF QUALITATIVE RESEARCH (CONTINUED)

Poverty: Portraits of Women and Children on Welfare. Again, the emphasis is not on the quantity of subjects but on the rich details, the subtleties and interactions that may be overlooked by others.

Exploratory: Qualitative researchers explore problems and phenomena about which little is known. Unlike quantitative research, seldom is there any interest in testing a hypothesis or theory. While quantitative researchers tend to be *deductive* (using a specific theory to make predictions about a particular situation), qualitative research is basically *inductive*—generating new theory from the observation of a special phenomenon or situation.

Value-free: The researcher's position is that of learner, not expert or specialist; he or she wants to know "What's going on here?" Assumptions and prior knowledge are held in abeyance until the latter stages of the analysis when they may then be compared to the findings (Morse & Field, 1995).

Another woman noted a particularly difficult situation:

> I was about seven months pregnant. ... [H]e started kicking me in the sides; I had a boot print on my side for months. ... I went to work; I did not know what else to do.
>
> Another woman who shared a car with her then boyfriend described missing work or report[ing] to her job as a waitress late because she "wait[ed] for him to return from work with the car from his shift. He was always late, or he would not show up at all sometimes." (pp. 6–7)

Qualitative researchers are flexible; their research goals or questions may be altered, even while data are being collected. While they usually have a methodology in mind prior to starting their project, they do not require that the research design and methodology be rigidly and unalterably stated before they begin to collect data. This fluidity allows qualitative researchers to generate hypotheses for later testing. In this sense, qualitative research is commonly regarded as being exploratory.

BOX 11.3 BOOKS WITH ETHNOGRAPHIC PERSPECTIVES

Ethnography is a type of qualitative research closely allied with cultural anthropologists. The goal of this type of research is to describe a culture or society from the perspective of the insiders—those living in it. The following books not only are interesting to read but also illustrate the necessity for a prolonged engagement approach that is characteristic of this type of qualitative research.

- ✓ Rawlence, B. (2016). *City of thorns: Nine lives in the world's largest refugee camp*. New York. NY: Picador.
- ✓ Knight, K. R. (2015). *addicted. pregnant. poor*. Durham, NC: Duke University Press.
- ✓ Holmes, S., & Bourgois, P. (2013). *Fresh fruit, broken bodies: Migrant farmworkers in the United States*. Los Angeles, CA: University of California Press.
- ✓ Ward, T. W. (2012). *Gangsters without borders: An ethnography of a Salvadoran street gang*. Oxford University Press.
- ✓ Bourgois, P., & Schonberg, J. (2009). *Righteous dopefiend*. Los Angeles, CA: University of California Press.
- ✓ Venkatesh, S. (2008). *Gang leader for a day: A rogue sociologist takes to the streets*. New York, NY: Penguin Press.

Reliability and Validity in Qualitative Studies

Qualitative researchers approach the issues of the reliability and validity of their findings somewhat differently than quantitative investigators. According to Neuman (2006), "Most qualitative researchers accept the basic principles of reliability and validity, but rarely use the terms because of their association with quantitative measurement" (p. 194). Belcher (1994) notes that three different strategies are used to establish trustworthiness or credibility, which "is analogous to establishing validity and reliability" (p. 128). These efforts can involve:

1. *Prolonged engagement*—investing sufficient time to not only learn about the culture, but also test one's understanding of it.
2. *Persistent observation*—to observe daily and keep records of the observations.
3. **Triangulation**—using multiple sources of information, methods, or observers to cross-check for inconsistencies or misinformation.

BOX 11.4 EVALUATING THE QUALITY OF QUALITATIVE STUDIES

Shek, Tang, and Han (2005) conducted a literature search of qualitative evaluation studies indexed in *Social Work Abstracts*. Drawing on criteria identified by previous qualitative investigators and writers, the authors developed 12 criteria to use for assessing the quality of the studies. What they found is instructive for those who aspire to create and present the best possible qualitative study. Here are some of their findings and conclusions:

*   The number and nature of participants were often not clearly stated.
*   The data collection procedures were not usually presented clearly, and the ability to audit the process of the study was missing—undermining the external validity of the study.
*   Honest reflection and discussion of biases or how biases might have been dealt with were not commonly found.
*   Triangulation across researchers in studies with multiple researchers fell short, resulting in the conclusion that "social work evaluators adopting qualitative methods do not appear to be very enthusiastic about the issue of reliability" (p. 190).

BOX 11.4   EVALUATING THE QUALITY OF QUALITATIVE STUDIES (CONTINUED)

- Peer checking was generally not mentioned as a way to check the interpretations of the researcher. (Peer checking involves having a colleague review one's data coding to confirm the categories and themes identified by the qualitative researcher.)
- Few studies mentioned alternative explanations, or looked for negative cases to disconfirm the findings, or limitations of the study.

To some extent, this list of frequent shortcomings reflects the difficulty of trying to standardize qualitative efforts and a need for journals to provide more guidelines for reporting and publishing qualitative research. Space limitations in journals may also force qualitative authors to abbreviate their work.

To this list, Padgett (2008) has added:

4. *Member checking*—going back into the field after data collection to verify with one or more participants regarding an interpretation or finding. Guba and Lincoln (1989) claim that member checks were the "single most critical technique for establishing credibility" (p. 293).
5. *Audit trails*—documenting the steps taken in one's data collection and analysis gives others confidence in the data.
6. *Negative case analysis*—looking in the data for any evidence that might disconfirm your finding or conclusion. Obviously, if you don't find any exceptions, then you can have more confidence in your findings.

Qualitative researchers have numerous ways of checking for reliability. For instance, if an informant were to reveal something that the investigator didn't think was true, he or she may want to ask other informants, get confirmation from the police or other officials, or view records or reports, newspaper accounts, or other forms of evidence. The importance of certain observations can be verified with different respondents within the same culture or confirmed again at a later time with the initial informant. Because qualitative researchers do not rely on a single source of information (such as a survey questionnaire or scale) but have "been there" themselves, they feel that qualitative research has greater validity than quantitative research.

It should not be overlooked that the differences in the way that quantitative and qualitative investigators view reliability and validity arise largely from basic assumptions about the notion of reality. For qualitative investigators, there is no single reality, but multiple ways of experiencing or viewing reality. Thus, notions like reliability or repetition of results that might hugely concern quantitative researchers are not always sought after with the same amount of energy by their counterparts. Rolfe (2006) states, "We should not expect either expert researchers or respondents to arrive at the same themes and categories as the researcher" (p. 305). This view is in marked contrast to the quantitative position.

In other words, the focus of reliability within qualitative research is only within that particular project. In quantitative research, the focus is both within and across other projects—for instance, with other studies that may have used the same instrument.

BOX 11.5   STEPS IN QUALITATIVE DATA ANALYSIS

1. The interviews, conversations, or responses are transcribed, and a written or electronic document is prepared.
2. The source material is carefully read, and key segments of text are highlighted.
3. Themes or categories and/or subcategories are coded (identified). In open coding, they are not pre-determined (as in a checklist), but emerge from an examination of the data. Many categories (for example, 20 to 40) may exist at this point.
4. Patterns are sought that make sense of the most important themes or categories. The researcher explains the significance that the themes or categories have for the research participants. Categories are refined to about three to eight (Thomas, 2008).

Focus Groups

A **focus group** is a small group of 8 to 15 individuals pulled together for a special evaluative or input purpose. They may be asked for their ideas regarding the design of a new service delivery program, for their evaluation of a well-established program, for their opinions about a revised BSW curriculum, and so on. Unlike personal interviews, focus groups generate interaction among participants, which may then result in valuable suggestions or recommendations as different perspectives are exchanged. Focus groups are relatively inexpensive and do not require a large investment of time for development or analysis of findings. This qualitative methodology is so popular it is likely that sometime in your career as a social worker, you may be called on to develop or lead a focus group. Focus groups tap the thinking of participants and elicit their ideas, attitudes, reactions, advice, and insights. Market research firms often use special rooms with one-way mirrors so that observers can watch and record the process when certain stimulus questions are presented. However, such facilities for focus groups are not used by most qualitative researchers in the social sciences.

Here is a brief summary of several studies using focus groups. Bronstein and McPhee (2009) were interested in how women transitioned from welfare to work when mandated mutual aid and information-sharing groups accompanied the benefits from the Temporary Assistance for Needy Families (TANF) program. Focus groups found the themes of connection and appreciation for information and resources, as well as many concrete hardships remaining unchanged.

Barnes (2008) conducted a focus group and in-depth interviews to obtain the perspectives of African American women on infant mortality. Some of the themes that respondents identified were: racism does exist within the medical system, our pain is often swept under the rug, and living with a constant source of stress.

Parish, Magana, and Cassiman (2008) conducted a series of focus groups with low-income mothers with disabilities. They spoke about the disincentives connected to working, about being burdened by the Supplemental Security Insurance (SSI) recertification process, the ongoing hardship experienced because social service benefits were inadequate, and about their inability to give their teenage sons and daughters the possessions and experiences that they wished.

BOX 11.6   EXAMPLE OF FOCUS GROUP RESEARCH

Survivors of major burn injuries can spend weeks—if not months—in the hospital, enduring multiple surgeries to graft skin, reduce scar tissue, and reconstruct facial features and/or amputated parts of the body. Their many lengthy encounters with health professionals establish their "credentials" as important participant observers of the health care system.

Purpose: The term *compassionate care* has received little attention in the research literature, and no literature could be located on the burn survivors' perspectives on the topic. This qualitative study asks the question, "What is compassionate care?"

Method: Two focus groups of adult burn survivors (n=31) were conducted at the Phoenix Society for Burn Survivors World Burn Congress. After completing a brief demographic questionnaire, open-ended questions were asked such as: a) Describe what comes to mind when you hear "compassionate health care" or "caring health care." How would you describe compassionate care? b) share examples of compassionate care you received from health care providers when you were recovering from your burn injury, focusing on the behaviors and personal characteristics that set those care providers apart from others; and c) reflect on and describe how the quality of care you received influenced your healing process. Participants contributed stories and examples that demonstrated instances when they experienced compassionate care. Each focus group was electronically recorded, transcribed, and content coded. Transcripts were read repeatedly, and themes were identified with open coding.

Data Analysis: Three major themes emerged: Respect for the person contained the secondary themes of establishing an empathic connection, restoring control to the patient by allowing choice, providing individual care, and going above and beyond the care provider's duties. Patients often felt ignored or disregarded—as simply objects on which medical procedures were performed. This came about because "no one looked at me. They looked at my body, but they didn't look at my eyes. And I remember feeling like I wasn't really there." In contrast, one burn survivor said "everything was wrapped" (in bandages) except for the toes on her right foot. She remembered one care provider who touched her toes while talking to her and "that meant more than anything" (p. 775).

A survivor burned as a child talked about the staff having "tea parties" in her room to get her to eat and drink. They also brought in water guns and surprised her with someone dressed up as an elf. Another woman talked about staff giving up their weekend to sit with her when she was transitioned to another unit.

Good communication, the second theme, involved explaining what they were going to do—what a medical procedure would involve. One survivor noted, "They (the burn team) may do a procedure a thousand times but just remember that the patient doesn't know that procedure" (p. 777). The third primary theme, provision of competent care, was expressed well by the participant who said this about one of her nurses: "He really took care of me and my husband said that when this nurse was on duty he always felt safe. He inspired trust" (p. 777).

Summary: "... compassion goes beyond feeling empathy and requires the care provider to take the patient's perspective—it demands that we take the time to communicate and understand what the patient's needs are" (p. 779).

Steps in Planning and Conducting a Focus Group

Step 1:

Decide on the problem to be solved or the specific questions that need to be answered. For the most part, these will be open-ended questions like "What do you think about the new program?" or sentence completions like "What I like best about the new program is ..." It is a good idea to list all of the questions to be raised in the session ahead of time. (*Note:* This is called preparing a discussion guide.)

Step 2:

Decide on the group of clients or participants to be invited. The reason underlying your study will suggest who ought to be asked to attend. (*Note:* Insofar as is possible, participants should be randomly selected to get a good representation of the clientele or target group.) Once details are finalized, mail invitations and follow up with telephone reminders.

Step 3:

Locate a facility large and quiet enough to accommodate approximately 15 participants. (*Note:* The recommended size for a focus group is 6 to 12 people; however, anticipate that you will lose about 2 participants to attrition for every 12 you invite, so you might want to expect a little attrition.)

Step 4:

Decide upon the moderator, the person who presents questions to the group. (*Note:* The moderator does *not* join the discussion but should ask probing questions when additional information is needed to clarify participants' comments.)

Step 5:

Consider whether you want to record the session; if you do, then make arrangements for the equipment. (*Note:* You may want to use a typed transcript when analyzing the data.) If recording seems too intrusive, the facilitator should have an assistant to take notes. Other issues to think through are whether you will provide light refreshments, name tags, or incentives for participation. You may also want to consider the possibility of conducting more than one focus group.

Step 6:

You might want to have some sort of icebreaker exercise so that participants will feel comfortable with each other. After introductions, you will want to explain the general purpose of the session and what is expected of the participants (for example, the necessity for candor and honesty). Explain that there are no right or wrong answers, that you are interested in each and every person's own thoughts and experiences. Consider providing each person with paper and pen. You might want to have them jot down the first two or three words that jump into their minds when a question is asked. (This will help the group from being swayed by someone holding a strong position on a given issue.) If there is a possibility that sensitive information might be revealed, then the group should be urged to respect confidential information.

Step 7:

Analyze the data. You may want to examine a transcript of the proceedings for writing about the key themes that emerged. A more rigorous approach would be to give the transcripts to two or three different

BOX 11.7   SELECTED STUDIES INVOLVING FOCUS GROUPS

✓   Wong, A. G., Maharaj, A., Brown, E., Davis, C., & Apolinsky, F. (2014). Social support sources, types, and generativity: A focus group study of cancer survivors and their caregivers. *Social Work in Health Care, 53*(3), 214–232.

✓   Baruth, M., Sharpe, P. A., Parra-Medina, D., & Wilcox, S. (2014). Perceived barriers to exercise and healthy eating among women from disadvantaged neighborhoods: Results from a focus group assessment. *Women & Health, 54*(4), 336–353.

✓   Pritchard, A. J., Jordan, C. E., & Jones, L. (2014). A qualitative comparison of battered women's perceptions of service needs and barriers across correctional and shelter contexts. *Criminal Justice and Behavior, 41, 7*, 844–861.

✓   Stolz, H. G., Brandon, M. D. J., Wallace, H. S., & Roberson, P. N. E. (2013). Understanding and addressing the needs of parenting educators: A focus group analysis. *Families in Society: The Journal of Contemporary Social Services, 94*(3), 203–210.

✓   Badger, K., & Royse, D. (2012). Compassionate care: The burn survivor's perspective. *Journal of Burn Care Research, 33*(6), 772–780.

individuals to read in order to protect against your bias seeping in. At a minimum, the report should identify the key points and major themes arising from the group's discussion.

Points to Keep in Mind About Focus Groups

Focus groups provide qualitative data; they do not yield statistically significant results. Rather than establishing definitive "proof" or evidence, it is best to remember that the data represent nothing more than the thinking of 8 or 10 or 12 individuals who were present on a given day. Another group might have a completely different set of opinions. In this sense, a focus group is like having a conversation with several people—if one is asking the right questions, listening, and observing (that is, taking note of body language and facial expressions), then there is an opportunity to learn something that otherwise might not be known. To make up for the fact that small sample sizes are always a limitation of focus groups, two, three, or four focus groups might be conducted with different groups of individuals to ensure that the responses being obtained are fairly widely held. In fact, the previously cited study by Pritchard, Jordan, and Jones (2014) involved 10 focus groups and 96 different individuals. When focus groups work well, it is because the facilitator is able to keep the participants on task, the group members feel they can respond freely, and good questions have been crafted.

The Problem with Qualitative Research

Qualitative researchers are at a disadvantage when it comes to having their research funded and published. This is a serious problem for the social work student or new professional who may be working toward either of those two goals. Here are a couple of excerpts from qualitative researchers who make these same points. "Quantitative research has become the normative mode of inquiry taught in universities, and quantitative researchers have tended to dominate review panels of funding agencies and the editorial boards of prestigious research journals" (Morse & Field, 1995, p. 3). Padgett (1998b) acknowledges that there are many sound reasons for conducting qualitative research, but also has written that "if you are concerned with scientific utility and with procuring research funding from government or private foundations, proposing a qualitative study will probably reduce your chances of success. It is better to think of qualitative research as a labor of love than as the fast track to the researcher's hall of fame" (p. 11).

The very characteristics of qualitative research (for example, little structure, few guidelines) that make it exciting and innovative may also make it difficult for the qualitative investigator to compete against the quantitatively oriented project for resources. This is not to say that this situation is right or fair, but simply to inform you that qualitative research might not always be viewed with the same amount of respect as quantitative research. Because it does not produce generalizable knowledge, many academics in the positivist tradition question its value.

As we've discussed previously, in some situations, qualitative methods are superior to quantitative approaches. However, the decision to use qualitative methods should not be made quickly. Certainly, the wrong reason to choose a qualitative approach would be because it doesn't require knowledge of statistical procedures or sampling designs, or because one doesn't have to be overly concerned with reviewing all the relevant literature. Like anything else, there is good qualitative research and there is bad. Despite fewer funding and publication opportunities for qualitative studies, these approaches remain popular with social workers.

ANXIETY CHECK 11.2

D'aaron, one of Bill and Sophia's classmates, recently started working in a pawnshop on the weekends to help with his expenses. He began keeping notes on the stories he heard from the store's customers about the reasons they were pawning their items, and he incorporated comments about their physical appearance and demeanor. Sophia pointed out that he was behaving like a participant observer and that he should write a manuscript about the world of those who pawn items. Is she correct? Could this be a qualitative research project?

[Answer is at the back of the book.]

The Great Debate

In the 1950s and 1960s, a debate began in professional journals regarding the relative virtues of quantitative and qualitative methodologies. In essence, advocates for the use of quantitative methods believe that qualitative methods will not produce the knowledge needed to document effectiveness and to guide practice. Interviewing a handful of people does not produce science, they say.

On the other hand, those who advocate for greater use of qualitative approaches argue that the trend toward empiricism results in research that is too restrictive and superficial because of the tendency to investigate only those aspects that can be operationally defined and measured. They say that instead of looking at the whole situation, empiricists fragment a situation and focus on what they can easily count. In the empiricists' quest for "objectivity," important interactions between participants and other details are often overlooked.

Which viewpoint is right? What is the most appropriate research method for social work? Actually, the debate should not be about which side is right. There are limitations associated with both quantitative and qualitative approaches. As a researcher-in-training, you should learn how to use both approaches. Social workers can use both methodologies profitably in their practice, and each approach can be used to enrich the findings of the other.

Actually, the debate has been somewhat resolved in that it has become common for social work researchers and evaluators to use **mixed methods** of research—for instance, employing both quantitative surveys and qualitative interviews with a few participants or a focus group—to ensure the conclusions have both breadth and depth. Qualitative and quantitative approaches can complement each other and certainly improve the researcher's ability to comprehend the phenomenon or program in question. It is more important to recognize the strengths and advantages of each perspective than to insist on the superiority of one approach over another.

The nature of the study and the questions you want to ask should suggest the most relevant strategy. Under some circumstances, investigators ought to employ qualitative approaches and under others, quantitative. The methodology must fit the questions that one wants to explore.

Here are some ways qualitative and quantitative approaches can work together: a) qualitative methods can be used at the initiation of a project to develop hypotheses and/or quantitative measures and instruments; b) a quantitative study is conducted, but a qualitative approach is also implemented to further expand the results of the quantitative investigation; c) a qualitative investigation is conducted, along with quantitative methods to supplement the qualitative findings. When both qualitative and quantitative methods are used, there is an opportunity to cross-validate the findings.

ANXIETY CHECK 11.3

Name two ways D'aaron could establish the reliability of his findings (see Anxiety Check 11.2).

[Answer at the end of the book.]

BOX 11.8   EXAMPLES OF MIXED-METHODS STUDIES IN THE LITERATURE

✓   Kidd, S. A., Frederick, T., Karabanow, J., Hughes, J., Naylor, T., et al. (2016). A mixed methods study of recently homeless youth efforts to sustain housing and stability. *Child & Adolescent Social Work Journal, 33*(3), 207–218.

✓   Hoefer, R., & Silva, S. M. (2014). Assessing and augmenting administration skills in nonprofits: An exploratory mixed methods study. *Human Service Organizations: Management, Leadership, & Governance, 38*(3), 246–257.

✓   Chaumba, J. (2013). The use and value of mixed methods research in social work. *Advances in Social Work, 14*(2), 307–333.

✓   Lawrence, C., Zuckerman, M., Smith, B. D., & Liu, J. (2012). Building cultural competence in the child welfare workforce: A mixed methods analysis. *Journal of Public Child Welfare, 6*(2), 225–241.

It is shortsighted to dismiss qualitative research (or quantitative, for that matter) prematurely. Each of these approaches has its place, and the contributions of both have been highlighted in a way that is succinct and profound:

> The methods are analogous to zooming in and zooming out with a lens. To the extent that they are reproduced objectively, wide-angle, telephoto, and microscopic views must be simultaneously valid, and zooming from different directions merely focuses attention on different facets of the same phenomenon. ... There are no grounds, logical or otherwise, for calling any view simple. We can start anywhere and zoom in to infinite detail or zoom out to indefinite scope. (Madey, 1982, pp. 83–83)

Qualitative approaches are valuable tools for helping social workers to understand their clients and the world in which they live. As you encounter social problems that need investigation, consider the method—whether qualitatively or quantitatively oriented—that will best help to answer the questions that you have.

Key Terms

open coding

grounded theory

constant comparative analysis

member checking

negative case analysis

peer checking

mixed methods

theoretical saturation

focus group

case study

ethnography

triangulation

audit trail

participant observer

SELF-REVIEW

(Answers are at the end of the book.)

1. Which group believes the world can be objectively determined—that there is only one reality?
   a. Quantitatively oriented researchers
   b. Qualitatively oriented researchers
   c. ethnomethodologists

2. Which of these characteristics does not describe qualitative research?
   a. no intervention
   b. use of participant observation
   c. large sample sizes
   d. journalistic narrative

3. Which of these characteristics does not describe qualitative research?

    a. diminished importance of literature review
    b. in-depth interviewing
    c. exploratory
    d. concern with instruments and measurement

4. For each of the research questions that follow, indicate the most appropriate research approach (qualitative or quantitative).

    a. You want to know how much time the average felon spends in prison.
    b. You want to know how prisoners experience the power wielded by their prison guards. You convince the warden to let you go undercover as a prisoner for two weeks.
    c. To understand the influences that shape criminal behavior, you develop a survey and administer it to 500 prisoners in a maximum security prison.
    d. To understand the influences that shape their criminal behavior, you interview five prisoners in depth awaiting execution on death row.
    e. After advocating for college classes to be offered at a nearby minimum security prison, you follow the first 60 prisoners until they complete one class and leave prison. You want to know if they are less likely to be rearrested than other prisoners.

5. List three reasons that an investigator might want to employ qualitative research methods.
6. T or F. Qualitative interviewers need to avoid *yes* and *no* questions.
7. T or F. Qualitative interviewers prepare very detailed questionnaires.
8. T or F. In a qualitative observational study, the observer probably wouldn't attend to body language or nonverbal communication.
9. What is theoretical saturation?
10. What is member checking?
11. T or F. For qualitative investigators, there is no single objective reality.

QUESTIONS FOR CLASS DISCUSSION

1. Suppose you want to know what it is like to live in poverty. Consequently, you interview an impoverished person one Saturday afternoon. How do you think it would be different from an ethnographic study of impoverished persons?
2. Which research approach has the greatest potential for advancing social work practice? (List arguments for and against qualitative and quantitative approaches.)
3. What are the pros and cons associated with not doing a thorough literature search before beginning a qualitative study?
4. Discuss any books, movies, or plays that recently may have helped you better understand the life of a unique person or group of persons.
5. Share life experiences that have given you insight into other cultures. What special worldviews or vocabularies were discovered?
6. Into what situations or settings would you like to go in disguise? What would you learn that you couldn't learn without a disguise?

7. Discuss how qualitative research is different from research employing a single-system design.
8. Describe a study where you might employ a mixed-methods approach.
9. What participant-observation study would you like to conduct? What do you think you might learn?
10. How might the Madey (1982) quote apply to social work practice?
11. Group project: View the film *Rabbit-Proof Fence* (2002) about three aboriginal girls taken from their families in 1931 by the Australian government. Propose a qualitative research project that could have been conducted.

RESOURCES AND REFERENCES

Barnes, G. L. (2008). Perspectives of African-American women on infant mortality. *Social Work in Health Care, 47* (3), 293–305.

Belcher, J. R. (1994). Understanding the process of social drift among the homeless: A qualitative analysis. In Edmund Sherman and William J. Reid (Eds.), *Qualitative research in social work*. New York, NY: Columbia University Press.

Berrick, J. D. (1995). *Faces of poverty: Portraits of women and children on welfare*. Cary, NC: Oxford University Press.

Bronstein, L. R. & McPhee, D. (2009). Goals for group work with women transitioning from welfare to work. *Social Work with Groups, 32* (1/2), 96–108.

Calvey, D. (2008). The art and politics of covert research: Doing "situated ethics" in the field. *Sociology—Journal of the British Sociological Association, 42*(5), 905–918.

Caudill, W., Redlich, F. C., Gilmore, H. R., & Brody, E. B. (1952). Social structure and interaction processes on a psychiatric ward. *American Journal of Orthopsychiatry, 22*, 314–334.

Davidson, B. (1997). Service needs of relative care givers: A qualitative analysis. *Families in Society, 78*, 502–510.

Deane, W. N. (1961). The reactions of a nonpatient to a stay on a mental hospital ward. *Psychiatry, 24*, 61–68.

Drisko, J. W. (2005). Writing up qualitative research. *Families in Society: The Journal of Contemporary Social Services, 86* (4), 589–593.

Earl, A., Crause, C., Vaid, A., & Albarracin, D. (2016). Disparities in attention to HIV-prevention information. *AIDS Care, 28*(1), 79–86.

Estroff, S. (1981). *Making it crazy: An ethnography of psychiatric clients in an American community*. Berkeley, CA: University of California Press.

Farber, N. K. (2006). Conducting qualitative research: A practical guide for school counselors. *Professional School Counseling, 9*(5), 367–375.

Gall, M. D., Borg, W. R, & Gall, J. P. (1996). *Educational research: An introduction*. White Plains, NY: Longman.

Goldman, A. R., Bohr, R. H., & Steinberg, T. A. (1970). On posing as mental patients: Reminiscences and recommendations. *Professional Psychology, 1*(5), 427–434.

Guba, E. G., & Lincoln, Y. S. (1989). *Fourth generation evaluation*. Thousand Oaks, CA: Sage.

Ishiyama, T., Batman, R., & Hewitt, E. (1967). Let's be patients. *American Journal of Nursing, 67*, 569–571.

Madey, D. L. (1982). Some benefits of integrating qualitative and quantitative methods in program evaluation, with illustrations. *Educational Evaluation, 4*(2), 223–236.

Morse, J. M., & Field, P. A. (1995). *Qualitative research methods for health professionals*. Thousand Oaks, CA: Sage.

Neuman, W. L. (2006). *Social research methods: Qualitative and quantitative approaches.* Boston, MA: Allyn & Bacon.

Padgett, D. K. (1998b). *Qualitative methods in social work research.* Thousand Oaks, CA: Sage.

Padgett, D. K. (2008). *Qualitative methods in social work research.* Thousand Oaks, CA: Sage.

Padgett, D. K., Henwood, B. F., & Tsemberis, S. J. (2016). *Housing first: Ending homelessness, transforming systems, and changing lives.* New York, NY: Oxford University Press.

Parnish, S. L., Magana, S. & Cassiman, S. A. (2008). It's just that much harder: Multilayered hardship experiences of low-income women with disabilities. *Affilia, 23* (1), 51–65.

Rolfe, G. (2006). Validity, trustworthiness, and rigour: Quality and the idea of qualitative research. *Journal of Advanced Nursing, 53*(3), 304–310.

Rosenhan, D. L. (1973). Being sane in insane places. *Science, 179*(Jan.), 250–258.

Shek, D. T. L, Tang, V. M. Y., & Han, X. Y. (2005). Evaluation of evaluation studies using qualitative research methods in the social work literature (1990–2003): Evidence that constitutes a wake-up call. *Research on Social Work Practice, 15*(3), 180–194.

Spicher, P. (2011). Ethical covert research. *Sociology—Journal of the British Sociological Association, 45*(1), 118–133.

Swanberg, J., & Logan, T. K. (2005). Domestic violence and employment: A qualitative study. *Journal of Occupational Health Psychology, 10*(1), 3–17.

Thomas, D. R. (2008). A general inductive approach for analyzing qualitative evaluation data. *American Journal of Evaluation, 27*(2), 237–246.

Yin, R. K. (2015). *Qualitative research from start to finish.* New York, NY: Guilford.

ASSIGNMENT 11.1

Designing a Qualitative Research Project

Objective: *To gain firsthand experience with participant observation.*

Before attempting this assignment, it will be important for you to get *prior approval* from your instructor for your idea. The directions are simple: Spend a minimum of four hours (eight is preferable) observing a group of people, a way of life, or a situation that you would like to know more about. For instance, to learn more about the stresses that police officers are under, contact the community relations officer of your local police department and see if you can arrange to spend a shift riding with a patrol officer or observing intake at the jail. To learn more about life in a nursing home, contact the social service department and ask to spend a day in their common room conversing with them. (*Note:* This is not about shadowing the social worker and her daily activities, but trying to understand what life must be like for the residents.) To understand what it might be like to be a stroke victim or to be physically disabled, borrow a wheelchair and spend a day in it going about your usual activities. To get a little perspective on the life of a homeless person, serve meals at a homeless shelter. You must use good judgment for this assignment and not attempt anything that might be dangerous. When contacting social service agencies, homeless shelters, and so forth, always identify yourself as a student and ask permission.

1.   Whom do you plan to observe?

2.   What agency or department do you need to secure permission from? Have you already obtained permission?

3.   What is your plan for participant observation?

4.   What did you learn from your observation?

5.   What did you learn about yourself in this participant observation?

ASSIGNMENT 11.2

Obtaining an Oral History

Objective: *To gain firsthand experience with in-depth interviewing.*

For this assignment, you will need to think not only about a topic, but a person who would be most likely to have information about that topic. For instance, you might want to interview someone who lived during the Vietnam War era to ask about how life was different then than it is now. You could interview an international student or a recent immigrant to this country to ask about their life experiences. Persons recovering from alcoholism or drug addiction might also make good informants about life on the streets. You may want to record your interview. Get prior approval from your instructor before beginning your interview.

1. What topic is being explored?

2. Give a brief background on the person interviewed:

3. List all of the questions you asked:

4. Discuss the most important things you learned from this oral history:

ASSIGNMENT 11.3

Reading a Qualitative Research Article

Objective: *To see how authors construct a qualitative research report*

Read the article by Barnert et al. (2015), "Incarcerated youths' perspectives on protective factors and risk factors for juvenile offending: Qualitative analysis." *American Journal of Public Health, 105*(7), 1365–1371. (Your instructor may allow you to read another article of your choosing.)

1. How did the authors select the participants to be interviewed?

2. Did the number of participants seem sufficient? Why or why not?

3. How did the study convince you that it was credible?

4. If you were to conduct the same study in a different facility, do you think you would obtain the same findings? Why or why not?

5. If you were conducting this study, is there anything you might want to do differently? Or do you have questions that the study did not answer?

CHAPTER 12

Program Evaluation

A s a social work practitioner, it is good to recognize situations that can trigger or foster interest in starting a program evaluation.

Influences from the Top: a) Funding sources may require some type of program evaluation as a condition of providing new or continuing money supporting an intervention—especially a new one; b) administrators, board members, and others may hear complaints or rumors in the community that a program is not "good." As I write this, the VA system nationally has received criticism and been in the news because of complaints about long waiting times and veterans being denied services; c) sometimes budgetary cutbacks force decision makers to examine programs with an eye to significantly curtailing or closing programs that don't appear to meet expectations.

Influences from the Middle: a) Managers and clinical directors may attend a conference, training session, or read about programs in other locations that have better results than the ones they manage or direct causing a concern; b) staff turnover, vacant positions, poor employee morale, or other organizational problems can cause managers or directors to become worried about the effectiveness of their programs; c) programmatic concerns from the agency direct or board of directors can be handed to the middle managers or directors to investigate.

Influences from the Practitioner: a) Practitioners wanting to know how they are doing and interested in evaluating programs in their agency can advocate for a program evaluation or even begin one themselves; b) pilot or innovative programs may need a program evaluation before they can be expanded to treat a large group of clients; c) practitioners may attend a conference, training session, or read about programs in other locations that seem to have better results than the ones at their own agencies—data may be needed for comparison.

Most often, program evaluation starts with a specific problem or question to be answered, such as: "Is our outpatient treatment program effective?" or "Are we as successful with our group counseling program as with our individual counseling?" Program evaluation, then, provides key information that can aid in decision making and launch efforts to improve its effectiveness.

Program evaluation is used to decide whether a program has worth or merit. Although it uses the research methodologies already covered in this text, its focus is not on generating basic science or new generalizable knowledge, but on concluding or reaching a decision about the value of a program. In fact, program evaluations are sometimes referred to as **summative evaluations**—a reflection of interest in condensing information about a program's outcomes to make an overall determination about the effectiveness of a program and from there to decide its fate. Because programs vary tremendously, there is no one "recipe" or cookbook approach to designing program evaluations. Instead, each evaluation tends to be individually tailored to address the unique concerns or characteristics of the program. This chapter will give you an overview of several ways that program evaluation can be approached.

BOX 12.1 PROGRAM EVALUATION ATTEMPTS TO ANSWER SUCH GENERAL QUESTIONS AS:

- Are clients being helped?
- Is there a better (cheaper, faster) way of doing this?
- How does this effort or level of activity compare with what was produced or accomplished last year? (Did we achieve our objectives?)
- How does our success rate compare with other agencies' success rates?
- Should this program be continued?
- How can we improve our program?

Why do we need to conduct program evaluation? The best argument for evaluating social service programs comes from an analogy suggested by Martin Bloom: Running a program without evaluating it is like driving a car blindfolded. You certainly are going places, but you don't know where you are or who you've endangered along the way. Program evaluation provides accountability. It can be used to assure the public, the funding sources of programs, and even the clients themselves that a particular program works and that it deserves further financial support. Program evaluation can be used to ensure that certain expectations are met, that efforts are appropriately applied to the identified needs, and that the community is better off because the program is having a positive effect.

There are many other reasons for evaluating a program. In addition to providing a reassuring level of accountability to clients and the public, program evaluation may be used to meet accreditation standards, and provide information for managing programs and monitoring their effects. Ultimately, program evaluation benefits clients by informing us whether they are being helped.

Program evaluation is an important phase in the development of a program. Ideally, every program should be examined, and what is learned from these efforts should go back to the managers and service providers to enable them to continually improve the effectiveness and efficiency of their activities.

Thinking About Conducting a Program Evaluation

Think about a social service program with which you have been associated. Perhaps it was an agency where you volunteered or were employed. Maybe you are currently there in a field practicum. Suppose that one day the agency director calls you into her office and says, "I've just received a letter from our major funding source informing us that we must provide them with results of a program evaluation within the next 90 days or risk losing our funding. There's nobody here with that kind of expertise, but since you are taking that research course at the university, I'm hoping you'll agree to be the leader on this. Let's meet again tomorrow and toss around some ideas about how to proceed. Maybe you can sketch out a rough plan for us?"

Although this scenario may seem a bit unlikely to you now, over the years, I've had a number of phone calls from students who have described being in a similar situation and frantically have asked, "What do I do now?" Indeed, what kind of an evaluation plan would you recommend if you were put in such a spot? By this point in the book, you are in a little better place than Sophia and Bill were when they first learned about the focus of their practicum. Still, let's see if the following issues would be on your radar.

Considerations Before Beginning a Program Evaluation

Before you can realistically begin planning a program evaluation, you must address a few questions:

> **BOX 12.2   CONSIDERATIONS BEFORE BEGINNING A PROGRAM EVALUATION**
>
> - How much time do you have to complete the evaluation?
> - What resources (staff, money, etc.) are at your disposal?
> - Who is the audience that will be reading the evaluation report? (Will they be clients/consumers, practitioners, or researchers?)
> - What is the purpose of the evaluation? (Are there certain questions that must be answered? How rigorous does it have to be?)

In the above scenario, the expectation of a completed project within 90 days would impose some limitations on the type of evaluation that could be conducted. There probably wouldn't be time to do a **prospective** (going forward into the future) **study** (for example, starting a new group or intervention and then capturing posttest data). You'd be more likely to do a **retrospective study**, looking back over already collected, existing data. Generally, the more time that is available for planning, the more control you have and the more sophisticated the design can be.

Resources are a major consideration. If you are informed that no funds are available for the evaluation, that situation will likely result in a simpler effort than one where standardized, copyrighted instruments might be purchased or consultants employed. If clerical help is available, or if an evaluation committee can be formed, then more might be proposed than if you have no assistance.

It is important to know the **audience** when writing the evaluation report. A report being prepared for consumers or the general public could be less complex and use a different writing style than a report going to a professional journal. Consumers may not want to read about *t*-tests and chi-squares—or at least would need help interpreting them; professionals with PhDs may have different expectations and may expect you to address sampling design, sample size, the psychometrics of instruments, and so on. The purpose of the evaluation is directly tied to how you write the report.

When selecting an evaluation design, the factors of time, resources, audience, and purpose must be weighed simultaneously, insofar as is possible. However, the purpose of the evaluation has an overarching influence for this reason: The results of an evaluation can be used to promote or to denigrate programs. If the required evaluation is viewed by your agency management as so much busy work, then the effort and energy put into it will be minimal. On the other hand, if there is a perception that the agency's principal funding source may be looking for reasons to eliminate programs, your agency will want to do the best job possible given the constraints of time and resources. Sometimes, by empirically demonstrating the superior job they do, agencies can position themselves to receive more funding for continuing or special projects. And, of course, the more competition there is for scarce funds, the more attention will be given to the program evaluation.

Types of Program Evaluations

Program evaluation is not a single methodology, but instead refers to a broad category of approaches that vary considerably and supply a wide range of different kinds of information. This next section describes some of the more common types of evaluation, ranging from the fairly basic to outcome and **cost-effectiveness** studies.

Patterns of Use Studies

- Answers the question "Whom are we serving?"
- Focuses on the characteristics of clients
- Is descriptive
- Allows for the monitoring of specific objectives
- Allows agencies to target services precisely where needed
- Helps to identify new patterns and trends

Patterns of use (also known as client utilization) data is the most basic information that every agency and program should be able to report; it is a prerequisite before designing more elaborate evaluations. Every director of a program must have access to such descriptive data as: How many clients were served in the past 12 months? How many were low income? How many were females? How many were over the age of 65? Who referred these clients? Where do they live? What are their problems? How many have dropped out? What is the average length of their stay with us?

As indicated in Table 12.1, this type of data inform only about those clients who have expressed a need for the program by appearing at the agency. They do not say anything about those who *could have* benefited from the program but who did not request it. They also do not allow you to conclude that the program is good, effective, or efficient. While the data inform about the number of clients served and allow you to establish who the recipients of the services were, they tell you nothing about the quality of care clients were provided. Even though many social service agencies report descriptive client utilization data in their annual reports, such information by itself should not be considered an evaluation of the agencies' activities or programs.

Patterns-of-use data are best used for indicating pockets of clients who are within the agency's target group for services but who are not being adequately served for some reason. For instance, in Table 12.1, it is apparent that the Happy Healthy Thinking Project is serving women predominantly. Now, it may have been designed to serve this population, but if it was conceived for both genders, then it is obviously underserving men. Similarly, the program is serving fewer minorities than their representation in the community would warrant and proportionately fewer children than might be expected. Could this be a problem? Also, the program seems to be doing a great job of reaching older adults but not very well in serving low-income clients. In fact, the clients' median household income is higher than the average for the community.

Other possible areas to examine are the extremely low number of referrals that come from other professionals and organizations in the community and the fact that clients appear to drop out after only a few sessions. Such data should concern program managers.

Patterns-of-use data inform and allow directors and managers to conduct **program monitoring**—that is, to inspect the extent to which a program reaches its target population with the intended intervention. Despite bright, capable staff, programs without guidance from management can wander off course at times.

TABLE 12.1 Client Utilization Data Past Year

	Clients Served	Census Representation
Number of clients served this year	1005	
Female clients	693 (69%)	31%
Minority admissions	181 (18%)	22%
Clients under 18	50 (5%)	13%
Clients 55 and older	402 (40%)	27%
Low-income households	120 (12%)	27%
Median household income	$43,985	$25,221
Prior mental health services	89 (17%)	
Dual diagnosis	120 (12%)	
Self-referrals	974 (97%)	

Average number of treatment episodes: 2.3

With the data from Table 12.1, it would be possible to develop concrete, measurable **objectives**. For example:

1. To increase minority admissions to 25% of clients served by December 31, 2021.
2. To increase admissions of low-income clients to 30% of those served by December 31, 2021.
3. To decrease self-referrals to 75% of all those served by December 31, 2021.
4. To reduce the percentage of clients who don't return to 30% by June 30, 2021.

Notice that these objectives are:

- Specific—they state a desired result.
- Measurable—they are easily verified.
- Referenced to a date—they indicate when results can be expected.

Objectives are different from **goals**, which are broad, general statements of direction. For instance, the Happy Healthy Thinking Project might state any or all of the following goals: *(1) To assist all of those needing mental health services to lead a more productive and satisfying life; (2) To provide the highest quality rehabilitative and strength-based services for consumers in the community; (3) To promote health and quality of life for all members of the community; (4) To eradicate suicide from the community.*

Note that goals may be idealistic and not easily obtainable—but that doesn't mean that they aren't worthwhile. Goals lay out the intent or general focus, while objectives relate more to specific benchmarks that might indicate the agency or program is on its way to meeting its goal. Objectives provide for pragmatic accountability. Once program objectives have been developed, program monitoring takes on a new importance.

The problem with relying on the program's own objectives as a way to determine how the program is doing is that whoever developed the objectives may have made them so easy to accomplish that they are essentially worthless. For instance, it sounds great if a program objective states that 500 new clients would be served next year. However, would you feel the same way if for each of the past two years the agency served 520 new clients? Ideally, a program should have to stretch a bit to meet its objectives. Objectives should be attainable, but not be so easy to reach that no special effort is required. And note with that objective, we will still have no idea about how "good" or effective the program was.

If the agency thinks that the principal funding source would be happy with the kind of data provided in Table 12.1, then there may be no need to go further. But if the agency has a management information system in place and someone is already responsible for program monitoring, another type of program evaluation might be needed.

Formative and Process Evaluation

- Answers the question "What would make this a better program?"
- Is primarily narrative and essentially qualitative
- Is most often used with new programs still being developed

Like program monitoring, **formative evaluation** is not specifically concerned with the worth of a program. As its name suggests, it focuses on improving programs. Formative evaluations are used to modify or shape programs that are still in development. They tend not to rely on statistics or analysis of numerical data. In this sense, they are much more qualitative than quantitative and usually don't conclude whether a program is successful. However, they may describe the experiences of clients and staff.

There are several ways to conduct a formative evaluation. One avenue might be to obtain **expert consultation**. This could be a person with a national reputation in the field in which the program is based; it also could be someone with a statewide or regional reputation. You could even use a social worker or agency director from a similar agency in the same town, as long as his or her program has a "good" reputation. The person would visit the agency to review operating policies and procedures, interview clients and staff, tour the facility, and maybe even meet with board members and reflect on aspects of the program. Maybe the person will notice that staff members have to share offices, that there aren't enough computers, or that the agency is not in a location that is accessible to clients who have to rely on public transportation. Depending on the expert, his or her interest, and your instructions, other aspects of the program such as staff caseloads or turnover rates might be examined. What could come from this approach could be a list of specific recommendations for the agency to address in order to improve the program.

If money is not available for experts and no one can be found to do a formative evaluation for free, there are still two other avenues. A second idea is to *locate model standards* from national accrediting or advocacy organizations. For instance, the Council on Accreditation (COA) is a nonprofit organization that has been accrediting human services since 1977. It has developed a vast array of standards for close to 50 different services, from Adoption to Youth Independent Living. These standards are quite specific and address everything from the facility itself to the number of staff. Their standards can be accessed from their website: **http://coanet.org/standards/standards-for-public-agencies**. You may find a set of standards there that could be applicable to your situation.

Also, don't overlook the possibility of finding a relevant program evaluation from a literature search. Such studies might provide rough guidelines for your program and what you might expect in terms of clients who drop out or relapse. For instance, I came across these two articles:

✓ Boal, A., & Mankowski, E. S. (2014). Barriers to compliance with Oregon batterer intervention program standards. *Violence & Victims, 29*(4), 607–619.

✓ Boal, A., & Mankowski, E. S. (2014). The impact of legislative standards on batter intervention program practices and characteristics. *American Journal of Community Psychology, 53*(1–2), 218–230.

A third approach to formative evaluation is to form a temporary, or **ad hoc committee** to study the issue—sometimes known as a **blue-ribbon committee** when dignitaries or other high-status persons are included. This task force could be composed of professionals, staff, board members, and even clients and university professors. The group could decide to host one or more focus groups to learn how the program could be improved. Or the group might want to interview a sample of clients or to develop a questionnaire to elicit clients' input as well as the staff's. It is important to use open-ended questions and to allow the respondents to be anonymous. The committee might want to visit other similar agencies to view their operations—maybe even talk with their current consumers. When a blue-ribbon task force is carefully chosen, a richness of ideas can emerge as participants share their thinking, experiences, and hopes for the program.

A fourth approach would be for the organization to hire an evaluator to assist in collecting the kind of formative data the agency's staff or board of directors desire to have.

Formative evaluation can also be known as **process evaluation**; however, not all process evaluations are formative. Sometimes, process evaluations are done at the conclusion of a project to get some idea of why the program did or did not work the way it was intended.

Like formative evaluation, process evaluations are also primarily narrative. They often describe the decisions and key events in the development of a new program. The federal government likes process evaluation—especially with research and demonstration projects—because this type of information is valuable to those who are interested in implementing or replicating a similar program in a different community. It makes sense: Why reinvent the wheel? Unlike formative evaluation, process evaluation ought to address what has been learned while launching and operating a program, consider what mistakes should not be repeated, and provide advice for others interested in implementing the same approach.

Once again, note that the focus of process evaluation is not so much on the number of client successes that were experienced (although this can be a part of the evaluation report) but rather on what happened and why. In this sense, a process evaluator has a role not unlike that of a journalist. However, the process evaluation can also include client utilization data, consumer feedback data, even client outcome data. Although most often qualitative in nature, process evaluations can incorporate quantitative components as well. You can see why it is important to have a clear understanding of the purpose of the evaluation. Here are several examples that might be of interest:

✓ Mye, S. C., & Moracco, K. E. (2015). "Compassion, pleasantry, and hope." A process evaluation of a volunteer-based nonprofit. *Evaluation and Program Planning, 50,* 18–25.

✓ Miller, T., Chandler, L., & Mouttapa, M. (2015). A needs assessment, development, and formative evaluation of a health promotion smartphone application for college students. *American Journal of Health Education, 46*(4), S1 207–215.

✓ Edelen, M. O., Tucker, J., & D'Amico, E. (2015). Spreading the word: A process evaluation of a voluntary AOD prevention program. *American Journal of Addictions, 24*(4), 315–322.

✓ Damush, T. M., Miller, K. K., Plue, L., Schmid, A. A., Myers, L., Graham, G., & Williams, L. S. (2014). National implementation of acute stroke care centers in the Veterans Health Administration (VHA): Formative evaluation of the field response. *Journal of General Internal Medicine, 29*(4), S845–S852.

BOX 12.3   QUESTIONS AND DATA SOURCES USEFUL IN PROCESS EVALUATION

Why was the program started? By whom?

What needs was the program designed to address?

How well have various agencies and organizations worked together?

What key decisions were made as the program was developing?

How did implementation differ from plans presented in the proposal?

What theory or principles is the program based on?

What is the program? What are its major components?

How has the program changed over time? What problems have been experienced?

What changes are planned for the immediate future? Why?

What are the characteristics of the clients using the program?

Is the program serving the intended population? If not, why not?

How are clients being recruited?

How satisfied are clients with the program? Why or why not?

BOX 12.4   SOURCES OF INFORMATION FOR PROCESS EVALUATION

Data Sources	*Persons to Contact/Interview*
Comparison data: Local, state, or national data from the census, needs assessments, reports from state departments of health/mental health, and so on; data from journal articles	Key informants in the community (for example, doctors, judges, ministers) who refer to or know about social services, key community leaders, administrators and staff of collaborating agencies
Agency data: Program documentation, agency agreements, correspondence and relevant memos, minutes from board and committee meetings	Clients, staff, program directors and administrators, board members, community forums
Agency documents: Treatment manuals or protocols, information provided to clients, agency brochures; tapes made during therapy	Personal observations of the program (for example, attending support group sessions), attending staff meetings, attending board meetings
Agency documents: Case record reviews, annual reports, program documentation, reports of any client interviews or agency surveys, needs assessments, files of client complaints or adverse events	Focus groups with clients, focus groups with staff, focus group with board members, focus group with key informants

Consumer Satisfaction Surveys

- Answers the question "Are clients pleased with our services?"
- Is easy to interpret
- Is inexpensive
- Allows trends to be monitored
- Is client centered
- Can be implemented quickly

When asked to plan a program evaluation, many students have a tendency to think first of **client satisfaction surveys**, and for good reason. They have great face validity—simply assessing whether clients are pleased or displeased with their services. These surveys are among the simplest and most frequently used evaluation methodologies. They do not require a lot of research expertise, expense, or planning, and once developed, the same instrument can be used over many years. What's more, obtaining client feedback is a democratic grassroots approach that values input from those receiving the services. There is no assumption that staff members or the administration knows best. Clients have the opportunity to comment negatively or positively about experiences with the agency.

With these points in its favor, what is the argument against making consumer satisfaction the principal component of an agency program evaluation effort? Just this: In practically every study, clients say that they are satisfied with services. The vast majority of published consumer satisfaction studies show that clients almost invariably report high levels of satisfaction. Not much has changed since Lebow (1982) noted many years ago that high satisfaction rates come from clients who "have little choice of facility, type of treatment, or practitioner" (p. 250).

High satisfaction rates are found not just in the United States. They have been reported, for example, in studies from New Zealand, Australia, the Philippines, Canada, and with French-speaking psychiatric outpatients in Montreal. Even psychiatric patients admitted involuntarily indicated satisfaction in Ireland (Smith et al., 2014).

There can be several reasons why this type of program evaluation tends to reveal positive findings. First, client feedback instruments are often "homemade" within an agency, and very little is known about their reliability or validity. Second, they tend to have a selection bias—clients who are dissatisfied with services often drop out early and may not receive or return questionnaires. Further, clients are in a vulnerable position and may not want to risk saying something negative for fear that they might lose their social worker or therapist—or even services at a future point. This vulnerability can sometimes be experienced even when those being surveyed are not clients. I once conducted a survey of high school principals and guidance counselors and found that they were hesitant to give negative feedback about an agency. They feared that too much criticism might result in the funding agency "pulling the plug," and then this group of school administrators and guidance counselors would have one less resource in the rural community where they could refer students who needed services. You might say that they were of the opinion that even a poor resource was better than none at all.

While it is often convenient to mail client satisfaction forms, there could be several problems with this approach. Many social work clients move frequently and do not leave a forwarding address. And there is the issue of confidentiality if they did not want it known to others in their household that they were receiving services. Also, clients with lower levels of educational achievement will not be as responsive to

---

BOX 12.5   EXAMPLES OF CLIENT SATISFACTION STUDIES IN THE SOCIAL WORK LITERATURE

✓ Drabble, L. A.; Haun, L. L.; Kushins, H., & Cohen, E. (2016). Measuring client satisfaction and engagement: The role of a mentor parent program in family drug treatment court. *Juvenile and Family Court Journal, 67*(1), 19–32. *[Note: you can see the scale they used at **https://docs.google.com/viewer?a=v&pid=sites&srcid=c2pzdS5lZHV8Y3ctcGFydHxneDo1OWMxOGVmNzgwYzljZTVh**].*

✓ Schuman, D. L., Slone, N. C., Reese, R. J., & Duncan, B. (2015). Efficacy of client feedback in group psychotherapy with soldiers referred for substance abuse treatment. *Psychotherapy Research, 25*(4), 396–407. *[Note: This article adds to the "growing research base … showing substantial improvements in treatment retention and outcome when therapists have access to systematic client feedback" (p. 403).]*

✓ Tsai, J., Reddy, N., & Rosenheck, R. A. (2014). Client satisfaction with a new group-based model of case management for supported housing services. *Evaluation and Program Planning, 43*, 118–123.

✓ Hsieh, C.-M. (2014). Beyond multiplication: Incorporating importance into client satisfaction measures. *Research on Social Work Practice, 24*(4), 470–476. *[Note: A technical article on the use of importance weighting scores that employ the CSQ-8 and two other measures of client satisfaction.]*

✓ Huisamen, A., & Weyers, M. (2014). Do social workers really make a difference? Measuring client satisfaction in an occupational setting. *Social Work, 50*(1), 1–18.

---

mailed questionnaires as those with higher levels of education. You'll remember the earlier discussion about response rates. While it would be wonderful to have 85% of respondents saying they are "very satisfied" with a program, but if only 30% of those eligible return their survey forms, what would you conclude? Would you wonder about the experiences of the 70% who did not respond?

Despite the generally positive bias and the problems associated with collecting representative samples of clients, there is much to recommend client satisfaction studies as one means of evaluating a program. Because professionals do not experience the agency in the same way as the clients, it is important to ask clients to share their experiences. The receptionist may be rude; a coworker may be insensitive, inattentive, or engaged in questionable practices. You need to know if clients have been mistreated, if their problems have been addressed, and if they feel they have been helped. If you don't ask questions like those listed in Figure 12.1, then you'll never know how clients might respond. Notice the use of both open-ended and closed-ended questions.

Client satisfaction studies should be used within agencies as *one* component of a comprehensive evaluation strategy. It is not recommended as the only means of evaluating a program, but as one way to gather supplemental information from the client's perspective. If you and the agency decide to conduct a client satisfaction study, here are a few recommendations:

• Use a scale that has known reliability and validity. One example is the Client Satisfaction Questionnaire (CSQ-8, Larsen, Attkisson, Hargreaves, & Nguyen, 1979) that has been used in a great number of studies. You might want to look at the surveys that have been prepared for the state of Washington's Division of Social and Health Services, Division of Behavioral Health and Recovery. On their extensive *Child/Family Consumer Survey 2014 Toolkit*, you will find their mail questionnaire and questions used in telephone interviews. The items measure *General Satisfaction* (5), *Voice in Service Delivery* (3), *Satisfaction with Staff* (5), *Perception of Outcome* (6),

1. How would you rate the quality of the services you received?

   Poor   Fair   Good   Excellent

2. How satisfied are you with the help you received?

   Very satisfied   Mostly satisfied   Mildly dissatisfied   Quite Dissatisfied

3. If a friend needed similar help, would you recommend our program?

   Yes, definitely   Not sure   No, definitely not

4. Did the staff treat you with courtesy and consideration?

   Always   Most of the time   Not very often   Not at all

5. Have the services you received help you to deal with your problems better?

   Yes, a great deal   Yes, somewhat   No, didn't seem to help   No, made things worse

Open-Ended Questions:

6. How could our program be improved?

7. What did you like best about this program?

8. What did you like least about this program?

FIGURE 12.1 Examples of Client Satisfaction Questions

Access (2), *Cultural Sensitivity* (4), and *Appropriateness of Services* (6). There are also three open-ended items (e.g., "What two things do you like the most about the mental health services you received?" (Find the website at: **http://depts.washington.edu/pbhjp/sites/default/files/2014%20 CFCS_Toolkit.pdf**)

Once you start reading the literature in your area, you will find many examples of client satisfaction instruments in published studies. Another alternative is to go to the website **www. walmyr.com** (under "Sample scales," use the dropdown menu to select the Client Satisfaction Inventory). The use of a scale that is known to have good psychometrics will eliminate many of the problems found in hastily designed questionnaires.

- Use the same instrument on repeated occasions so that you will have a baseline and trend data to find any periods of low satisfaction. "Low" client satisfaction rates may differ somewhat from agency to agency, but rates indicating that only 65% to 70% of clients are satisfied probably mean the program needs close inspection.

- Encourage client satisfaction surveys to be conducted regularly to minimize "bugs" in the system and to routinize the evaluation process.

- To reduce the problem of selection bias, consider using a "ballot box" approach, where one week every month or quarter each client coming into the agency is given a brief questionnaire and asked to complete it.

- Use at least one open-ended question to give consumers the opportunity to inform you about problems you did not know about and could not anticipate.

Outcome Evaluation (or Summative Evaluation)

- Answers the question "Are clients being helped?"
- Is often based on group research designs
- Is the type of evaluation every program should conduct
- Requires that indicators of client "success" or "failure" be well conceptualized

Outcome evaluation, also known as impact or effectiveness evaluation, often makes use of quantitative group research designs. Typically, this approach uses a control group, random assignment of clients, and involves pre- and posttesting as a way to obtain hard objective data on the performance of a program. Outcome evaluation attempts to demonstrate that a program did make a difference, that clients were helped and did improve. The successful outcomes of a program should not be confused with "output." That is, an agency could "graduate" or "process" any number of clients during a year, but outcome evaluation is concerned with the extent to which these clients change or improve.

Beutler (1993) lists principles, and Peterson and Bell-Dolan (1995) mention some "commandments" that not only are a good review of what we already have covered, but also suggest key considerations for when an outcome study is being planned.

1. *Employ a control or comparison group whenever possible.* The essence of program evaluation is comparison. How well did the program do? The comparison group provides the basis for answering this question by furnishing the contrast that allows the evaluator to observe for threats to the internal validity such as maturation, history, effects of testing, and so forth.

2. *Client samples should be representative.* Invalid conclusions can arise from convenience samples and those where the sampling procedures produce a selection bias.

3. *Random assignment for controlling treatment groups is strongly recommended.* If random assignment is not possible, check pretreatment data to determine if there is group equivalence. Also, take steps to keep subjects from dropping out of the study (minimize the threat of mortality) because this can change the equivalence between groups. Start with a sufficient group size to support the statistical analyses you want to conduct and to protect against loss of subjects in the final stages of the evaluation.

4. *Outcome measures should have demonstrated reliability and validity.* If instruments are needed, it is recommended that only those with adequate reliability and validity be employed. Additionally, multimodal measurement (using multiple instruments and measuring more than one domain) is more likely to detect an intervention's effects than a single instrument.

5. *Interventions need to be standardized and applied as uniformly as possible.* Develop treatment protocols to ensure that clients with the same problems consistently receive the same treatment from practitioners.

6. *Samples of therapists providing the intervention must be large enough to be representative.* While researchers often worry about whether they have large enough samples of clients, too few worry about whether they have an adequate sample of therapists who are providing the treatment being evaluated. Small, inadequate samples of therapists also limit the evaluator's ability to understand whether the intervention worked in the intended way.

7. *Assessment of clinical meaningfulness should accompany computations of statistical significance.* It is entirely possible to obtain differences in average scores that are statistically significant but that

have no real meaning clinically. In other words, clients' scores may improve, but not so much that it would be noticeable to the client, to his or her family, or to the therapist.

Cost-Effectiveness and Cost Analysis

- Answers the question "What does it cost to help a client?"
- Focuses on desired program outcome (success) indicators
- Allows policy makers to look simultaneously at the expense of running a program (efficiency) and its success (effectiveness)

To set this type of evaluation in perspective, it would be helpful to read the article by Eamon, Wu, and Zhang (2012), which shows public benefit programs actually give greater benefit than just to those who receive direct assistance. (And students interested in policy should love it!) The authors share the results of major studies that show, for instance:

> ... for each dollar spent on WIC, Medicaid saved an estimated $2.91. (p. 20)
>
> The analysis estimated that the states would spend a total of $132.1 billion on Medicaid, resulting in a $367.5 billion increase in business activity (measured by the value of the goods and services produced). In other words, an average of $3.4 million in increased business activity would be generated for every million dollars a state invests in Medicaid. (p. 17)
>
> ... a study estimated that Medicaid spending in Texas created 474,420 permanent jobs; and the $49.5 million Medicaid cuts enacted in the 2003 legislative session in Florida, resulted in 1732 lost jobs and $59 million in lost wages. (p. 18)

Johnson-Motoyama, Brook, Yan, and McDonald (2013) conducted a **cost analysis** of the Strengthening Families Program (SFP) in Kansas. The purpose was to see if the program reduced the amount of time children spent in out-of-home care when their parents or caregivers were substance involved. The study found children whose caregivers were involved with SFP spent 190 days fewer in out-of-home care, saving approximately $16,340 per child in state and federal out-of-home care costs. It costs $8.75 per child each day for the program, and that was about one-tenth the cost of the $85.70 cost for each day in out-of-home care. Further, for each dollar invested in SFP, the benefits ranged from $9.15 to $25.35, depending on the level of out-of-home care cost and the SFP staffing model. This is powerful information!

Similarly, Sharp and colleagues (2014), concerned with the problem of youth violence, have estimated that a brief 30-minute intervention by a social worker when an at-risk adolescent has been brought into the hospital could cost as little as $10.08 to prevent the adolescent from engaging in a subsequent act with a violent consequence. The savings are immense. "Nationally, an average ED (emergency department) visit costs $1,349, an average pediatric ED visit for a firearm injury costs $3,642, and if admitted to the hospital, the mean charge is $70,164" (p. 452). (Other information on the SafERteens studies can be found with Walton et al., 2010 and Cunningham et al., 2012.)

Rizzo and Rowe (2006), in a review of 40 articles on the cost-effectiveness of social work services in aging, conclude, "[T]he current body of outcome studies ... provides convincing empirical evidence that social work services can have a positive and significant impact on quality of life and health care costs and use for aging individuals" (p. 72).

Toseland and Smith (2006) report on a health education program (HEP) designed for spouse caregivers of frail older adults with chronic illnesses. This study was designed to learn if the social work intervention would result in reductions in outpatient, inpatient, and total health care charges at a participating HMO. The study found that overall, the intervention saved the HMO $309,461 on caregivers and care recipients during the study period. Care recipients whose spouses participated in HEP cost the HMO an average of $1,418 per person versus an average of $5,760 for those receiving the usual care (the control group).

Cost-effectiveness and cost-analysis studies allow the evaluator not only to compare the success rates of different programs, but also to examine these rates in terms of their costs. These studies could be classified as a type of outcome evaluation but have been given their own category in this book to highlight their distinctive quality of factoring in program costs.

Some examples of cost-analysis studies you may want to examine are:

✓ Morgan, T. B., Crane, D. R., Moore, A. M., & Eggett, D. L. (2013). The cost of treating substance use disorders: Individual versus family therapy. *Journal of Family Therapy, 35*, 2–23.

✓ Maher, E. J., Corwin, T. W., Hodnett, R., & Faulk, K. (2012). A cost-savings analysis of a statewide parenting education program in child welfare. *Research on Social Work Practice, 22*, 615–625.

✓ Basu, A., Kee, R., Buchanan, D., & Sadowski, L. S. (2012). Comparative cost analysis of housing and case management programs for chronically ill homeless adults compared to usual care. *Health Services Research, 47* (1, Pt. II), 523–542.

✓ Butcher, Tossone, and Kretchmer (2016) have completed a 10-year evaluation of a behavioral health/juvenile justice initiative in Ohio that is very comprehensive and complete. It evaluates the project a number of different ways (e.g., cost analysis, client satisfaction, recidivism, reduction in out-of-home placement, reduction of trauma symptoms and substance use, etc.) Look over the report to see how an excellent report is crafted. Find this report at:

http://begun.case.edu/wp-content/uploads/2016/04/BHJJ-Evaluation-2016-Statewide-and-County-Results.pdf.

Steps in Conducting a Cost-Effective Study

1. *Operationalize program success.* Think, for example, of a program designed to provide supported employment for persons with severe disabilities due to mental illness. What would success be? Transitioning to the competitive job market? Fewer hospitalizations? Being employed at least 20 hours a week for at least 40 weeks a year?

2. *Prepare to gather program outcome data.* In a retrospective evaluation, this step involves identifying the sample of clients to be included in the evaluation and deciding how many years to examine. If there are many clients, a random sampling strategy may be developed.

3. *Gather client outcome data.* This step typically involves contacting former "graduates" of the program to determine how many meet the criteria for success.

4. *Compute the program costs.* The total costs for operating the program need to be computed. Costs include such items as personnel salaries and benefits, facility rent, and maintenance (heating, air conditioning, electricity, insurance, phones, travel, and so on).

5. *Compute the cost-effectiveness ratio.* The cost-effectiveness of a program is computed by dividing its total cost by the number of client successes. For instance, a program that expended $200,000 and had 400 successes costs $500 for each successful client.

As you can see, this type of evaluation supplies superior information for decision makers and enables them to choose the best programs. Those programs with substantial costs that produce few positive effects can be discontinued, and the resulting cost savings can be applied to more effective interventions.

ANXIETY CHECK 12.1

Willa is a recent MSW graduate and has been asked by the director of her agency to identify 10 of their recent clients who became outstanding successes in five sessions or less. Further, the director wants to use this information in a new marketing campaign to attract more self-pay clients to the agency. Willa is expected to compute a cost-effectiveness study to use in the marketing effort based on the 10 clients. From a research standpoint, would the cost-effectiveness study be unbiased? From a research ethics perspective, would Willa be representing the agency correctly?

[Answer is at the end of the book.]

Other Models

Cost analysis is not limited to cost-effectiveness studies. There are cost-benefit analyses, cost-utility analyses, and cost-feasibility analyses, to name a few. Unlike cost-effectiveness studies, in cost-benefit analyses, effort is made to measure both costs and benefits in monetary units. However, sometimes it is difficult to measure the absolute benefit of interventions. Many benefits are intangible and cannot be easily converted to a dollar value (e.g., improved self-esteem, reduced human suffering, or the value of a new park); often, these studies make estimates that you may not feel are defendable. Such findings should be viewed cautiously until you check their assumptions and methodology.

As social workers, we need to examine our interventions in terms of their cost-effectiveness. The profession of social work will be enhanced to the extent to which we can show a skeptical public that costs to society are far greater when evidence-based interventions are inadequately funded than when sufficient funds are provided for prevention and remediation programs. Important programmatic decisions should not be made without evaluation data. To the extent that we can successfully identify the most efficient *and* effective programs, the prestige of the social work profession will be enhanced.

BOX 12.6   STUDIES WITH A QUALITATIVE FOCUS/COMPONENT ON COST

- ✓ Henry, D., Bales, R., & Graves, E. (2007). Ethnography in evaluation: Uncovering hidden costs and benefits in child mental health. *Human Organization, 66*(3), 315–326.
- ✓ Kenealy, T. W., Parsons, M. J. G., Rouse, P. B., Doughty, R. N., Sheridan, N. F., Hindmarsh, J. K. H., ... & Rea, H. H. (2015). Telecare for diabetes, CHF or COPD: Effect on quality of life, hospital use and costs: A randomized controlled trial and qualitative evaluation. *PLOS ONE, 10*(3), 1–21.

There are numerous models from which to pattern a program evaluation. Some of the differences among these approaches are subtle, others are not. In planning an evaluation, you need to select a model that makes sense to you, one that will answer the questions that stimulated the study. In this chapter, the goal has been to familiarize you with just a few of many designs. For example, a mixed-methods or qualitative evaluation might be undertaken either with focus groups or participant interviews.

ANXIETY CHECK 12.2

For each of the types of program evaluation listed below, identify whether it is primarily quantitatively or qualitatively oriented.

   Patterns of Use
   Formative/Process Evaluation
   Consumer Satisfaction
   Outcome Evaluation
   Cost-Effectiveness

[Answers found at the end of the book.]

Program Evaluation with Qualitative Approaches

At times, a qualitative approach is exactly what is needed to diagnose problems within a program or agency. Reflect on these questions: "How do clients experience your agency? Is the receptionist pleasant and courteous? Does the staff treat clients with respect? What would it be like to be a client at your agency?" Funding sources often request the recipients of their funds to supply process evaluations, which tend to be primarily narrative descriptions and may provide information about what it took to start up a new intervention, problems encountered along the way, the staff and clients' experiences with it, and so forth.

We've all experienced staff who were rude or not helpful—secretaries who wouldn't answer the phone because they were on a break, receptionists who said hurtful things to clients. I've personally observed counselors who would not see their clients early even if the counselors were available; I've been in buildings where the walls were so thin that voices from the next office traveled through the walls; buildings where there wasn't enough parking; and buildings where there were no handicapped-accessible facilities. Qualitative researchers posing as clients could provide information about an agency that administrators might otherwise never receive.

Qualitative investigators conducting a program evaluation of an agency or program would not be counting successful clients or documenting how much clients had improved. Their interests would be in how clients' lives have changed as a result of the intervention they've received. The qualitative program evaluator would be looking for the values or benefits that the intervention provided for clients. As Goldstein (1997) notes, "It is not how to count but what counts in peoples' lives that will begin to enlighten and shape the course and nature of our inquiries" (p. 452). The qualitative investigator would help the program or agency to see itself by capturing the clients' experiences as they reported in their own words.

In a qualitative program evaluation, there is no formal model for the investigator to follow. The approach to be followed and the data to be gathered depend on what it is that the investigator wishes to learn.

BOX 12.7   QUALITATIVE EVALUATION OF A PROSTITUTION DIVERSION PROJECT

Commercial sex workers in Salt Lake City, Utah, arrested for prostitution offenses had the opportunity to be diverted from jail by participating in a 16-week, three-phase program that involved individual and group counseling. A review panel assessed attendance and progress every two weeks.

All participants were paid $20 an hour, and interviews lasted between one and two hours. At the time of the study, 24 sex workers had been enrolled in the program and 12 consented to the semi-structured qualitative interviews. The sample also consisted of 19 service providers. A professional transcriber transcribed the audiotaped interviews, which were then coded with open-coding and in-vivo techniques (where codes are conceptual names or phrases taken from participants' comments).

The sex workers made a number of recommendations about the program. One of the more interesting was about the interventions they received—interventions that sometimes came across as being not well structured or coherent (for example, there was no treatment manual or standard approach). As one sex worker observed,

> Even walking in, the counselors, they just kind of "winged" it, you know. They did the group like they were supposed to, but they really "winged" it. And any materials that they brought in, it was their own. ... It was things that they found that they thought would help us. (p. 212)

Sex workers also identified a problem in that some of the participants who attended sessions were high but were not asked to leave, and there appeared to be no consequences for their actions. These two specific observations were made:

> You know, they got to sit there ... and it was kind of a distraction, and ... it gives you the urge to use watching somebody else ... that's that way. ... And I think [it] was a really big distraction for me. ... And that's what I think they need to change when somebody comes in there like that. (p. 215)
>
> I have a lot of treatment under my belt. ... And to go share my stuff with clean and sober people that I know are clean and sober is one thing. But to just go give all this to people who are unpracticed and using is pretty unusual. (p. 215)

Another telling finding was that none of the service providers or sex workers was able to refer to written documents or explicit verbal instructions regarding the intended objectives of the program. It is apparent from reading even this small portion of Wahab's article that the qualitative evaluation contained important information that could improve the diversion program. Did you read anything here that might concern you as a service provider or administrator?

Source: Wahab, S. (2005). Navigating mixed-theory programs: Lessons learned from a prostitution-diversion project. *Affilia, 20*(2), 203–221.

Note: You may wish to read a more recent qualitative program evaluation along this line by Preble, Praetorius, and Cimino (2016). Supporting exists: A best practices report for a sex worker intervention. *Journal of Human Behavior in the Social Environment, 26*(2), 162–178.

Qualitative research approaches are superior to quantitative methods in some instances. For example, an excellent test to see whether an antidiscrimination ordinance in a community is effective is to have a person of color make application to rent an apartment, and then, an hour or so later, a white person also makes an application. If the first person was informed there were no vacancies, but the second person was shown a vacant apartment, then there is good evidence of discrimination—much better information (and evidence) than would be obtained by conducting a survey of apartment managers and asking if they discriminate.

Practical Considerations for a Smooth Evaluation Process

While the conceptualization of the evaluation design often seems like the most difficult part, any number of factors can influence the choice of a design—even the political climate within the agency. Ideally, it is helpful to know something about a program's history and its personnel before beginning to evaluate it. As a new staff person, student intern, or contract evaluator, however, you may not have the opportunity to gain "inside" information. So, what can you do?

First and foremost, whether you are planning a qualitative or quantitative evaluation, you need to keep in mind that all evaluation is inherently threatening. Practically everyone feels uncomfortable when they are being evaluated—especially when the evaluator is someone unknown. People are even more threatened when they think the evaluator may not like them or might want to eliminate their jobs. Therefore, you must be sensitive to the feelings of those who may be affected by the findings of the program evaluation. Try not to create anxiety within the staff. Communicate frequently with involved personnel. Avoid surprises. If at all possible, involve staff in planning the evaluation. Ask for their ideas. Remember that evaluations are a political activity—someone may have a vested interest in making one program look good at the expense of another. Some policy makers may hope to use the program evaluation to justify cutting a particular program's budget.

Second, expect that obstacles and objections to the evaluation effort will arise. Even staff members who should be supportive may have strongly held, but erroneous, beliefs about the evaluation. There may be political alliances and defenders of the status quo who view the evaluation as terrifying because it will bring about change from the way things "have always been done." As a result, some staff may overtly not cooperate, and others may conveniently "forget" to complete assignments or forms. Other staff will be too afraid to reply honestly for fear of being recognized.

Third, it is recommended that you develop a contract, or, if that seems too formal, then a detailed memo describing your understanding of the following:

1. The *purpose* of the evaluation, including questions to be answered or hypotheses to be tested. You may also want to list the evaluation design to be used.
2. The *audience* for whom you will be writing the evaluation report. (Will it go only to the program director, or the whole staff, the board of directors, the public?)
3. The *amount of time* you have to conduct the evaluation and write the final report.
4. The terms of your *reimbursement* or the amount of time that you will be released from your regular duties to conduct the evaluation.
5. The *budget* or amount that you can spend purchasing standardized instruments, visiting other programs, photocopying, providing snacks or incentives to participants, and so on.

Don't be afraid to negotiate if you feel that you need more time or funds to do the job right. Put it all in writing, even the issue of who will have access to the data for purposes of publication. You may want to state that you will have first opportunity to use the data, or ask for something like six months of exclusive use if you want to write a manuscript for publication.

Key Terms

audience

ad hoc committee

prospective study

retrospective study

program monitoring

formative evaluation

process evaluation

cost-benefit analyses

objective

summative evaluation

cost analysis

patterns of use

goal

blue-ribbon committee

client satisfaction survey

cost-effectiveness

program evaluation

expert consultation

SELF-REVIEW
(Answers at the end of the book.)

1. Which type of evaluation design answers the question "Whom are we serving?"
2. Which type of evaluation design answers the question "What would make this new program better?"
3. Process evaluations are primarily:

   a. narrative
   b. statistical
   c. hypothetical

4. Which type of evaluation design answers the question "How pleased are clients with our services?"
5. Which type of evaluation design answers the question "Are clients being helped?"
6. Which type of evaluation design answers the question "What does it cost to help a client?"
7. T or F. The focus of process evaluation is not so much on the number of client successes as on what happened during the development of the program and why.
8. The main reason client satisfaction data can't be considered "proof" that a program is effective is _____.
9. Another name for an evaluation type that examines client utilization data is _____.
10. List four considerations to keep in mind when planning a program evaluation.
11. How does a qualitative program evaluation differ from a cost-effectiveness study?

QUESTIONS FOR CLASS DISCUSSION

1. The following could be called Exemplars of Poor Evaluation Designs. What is wrong with each of the following plans for evaluating programs?

    a. The agency is a halfway house run by the Department of Corrections. Residents are all young men who have been in prison for the first time and are now on parole in a prerelease program. In this program evaluation, three new residents who have outward signs of depression will be selected and compared with two other residents who are not depressed. The Zung Self-Rating Depression Inventory will be the instrument used to determine if a caring attitude by the program staff and conjugal visits can help with adjustment from prison to the larger community. A pretest-posttest design will be employed.

    b. A school has developed a latchkey program for students in the elementary grades. Parents who want to participate must contribute $50 a week for the program for each child enrolled. A preexperimental (posttest-only with nonequivalent groups) design will be used to compare students enrolled in the program with other students who could benefit from it but whose parents can't pay the fee. At the end of the school year, comparisons will be made on the variable of academic achievement. The principal handpicks the students who will be in the control group based on low reading and math scores.

    c. A family preservation program wants to conduct an outcome evaluation. A student intern is given the names and phone numbers for the last 50 closed cases. Success is defined as "no subsequent abuse." The student is instructed to call the 50 former clients and, after introducing herself, to ask if there has been any subsequent abuse in the families since the cases were closed. If she receives an affirmative response, there is another set of questions she is supposed to ask.

2. What conditions present in an agency would make it ripe for evaluation, in your opinion?
3. What conditions present in an agency would make it difficult to conduct an evaluation there?
4. Does evaluation always have to be threatening? When would it not be?
5. Idea for group projects: Allow students to divide into groups, and then select one of the types of evaluation in the Butcher, Tossone, and Krethmar (2016) 10-year evaluation of a behavioral health/juvenile justice initiative in Ohio. They can summarize the findings and report back to the class. Do all of the groups report positive findings? Here is the website for the report:

    http://begun.case.edu/wp-content/uploads/2016/04/BHJJ-Evaluation-2016-Statewide-and-County-Results.pdf

RESOURCES AND REFERENCES

Beutler, L. E. (1993). Designing outcome studies: Treatment of adult victims of childhood sexual abuse. *Journal of Interpersonal Violence*, 8, AQ2-A1A.

Cummings, B., Mengistu, M., Negash, W., Bekele, A., & Ghile, T. (2006). Barriers to and facilitators for female participation in an HIV prevention project in rural Ethiopia: Findings from a qualitative evaluation. *Culture, Health, & Sexuality, 8*(3), 251–266.

Cunningham, R. M., Chermack, S. T., Zimmerman, M. A., Shope, J. T., Bingham, C. R., Blow, F. C. & Walton, M. A. (2012). Brief motivational interviewing intervention for peer violence and alcohol use in teens: One-year follow-up. *Pediatrics, 129* (6), 1083–1090.

Eamon, M. K., Wu, C.-F., & Zhang, S. (2012). Reframing the benefits and beneficiaries of public benefits programs. *Children and Youth Services Review, 34,* 15–26.

Goldstein, H. (1997). Shaping our inquiries into foster and kinship care: Editorial note. *Families in Society, 78,* 451–452.

Johnson-Motoyama, M., Brook, J., Yan, Y., & McDonald, T. P. (2013). Cost analysis of the strengthening families program in reducing time to family reunification among substance-affected families. *Children and Youth Services Review, 35,* 244–252.

Larsen, D. L., Attkisson, C. C., Hargreaves, W. A., & Nguyen, T. D. (1979). Assessment of client/patient satisfaction: Development of a general scale. *Evaluation and Program Planning, 2,* 197–207.

Lebow, J. (1982). Consumer satisfaction with mental health treatment. *Psychological Bulletin, 91*(2), 244–259.

Peterson, L., & Bell-Dolan, D. (1995). Treatment outcome research in child psychology: Realistic coping with the "Ten Commandments of Methodology." *Journal of Clinical Child Psychology, 24,* 149–162.

Rhodes, P., Brown, J., & Madden, S. (2009). The Maudsley model of family-based treatment for anorexia nervosa: A qualitative evaluation of parent-to-parent consultation. *Journal of Marital and Family Therapy, 35*(2), 181–192.

Rizzo, V. M., & Rowe, J. M. (2006). Studies of the cost-effectiveness of social work services in aging: A review of the literature. *Research on Social Work Practice, 16*(1), 67–73.

Royse, D., Thyer, B., & Padgett, D. K. (2016). *Program evaluation: An introduction to an evidence-based approach.* Boston, MA: Cengage Learning.

Sharp, A. L., Prosser, L. A., Walton, M., Blow, F. C., Chermack, S. T., Zimmerman, M. A., & Cunningham, R. (2014). Cost analysis of youth violence prevention. *Pediatrics, 133*(3), 448–453.

Smith, D., Roche, E., O'Loughlin, K., Brennan, D., Madigan, K., Lyne, J., ... & O'Donoghue, B. (2014). Satisfaction with services following voluntary and involuntary admission. *Journal of Mental Health, 23*(10), 38–45.

Toseland, R. W., & Smith, T. L. (2006). The impact of a caregiver health education program on health care costs. *Research on Social Work Practice, 16*(1), 9–19.

Walton, M., Chermack, S. T., Shope, J. T., Bingham, C. R., Zimmerman, M. H., Blow, F. C. & Cunningham, R. M. (2010). Effects of a brief intervention for reducing violence and alcohol misuse among adolescents: A Randomized Controlled Trial. *JAMA, 304,* 527–535.

ASSIGNMENT 12.1

Designing a Program Evaluation

Objective: *To gain experience considering the critical elements going into a program evaluation.*

Five different programs could benefit from an objective outcome evaluation. While you may wish to employ a scale or standardized instrument, all of these programs may also be evaluated by changes in clients' actual behaviors. (*Note:* Your instructor will inform you if he or she wants you to find an instrument.) Choose one of the topics that follow, and then answer the questions.

Program Examples

- A peer educator–led eating disorders education and prevention program
- A token economy system in a state psychiatric hospital
- A program to prevent juvenile arsonists from recidivating
- An alternative education program for expelled youth
- A divorce adjustment group for young children

1. List at least two questions that you think would be important to answer about this program.
2. Operationally define your dependent variables(s). How will success be determined?
3. Describe a program evaluation design and methodology for collecting your data. Be sure to address how the sample is to be selected.
4. What limitations might your study have?

ASSIGNMENT 12.2

Reading a Program Evaluation

Objective: *To gain experience reading a program evaluation and critically thinking about it.*

This is a two-part assignment. The first step requires that you search the literature for an article in one of the professional journals that evaluates a program. Be careful to choose a piece that contains data (that is, tables) and doesn't just talk about the need for program evaluation. Then, you will need to closely read the article to answer the following questions. (Your instructor may want the whole class to read the same article; if that is not the case, he or she may want you to append a photocopy of the article you read to this assignment.)

1. Which article did you read? (Provide the complete citation in APA format.)
2. What is the major question that this program evaluation seeks to answer?
3. How was the dependent variable(s) operationalized?
4. Briefly describe the methodology used to determine if the program was successful.
5. Did the study involve a sample of clients? If yes, how many were in the sample? Was the sample size adequate?
6. What did you learn about evaluating a program of this type? (Be as specific as possible.)
7. What possible limitations does this study have?

ASSIGNMENT 12.3

Critically Reviewing an Evaluative Study

Objective: *To gain experience reading a program evaluation and critically thinking about it.*

In Chapter 5, Sophia and Bill discovered at least four different studies that attempted to reduce HIV risk among incarcerated women and youth as well as women receiving substance abuse treatment in an urban community. Go back to that chapter to find the citations for Amaro et al. (2007), Goldberg et al. (2009), Knudsen et al. (2014), or Leukefeld et al. (2012). Choose one of these articles (that you did not read earlier), and answer the questions below.

1. Which article did you report on? Use the full APA citation.
2. Did the authors give you an understanding of the theoretical orientation on which the intervention was based? What was it?
3. Did the authors, in your opinion, draw an adequate sample? Why or why not?
4. Discuss the instruments that the authors used. Were they psychometrically sound?
5. Do the reported results make sense and seem trustworthy? How so?
6. What do you make of the study's limitations? Could the study have been conducted with fewer or less serious limitations? If so, explain.

CHAPTER 13

Interpreting Statistics and Data Found in Research Reports

S ATURDAY MORNING. SOPHIA was still in her pajamas, making out a list of things to pick up from the supermarket later that morning when her phone rang.

"Hey," Bill said brightly, in that voice that suggested he had a problem or needed a favor. "Have you started studying for the quiz in research methods?"

"Not yet."

"When are you going to start?" True to form, Bill was quick to make his requests known.

"I don't know. I don't have anything in the refrigerator. I was planning on shopping this morning and studying in the afternoon." Sophia thought she'd play with Bill a bit. "Why are you asking?"

"Well, I think I need some help. I started looking at my lecture notes last night, and the stuff I wrote down doesn't make sense to me now."

Teasing him a bit more, Sophia asked, "And what does that have to do with me? Don't you have a book?"

"Oh, come on. Can I study with you? I think if you helped me with a couple of questions, I could begin to understand what I need to know."

"Fine. But you owe me." She waited until she heard Bill's acknowledgment of his debt, and then she said, "I'm going to start studying about one. You can come over then."

A Little Talk About Understanding Statistical Concepts

Like Bill, your reaction to reading the title of this chapter might be "Oh, no! Not statistics! I don't understand statistics! I can't do math."

I understand. If you feel lost when it comes to interpreting research articles, I can tell you with some authority that I have been lost too. As an undergraduate, I was lost in my first statistics course. The instructor tossed statistical terms up in the air like someone throwing confetti at a New Year's Eve party. In his class, I not only had no understanding of what he was talking about but also not even a clue as to where to grab hold to begin to comprehend his lectures. Because I was "fogged in" about almost everything the instructor was talking about, I dropped that course before midterm and signed up for a statistics course in a different department the next semester. Fortunately for me, the new instructor used examples and applied problems that made sense. My confidence grew, and I mastered what the instructor required us to learn.

That's what this chapter is all about—helping you to become more confident in grasping the statistical concepts and statements you will encounter when reading a research article or report you need to comprehend. This chapter's aim is to help you *understand* the most frequently used statistical concepts found in professional articles and reports. Except for the simplest of statistics, the chapter will not discuss or worry you with the calculation of these useful tools.

However, I want to emphasize that all of the statistics we discuss in this chapter can be computed easily by one of three ways: First, most universities have the Statistical Package for the Social Sciences (SPSS) available in computer labs or allow students to download it. The program's drop-down windows make it very user-friendly. Student versions can also be purchased, often from college bookstores. Second, there are interactive web pages that allow you to use free of charge a large range of statistical procedures that work well—and usually without having to register or sign up. Explore **https://statpages.info** to see for yourself. Third, almost all computers and laptops have a version of Excel installed, which can be used to analyze data as well. Although without a guide of some sort, it is not as intuitive for the student to use as the two previous methods. Regardless of which approach your instructor or you prefer to use, what is most important is that you realize that there is no reason to fear checking out an app or interactive page to produce a statistic. Really! In fact, you might want to do that with several of the examples in this chapter. You just might be surprised how effortless it can be. Don't worry about calculating or computing "a bunch of numbers" for now. It is more important to grasp what these procedures can tell you about the data and why the authors of research publications used them.

Before we get too much further into the chapter, a slight mental reframe might be necessary. Instead of thinking about how difficult it is to learn statistical concepts, look for a way to connect with the content. Maybe you have some topic that you would like to know more about. Perhaps you could see yourself applying a particular statistical tool to conduct research about that topic. At any rate, look for connections and linkages and you'll find that the content will be so much easier to remember. You'll see what I mean in the next paragraph.

Univariate Statistics

One statistical term that is easy to learn is **univariate statistics**. It sounds strange but actually is simple to understand. Look at the first part of the word: *uni* means one as in unicycle. When you see univariate statistics, the author of the research publication will be examining the descriptive features of one variable at a time. In studies you are reading, you may see univariate statistics like those described in this section to help you understand the individuals from whom data were collected. These persons might be called the research participants, research subjects, or respondents. Univariate statistics can provide you with information about the age of the youngest and oldest persons in the study, the average age, the proportion who were African American or female, and so on. Univariate statistics might also be shown for the dependent variable in some instances. The author might compare scores obtained on a standardized test with the scores reported in another study and might want you to be able to compare the two sets of scores in terms of their differences or similarities.

In this section, we will be discussing the following terms and concepts:

- N and n
- Percentages
- Measures of central tendency (mean, median, mode)
- Ratio and interval data
- Range
- Standard deviation

N and n

In almost every professional journal article, you will encounter statistical abbreviations like this: **(n = 100).** The **n** represents the number of individuals in a study's sample. You can remember it easily because n is the first letter of the word "number." As you read a study, pay attention to whether that number changes. For instance, the study may have started off with a sample of 100 respondents, but six months later at the follow-up data collection or posttest, the n may have dropped precipitously (n = 20). This issue is important to note. If a study loses a large number of respondents, it is a threat to the internal validity of the study (see mortality/attrition in Chapter 5). A small **n** indicates the number of cases or participants (as in a particular sample), while a large **N** tells us that the statistic is referring to a larger group, such as the total number of cases in a study or the population of adult residents in a community.

Percentages

Percentages are always based on 100. In the previous example, if a study starts with a sample of 100 respondents and ends up with 20, then it has lost 80% of its respondents. You can compute this by dividing 20 by the original number of 100. That calculation produces 0.20, which times 100 equals 20%—those who stayed in the study. Subtracting 20% from 100% = 80% or those who dropped out. Anytime you divide a small number by a larger number, you can refer to that result as a percentage. For example, if you order a small personal pan pizza that is cut into three pieces and eat two of the three, then you have eaten 67% of the pizza (2 divided by 3 = 0.6667 or rounded up to 67%). Note that with calculating percentages, multiplying by 100 is often understood and not stated.

A proportion is essentially the same as a percentage—it just means identifying some part of a whole. That *whole* can be a sample, as can be seen in this question: *What percent of the sample is Hispanic?* A researcher might also examine a certain characteristic in a particular population, as in this question: *What percent of the residents of Indianapolis are over the age of 70?*

Average (Mean)

We all learned about averages in elementary school—so they should be familiar too. Let's say that you have had three quizzes in your favorite course. You obtained scores of 95, 85, and 90. What is your average quiz

EXAMPLE 13.1 How You Might See n, N, and % in a Study

	Total (N = 250)		New Clients (n = 200)		Returning Clients (n = 50)	
Demographics of Study	n	%	n	%	n	%
Females	145	58	130	65	15	30
Males	105	42	70	35	35	70
Age						
20–29	100	40	80	40	20	40
30–39	70	28	56	28	14	28
40–49	50	20	40	20	10	20
50+	30	12	24	12	06	12

score? The process involves adding the three scores together (95 + 85 + 90), which sums to 270. Since there were three quizzes, you divide the sum of the scores by the number of quizzes (270 / 3 = 90) and obtain the average score of 90. The average is the most commonly used form of what is referred to as measures of central tendency—ways of understanding the "typical case or value" to represent all of the data. (More about measures of central tendency in the next section.)

Don't be thrown by large numbers (10,000, 15,000, 20,000, 25,000, and 85,000). You add them together and then divide the sum in the same way by the number of values. In this example, the sum of the five numbers is 155,000; dividing it by the five values produces a mean of 31,000.

In professional journal articles, you may see the statistical symbol for mean as **M** or $\bar{x}$ (referred to as x bar). However, note that this symbol is associated with the mean of a sample. For instance, a mean of 31,000 could represent the average salary of the sample of five men in the treatment group of 20 referred to earlier who didn't drop out of treatment. Note that as you look back over the five salaries, there is no salary of $31,000. In fact, four of them are below that level and only one is above. One issue with the mean is that, as a representation of the typical respondent or value in the sample, it is pulled in the direction of extreme scores (the one salary of $85,000). Had the mean been computed on the four other salaries ($10,000, $15,000, $20,000, $25,000), the mean would have been $17,500, which is $7,500 more than the lowest salary and exactly $7,500 below the highest salary. It is this dependable characteristic that makes the mean a major statistic upon which other more sophisticated analytic procedures are based. Note though that researchers often remove extreme scores that are very different from the others (like $85,000) so that the mean is more representative. These extreme scores are known as **outliers**.

Ratio and Interval Data

You may never have thought about it, but certain types of quantitative variables that involve counting or measuring are known as interval and ratio data. Sometimes called **continuous variables**, you'll recognize them immediately. Ratio-level variables have true zeros. Say you are asked, "How many children do you have?" And if you have never had children, then a response of "none" is a true zero. Other examples might include test scores, years of military service, and so on. However, a lot of the concepts we measure in the social sciences do not have a true zero. For instance, even a person with the lowest self-esteem imaginable could not have zero self-esteem. Variables like weight and height, for all practical purposes, do not have a true zero. The basic feature of interval and ratio variables is that the units that represent their measure are equally spaced or occurring. That feature makes it easy to know that if a friend is 21 today, in another year, that person will be 22. Similarly, if a grandmother is 72, then four years ago, she was 68. And, finally, if you are making $10 an hour at your job and your employer gives you a $2-an-hour raise, then you will be making $12 an hour. Such is the beauty of interval and ratio data. It allows us to get accurate measurements and to compute such statistics as the mean number of years a sample of clients has been dealing with Post-traumatic stress disorder (PTSD) or their average score on a depression scale.

Researchers usually strive to obtain interval and ratio data because the more sophisticated statistical procedures require it. You need to recognize them as *one type* of data, because research publications are *not* going to announce that the information you are reading is based on interval data—it will be assumed that you know and recognize that. Statistical procedures generally treat interval and ratio levels of measurement the same, and the distinction is not an important one. Sometimes they are referred to as being at the interval/ratio level.

Other types of data will be discussed a bit later in the chapter under the heading of levels of measurement. In terms of univariate variables, means, medians, ranges, and standard deviations are all based on interval/ratio data. Having already discussed means, we discuss the others next.

Measures of Central Tendency

Besides the mean, two other measures of central tendency include the median and the mode. The **median**, like the median between lanes on an interstate highway, precisely divides the data in half—with half of the values falling below the median and half occurring above the median. Here's a sample of scores from the research methods quiz that Bill and Sophia collected from seven close friends: 82, 84, 85, 87, 90, 90, 96. The median is 87; can you explain why? (It is the middle score with three above it and three below.) The median is sometimes reported when there are extreme scores that would make the mean misleading. The symbol for median can be represented as **Mdn**. Note that to determine the median, the data must be arranged from low to high or high to low.

The **mode** is the most frequently occurring value. In the previous example, the mode is 90 because it occurs twice, and all the other scores only occur once. If Bill conducted a survey and found that 60% of respondents preferred chocolate ice cream, 25% favored vanilla, and 15% preferred strawberry, then the large group of respondents (chocolate lovers) would represent the modal group. You may find the symbol for mode shown as **Mo**.

Range

The range is used to illustrate the lowest and highest values within a distribution of values when the values or scores are arranged in order from low to high or high to low. Let's say you are looking at the intake data from women who have come into a shelter for victims of domestic violence over the last five years. You note that a small group were not allowed by their partners or husbands to work outside the home and claimed no income while about three residents claimed incomes of approximately $150,000. You are struck by the range running from $0 to $150,000, which confirms for you that domestic violence occurs across all social classes or income groups. By itself, the range often is not all that valuable for understanding the typical client. Wouldn't you prefer to know the average income for these women or the median or mode?

Standard Deviation

The standard deviation is just what its name sounds like—a statistic showing how much the average score deviates (or varies, either higher or lower) from the mean. To understand this concept, let's assume that you are working with court-involved teenagers in a residential center. Using the Child Report of Posttraumatic Symptoms (CROPS), a 25-item instrument that allows respondents to report such symptoms as feeling alone, sad, or depressed or having stomachaches, Crosby et al. (2017) reported the following information in Example 13.2:

EXAMPLE 13.2 How You Might See Standard Deviation and Mean in a Study

	Mean	Std. Dev.
Trauma Symptoms (Scores Range From 0 to 50)	23.05	10.66
White Students	24.56	10.66
African American or Other	22.15	10.62

Source: Crosby et al. (2017)

In Example 13.2, we can see that the white students reported slightly more symptoms, 2.41 symptoms more, than the African American and other students. However, there is very little difference in the standard deviations. Overall, the scores reported from the students in the residential school were slightly higher than those found with the first study of the CROPS using younger children (as young as third and fourth graders but no older than eighth graders, median age 11.5). In that study, Greenwald and Rubin (1999) reported a mean CROPS of 19.7 with a standard deviation of 10.4. Since the students in the residential treatment program were older (15.5 years), it is logical that they might have had a longer time to experience trauma and thus to self-report higher mean symptom scores.

The standard deviation is useful when examining studies *with similar means*. For instance, assume you have administered the CROPS to two different samples of teenagers being treated for issues associated with childhood trauma. Let's say that the six teens in Group A had a mean score of 15.3 and that teens in Group B had a mean score of 15.0. The two groups seem very similar at this point. However, when we look a little further, the teens in Group A had a standard deviation of 1.03 and the teens in Group B had a standard deviation of 9.74. How could that be? It can happen when the scores or values in each study have a different dispersion. For instance, they could be packed somewhat closely together in Group A with scores (14, 15, 15, 15, 16, 17) perhaps suggesting that maybe they were siblings who experienced the same type of child maltreatment. Note that researchers may describe low standard deviations in a sample as a **homogeneous sample**—meaning similar. In contrast, teens in Group B with scores of (4, 7, 10, 17, 23, 29) had scores that varied much more (referred to as being a **heterogeneous sample**). The scores that are closer together in Group A yield a much lower standard deviation of 1.03 because they don't differ that much on average from the mean, while the standard deviation in Group B (9.74) reflects a dispersion pattern of scores being more spread out and not being as close to the mean as the scores in Group A.

The symbol for standard deviation may appear as **SD**.

Example 13.3 illustrates how researchers may provide several descriptive statistics in a single table. Triantafyllou, Wang, and North (2019) have investigated the duration of intimate partner violence and factors that might prevent women from leaving abusive relationships. A few variables have been selected from their study of women applying to a Texas shelter for female domestic violence victims.

Over their lifetimes, women in the Triantafyllou et al. (2019) study had lived in abusive relationships an average of 11 years and in nonabusive relationships less than 4 years. The higher mean associated with years in abusive relationships (8.7) compared to the mean of years in nonabusive relationships (3.6) indicates that these women were in abusive relationships more than twice as long as they were in nonabusive relationships. Also, the standard deviation for years in abusive relationships shows a more heterogeneous data pattern than the years in nonabusive relationships. This is also indicated by the greater range in the

EXAMPLE 13.3 How You Might See Mean, Median, Standard Deviation, and Range in a Study

Variable	M	(SD)	Median	Range
Lifetime # abusive relationships	1.4	0.6	1	1–4
Total lifetime years of abusive relationships	11.1	8.6	9	1–42
Averaged years of nonabusive relationships	3.6	3.2	2	1–17
Averaged years of abusive relationships	8.7	8.1	7	1–42

data for the abusive relationships. Thus women in nonabusive relationships with a standard deviation of 3.2 indicates (if we could see the actual data) that most were pretty similar in the short lengths of time they remained in nonabusive relationships. In this sample, the lengths of time in abusive relationships were not as compacted or clustered together; there was more variability with some women staying longer and some women staying shorter times.

Bivariate and Multivariate Analysis

Bivariate analysis involves a focus on two variables at a time. This is also easy to remember because just as univariate will remind you of the one-wheeled unicycle, bivariate can bring to mind the *two* wheels of a bicycle.

In this section, we will be discussing several statistical terms and concepts when researchers report procedures that involved *two* variables at a time. We'll continue learning what information interval/ratio variables can provide us until we arrive at the statistical procedure known as chi-square, which uses a different type of data that we will learn about a bit later in the chapter. The section will discuss the following:

- Coefficient of correlation (r)
- Coefficient of determination (r^2)
- Statistical significance ($p < .05$)
- *T*-test (t)
- ANOVA
- Reliability (internal consistency)
- Effect size
- Multiple regression (R^2)
- Levels of measurement (again)
- Chi-square (X^2)
- Odds ratio (logistic regression)

Coefficient of Correlation

Students and researchers who have obtained quantitatively measured variables of interest that they want to examine may wish to know the relationship (or strength of relationship, if any) between two of them. While computing a correlation of coefficient is laborious using a calculator, it is extremely easy and fast with most statistical software. The correlation coefficient is one of the easiest bivariate statistics to understand and is frequently found in research publications.

Let's start by briefly discussing a study that actually used this type of statistic.

Some researchers have proposed an explanation of child physical abuse and neglect by suggesting parents and caretakers can have flawed social information processing (SIP) that may not allow good perception or interpretation of child behavior. For these parents, negative attributions (e.g., blame) may be associated with a child's behavior, even when the behavior was unintentional or accidental—such as spilling a cup of milk. Similarly, parents can possess distorted, unrealistic expectations of children and have poor problem-solving abilities.

Azar, McGuier, Miller, and Hernandez-Mekonnen (2017) gathered data from low-socioeconomic mothers with histories of perpetrating child neglect. Their study's variables came from standardized instruments that measured the mothers' IQ (Wechsler Adult Intelligence Scale-IV), negative intent attributions to their children (Child Vignettes), problem-solving abilities in parenting situations (Parent Problem-Solving Inventory), cognitive flexibility (Alternate Uses Test), and preservative errors or continuing to use a rule for decision making that is no longer correct (the Wisconsin Card Sorting Test)—to name a few of the measures used in the study. Example 13.4 is a portion of what they discovered and reported in their article:

EXAMPLE 13.4 How You Might See Correlations in a Study Correlations Between Maternal IQ and SIP Deficit

	Negative Intent Attributions to Children	Parental Problem Solving	Cognitive Flexibility	Perseverative Errors
Maternal IQ	−.32**	−.35**	.42**	−.54**
Neg. Intent Attributions		.15	−.23	.17
Paternal Problem Solving			−.30	.265
Cognitive Flexibility				−.30

*p < .05 **p < .01

Interpreting the correlations. Correlation coefficients (*r*) like those presented in the table form what's known as a **correlation matrix** (a table of correlations) and can range from .00 to 1 (a perfect linear relationship). The higher the value, the stronger the relationship between two variables. Correlation coefficients can be positive or negative. A positive correlation like that between Maternal IQ and Cognitive Flexibility (*r* = .42) means that, within the group of mothers in the study, those with higher IQ scores also had higher cognitive flexibility scores. One can also interpret the correlation as indicating that those with lower IQs had less cognitive flexibility capability. This is what a positive relationship means between two variables—that they both either increase (or decrease) in the same direction. In a matrix, only half the data are presented because the correlation between Parental Problem Solving and Cognitive Flexibility, for instance, is the same as between Cognitive Flexibility and Parental Problem Solving, so there is no need to repeat it. Any variable correlated with itself will always be 1.

As we look at the correlations, however, we notice that six of the 10 have a negative sign in front of them. This means that the two variables tend to go in different directions. The correlation of −.35 between Maternal IQ and Parental Problem Solving indicates that as the mothers' IQs went up, they were less likely to have difficulties with problem solving as parents. The reverse is also true, that mothers with lower IQs tended to have more difficulties with problem solving as parents.

Keep in mind that the correlations obtained from a study are simply a reflection of the instruments used to collect data, the procedures (when, where, and how the data were collected), and the particular individuals in the study's sample. The correlations do not represent all mothers or even all highly disadvantaged mothers of young children with histories of perpetrating child neglect. To say so would be generalizing beyond what the data can support or **overgeneralizing**. The correlations are simply information obtained from one study.

Within this study of 145 individuals, there were some mothers who did not fit the pattern suggested by the correlation. How do we know this? Another statistic can inform us more precisely as to the extent to which the two variables are related —**the coefficient of determination (r^2)**. Without getting into the mathematics, if one squares the correlation coefficient (i.e., .42 times .42), the product of that multiplication (.1764) means that the proportion of variation in one variable explained by the other is approximately 18%. Similarly, the correlation of .54 (we can ignore the minus sign) explains only 29% (.54 times .54 = .2916) of the variation shared by Maternal IQ and Perseverative Errors. In other words, with a correlation of .54, one still is not explaining 71% of the variability between the two variables.

Even though a fairly low correlation can begin to suggest a pattern in the data, which might be worthy of further exploration in a future or more refined study, you can see how even a much higher correlation (for example. .70) still explains only 49% of the variation. To make sense of the strength of correlation coefficients, researchers often refer to their **magnitude**. Table 13.1 is helpful in understanding how researchers interpret or view the strength of a correlation coefficient.

TABLE 13.1 Quick Guide for Interpreting the Strength of Correlation Coefficients

Correlation Coefficient	Interpretation of Strength
Under .20	Very weak correlation
.20 to .40	Small correlation
.40 to .70	Moderate correlation
.70 to .90	Strong correlation
.90 +	Very strong correlation

You may sometimes see the letter **r** used to represent the term correlation. And there is one other thing. We are also usually provided additional information that allows us to understand how likely a role chance played in producing the value or magnitude of the correlation coefficient. This concept is explained next.

Statistical Significance

In everyday conversation, when we talk about something being significant, we mean it as "important to us." There are significant others; significant events, such as births, marriages, deaths; and, perhaps, even significant new responsibilities or significant increases in one's salary. However, in research articles and reports, the term "significant" has only one meaning—it indicates that a finding did not likely occur by chance.

A frequently used rule of thumb in the social sciences is based on setting a significance level at .05. At this level, the researcher would report significant findings only if the statistical software indicated probability (p) that the findings would have occurred by chance less than five times out of 100. This is written $p < .05$ and is stated as "probability is less than .05." In other words, 95 times out of 100, we would be correct in assuming that the findings were not a fluke but represent a real pattern in the data. A fluke is a random event that cannot be planned for or expected—like finding a $100 bill on the street.

A finding of significance or a significant difference is considered a real difference. For example, you could compare the average weight of two different groups of athletes with a null (no difference) hypothesis and set the significance level at .05. And if you compared two groups of varsity basketball players from two different high schools, you might truly find not much difference in their average weights—maybe you would obtain a $p = .71$, indicating that the same results would very likely be obtained many, many times out of 100 if you wanted to make that many comparisons.

On the other hand, what if you compared ballerinas as a group (let's say at an average weight of 110 pounds) and compared their weight to the average of professional football players? With these two groups, we would expect a significant difference or the probability of their having the same average weight occurring very, very rarely. That occurrence might be something like $p < .001$ (one in 1,000 times) or $p < .0001$ (one in 10,000 times) or maybe even more remote. When a finding is not significant, its lack of significance is usually written $p > .05$ (probability greater than .05).

Even correlations can be understood in terms of whether they are significant or not, and it is important for this reason: one has much less confidence that the correlation is not an accident or a fluke when it is significant. Obtaining a correlation of .25 that is not significant ($p > .05$) means that we shouldn't make too much of the correlation—even if it supports our hypothesis, because we might not be able to achieve it again if we were to repeat the study with a similar sample. Generally, correlations obtained from larger, more representative samples will be significant. Note that in the correlations selected from the Azar et al. (2017) study, all of the correlations were significant at $p < .01$ from a sample of 145 mothers. This means that the relationship between the portrayed sets of two variables would have occurred *by chance* only once in 100 times.

T-Test

Imagine that the supervisor in your practicum asks you to find a consumer feedback instrument that could be used to evaluate how satisfied clients are with the agency's programs. You find a tool you like that asks easy questions, such as, "Would you recommend our agency to a friend?" And, "Would you return here if you needed help again with the same problem?" Let's further assume that clients could respond with a scale that ranged from 0 (Not at All Satisfied) to 100 (Highly Satisfied), and they could choose any number between 0 to 100 to indicate their level of satisfaction or dissatisfaction. Let's further assume that you want to compare the overall client satisfaction scores of men and women.

When you have measured the dependent variable at the interval or ratio level (the client satisfaction scores) and have two groups (and only two groups—never more), then the appropriate statistic is the *t*-test.

Let's consider a sample of 10 women who completed the client satisfaction form and gave the agency an average rating of 90 while a sample of 10 men gave the agency an average rating of 76.8. These look like significant differences, but are they? And how would you tell?

With an interval- or ratio-level dependent variable and two groups, you would use the *t*-test and further choose the one designed for **independent samples**. The best way to think about independent samples is this: the data drawn from the men was in every way totally independent of the data obtained from the women—there was no connection between the men and women that would have influenced the other's ratings.

In a research publication, the results of the *t*-test could be shown in a format something like Example 13.5:

EXAMPLE 13.5 How You Might See *T*-Test Results in a Study

Gender	*n*	Agency Satisfaction Ratings Mean	Std. Dev.	*t*	Sig.
Women	10	90	6.342	4.05	.001
Men	10	76.8	8.135		

In this example, you can see that not only were the means different, but the standard deviations were too. That is to say that the women evaluated the agency in a different way (with more similar ratings) than men. This can be seen when we look at the actual ratings each group awarded. Women's ratings were more homogeneous: 89, 94, 96, 95, 92, 88, 85, 91, 95, 75. Men's ratings varied more and were more heterogeneous at: 75, 60, 79, 69, 81, 82, 74, 90, 77, 81. What informs the reader that these scores were, in fact, statistically significant or different is the .001 under the abbreviated heading for significance (Sig.).

The *t*-value of 4.05 won't mean anything to you or most other people (except interested researchers) but is something of a carryover from the days when *t*-tests were calculated manually and one used a table in the back of a statistics book to look up the *t*-value along with the degrees of freedom (the value in the following parentheses of 18 obtained from the SPPS printout of results) to see if one's calculation of a *t*-test produced a significant finding. Researchers often present a summary statement of the *t*-test results in this format: $t(18) = 4.047, p < .01$. The degrees of freedom in this example is the number of cases minus two (18).

Another type of *t*-test is designed for situations where there is one sample that is examined, compared, or measured at two different times. For instance, staying with the earlier example, suppose your supervisor asks you to see if the men's level of satisfaction improves three months after their initial ratings. Since we are looking at one group of participants (men) at two different times, the independent group type of *t*-test is not appropriate, because the same group is providing both sets of data (which we'll call Initial Rating and 90 Day Ratings). The *t*-test to be used in this situation is known as **paired samples** because fictitious Joe Smith's initial ratings are matched with his ratings three months later; Tom Wilson's initial ratings are paired with his own ratings three months later, and so on. In Example 13.6, five more men were identified and added to the study group for a total of 15.

EXAMPLE 13.6 How You Might See Paired Samples *T*-Test Results in a Study

	Mean	*n*	Male Clients' Satisfaction Ratings, Initial and 90 Days Std. Dev.	*t*	Significance
Initial Rating	76.9	15	7.64	–1.169	.26
90 Day Rating	77.13	15	7.52		

Even though the men's 90-day ratings were slightly higher, computing the paired samples *t*-test reveals that they were not high enough to state that they were significantly higher at the second assessment. Sometimes one finds slight differences that aren't big enough to say that it is a real difference.

In this example, the significance level larger than .05 means that these results could have occurred by chance or, more practically speaking, simply that the ratings weren't that different. Seeing the standard deviations at very similar levels also suggests that the men tended to be consistent in their patterns of rating the agency.

In research reports of data using *t*-tests, you may find the results from the paired samples *t*-test presented this way: $t = -1.169$ (14), $p = .26$. Since there is only one sample, the degrees of freedom (14) is one less than the number of cases.

ANOVA

ANOVA stands for analysis of variance and is sometimes referred to as one-way analysis of variance. As a consumer of research reports, what you need to know is that it, like the *t*-test, needs an interval-/ratio-level dependent variable, but it is different in that it can accommodate three, four, five, or more groups. This makes it very handy, for instance, when a researcher wants to analyze a dependent variable by age groups (e.g., 20–39, 40–59, 60–79, 80+) with four groups instead of two.

In Example 13.7, Griffiths, Royse, and Walker (2018) have looked at the number of unhealthy habits or behaviors (such as eating too much fast food or not exercising) that child protective service workers developed as a result of work-related stress, secondary traumatization, and so forth. The survey instrument allowed the authors to group respondents into three groups: those who listed presumed health consequences of their stress but who didn't provide any information about their own unhealthy habits, those who listed one or two unhealthy habits, and those listing three or more unhealthy habits.

EXAMPLE 13.7 How You Might See One-Way ANOVA Results in a Study

Variable	No Mentions (n = 57)	1–2 Mentions (n = 283)	3 + Mentions (n = 51)	Total (n = 391)	F	p
Age (yrs)	40.3	37.1	37.96	37.7	2.49	0.08
Years at Agency	5.7	8.4	9.1	8.1	3.3	0.04
Intent to Leave Scale	1.9	2.7	2.8	2.6	11.9	0.00
Health Status Rating	1.9	2.5	2.98	2.5	29.0	0.00

Reading this excerpt from their table, the *F-ratio* at the far right (2.49) is produced when calculating an ANOVA. Again, it won't mean anything to you; however, smaller *F* values are not as likely to be significant as larger values. Like the *t*-value, it is a holdover from the days when researchers had to look up the *F*-value in a table found in a statistics book. Again, reading across the first row of data, we see that there was no significant difference ($p > .05$) in Age reported in the probability column. To explain this, when participants in the study were formed into three groups (those who made no mention of unhealthy habits, those making one or two mentions, or those making three or more mentions), they did not significantly vary in terms of the average age of those in each group. That is, while it is logical to suspect that older respondents might have developed more unhealthy behaviors than younger employees, the average ages in each group (40.3, 37.1, and almost 38) were not different enough to be significant—although they were trending in that direction (.08 is not that far from .05).

By calculating ANOVA on the other three dependent variables, we can see that there were significant differences, and it was reported this way in the article:

However, a significant pattern of differences emerged when exploring unhealthy habits and tenure, intention to leave, and self-reported health. Specifically, as the number of unhealthy habits increased, child welfare workers were more likely to leave the agency and had a worse perception of their self-reported health. Not surprisingly, longer tenure at the agency was associated with higher quantities of unhealthy habits. (Griffiths et al., 2018, p. 51)

You may see the summary results of a one-way ANOVA written in this APA format: $F (2, 22) = 9.65$, $p < .001$. Note that with this statistical procedure, a data readout produces the two values within the parentheses (2, 22), which represent the degrees of freedom for the comparisons made between and within groups. It is not essential that you understand the degrees of freedom to recognize whether the ANOVA procedure found overall significance or not. The one-way ANOVA simply indicates that there were significant differences among groups. It does not tell you, for example, with three groups being compared, if the major differences were between group 1 and group 2, between groups 1 and 3, or between groups 2 and 3. Whenever overall findings of the one-way ANOVA are significant, the research report may describe computing a **post hoc test** to locate the comparison that produced the major effect. The post hoc test is easy to request with most statistical software and seeing the group means will help with interpreting the data. The Scheffe test or Tukey procedure are commonly used.

Reliability

When trying to evaluate how well a scale or measurement instrument performs in terms of being dependable or consistent, **reliability** or internal consistency data is sought. These values (often known as **Cronbach's alpha**) look like correlation coefficients except that they often range much higher. Typically, instruments with a reliability of less than .70 are not considered reliable enough to use for basic research. Instruments with an internal consistency of at least .80 are generally needed for basic research, and .90 is needed when important decisions are going to be made with the data (Nunnally, 1994).

In other words, scales with reliabilities of .40, .55, and so forth are weak and shouldn't be used because they can't be depended on to provide accurate readings with similar populations. If you were to use a scale with low reliability, you would get data with it, but you wouldn't know if it was flawed information. In other words, if you were to repeat the data collection with the same sample, you might get different results because the instrument didn't perform well. This could come about because items composing the scale were imprecise or ambiguous, allowing misunderstandings and differences in interpretation. Read about or review this problem in Chapter 7.

In Example 13.8, all of the scales contained at least two items. That's because reliability cannot be computed for one item. However, it is possible to obtain acceptable levels of reliability with just two items. As a general rule of thumb, the strongest levels of internal consistency come from having multiple items, which give the researchers an opportunity to measure an overall concept by sampling different dimensions of the concept. Thus the Child Welfare Employee Feedback Scale (CWEFS) at 25 items is a composite of all seven subscales. The CWEFS indicates the respondent's summary level of satisfaction or dissatisfaction with each of the shown scales that have been found to be associated with child protection worker turnover. Higher scores indicate greater satisfaction. When evaluating an instrument, it is important to learn as much as you can about it—not just its reliability. You also want to know about efforts to establish its validity (read or review Chapter 6 for more detail) as well as the items or scales used to compose the instrument.

EXAMPLE 13.8 How You Might See Cronbach's Alphas in a Study

Item Means and Cronbach's Alphas for Subscales and Global Scale

Subscale	Item Mean	# Items	Possible Score	Alpha
Salary	1.87	2	2–10	.705
Workload	2.24	8	8–40	.885
Recognition	2.57	3	3–15	.790
Professional Development	2.85	4	4–20	.721
Accomplishment	3.53	2	2–10	.787
Peer Support	3.97	2	2–10	.806
Supervision	4.19	4	4–20	.919
CWEFS	2.90	25	25–125	.910

Source: Griffiths, Royse, Culver, Piescher, and Zang (2017)

In Example 13.8, respondents could rate items from the instrument on a Likert scale (Strongly Disagree = 1, Disagree = 2, Neutral = 3, Agree = 4, Strongly Agree = 5). The low mean rating for Salary indicates that, overall, the respondents were somewhere between strongly disagreeing and disagreeing that they were satisfied with their salaries. On the other hand, they had the highest level of satisfaction with their supervision. All the subscales had acceptable levels of internal consistency, and one can see that the subscales composed with the most items generally had the highest reliability. The possible scores (or range of score values) are computed by multiplying the number of subscale items times the lowest possible rating (1) and the highest possible rating (5).

Effect Size

Once you get deep into a literature review on a particular topic, you may come across a research publication that is actually a study of studies. These may be known as **meta-analyses** or **systematic reviews**. Either the meta-analysis or the systematic review will be a great finding for you in your evidence-based practice, as each type of these studies searches the previous literature on a narrow topic (such as the effectiveness of a particular intervention) and summarizes the findings.

Let's focus on the meta-analysis first. This research approach generally seeks studies containing quantitative data that may vary in terms of samples of different sizes, in different settings, or with different client populations. Having a large pool of studies provides a better estimate of treatment effectiveness available from the program or intervention being investigated.

In a meta-analysis, once all of the pertinent studies have been gathered, then a statistical process is used to create an effect size to summarize whether, for instance, an intervention was able to show a large, medium, or small effect. The **effect size** can be computed several different ways. One popular approach involves subtracting the control group's mean from the intervention group's mean and dividing by their pooled (average) standard deviations. Interactive sites on the Internet exist if you want to calculate this for studies you collect. The author(s) of a meta-analysis will use a statistical procedure to calculate effect size and then report these for each included study. Commonly used guidelines suggest that effect sizes under .2 are small, those at .5 or higher are medium or moderate, and those at .8 or higher are large effects.

For an example of a meta-analysis on the effectiveness of parent-child interaction therapy (PCIT), see Kennedy, Kim, Tripodi, Brown, and Gowdy (2016). In their article, the authors located two studies that looked at whether PCIT reduced physical abuse recurrence. Combining the results of both studies produced a medium effect size estimate of .52, suggesting that parents in the PCIT groups scored .52 standard deviation units above those in the groups receiving the usual treatment. They also located four studies that employed PCIT and used the Parenting Stress Inventory as the dependent variable. These studies produced an effect size of .35—small effect. There was also a similar finding using the Child Abuse Potential Inventory as a dependent variable. The researchers estimated the effect size as .31—a small effect but unlike the other two, it was not significant (p = .053). When reading meta-analyses, pay attention to whether the results are significant—this is true for every quantitative statistic too! Read the discussion and limitations section from Kennedy et al. (2016) to get a better understanding of factors that may be in play when trying to determine the effectiveness of PCIT.

Systematic reviews may contain meta-analyses, or they may not. A systematic review has a "clearly formulated question" that follows a very rigorous, detailed methodology (www.Prisma-statement.org). On the PRISMA website, see the flowchart where each step is carefully described. The systematic review generally attempts to collect every piece of literature pertinent to the question and delineates the search strategy and terms used in the search as well as the criteria employed for including or excluding studies. Risk of bias will also be examined for the studies being discussed. It may examine small and qualitative studies if the literature on the topic is very small, or it may not. The systematic review most generally will discuss the quality of the study in terms of the research design, sample size, measurements made or used, etc. Systematic reviews may contain a meta-analysis and focus only on studies with numerical data, but not every systematic review will involve a meta-analysis—so you may not see any effect sizes discussed.

For a recent example of a systematic review entitled "Self-Care Practice in Social Work Education: A Systematic Review," see Griffiths, Royse, Murphy, and Starks (2019). The authors discovered that between 2006 and 2016, only four peer-reviewed articles using quantitative instruments had been published that examined the effectiveness of teaching a self-care intervention to social work students. These four studies all involved mindfulness training and are identified for the reader.

Multiple Regression

The concept of multiple regression can be explained simply: it is when several independent variables are used to see which one, or set of these, does the best job of predicting the dependent variable. This is not a statistical procedure that can be performed manually; one must use a software program like SPSS to compute the statistic. Note that while you could perform a multiple regression with one independent variable to see how well it predicts a dependent variable, normally, researchers test three to eight or more variables. Sample size becomes an issue if there is interest in a very large number of predictors.

When multiple regression results are presented in a research publication, the main thing you want to look for is R^2. This is a single summary measure of how much variation the statistically significant predictors explain in the dependent (criterion) variable. A reported R^2 of .26 (after multiplying times 100) explains 26% of the variability of the significant predictors with the dependent variable. R^2 is a way of saying how well the regression model with its set of predictors worked overall. A model with an R^2 of 44% is explaining more variation (predicting better) than a model with an R^2 of 13% or 26%.

R in a multiple or multivariate regression can be understood like a correlation coefficient except that it represents all of the independent variables and their combined relationships with the outcome or dependent variable.

The *F* is the *F*-value for the model that has a corresponding significance level. You know by now that a finding of $p > .05$ means that the set of independent variables being employed did not achieve significance. In that case, there is not much more to interpret. If a table of the predictor variables is presented, then only those that have a significant *t*-value have contributed to the R^2.

The reported *B* values in Example 13.9 are known as the *b* coefficients or partial slope. They reflect the relationship to the dependent or criterion variable after the effects of the other variables are removed. If these values are large, for example, 1.8 for a particular independent variable, that would indicate an increase of 1.8 points in the dependent variable for every one unit of increase in the independent variable while holding constant the effect of the other predictor variables. Technically speaking, that statistic isn't as useful as the β or standardized beta weight represented by the Greek letter for b (*beta*).

Standardized beta weights (also known as beta weights or beta coefficients) have, as their name suggests, had their values adjusted statistically so that one predictor variable does not carry more weight than another because of differences in the way the variables were measured. For instance, an independent variable representing respondents' household income might have scores ranging from $10,000 to $95,000, while the age variable might range only from 35 to 50 and the number of children from one to five. These standardized weights can indicate that for every increase in standard deviation in the independent variable, the dependent variable increases by the amount indicated in the table (holding constant the other variables).

The *t*-values represent the values obtained from *t*-tests that together with the associated asterisks (or lack of them) indicate whether the predictor variable made a significant contribution to the multiple regression model. Let's look at Example 13.9 to see these statistics in a publication by Elizabeth Wahler in her 2015 study "Social Disadvantage and Economic Hardship as Predictors of Follow-Up Addiction Severity after Substance Abuse Treatment: Does Referral to Treatment by the Criminal Justice System Matter?"

A little background is needed before we look at a multiple regression table from her study. From a previous study of almost 1,100 participants involved in entering substance abuse treatment, 560 entered voluntarily and 539 were referred by some component of the criminal justice system. Those who consented were also interviewed 12 months later. In Example 13.9, we see a portion of a table Dr. Wahler produced when she examined the predictors of alcohol addiction severity (measured by the Addiction Severity Index) for those who entered treatment voluntarily. She performed several multiple regression procedures called models.

In this excerpt, the first three variables are control variables, and a multiple regression was computed with them first. **Control variables** are those that the researcher wants to hold constant. For instance, since the alcohol and drug use of respondents might vary by their age, age can be established as a control variable to hold its effect constant. That makes it easier to see the contribution of the other variables. As a set, the control variables explained 18% of the variation between the variables and the dependent variable in the first model (which is not presented—you may want to see the full set of tables in Wahler, 2015). That model was significant; however, the only significant predictor was the variable representing the initial or baseline alcohol addiction severity score.

Wahler then added gender, education level, employment status, race, and income to represent social disadvantage in the second regression model but only education and race were significant predictors. These variables increased the R^2 by .026 points. In a third model, Wahler added in an economic hardship

EXAMPLE 13.9 How You Might See Multiple Regression Results Reported Ordinary Least Squares Regression for Alcohol Addiction Severity (Model 4)

Variables	B	β	t
Age	.000	−.010	−.26
Initial Alcohol ASI	.236	.388	9.80***
Initial Drug ASI	−.034	−.033	−.85
Gender	−.020	−.058	−1.45
Educational Level	.008	.091	2.35*
Employment Status	.013	.048	1.17
Race	.053	.135	3.50***
Income	−.000	−.012	−.31
Economic Hardship	−.005	−.070	−1.67
Perceived Stress	.003	.166	3.93***
F			16.44***
R^2			.23

*$p \leq .05$ **$p \leq .01$ ***$p < .001$

variable, which turned out not to be significant. In the final fourth model (the portion of the table in Example 13.9), perceived stress was entered and was significant. Thus the final model had four significant predictors and explained 23% of the variation between the variables and the dependent variable of alcohol addiction severity. The summary of the final regression model in APA format was $R^2 = .23$, $F = 16.44$, $p \leq .001$.

Levels of Measurement (Again)

With the exception of the mode, all of the statistics and concepts we have discussed thus far have relied upon interval/ratio (numerical) data. Now we need to broaden our horizons a bit and recognize the other types of variables that we might use and encounter in research.

Nominal data are those items that are best thought of as named or categorical variables. Most of the independent and sociodemographic variables that a client might have to complete on an agency's intake or application form are of this variety—for instance, gender, race/ethnicity, marital status, employment, and whether one is a veteran, has insurance, has visited the agency previously, and so on.

Such items as these don't vary along continuous intervals but differ by a classification or group status. To take employment as an example, one could be employed or not employed. Or a little more information would be available if we knew if those employed were employed full-time or part-time and if those unemployed were retired, disabled, or looking for work or not looking. Such variations of nominal variables are known as their **attributes**.

It makes no sense to try and average categorical or named data in the same way as we might do when the ages of our clients are known. How do you average male and female? Or how do you average employed and unemployed in a sample of college students to provide a profile? The short answer is—you don't. Instead, you might count the five employed students and the 10 unemployed students and let the modal category represent the typical student.

Sometimes researchers take interval-level data and then create nominal or interval groups. For instance, a database containing information about clients of a mental health system may contain data on the number of prior hospitalizations, but a researcher may want to categorize the patients in terms of no prior hospitalizations and those with prior hospitalizations—creating two nominal groups.

The mode works well for nominal data and for **ordinal data**, which are like the nominal items only there is a definite order to them. For example, let's say you and a colleague are reviewing the amount of clinical progress your clients have made in a six-week treatment program. You might decide to rate the clients in terms of three categories: Good Progress, Medium Progress, and Poor Progress. Although there is an order to these ranks, you can think of ordinal data as being nominal when you want to determine if there is a significant association between clients' clinical progress and whether they would return to the agency. And for that statistical procedure, we need to learn about chi-square.

Chi-Square

When you have variables that are nominal or ordinal and you want to determine if there is an association or statistical difference among the groups, the appropriate bivariate statistic is chi-square. A wonderful feature of the chi-square procedure (also known as crosstabs) is that if the sample size is large enough, the number of groups or categories don't really matter. The only thing you need to watch is that the number of cells with an expected count of participants less than five cannot exceed 20% of the cells. (And in SPSS, the software will give you a statement informing you of that issue so that you can combine or reduce the number of cells or categories if needed.) The values produced by the chi-square procedure is often represented by the symbol X^2.

EXAMPLE 13.10 How You Might See a Chi-Square Table in a Study

Progress Made	Would Return to Agency %	Would Not Return to Agency %	Totals
Good	15 (79%)	4 (21%)	19
Medium	10 (62.5%)	6 (37.5%)	16
Poor	5 (33%)	10 (67%)	15
Totals	30	20	50

Chi-Square = 7.3, p=.026

Once again, the value of the chi-square (7.3) in Example 13.10 won't mean a great deal to you, but what is interesting about the table is that you can actually visually see a pattern in the data. The majority of those clients making a good amount of progress and a medium amount of progress would return to the agency for services. However, of those who made the least progress, the largest proportion (two thirds) *would not* return to the agency for services. These distinctive attitudes about returning or not are why the chi-square is significant. If approximately equal proportions of clients would return for service regardless of their progress, then the chi-square would not have been significant. The APA format for writing the summary results of the chi-square for the data presented in Example 13.10 is $X^2 = (2, N = 50) = 7.33, p < .05$ (where the 2 inside the parentheses represents the degrees of freedom [as one less than the number of groups] and the 7.33 is the actual chi-square value).

Odds Ratio (Logistic Regression)

Discussion of logistic regression is placed here, after chi-square, because it also involves nominal-level dependent variables that are in a binary (0 or 1), either/or format, such as being diagnosed or not diagnosed, passing or failing, or having previous arrests or no arrests. However, logistic regression also allows independent variables to be at either the interval or nominal level as it weighs which ones best predict the outcome (dependent) variable.

Each independent variable is weighed in an equation that results in a table producing a probability level for each variable and an odds ratio. The odds ratio is an expression of the contribution the independent variable makes relative to the outcome variable.

Garcia, Gupta, Greeson, Thompson, and DeNard (2017) have used a large data set (the National Survey of Child and Adolescent Well-Being) to examine adverse childhood experiences among children involved with the child welfare system. The researchers used logistic regression to look at the predictors of children diagnosed or not for internalizing behavior problems (mood disturbance, including anxiety, depression, and social withdrawal), externalizing behavior problems (delinquent and aggressive behavior), or total behavior problems. Excerpts from some of the findings presented in its tables are provided in Example 13.11.

EXAMPLE 13.11 How You Might See Logistic Regression Results in a Study Factors Associated With Internalizing Behaviors

Variable	OR	95% CI	p
Child Victim of Physical Abuse	.37	[0.23–0.60]	< .01
Child Victim of Sexual Abuse	1.89	[1.03–3.47]	0.04
Child Placed in Foster Care	1.74	[0.88–3.43]	0.11

Factors Associated With Externalizing Behaviors (Continued)

Variable	OR	95% CI	p
Child Victim of Sexual Abuse	2.17	[0.823–5.78]	0.12
Gender Female	.54	[0.34–0.86]	0.01

Here's how to interpret these logistic regression statistics: In the odds ratio, OR, column, children who were physically abused were less likely to be diagnosed with internalizing behaviors than the reference category of children who never developed or had improved behavior between the first survey and the second one 12 months later. Reference categories are always coded 1, so .37 is less than 1; thus physically abused children were less likely than the reference group to be diagnosed with internalizing behaviors.

The CI column refers to the confidence interval around the .37, and you can think about this as being like a low-high range if you need to be 95% confident about the odds ratio.

The table also reveals that internalizing behaviors are more likely to be diagnosed when the child has been sexually abused. In fact, the odds ratio says that these children are 1.89 times more likely to be diagnosed with internalizing behaviors than the reference group. Both abuse variables were statistically significant for internalizing behaviors but being placed in foster care was not.

In terms of the externalizing behaviors, we can see that female children are significantly less likely to receive this diagnosis than those in the reference group (male children who are coded 1). To clarify, the female children's OR at .54 is much lower than the reference group (where male children are coded 1). We can also see that child victims of sexual abuse produce a relatively high odds ratio (more than two times the reference group), but it is not statistically significant for externalizing behaviors.

Key Terms

Univariate statistics	P
N, n	*t*-test (independent and dependent samples)
Percentage	ANOVA
Mean	Post hoc test
Outliers	Reliability (internal consistency)
Continuous variables	Cronbach's alpha
Median	Meta-analysis
Range	Systematic review
Standard deviation	Effect size
Homogeneous	Multiple regression
Heterogeneous	Control variables
Bivariate	Nominal data
Correlation coefficient	Attributes
Overgeneralizing	Ordinal data
Coefficient of determination	Chi-square
Magnitude (of a correlation coefficient)	Logistic regression
Statistical significance	Odds ratio

SELF-REVIEW
(*Answers are at the end of the book*)

1. Which measure of central tendency is affected by extreme scores?
   a. median
   b. mode
   c. mean
   d. stetactic harmony

2. Labeling clients' progress after intervention as "improved" or "not improved" would be using what level of measurement?

3. Labeling clients' progress after intervention as "major improvement," "slight improvement," or "no improvement" would be using what level of measurement?

4. What is an attribute?

5. A chi-square cross-tabulation is associated with which level of analysis?

    a. multivariate
    b. bivariate
    c. univariate
    d. trivariate

6. Juanita runs an outpatient clinic for teens with problems at home. She claims that 60% of the clients are "improved" after six visits and that only 40% are "not improved." What statistical procedure would she use to see if males made more improvement than females?

    a. chi-square
    b. *t*-test
    c. one-way analysis of variance
    d. frequency distribution

7. In a self-esteem group Sue was leading, the participants' mean score at pretest was 35.6 and 41.1 at posttest. She wants to know if this is a statistically significant improvement. With this interval data, Sue would use what statistical procedure?

    a. chi-square
    b. *t*-test for paired samples
    c. one-way analysis of variance
    d. *t*-test for independent samples

8. Using the same posttest data as in #7, Sue wants to examine her clients' improvement by the variable of attendance. She divides her clients into three groups: those with "good" attendance, those with "average" attendance, and those with "poor" attendance. With these three groups instead of two, what statistical procedure should Sue employ?

    a. chi-square
    b. *t*-test
    c. one-way analysis of variance
    d. standard deviation

9. T or F. Using the appropriate statistical test, Carolyn obtained a probability of .90. This indicates that her findings are statistically significant.

10. What does $p > .05$ mean?

    a. a statistically significant difference
    b. differences between or among means were not statistically significant
    c. that the odds of obtaining approximately the same means could happen by chance more than five times in 100
    d. both b and c are correct
    e. none of the above are correct

11. How much variation between two variables does a correlation coefficient of .35 explain?

    a. about 30%
    b. about 20%
    c. about 12%
    d. less than 5%

12. Susan recently reviewed the records of clients who had been in her program at least 6 months and classified their progress as follows: good progress, moderate progress, and minimal progress. Has she created an interval variable?

13. Earlier in the chapter, it was explained that Bill collected data on ice cream preferences: chocolate, vanilla, and strawberry. Which measure of central tendency would be most appropriate to use?

QUESTIONS FOR CLASS DISCUSSION

1. What are the limitations associated with doing correlational research? What can't it tell you?
2. Why is it important for social work researchers to be able to conduct their own statistical analyses?
3. Is it possible to write a credible, professional evaluation of a program's effectiveness without using statistical analysis? Explain. Under what circumstances?
4. Which aspect of statistical analysis is most difficult to understand? Which is the easiest?

REFERENCES

Azar, S. T., McGuier, D. J., Miller, E.A., & Hernandez-Mekonnen, R. (2017). Child neglect and maternal cross-relational social cognitive and neurocognitive disturbances. *Journal of Family Psychology, 31,* 8–18.

Crosby, S. D., Somers, C. L., Day, A. G., Zammit, M., Shier, J. M., & Baroni, B. A. (2017). Examining school attachment, social support, and trauma symptomatology among court-involved female students. *Journal of Child and Family Studies, 26,* 2539–2546.

Garcia, A. R., Gupta, M., Greeson, J. K. P., Thompson, A. & DeNard, C. (2017). Adverse childhood experiences among youth reported to child welfare: Results from the national survey of child & adolescent wellbeing. *Child Abuse & Neglect, 70,* 292–302.

Greenwald, R. & Rubin, A. (1999). Assessment of posttraumatic symptoms in children: Development and preliminary validation of parent and child scales. *Research on Social Work Practice, 9,* 61–75.

Griffiths, A., Royse, D., Culver, K., Piescher, K. & Zang, Y. (2017). Who stays, who goes, who knows? A state-wide survey of child welfare workers. *Children and Youth Services Review, 77,* 110–117.

Griffiths, A., Royse, D., Murphy, A., & Starks, S. (2019). Self-care practice in social work education: A systemic review of interventions. *Journal of Social Work Education, 55,* 102–114.

Griffiths, A., Royse, D. & Walker, R. (2018). Stress among child protective service workers: Self-reported health consequences. *Children and Youth Services Review, 90,* 46–53.

Kennedy, S. C., Kim, J. S., Tripodi, S. J., Brown, S. M., & Gowdy, G. (2016). Does parent-child interaction therapy reduce future physical abuse? A meta-analysis. *Research on Social Work Practice, 26,* 147–156.

Nunnally, J. C. (1994). *Psychometric theory.* New York, NY: McGraw-Hill.

Triantafyllou, D., Wang, C., & North, C. S. (2019). Correlates of duration of intimate partner violence among women seeking services at a domestic violence support center. *Journal of Interpersonal Violence, 34,* 1127–1138.

Wahler, E. A. (2015). Social disadvantage and economic hardship as predictors of follow-up addiction severity after substance abuse treatment: Does referral to treatment by the criminal justice system matter? *Alcoholism Treatment Quarterly, 33,* 6–27.

Credit

ASSIGNMENT 13.1

Analyzing Data (Suitable for a Group Project)

Objective: *To obtain firsthand experience with entering data and performing statistical procedures on the computer.*

Before beginning this assignment, you will need to collect some raw data. If you are interning at a social service agency, perhaps you can look at the last 50 admissions to the agency in terms of age, gender, race, and so on. Or there may be some other project that needs your assistance. Of course, it will be important to get your supervisor's permission if you are using real client data, as it will be important to protect their personal information. Alternatively, your research methods instructor may direct you to conduct a small survey of classmates using either the scale you created in Assignment 5.1 or the instrument that you discussed in Assignment 5.3. If SPSS or other statistical software are not available to you, a comprehensive collection of interactive statistical computation pages is maintained by John Pezzullo at **https://statpages.info**.

1.   State a hypothesis.

2.   What is your dependent variable? Is it nominal, ordinal, or interval/ratio?

3.   What variable or variables will you use to analyze the dependent variable? (For each variable named, identify the level of measurement.)

4.   What statistical procedure(s) will you be performing?

5.   What are your findings? (Your instructor may also want you to submit a printout of your table or findings.)

ASSIGNMENT 13.2

Analyzing Data (Suitable for a Group Project)

Objective: *To obtain firsthand experience with entering data and performing statistical procedures on the computer.*

Enter the data from the next page into the statistical software that you intend to use. If SPSS, SAS, or other similar software are not available to you, a comprehensive collection of interactive statistical computation pages is maintained by John Pezzullo at **https://statpages.org**. Once you have entered the data, you can test hypotheses that there are differences, for example, in

- clients' ratings of services by gender, age, income, or marital status
- clients' ratings of case managers by gender, age, income, or marital status
- clients' incomes by gender, age, or marital status
- clients' ages by gender, marital status, or income
- clients' willingness to recommend the agency to friends by program type, gender, or marital status
- program participation by gender, age, marital status, or income

You might also want to see if there is a correlation between age and income. Your instructor may tell you which statistical procedure to use or possibly which hypothesis to test. Follow these instructions:

1. Write your hypothesis or hypotheses here.

2. What is your dependent variable? What is its level of measurement?

3. What statistical procedure did you use? Why?

4. Describe your findings.

Data for Assignment 13.2

Service	Gender	Status	Age	Reported Income	Rating of Services	Would Recommend Agency	Rating of Case Manager
Case Manage.	Male	Married	86	$12,000	Good	Yes	4
Case Manage.	Male	Married	83	$17,000	No Info.	No Info.	No Info.
Homemaker	Male	Widowed	77	$15,000	Good	Yes	4
Homemaker	Female	Divorced	65	$11,850	Excellent	Yes	5
Meals	Male	Separated	92	$10,000	Excellent	Yes	5
Transport.	Female	No Info.	78	$9,775	Good	Don't Know	3
Transport.	Female	Separated	68	$14,000	Fair	No	2
Case Manage.	Male	Widowed	69	$17,000	Excellent	Yes	5
Case Manage.	Female	Widowed	70	$13,680	Good	Yes	4
Case Manage.	Female	Widowed	75	$13,500	Fair	Yes	4
Case Manage.	Male	Divorced	85	$19,950	Poor	No	1
Transport.	Female	Separated	71	$18,100	Good	Yes	4
Meals	Male	Divorced	84	$13,000	Excellent	Yes	5
Meals	Male	Widowed	90	$17,750	Excellent	Yes	5
Meals	Female	Married	68	$14,000	Good	Yes	4
Case Manage.	Male	Married	83	$13,000	Good	Yes	4
Transport.	Male	Divorced	73	$18,000	Poor	No	2
Transport.	Female	Married	79	$14,333	Fair	Don't Know	3
Homemaker	Male	Separated	87	$17,250	Excellent	Yes	5
Homemaker	Female	Widowed	66	$14,400	Excellent	Yes	5
Transport.	Female	Widowed	74	$14,800	Good	No Info.	3
Transport.	Female	Separated	83	$12,565	Good	Yes	4
Meals	Female	Married	75	$19,000	Good	Yes	4
Meals	Female	Separated	66	$16,000	Good	No Info.	3
Transport.	Male	Separated	67	$18,000	Fair	Yes	3
Transport.	Female	Widowed	87	$12,000	Good	Yes	4
Homemaker	Male	Divorced	68	$10,000	Good	Yes	4
Meals	Male	Widowed	65	$9,000	Excellent	Yes	5
Meals	Male	Married	84	$20,000	Poor	No	1
Homemaker	Male	Separated	74	$19,000	Fair	Yes	2
Homemaker	Female	Widowed	80	$22,000	Good	Yes	3
Homemaker	Female	Widowed	82	$11,950	Excellent	Yes	4
Case Manage.	Male	Married	81	$17,600	Good	Yes	5
Case Manage.	Female	Married	72	$20,250	Good	Yes	4
Case Manage.	Female	Married	76	$22,000	Excellent	Yes	4
Case Manage.	Female	Married	82	$17,800	Good	Yes	5
Case Manage.	Female	Married	90	$15,000	Fair	No Info.	No Info.
Meals	Male	Divorced	72	$14,000	Fair	Yes	4

Meals	Male	Widowed	79	$11,000	Excellent	Yes	4
Transport.	Female	Married	70	$12,050	Fair	Yes	2
Meals	Female	Widowed	80	$12,000	Fair	Yes	5
Meals	Female	Widowed	78	$11,600	Good	Yes	4
Homemaker	Male	Widowed	79	$11,300	Excellent	Yes	5
Homemaker	Female	Widowed	77	$12,900	Good	No Info.	3
Homemaker	Female	Divorced	68	$10,800	Good	Yes	4
Case Manage.	Male	Divorced	71	$10,400	Good	Yes	4
Case Manage.	Female	Widowed	70	$10,200	Excellent	Yes	5
Case Manage.	Female	Widowed	77	$9,600	Excellent	Yes	4
Case Manage.	Female	Divorced	66	$9,800	Good	Yes	4
Transport.	Male	Widowed	64	$10,900	Fair	No	2
Case Manage.	Female	Separated	65	$20,000	Fair	No	1
Case Manage.	Female	Widowed	70	$10,800	Excellent	Good	5

CHAPTER 14

Professional Writing

Proposals, Research Reports, and Journal Articles

There are three good reasons why a chapter on writing is at the end of a book on research methods. First, at some point in your career as a social worker, you may want to apply to a funding source for monies to develop some new intervention or expand services for your clients. The larger the scale of the effort you have in mind, the greater the likelihood that you could benefit from external funding. Grant writing often falls to staff who are knowledgeable about research because funding sources usually expect an evaluation component to be built into the proposal.

Guess what? Completing a social work program that requires at least one research course makes you "knowledgeable." That is, your research course may be viewed by your supervisor as more relevant and valuable than that of other staff members who completed their courses years ago. Or maybe, as the most recent hire, your caseload isn't as heavy, and you might have more time to devote to writing a grant proposal.

Second, social workers (particularly those with MSW degrees) can get assigned to committees or projects that involve a needs assessment, program evaluation, or the reporting of some kind of data collection. These reports may be the agency's yearly report about the characteristics of clients who are using the agency's services, or may involve studies of staff utilization and caseload changes over time. Reports might need to be sent to United Way or some other funder outside of the agency.

Third, perhaps you'll be part of a group interested in drafting a manuscript for a professional journal. At any rate, you'll be preparing yourself for big future dividends if you learn what is needed to write a proposal for a research project and can report the project's findings. Whether you are writing a grant proposal or reporting the results of a program evaluation, the elements that you must address are similar. Note that proposals are written in future tense—something you hope to do—while reports are written in past tense (data collected, findings obtained). This chapter presents an overview of the important components needed when writing a proposal or reporting a research effort.

As a result of her research practicum at the prison, Sophia wanted to learn more about writing grant proposals, and Mrs. Simpson was able to arrange for Sophia to obtain a workshop on the topic being provided downtown. Meanwhile, Bill volunteered to take the lead in writing up the evaluation report on their HRAP program for the warden. During the summer break, Bill and Sophia wanted to take that report and revise it for submission to a professional journal. Although they were a little nervous about these writing projects, they wanted to see if they could apply what they had been learning and at the same time possibly add a publication to their résumés.

Writing Grant Proposals

Most research grant proposals require that your application addresses the various components of a research project that we discuss in this chapter. Not only do you need good written communication skills to write a persuasive grant application, but you also need to understand what is required of the grant writer—such as how to prepare need statements, work plans, budget justifications, and so forth.

The information in this section is presented to help you prepare for the time when you write a grant proposal. A successful grant proposal has three essential elements:

- A compelling idea
- A funding source interested in that idea
- A plan or statement of methodology explaining how the project will be carried out

What is a compelling idea? Generally, grant writers must convince the prospective funding source that there is a real, substantial problem of some kind and that the agency or researcher has a new or innovative approach that stands a reasonable chance of making an impact. The researcher most involved with writing the grant is known as the **principal investigator** or the PI. Federal agencies (and sometimes state agencies and foundations) announce their intentions to fund specific research or programs. These announcements are known as requests for proposals and are generally referred to as **RFP**s. These RFPs usually contain all of the instructions you need to prepare a grant proposal—giving precise details as to what the funding source is and is not willing to fund, as well as information like how long particular sections of the proposal may be. When no current RFP has been issued, researchers and program developers often write **letters of inquiry** to logical funding sources to determine if the agency or foundation would be willing to receive a proposal regarding a specific topic. A compelling idea may be something never tried before or an approach that has been around for awhile and given a fresh twist. Once you have a good idea that warrants further development and a firm funding source possibly interested in underwriting the expense of your project, then your next step is to begin thinking about writing the grant proposal. If possible, forming an advisory group or committee could be of assistance.

Nonprofit agencies may write grants to plan a new program, for seed money to start a new program, and sometimes for equipment, facilities, or special needs. Sometimes, the funding request is to continue a worthwhile program that is running out of funds or has lost funding. For this type of funding, a good resource is the **www.foundationcenter.org**. Foundations, not the federal government, are most likely to best source for this type of grant.

For research monies, the federal government is the best source as there is a wide variety of types of funds ranging from the R01 or major research grants that typically are funded for three to five years, smaller R03 grants (for pilot studies, feasibility studies, secondary analysis), and a host of others. It will be important to make sure you and/or your agency meet the eligibility guidelines, before beginning to write one of the proposals. Go to **www.grants.gov**; this is a very valuable website that allows you to locate specific grant opportunities available from the federal government. You can search by topic or by the sponsoring federal agency. The Grants Learning Center provides basic helpful information on grant terminology, eligibility guidelines, and Grants 101. Check it out!

These are the seven components that typically form the core of a grant proposal:

Problem/Need Statement: This section of the proposal describes the magnitude of the problem that your compelling idea would address and furnishes background information about the reasons the proposal should be funded. It is important in this section to be knowledgeable about the literature on the program or problem. You are expected to be an expert and well informed about the efforts of others with regard to this problem. It is necessary to include statistics showing the extent of the problem and possibly statements from local, state, or other prominent authorities supporting the proposal. Describe the target population well. If your project involves the creation of a new program or service, you may want to address any prior research or planning connected to the need/problem. In the absence of prior efforts, you may want to conduct a quick needs assessment or data collection to show evidence of the need in the community. Reviewers of your proposal will want to know who will benefit from your program and what impact it is expected to make on the problem. Generally speaking, new and original ideas will get a lot further in the process than ideas that have been around for a long while. Make sure that the innovative and unique facets of your project stand out. It is critical that your project's purpose be clearly stated, and further, that it be consistent with the RFP guidelines or the funding source's priorities.

Qualifications of the PI and/or Organization: The RFP may require that you provide a description of your and the organization's credentials that establish capability to handle the project. It is helpful sometimes to have a more senior person who has been successfully funded in the past be the lead PI or at least to be a mentor and possible co-PI. Similarly, inexperienced proposal writers occasionally are advised to conduct a small-scale project, or **pilot project**, first to gain experience before tackling a larger project and proposal.

If asked, carefully address the capacity of your agency to deliver the proposed program or to conduct the research. You may want to discuss your agency's mandate for services, the programs offered, geographical service area covered, the makeup and qualifications of staff, their accomplishments, and such details that would convince the funding source of your agency's ability to launch and support the project. List any agency accomplishments or achievements, and summarize any outcome evaluation studies or reports that relate to the proposal. If the proposal will involve a slightly different clientele, it is important to show how these clients will be reached and how the program will complement the agency's mission. If your agency has a great deal of experience with this type of problem or client group, make sure to highlight it. Readers of your proposal will be looking for indications of the agency's competence and capacity. Working relationships and partnerships with other agencies are good to include, as is any success in securing prior grants. From time to time, it is essential to describe your agency's facilities.

Proposed goals and objectives: Describe your work plan, listing the goals and measurable objectives associated with the project, along with dates showing when key events or activities will take place. The goals and objectives must relate to what you hope to accomplish with the project. Don't create a set of inconsequential tasks that roam away from the project; key tasks should be directly related in a meaningful way. Be realistic in your plans.

Program Design & Strategy: In this section, fully describe what will take place if you receive funding. If the proposal centers on expansion of services or development of a new program, this section will address the activities associated with creating the new program or increasing service delivery. Consequently, you'll need to discuss such items as hiring new staff, training them, acquiring/renting space, design of the program, how prospective clients will be informed, evaluation of the program, and so on. If the proposal is to support a research project, you will need to explain your methodology, measurement of variables, recruitment of participants, how the data will be analyzed, etc. You may be asked to provide a **Gantt chart** showing a time line for completion of the various tasks.

Impact/Outcomes/Evaluation: Almost all funding sources expect a program evaluation of some sort. They will probably want to know how you plan to measure the project's success. This section builds on and benefits from the clearly stated objectives previously listed. Discuss your intended outcomes, the potential impact the program or research could have. If, for example, you will be surveying clients or reviewing client records for indications of success, this is the place where you will discuss your evaluation plan and methodology. With research proposals, place instruments that will be used in the **appendix**. Consider, too, the way that data will be collected and analyzed. The RFP might require a process evaluation, which, as we learned earlier, is a narrative description addressing such concerns as how the project developed, the key decisions that were made, the activities that took place, and what resulted.

Budget: Every proposal will need to contain a budget that identifies all major expenses (for example, staff salaries and benefits, rent, supplies, photocopies, utilities, office furniture, etc.). It will also likely be necessary to list in-kind contributions (that is, what your agency donates in the way of staff's salaries and benefits, office space, equipment, etc., as well as what volunteers or others in the community may donate).

Sustainability/Future Funding: Increasingly, funders are asking for information about how the project may be sustained or continued after the grant funding period ends. Even though you may not have well-developed plans for placing here, you will need to speculate about possible sources of funds.

In addition to the key components already identified, it is often necessary to show that you have community support from key agencies and professionals in prominent positions. Letters of endorsement are particularly important from those providing in-kind support such as the contribution of staff to the project.

Once your proposal has been drafted, it might be a good idea to get someone not involved with the project to read and critique your work so that you can revise it and make the best possible presentation. Take care to be neat and eliminate all spelling and grammatical errors. Make sure that it is delivered to the right location prior to the submission deadline. Finally, make sure that you have followed all of the directions exactly, made the proper number of copies, and written an interesting cover letter to accompany the proposal. Then you wait—sometimes several months—before announcements are made about the funding awards. If you are among the lucky ones, then you can start developing and testing your ideas. Later, you will probably be required to write a report to communicate what you learned from the implementation of your project.

You will improve your chances of writing a successful grant if you find a mentor—someone with a track record of securing funds from grants. Even better would be a mentor whose interest and expertise are in the same area as the proposal you would like to write. Also, you may want to review some of the books available on the topic such as those by Coley and Scheinberg (2013) and Karsh and Fox (2014), but there are many others. And there are many Internet resources available for free, such as "Writing a Successful Grant Proposal" at **https://www.mcf.org/sites/default/files/files/pages/writingagrantproposal.pdf.**

Writing Research Reports

Let's imagine that you have conducted some exciting research and want to communicate your findings. Even if the results didn't turn out quite as expected, you might be prompted to write about your research because the agency executive asks you to give a report to the agency staff or board of directors, or because the grant or funding source requires a formal evaluation report. Your **audience** may run the gamut from friendly coworkers inside your agency to citizens in the community and federal bureaucrats you've never

BOX 14.1 COMPONENTS OF A RESEARCH REPORT

1. Introduction
   a. description of problem
   b. statement of research question or hypothesis
   c. significance of problem and rationale for studying it
2. Literature review
   a. theoretical and historical perspectives
   b. identified gaps in literature
   c. reiteration of purpose of study
3. Methodology
   a. research design and data collection procedures
   b. characteristics of subjects
   c. sampling design
   d. description of instrumentation
   e. data analysis procedures
4. Findings (results)
   a. factual information presented
   b. statistical and practical significance discussed
   c. tables, charts
5. Discussion
   a. brief summary of findings
   b. explanation of unexpected findings
   c. applications to practice
   d. weaknesses or limitations of research
   e. suggestions for future research
6. References
7. Appendixes

met. What would you need to tell them? What format would you follow? The purpose of this section is to show you how to conceptualize and prepare a report of research findings. Please note that the essential elements of a research report with quantitative data are essentially the same—whether you are writing a report, thesis, or professional journal article. However, reports of qualitative research may not conform to this outline. Each of these major categories of presentation will be explained in more depth.

The Introduction

The purpose of the *Introduction* is to place the research question or problem within some context or frame of reference. This generally entails describing the problem and the extent to which it affects people. For instance, if your project is about developing services for bereaved parents who have experienced the murder of a child, a logical starting place would be recent estimates of the number of parents affected this way. Is it 15,000 or 75,000? Has it been increasing lately or falling off? Your reader should understand the scope of the problem and the kinds of difficulties experienced by these parents.

There are many ways to begin a report, and the nature of your topic may suggest an approach. In order to hook a reader's interest, you may want to start with a question like this: How involved is social work in the criminal justice field? Are social workers less involved with criminal justice than in the past?

View the Introduction as an opportunity to stimulate the readers' interest in your topic. Tell readers how your research or program is different and why innovative methods are needed. You might start with what is known about a problem and then move to what is not known about it. Controversies work, too. Briefly present the debate, as it can serve as the stage to highlight your project.

When you have finished writing the Introduction, read it over to make sure that you have:

- Articulated some interesting problem or issue
- Identified your specific research question or hypothesis
- Offered a rationale for your study (explain why it is needed and unique)

The easiest research reports to read are those that engage the reader's interest. What needs to be fixed? What don't we know about a problem? Present this information early in the Introduction instead of burying it somewhere in the report. Material discussed in your Introduction makes more sense when the reader has a clear understanding of the problem prompting your investigation. Don't be afraid to let your enthusiasm for the topic (or the significance of the problem) be shown. There's no point in writing so dispassionately that no one will care about your conclusions.

The Review of the Literature

The *Literature Review* section of a report or journal article is where relevant studies and theoretical explanations of the problem or phenomenon of interest are summarized. You need not describe every study that has ever been conducted on your topic. Cite only the most pertinent ones. Summarize the major findings; it is not necessary to give every nuance or detail. For example, consider the following fictitious excerpt:

> While relatively little has been written in the social work literature about shoplifting, it is a topic of interest to those who work in the criminal justice system because of the seemingly complex dynamics involved. Financial need does not always appear to be a significant factor. Almost all of the studies have shown that poverty is not a major explanation for

shoplifting (Mills, 2008). Shoplifters tend to come from all economic classes (Hunt, 2007), and the overwhelming majority of persons caught shoplifting do not intend to resell the item (Book & Vurm, 2010). It has also been noted that in only a minority of cases is shoplifting associated with mental illness, and the majority of arrested shoplifters do not have any psychotic features (Doktor, 2012). Recent studies have shown that shoplifters are not apprehended differentially by race, sex, or age when control variables are employed. (Mills, 2008; Vurm, 2015)

From this brief example, we can learn that theories based on economic deprivation or mental illness have not been found to explain shoplifting. Further, explanations involving a greater level of absentmindedness among the elderly do not seem viable. Because these theories have been tested and then discarded, the way is open for a new theoretical explanation—perhaps that shoplifting is a help-seeking activity unconsciously motivated by high levels of stress.

This passage also demonstrates how quite a few studies can be summarized in a short amount of space. Learn to summarize succinctly other studies and articles. Don't provide irrelevant information. For example, it is usually inconsequential whether the studies were conducted in Ohio or New York State. It is more important that the literature review show trends in the major findings of these studies. However, the location, methodology, sample size, and other facets of the earlier research can take on more importance if you are replicating a study or want to note how your study is different from or similar to that of other research. Please don't take all of your information from the abstract. Your job is to be knowledgeable of the literature. It can be embarrassing if you are asked by your professor or by a reviewing committee to provide more information about an article you didn't read. Also, avoid citing lengthy passages of an article—professionals don't do that.

In reviewing the literature, you may find a number of competing theories. Even though you may not subscribe to all of them, you still owe it to your readers to give a balanced presentation and to acknowledge rival theories or explanations. This background helps provide some of the controversy or interest that can make reading your article or report more enjoyable.

Because research is usually conducted on topics where not much is known, the review of the literature section helps justify your research by pointing out gaps in our knowledge base. Here's the way one set of authors handled it:

> Using randomized controlled trials (RCTs) to evaluate behavioral interventions with releasing prisoners is rare. Farrington and Welsh (2005) found that only 14 studies published between 1984 and 2005 with sample sizes of 100 or more that used RCTs with incarcerated populations. Although RCTs are widely recognized as the gold standard for evaluating intervention effectiveness, the use of RCTs is similarly rare in studies of interventions developed by social workers. … As a result, few researchers have published lessons learned from their trials of interventions with releasing prisoners. The current study adds to this limited literature by presenting challenges, successful strategies, and recommendations … (Pettus-Davis, Howard, Dunnigan, Scheyett, & Roberts-Lewis, 2016, p. 35)

After you have reviewed the relevant literature and noted the gaps in knowledge on a particular problem or topic, you may want to restate the purpose of your study. This will assist the reader in assimilating the potpourri of literature you have just presented.

When you finish writing your review of the literature section, look it over to make sure that you have:

- Covered all of the major studies in the field
- Included the most recent studies and looked for gaps (if all of your references are dated between 1988 and 2002, then you probably need to look a little further)
- Summarized what is *not known* about the problem and you have reminded the reader of your specific interest

When you have done these things, then you are ready to begin the methodology section.

The Methods Section

The *Methods* section of the report describes in detail how you conducted the study. In this section, the reader learns how you collected the data. Typically, the following are described:

1. *The research design.* Explain: was it an RCT, a nonequivalent control group design, a survey of some sort?
2. *The subjects.* How were they recruited or selected? Random or convenience sampling? What was special or unique about the subjects?
3. *Data collection procedures.* Did you use electronic questionnaires, personally interview the respondents, use secondary data?
4. *The instrumentation.* What instruments did you use? Have the instruments been used in a similar application before? What is known about the instruments' reliability and validity?
5. *Data analysis.* What statistical procedures did you employ?

You should give sufficient information in this section to allow another investigator to replicate the study. Commonly, subsections and subheadings are used to differentiate the various components of the methodology. This is an example of how one set of authors briefly describes their survey of veterans attending a community college:

STUDY DESIGN

> The specific objective of the study was to assess health risks in a group of community college veterans utilizing a cross-sectional health assessment survey. No personal identifiers were collected during this study. The protocol was granted an exemption by the Institutional Review Board and approved by the Research and Development Committee at the Louis Stokes Cleveland VAMC and was approved by the Institutional Review Board at Cuyahoga Community College (Tri-C) in Cleveland, Ohio. (Misra-Hebert, Santurri, DeChant, Watts, Sehgal, & Aron, 2015, p. 1059)

Authors use somewhat different approaches in describing their subjects. However, your readers will typically be interested in how many subjects you had, how you selected them, and something about their personal characteristics. Here's additional information the authors presented:

Study Setting

This study was conducted at the campuses of Tri-C in collaboration with the Tri-C Department of Veterans Services and Programs. Tri-C is the largest public community college in

Ohio with four main campuses, serving over 60,000 students annually.14 Study Participants The study population included all identified student veterans enrolled at Tri-C in Spring Semester 2013 (978 students). Of note, an estimated 83% of veterans enrolled at Tri-C in the spring semester 2012 utilized the post-9/11 GI Bill benefits available to those who served after September 2001 (personal communication, Tri-C Office of Institutional Research). Population sampling for all enrolled veteran students was used. (Misra-Hebert, Santurri, DeChant, Watts, Sehgal, & Aron, 2015, p. 1060)

You might find this part of the description more interesting:

Data Collection Survey questions (available from authors upon request) included those used with permission from the National Health Study for a New Generation of U.S. Veterans Questionnaire, a national survey tool currently in use for recent veterans,[15] and additional questions added by the research team. Specific measures in the survey included 1. Demographic information including self-reported biometric data and descriptive information about branch of service and deployment (questions 1–6, 8–9, and 26–33) 2. Utilization of health care services (questions 7 and 13–14) 3. Medical history (questions 10–12 and 15) 4. Health behaviors (questions 22–25 and 34–38) 5. Health status (questions 16–21)…. The survey was sent to 978 veterans in Spring Semester 2013. An introductory e-mail letter with a link to the electronic survey was sent to students requesting voluntary participation. Over the next 2 weeks, a reminder was included in an electronic newsletter and an e-mail reminder was also sent. An invitation was then sent by mail with a paper survey and postage paid return envelope as well as a link to the electronic survey, with a $5 grocery store gift card to all veterans requesting their participation in the survey. This incentive amount was chosen based on previous studies.[20-22] As the survey was anonymous, the gift card was sent to all students. After 2 weeks, an e-mail reminder was sent (without survey link), with a final e-mail reminder after 10 days. Results include responses received up to 1 month after the final reminder (April, 2013). (Misra-Hebert, Santurri, DeChant, Watts, Sehgal, & Aron, 2015, p. 1060)

Readers will also be interested in the instruments or measures used in the study. Typically, you identify the source reference for the instrument and discuss its reliability and validity, as in the following example from Craig and Sprang (2014) from their study about children in trauma treatment:

Measurement

The UCLA PTSD Reaction Index (UCLA PTSD-RI; Steinberg, Bryer, Decker & Pynoos, 2004) consists of three parts. Part I assesses traumatic experiences that lead to subsequent questions that help the child recall details of the traumatic event (Criterion A1). Part II includes questions related to A1 and A2 criteria which are scored "yes" or "no." Part III asks about the frequency of PTSD symptoms during the past month (rated from 0 = none of the time to 4 = most of the time). These items map directly onto the DSM-IV PTSD criterion B (intrusion), criterion C (avoidance/numbing), and criterion D (arousal). Twenty of these items assess PTSD symptoms: two additional items assess associated features—fear of recurrence and trauma-related guilt. A cut-off of 38 or greater for a single incident traumatic event has the greatest sensitivity (0.93) and specificity (0.87) for detecting PTSD (Rodriguez, Steinberg, Saltzman, & Pynoos, 2001a, 2001b). The UCLA PTSD RI DSM-IV version demonstrates good convergent validity as evidenced by moderately high correlations of .70 with the PTSD Module of the Schedule for Affective Disorders and Schizophrenia for School-Age Children (Epidemiologic version) and .82 in comparison with the Child and Adolescent Version of the Clinician-Administered PTSD Scale. Roussos et al. (2005) reports a test-retest-reliability coefficient of .84 for the DSM-IV version and a Cronbach's alpha falling in the range of .90, suggesting good internal consistency (Craig & Sprang, 2014, pp. 931–932).

Usually, only a paragraph or two is needed to inform the reader about the way in which the data were analyzed. Here is a description of the analysis from an article about recidivism among individuals who received corrections-based treatment and parole (Staton-Tindall, Harp, Winston, Webster, & Pangburn, 2015):

Analytic Plan

Descriptive statistics were generated for each variable of interest. Next, bivariate analyses were conducted to determine significant differences between rural and urban participants at treatment intake and to examine differences among rural and urban individuals who returned to custody during the 12-month follow-up period compared to those who did not. Chi-square analyses and ANOVA were used to determine statistical significance. Finally, a logistic regression model was used to examine if geographic location (rural vs. urban) differentiated the odds of recidivism one-year post-release. Demographic and behavioral health variables were included as controls in this model.

When you have finished writing your methodology section, look over the checklist below to make sure you have covered all of the essential questions.

BOX 14.2 CHECKLIST FOR METHODOLOGY SECTION

Have you:
□ Explained who the participants were? Their characteristics? How were they were recruited, assigned, or selected (if relevant)?
□ Identified what data were collected and analyzed? What measurements were used? Make sure key independent and dependent variables are identified.
□ Explained the design and how the data were collected (procedures)?
□ Made sure the reader understands how the methodology relates to the research question(s)?

When you have answered these questions, then you are ready to begin the Results section.

The Results

This section of the report or article contains what you actually discovered from conducting your research. The *Results* section summarizes the data. You do not present the raw data but aggregate or average scores.

Up to this point, you have not revealed your findings. Now it is time to exhibit your results. Your task in this section is to present the findings factually, without opinion. The facts must stand by themselves.

You can organize your findings in many ways. The most common practice is to present the major findings first. But if you have several hypotheses, report your findings relative to the first hypothesis, then move to the second hypothesis, and so on.

Many researchers and would-be authors often feel overwhelmed because there appears to be too much information to crowd into a single research report. This can happen when they have many hypotheses or have performed a large number of statistical analyses. However, not all findings are equally important.

Sometimes, it is helpful to get a blank sheet of paper and write down what you would report if limited to one major point. Then, ask yourself, "What is the second most important finding coming from this study?" This process continues until you have identified all of the important points. Once you have noted all the key findings, begin thinking about how to present them. Tables are helpful in that they visually break up the narrative while providing precise information that makes for dry reading if incorporated into the text.

Most research reports contain tables as a way of reducing verbiage. You may want to consider developing one or two tables for your research report. However, don't overdo it. Too many tables is almost as bad as not having enough. When multiple tables are employed, it is hard for a reader or reviewer to keep all of the main points in mind; the information tends to run together.

In the Results section, you will also report the outcomes of the statistical tests you have conducted. For example, if your studies found that MSW social workers received higher-quality assurance ratings than BSW social workers, it will be important to state if the difference in ratings is statistically significant. Do not allow your readers to conclude that a difference of three points, for example, is important if a t-test or other appropriate statistical test reveals no statistically significant difference.

If creating a table, take the time to prepare it so that the data displayed can be digested. Don't throw some numbers together and think you are done, as in the following table 14.1:

TABLE 14.1

Scale	Pretest Mean	Posttest Mean	t Value	Significance
A	5.308	4.809	2.15	.04
B	4.339	5.900	4.11	.001
C	6.663	5.323	2.84	.01
D	5.777	4.990	1.57	.13
E	6.191	7.42	1.92	.07
F	5.901	6.02	1.85	.80

Although this table might look neat and tidy, notice that it has no heading or caption. The reader has no idea what is being presented or what the scales represent. Do lower posttest mean scores suggest client improvement, or do they indicate that clients have gotten worse? The reader should not have to guess whether Scale A represents social maladjustment or if that concept is represented by Scale E.

If you are in doubt about how to present your findings in tabular form, consult the *Publication Manual of the American Psychological Association*, which is widely used by social work journals. The manual also demonstrates how to portray statistical data within the text. For instance, chi-square is shown this way:

There were no statistically significant differences among the four groups by race X^2 (6, $N = 1,003$) = 4.41, $p = .62$, or gender X^2 (3, $N = 1,003$) = 1.33, $p = .72$.

One-way analysis of variance is expressed in this manner:

There were no statistically significant differences in the number of referrals by group F (3, 1,002) = .75, $p = .53$.

Often, the characteristics of a study's sample are shown in the Results section. In an article on the health behaviors among residents of low-income housing developments, the authors described the respondents this way:

Respondents

A sample of 1937 households was selected from across 20 sites, of which 1679 were eligible. Of these 1679, 828 residents (49.3%) completed the survey. The number of completed surveys ranged across sites from 18 to 64. Most participants had completed high school or beyond (62%); were less than 50 years of age (65%); and identified themselves as either Hispanic (41%) or non-Hispanic Black (38%) ... Most were female (80%) and foreign-born (68%). A majority reported some level of financial hardship, with more than one-third not being able to make ends meet each month. An examination of these sociodemographic factors by housing development shows that the sites varied (p<.05) on all of these variables. (Harley et al., 2014, pp. 61–62)

When you have finished writing your Results section, look over it to make sure that you have:

BOX 14.3   CHECKLIST FOR RESULTS SECTION

☐ Presented the most salient findings that merit reporting.
☐ Not reported excessively or overanalyzed the data (don't clutter the report with every correlation or statistic that you produced—especially if they are not relevant to major findings).
☐ Used the appropriate statistical procedures and reported what you used.

When you feel that your findings are succinct and to the point, providing information directly related to your hypotheses or research question(s), then you are ready to move on to the Discussion section.

The Discussion

The *Discussion* section often begins with a brief summary of your findings. It is not necessary to go into a lot of detail—this information was just exhibited in the Results. Just address the major findings or the highlights of your study. Once that is done, you can begin to flesh out the findings. Perhaps you were surprised to find that the BSWs in your study performed better than the MSW employees; here is the place to elaborate the reasons for your surprise. You can reveal any unexpected findings—as well as what didn't go as planned.

Most importantly, the Discussion section should interpret the findings for the reader and address the relevance of these findings for practice. What do the findings mean or suggest to you? Do they suggest that BSWs have better skills or knowledge than persons with other undergraduate degrees? Does additional training seem to be indicated for the staff? What implications does your study have for practice or policy? Discuss findings that have practical significance—even if there was no statistical significance.

When presenting findings, one must be careful not to lead the reader into believing that the study has "proved" whatever point. In the social sciences, we usually "find evidence" that may "suggest that" certain relationships or variables may be involved.

The part of the Discussion section that many researchers do not like to write is the description of what did *not* go according to the research design. Sometimes, secretaries forget to mail follow-up reminders by the deadline for data collection. Clients drop out of programs and create smaller treatment samples than intended. Small glitches are common because we don't have the same degree of control that laboratory scientists have. So, you may need to admit to departures from planned research procedures. Any problems you encountered in collecting your data may well explain why you got the results that you did. For instance, someone forgetting to mail reminder postcards could have caused a lower response rate for one group than for another. A change in agency policies during the middle of your study could have changed staff morale or increased the proportion of employees who felt "burned out"—which in turn could have affected the quality of their work. Also, recognize biases that may have crept into your study or that you discovered too late to do anything about. These problems constitute a part of the Discussion section known as the **limitations**.

Your study may have significant limitations. Perhaps you had hoped for a representative sampling of social workers from all educational backgrounds, but you heard from 65% of the BSWs and only 10% of the MSWs. Thus, your study would be limited in how far you could generalize your research—especially to MSWs in the population.

Almost every study has some limitations—perhaps the most common one is some sort of selection bias. If it is hard for you to think of limitations, you may want to review the section in Chapter 5 on internal and external threats to the validity of a study.

Many authors conclude their research reports and journal articles by indicating areas for future research. In conducting their studies, researchers may have ideas about ways to improve procedures, instruments, the operationalization of variables, sampling techniques, and so on that would assist other researchers. This can be done, even if the current researcher does not have plans for further work in that area but wishes others to benefit from what has been learned in the process of conducting the present research.

Here is an example of how limitations were addressed in one study of life satisfaction after medical discharge for a traumatically acquired disability:

> There are several limitations of our study that merit consideration. We relied on self-report instruments for all measured variables. The LSI [Life Satisfaction Index], despite its utility in past research (McDowell, 2006), was first published in 1961 and may be considered dated

by some researchers. The data were collected from participants who were treated and discharged between the years 1989 to 1992 in one southeastern state in the United States. We
do not know the degree to which these features affect our results or their generalizability.
(Hernandez, Elliott, Berry, Underhill, Fine, & Lai, 2014, p. 189)

After your discussion section, you may want to prepare a separate section called *Conclusion*. Whether
you write a Conclusion section separate from your Discussion section is usually a matter of individual
preference. However, if your report is being prepared for a policy or advisory board, they will likely appreciate a listing of conclusions that have implications for actions that they may need to take. Be careful not
to become too exuberant and make claims that go beyond your data. When you have finished writing the
Discussion section, check to make sure that you have:

BOX 14.4 CHECKLIST FOR THE DISCUSSION SECTION

☐ Answered the questions that launched the study.
☐ Discussed the implications of your findings.
☐ Identified limitations of the study.
☐ Identified areas where future research is still needed.
☐ Not overgeneralized.

References, Appendixes, and Abstracts

Whenever other documents or resources have been cited, they need to be listed in the *References* section
at the end of the report or manuscript. References are usually listed according to APA style, alphabetically
by authors' names.

The *Appendix* is a section at the back of the report where you place a copy of instruments, written
instructions given to subjects, or important materials that may have been used during the course of your
study. Research reports generally are not considered complete without a copy of your instrument. If you
have many tables in your report, you may want to place those of lesser importance in the Appendix.

Abstracts are brief summaries. They usually accompany journal manuscripts, but are not always found
in research reports. Abstracts can be difficult to write because of the need to compress a complex manuscript into a few paragraphs. When you write an abstract, limit yourself to a paragraph to introduce the
study and no more than a paragraph to present each of your major findings. If you get stumped, look at
several abstracts in recent articles you've read or photocopied for examples.

An **executive summary** is like a long abstract (for example, two to five pages long) and is prepared
to present a quick overview of the project for board members, the news media, and so on. Formal
evaluation reports often contain executive summaries for those who may not have time to read the
full report.

Qualitative Research Reports

Because there are so many different types of qualitative research approaches, there isn't only one format
used when writing a qualitative research report. However, Drisko (2005) wrote an essay entitled "Writing

Up Qualitative Research" and states that a qualitative research report "… must always tell the story of the project, richly convey the views of others, and detail implications" (p. 589). DePoy and Gitlin (1998) say it this way: "Interpretative schemes are often presented in story-like fashion in which main themes and subtexts unfold as the story is told" (p. 292).

As we discussed earlier, qualitative research is different from the quantitative tradition, and that difference is noticeable right away: There is a heavy use of narrative as well as quotations from participants, which allows their views to "come alive to the reader" (Drisko, 2005, p. 592). Quantitatively oriented reports tend not to involve quotations from their research participants unless mixed methods of data collection were used, and seldom would quantitatively oriented investigators use quotations to the same extent as qualitative researchers. At the same time, it is important to remember that the qualitative researcher's job involves more than simply citing one quotation after another.

Qualitative reports also differ from quantitative reports in that qualitative researchers are expected to reveal their personal reactions, values, or biases that they recognize during the data collection. In fact, the qualitative researcher can write in first person (using "I" or "my" language), while this is not generally seen in quantitative reports.

Quantitative research reports often involve the testing of a theory or hypotheses, while the qualitative research report usually does not. Quantitative studies tend to have thorough reviews of the literature, whereas this is not essential for qualitative studies because of their inductive approach. Lastly, quantitative reports tend to include statistical analysis and tables; qualitative reports usually do not.

Luquis, R. R., & Cruz, I. J. (2006). Knowledge, attitudes, and perceptions about breast cancer and breast cancer screening among Hispanic women residing in south central Pennsylvania. *Journal of Community Health, 31*(1), 25–42.

Luquis and Cruz employed eight different focus groups, involving 56 Hispanic women total, and this is how they presented their first paragraph under the Results section:

> When asked about cancer in general, most women reported that when they heard the word cancer the first thing that came to mind was either "muerte" (death), "temor" (fear), and/or "enfermedad mortal" (fatal disease). For example, a participant said, "death, it is an incurable disease." In another group, a woman stated "the truth is that when you hear about cancer, one gets very scared, and the only thing that one thinks is that death will come soon." Another woman added, "I get very afraid because I have family members who died of cancer." However, a couple of participants acknowledged that cancer could be prevented and treated. (p. 34)

Later, in the Discussion section, the authors draw this conclusion:

> [M]ost participants reported that they have received no or minimal information about breast cancer from their health care provider or other sources (i.e., brochures, friends). This lack of information or misinformation might also reduce the likelihood that these women would practice breast cancer preventive behaviors. (p. 39)

Other examples of qualitative studies that are good examples to read and possibly use as models for writing are Wahab (2005) and Swanberg and Logan (2005). These examples were previously mentioned in Chapters 12 and 11, respectively.

Writing as a Practice Goal

Although writing for a professional publication may seem like an impossible goal, it starts with the desire to publish. Following that, it is helpful to have access to data to analyze. As social workers, you will have access to and create data for research as you practice. This information can be used to improve its quality, effectiveness, or efficiency. It does not flow automatically from your work with clients—it depends on you planning and organizing a research effort. Even then, many times social work research is never written up, but remains in file folders or on someone's desk until it becomes outdated or is thrown away. For the results of research to guide practice, the findings must be disseminated to colleagues and other professionals. Who will move our profession forward if you don't?

Writing about the successes and failures of interventions and about the problems of clients is clearly a responsibility of professional social workers. Indeed, the following passage is found in the National Association of Social Workers Code of Ethics (1999):

> 5.01 (d) Social workers should contribute to the knowledge base of social work and share with colleagues their knowledge related to practice, research, and ethics. Social workers should seek to contribute to the profession's literature and to share their knowledge at professional meetings and conferences.

Additionally, writing for professional audiences can also provide a great deal of personal satisfaction as well as recognition for your agency or university.

The basic structure and key elements needed to report research findings are the same whether one is writing a thesis, an evaluation report, or a journal article. Of course, there are some observable differences when we compare these three types of reports. For one thing, theses and dissertations tend to be much longer than journal articles. While manuscripts for journal articles must often be between 16 and 20 pages, research reports written for internal agency consumption and dissertations may have no set limit on the number of pages.

Writing for Professional Journals

This section of the chapter contains some suggestions for taking a research report and developing it as a journal article. First, when you prepare a manuscript, have a specific journal in mind. Become familiar with that journal. Are its articles written for the practitioner or for the scholar? Journals have different audiences (readerships). Those journals oriented more toward practitioners may expect case examples and vignettes, and they may contain fewer references. Academically oriented journals have readers who may expect sophisticated analytical procedures. You will have more success placing articles in a journal that you are well acquainted with (for example, knowing the style, format, and type of article that the journal tends to publish) than in an unfamiliar journal. Most social work journals use the APA style for formatting. You need to become proficient in the use of this style.

Practically all journals carry a statement informing readers and prospective authors of the types of articles that they would like to see. By reading such statements, prospective authors determine if their manuscripts would be appropriate for the journals. For instance, this is the information for authors found in *Social Work*:

> It is a professional journal dedicated to improving practice and advancing knowledge in social work and social welfare. The editorial board welcomes manuscripts that expand and evaluate knowledge of social work practice, social issues, and the social work profession.

Topics of interest:

- Research on social problems
- Evaluation of social work practice
- Advancement of developmental and practice theory
- Culture and ethnicity
- Social policy, advocacy, and administration **http://www.naswpress.org/authors/guidelines/04-journals.html**

Research on Social Work Practice describes its editorial policy this way:

> *Research on Social Work Practice* is a disciplinary journal devoted to the publication of empirical research concerning the assessment methods and outcomes of social work practice. Social work practice is broadly interpreted to refer to the application of intentionally designed social work intervention programs to problems of societal or interpersonal importance. Interventions include behavior analysis and therapy; psychotherapy or counseling with individuals; case management/care coordination; education; supervision; practice involving couples, families, or small groups; advocacy; community practice; organizational management; and the evaluation of social policies. At least one author of a submitted article must be a professional social worker, and/or the interventions evaluated must have been provided by professional social workers.

The journal will primarily serve as an outlet for the publication of the following:

1. Original reports of empirically based evaluation studies on the outcomes of social work practice,
2. Original reports of empirical studies on the development and validation of social work assessment methods, and
3. Original systematic reviews, including meta-analyses, of the practice-research literature that convey direct applications (not simply implications) to social work practice. The website of the Campbell Collaboration provides exemplary guidelines for the design and conduct of systematic reviews, and authors contemplating submitting such studies are urged to follow the Campbell Guidelines (see **www.Campbellcollaboration.org**). The two types of systematic reviews considered for publication are:

   A. Systematic reviews of the evidence-based status of a particular psychosocial intervention or assessment method, or
   B. Systematic reviews of several psychosocial interventions applicable to clients with a particular psychosocial problem.
       https://us.sagepub.com/en-us/nam/research-on-social-work-practice/journal200896 #submission-guidelines

Journals want original manuscripts that are clearly written, of timely interest, appropriate to the journal, of the right length, and in the correct style. Journal reviewers look for an adequate literature review, reasonable research design, and the correct use of statistical techniques. But beyond those considerations, reviewers must decide whether your manuscript makes a "contribution" to the knowledge base.

Reviewers may decide that your manuscript makes no contribution because of severe limitations in its generalizability, or because a more thorough literature review would have revealed the existence of studies similar to the one being reported.

You will probably increase your chances of publication if you find a journal that, in the last six years or so, has published similar (or somewhat related) articles to the one you are preparing. While this guideline is no guarantee that the journal will publish your article, at least it indicates that the journal has an interest in your topic. Study the articles that have recently appeared in the journal. Observe the reference style, the use of tables, the length of the literature review, and the general level at which the article is written.

Study the "Information for Authors." Sometimes, the instructions about manuscript preparation and the types of manuscripts that journals seek are contained within selected issues. Or you may want to look for that journal's information on the Internet. Information about the NASW journals (*Social Work*, *Health & Social Work*, *Children & Schools*, and *Social Work Research*) can be found at **www.naswpress.org.**

After you revise and polish your manuscript to the point where you think it is finished, set it aside. After several days, reread it. Make necessary revisions and prepare a clean copy. Share it with two or three persons whose opinions you respect. Find helpful readers who can give you constructive criticism without battering your ego. If you know that you are weak in the grammar department, seek a friendly reviewer who can assist.

Do not send your manuscript to more than one journal at a time. Sending out multiple submissions at one time is regarded as unethical. If your manuscript is rejected by the first journal you choose, do not be discouraged. A rejection does not necessarily mean that your manuscript is poorly conceptualized or written. It could be that the journal just accepted a similar article on the same topic last week. Or, it may mean that the journal is planning a special issue, and your manuscript does not fit their needs. Also, you may have submitted your article to an inappropriate journal.

Sometimes, busy reviewers may not take the time to read carefully enough to understand what you have written. Reviews are conducted "blind"—that is, you will not know who read your manuscript and will have no way of knowing whether the reviewer knew as much about your topic or your methodology as you do. So, even good articles can be rejected. If your first effort is rejected, dust off your pride and try to objectively read your manuscript again. Repair any problems indicated by the reviewers of the first journal, and submit it to the second journal of your choice.

Journal reviewers usually make one of three decisions: They accept the manuscript as it is; they accept it if the author makes certain changes; or they reject it. Even if the journal likes your manuscript, don't be surprised if you are asked to make certain revisions. Often, manuscripts are strengthened by the additional information that reviewers might request.

If your manuscript has been rejected three times, should you continue trying to get it published? This is the point at which I become frustrated and tired of working with one manuscript, and I quit. However, if you feel that yours is basically a good manuscript, and some of the reviewers have encouraged revision, then you should try it again.

Getting a manuscript published is like most other things in life that require practice. The more you practice, the better you will become at this activity.

Reading and Critiquing Research

Students sometimes have a tendency to believe that any research that manages to appear in print is "good" research. Unfortunately, some pretty shoddy research can be found in journals without too much difficulty. As I stated in the beginning of this book, one reason you are required to enroll in a research methods course is to help you recognize poor or inadequate research. Flawed research (if unrecognized) could lead you to conclusions that are not warranted and could be dangerous to your clients.

Using the major content areas of research reports, we can construct a set of criteria to use in evaluating research reports, journal articles, or manuscripts. (These criteria can also be used to double-check your manuscripts.) I'm indebted to Garfield (1984) for his observations and guidelines on this topic.

When evaluating a research report, you should find yourself answering "yes" to most of the following evaluative questions. Strong research articles will elicit a greater number of affirmative responses; weak articles will receive fewer. You can use these criteria not only to evaluate the research reports prepared by others, but also to check your own report or manuscript to ensure that you have included all of the crucial elements.

If you are serious about trying to get published, three points cannot be emphasized enough: (1) the importance of studying examples of other research reports and literature; (2) the critical need for social workers to publish their research results; and (3) the necessity to persevere when first efforts are rejected by journal reviewers.

BOX 14.5   CHECKLIST FOR EVALUATING RESEARCH REPORTS, ARTICLES, AND MANUSCRIPTS

☐ Does the Introduction provide a clear notion of:
- the problem
- the purpose of the research
- its significance

☐ Are hypotheses reasonable? Do they appear to logically follow from the review of the literature?

☐ Is the literature review:
- relevant to the study
- thorough
- current

☐ Is a research design stated?
- Do the subjects appear to have been selected without overt bias?
- If there is a control group, does it seem to be an appropriate group for comparison?
- Is the number of participants sufficient?

☐ Is there enough information on:
- the procedures
- operational definitions of the variables
- the reliability and validity of the instruments

☐ Are the findings discussed in terms of their implications and practical significance?
- Do the conclusions logically follow from the data?
- Are the appropriate statistical tests used?
- Has the author overgeneralized? Have limitations been recognized?

When you publish your research, you contribute to the knowledge base of social work and allow others to build on your research. Knowledge is an incremental process; it moves forward in small steps rather than large leaps. Any movement toward the goal of advancing social work knowledge starts with understanding the research process. Because knowledge can become outdated and obsolete with the passage of time, it is vital that social workers not only read research as a way of keeping up with new developments in the field but also engage in research and seek professional outlets for the dissemination of research efforts. Otherwise, as Williams and Hopps (1987) noted many years ago, "the profession does not advance, clients cannot thrive, and practice does not improve" (p. 376).

Key Terms

abstract	letters of inquiry
appendix	limitations
audience	pilot project
executive summary	principal investigator (PI)
Gantt chart	request for proposals (RFP)

SELF-REVIEW
(Answers are at the end of the book.)

1. T or F. The *Discussion* section of a research report is where the notable theoretical explanations of the problem are summarized.
2. Why are tables included in research reports? Would most manuscripts contain 10 or more tables?
3. T or F. The *Results* section of a research report contains only the findings the investigator has obtained; this is not the place for speculation or implications.
4. T or F. The study's limitations are presented in the *Methodology* section.
5. T or F. The *Introduction* is where a clear statement of the research problem is addressed so that the reader understands the study's purpose.
6. T or F. The usual length of manuscripts submitted to professional journals is 35 pages, exclusive of tables and references.

QUESTIONS FOR CLASS DISCUSSION

1. Discuss the ways in which a research report is similar to and different from the customary term paper.
2. Discuss what it is about a "good" journal article that makes it interesting or fun to read and what it is about some journal articles that make them dull and uninteresting.
3. How is writing for professional audiences different from writing for clients or friends?
4. Think about the various sections of the research report. What might be the most difficult section to write and which the easiest? Why?

RESOURCES AND REFERENCES

American Psychological Association. (2009). *Publication manual of the American Psychological Association* (6th ed.). Washington, DC: APA.

Coley, S., & Scheinberg, C. A. (2013). *Proposal writing: Effective grantsmanship.* Thousand Oaks, CA: Sage.

Craig, C. D., & Sprang, G. (2014). Gender Differences in Trauma Treatment: Do Boys and Girls Respond to Evidence-Based Interventions in the Same Way? *Violence & Victims, 29*(6), 927–939.

DePoy, E., & Gitlin, L. N. (1998). *Introduction to research: Understanding and applying multiple strategies.* St Louis, MO: Mosby.

Drisko, J. W. (2005). Writing up qualitative research. *Families in Society, 86*(4), 589–593.

Garfield, S. L. (1984). The evaluation of research: An editorial perspective. In A. S. Bellack & M. Hersen (Eds.), *Research methods in clinical psychology.* New York, NY: Pergamon.

Geever, J. C. (2012). *The Foundation Center's guide to proposal writing.* New York, NY: Foundation Center.

Goldberg, A. E., & Allen, K. R. (2015). Communicating qualitative research: Some practical guideposts for scholars. *Journal of Marriage and Family, 77,* 3–22.

Harley, A., Yang, M., Stoddard, A. M., Adamkiewicz, G., Walker, R., Tucker-Seeley, R. D., ... & Sorensen, G. (2014). Patterns and predictors of health behaviors among racially/ethnically diverse residents of low-income housing developments. *American Journal of Health Promotion, 29*(1), 59–67.

Hernandez, C. L., Elliott, T. R., Underhill, A. T., Fine, P. R., Berry, J. W., & Lai, M. H. H. (2014). Trajectories of life satisfaction five years after medical discharge for traumatically acquired disability. *Rehabilitation Psychology, 59*(2), 183–192.

Karsh, E., & Fox, A. S. (2014). *The only grant-writing book you'll ever need.* New York, NY: Basic Books.

Misra-Hebert, A. D., Santurri, L., DeChant, R., Watts, B., Sehgal, A. R., & Aron, D. C. (2015). A health assessment survey of veteran students: Utilizing a community college-veterans affairs medical center partnership. *Military Medicine, 180,* 1059–1064.

National Association of Social Workers (1999). *Code of Ethics.* Washington, D. C.: National Association of Social Workers.

Pettus-Davis, C., Howard, M. O., Dunnigan, A., Scheyett, A. M., & Roberts-Lewis, A. (2016). Using randomized controlled trials to evaluate interventions for releasing prisoners. *Research on Social Work Practice, 26*(1), 35–43.

Pyrczak, F., & Bruce, R. R. (2014). *Writing empirical research reports.* Glendale, CA: Pyrczak Publishing.

Staton-Tindall, M., Harp, K. L. H., Winston, E., Webster, J. M., & Pangburn, K. (2015). Factors associated with recidivism among corrections-based treatment participants in rural and urban areas. *Journal of Substance Abuse Treatment, 56,* 16–22.

Swanberg, J. E., & Logan, T. (2005). Domestic violence and employment: A qualitative study. *Journal of Occupational Health Psychology, 10*(1), 3–17.

Wahab, S. (2005). Navigating mixed-theory programs: Lessons learned from a prostitution-diversion project. *Affilia, 20*(2), 203–221.

Young, D. J., & Tamburro, A. (2014). *The writer's handbook: A guide for social workers.* Ogden Dunes, IN: Writer's Toolkit Publishing LLC.

Williams, L. F., & Hopps, J. G. (1987). Publication as a practice goal: Enhancing opportunities for social workers. *Social Work, 32*(5), 373–376.

ASSIGNMENT 14.1

Reading Agency Research Reports and Proposals

Objective: *To provide hands-on experience with evaluating and critiquing reports and grant proposals.*

In the practicum agency where you are interning, try to find an example of a research or evaluation report. Read this report, and use the following checklist to assess its various components. (Instructors: You may want to post a local research report or proposal electronically so that every student is reading the same document. Alternatively, a journal article could be used.)

CHECKLIST FOR EVALUATING JOURNAL ARTICLES AND MANUSCRIPTS

Title of the research report or article read?
Who prepared it?
Date?

THE INTRODUCTION
Does its introduction provide a clear notion of

a.	the problem	_Yes	_No
b.	the purpose of the research	_Yes	_No
c.	its significance	_Yes	_No

How could the introduction have been improved?

THE LITERATURE REVIEW
Is the literature review

a.	relevant to the study	_Yes	_No
b.	thorough	_Yes	_No
c.	current	_Yes	_No

Are the hypotheses/research questions reasonable? _Yes _No
Do they appear to logically follow from the review of the literature? _Yes _No

How might the literature review section have been improved?

THE METHODOLOGY

Is a research design stated? _Yes _No
Do the subjects appear to have been selected without overt bias? _Yes _No
If there is a control group, does it seem to be an appropriate group for comparison? _Yes _No
Is the number of participants sufficient? _Yes _No
Is there is enough information on
a. the procedures _Yes _No

b. operational definitions of the variables   _Yes   _No
c. the reliability and validity of the instruments   _Yes   _No

What additional information about this project's methodology would you like to have found in the report?

THE RESULTS

Are the appropriate statistical tests used?   _Yes   _No

Are the findings discussed in terms of their implications
   and practical significance?   _Yes   _No

Do the conclusions logically follow from the data?   _Yes   _No

Has the author identified limitations of the study?   _Yes   _No

How could the Results section have been improved?

ASSIGNMENT 14.2

Critiquing Grant Proposals

Objective: *To provide hands-on experience with evaluating and critiquing grant proposals.*

Obtain a copy of a recent grant proposal that has been written by a social service agency in your community or by a faculty member at your college or university. Read this proposal, and use the following headings and questions to assess its various components. Elaborate your responses with a reasoned reply. (Instructors: You may want to put a copy of a grant proposal on reserve or post it electronically so that every student is reading the same proposal.)

1. Problem statement: Is the problem real? Is the description of the problem compelling?

2. Qualifications of the organization: Does this section make a good argument for why this organization is particularly well suited to launch the project? Does it seem to have the necessary resources and staff?

3. Goals and objectives: Are the goals and objectives appropriate for the project? In your opinion, are they feasible?

4. Methodology: Does this section of the proposal clearly explain what the funding will provide in services or how the research will be conducted? Are these plans reasonable and built on best-practice models?

5. Evaluation plan: Will the plans to evaluate the project provide important process evaluation information or outcome data for concluding whether it succeeded? Is there anything else you would want to know?

6. Budget: Does the budget seem realistic, neither overinflated nor too skimpy?

7. Future funding plans: Is a practical plan described that would seem to provide for continued funding of this project?

Appendix A

Attitudes About Research Courses

1. Check the following courses that you have successfully completed in high school:

- Algebra I
- Algebra II
- Geometry
- Calculus

2. What is your age?_____

3. What is your gender?_____

4. Consider for a moment the extent (if any) of your fear of research courses. Indicate your fear on the following scale.

No Fear			Some Fear				Lots of Fear		
1	2	3	4	5	6	7	8	9	10

5. On the following scale, rate your perception of how useful you think research courses will be to you.

Not Very Useful			Some Use				Very Useful		
1	2	3	4	5	6	7	8	9	10

6. On the following scale, rate your interest in taking research courses.

No Interest			Some Interest				Lots of Interest		
1	2	3	4	5	6	7	8	9	10

To better understand your feelings about research, indicate whether the following statements are true or false.

7. T or F.   I dread speaking before a large group of people more than taking a research course.
8. T or F.   I would rather take a research course than ask a server to return an improperly cooked meal to the kitchen.
9. T or F.   My fear of snakes is greater than my fear of taking a research course.
10. T or F.   My fear of spiders is less than my fear of taking a research course
11. T or F.   I would rather take a research course than ask a total stranger to do a favor for me.
12. T or F.   My fear of research is such that I would rather the university require an additional two courses of my choosing than take one research course.
13. T or F.   I dread going to the dentist more than taking a research course.
14. T or F.   I fear a statistics course more than a research methods course.
15. T or F.   I have always "hated math."

The following symbols frequently appear in research studies that employ statistical analyses. To the best of your ability, identify the statistical symbol. If unknown, write "unknown." (Example: The symbol + means addition.)

16. *F* _____
17. *df* _____
18. *t* _____
19. *r* _____
20. X^2 _____
21. *x–* _____
22. SD, S _____

Appendix B

Drug Attitude Questionnaire

Please read each of the following items carefully. Rate your agreement or disagreement by checking the appropriate blank to the right of the question.

Response Key: Strongly Agree = SA   Agree = A   Undecided = U
                   Disagree = D   Strongly Disagree = SD

		SA	A	U	D	SD
1.	Using marijuana or beer often leads to becoming addicted to more harmful drugs.	□	□	□	□	□
2.	Drugs are basically an "unnatural" way to enjoy life.	□	□	□	□	□
3.	I see nothing wrong with getting drunk occasionally.	□	□	□	□	□
4.	Too many of society's problems are blamed on kids who use alcohol or drugs regularly.	□	□	□	□	□
5.	Even if my best friend gave me some drugs, I probably wouldn't use them.	□	□	□	□	□
6.	If I become a parent, I don't intend to hassle my kids about their use of drugs or alcohol.	□	□	□	□	□
7.	Certain drugs like marijuana are all right to use because you can't get addicted.	□	□	□	□	□
8.	It is not difficult for me to turn down an opportunity to get high.	□	□	□	□	□
9.	Marijuana should not be legalized.	□	□	□	□	□

		SA	A	U	D	SD
10.	It is not okay with me if my friends get high or drunk.	☐	☐	☐	☐	☐
11.	I would rather occasionally use drugs or alcohol with my friends than lose this set of friends.	☐	☐	☐	☐	☐
12.	Someone who regularly uses drugs or alcohol may be considered a sick person.	☐	☐	☐	☐	☐
13.	Most of my friends have experimented with drugs.	☐	☐	☐	☐	☐
14.	Personally, use of alcohol is more acceptable than use of drugs.	☐	☐	☐	☐	☐
15.	Any addict with willpower should be able to give up drugs on his or her own.	☐	☐	☐	☐	☐
16.	Either drug addiction or alcoholism leads to family problems.	☐	☐	☐	☐	☐
17.	Most Americans do not heavily rely on drugs.	☐	☐	☐	☐	☐
18.	Some experience with drugs or alcohol is important for a teenager in today's society.	☐	☐	☐	☐	☐
19.	Kids who use drugs are less popular than kids who do not.	☐	☐	☐	☐	☐
20.	Drugs or alcohol provide a good way to "get away from it all."	☐	☐	☐	☐	☐
21.	I think the legal drinking age should be lowered.	☐	☐	☐	☐	☐
22.	Teachers should place more emphasis on teaching American ideals and values.	☐	☐	☐	☐	☐
23.	It is all right to get around the law if you don't actually break it.	☐	☐	☐	☐	☐

Answers to Self-Review Questions and Anxiety Checks

Chapter 1

Anxiety Check 1.1: The statement which best reflect "generalization" is "B." One can only generalize from the sample to the group or population from which it was drawn—in this case only Napa County.

Anxiety Check 1.2: #3 doesn't belong. The correct steps in order are: 5, Forming an answerable question; 6, Searching for evidence; 4, Evaluating the evidence; 1, Integrating the critical appraisal with clinical expertise and client's individuality; 2, Evaluating the intervention.

Self-Review

1. a.
    to be an informed consumer; b. to maintain accountability; c. to meet CSWE standards; d. to be an ethical practitioner; e. to contribute fully to the profession.
2. a. Accreditation of social work programs
3. True
4. Empirically-based means to rely on research to guide assessments and the choice of interventions, and to gauge the effectiveness of those efforts. In practice, to call upon and use research as a tool to improve our efforts to impact problems.
5. Social work research is applied. We use it to improve the quality of our clients' lives.
6. A well-built question must have four features: a question seated within a particular client population, a possible approach or solution, an alternative course of action, and an idea of what would constitute "success."
7. Yes, without a population referent, the question might be too broad or vague
8. A systematic review is a focused literature review that examines all of the studies available to answer a single well-built question.

CHAPTER 2

Anxiety Check 2.1: Yes, both hypotheses conform to the model.

Anxiety Check 2.2: The hypothesis is acceptable.

Anxiety Check 2.3: No evidence that observation of self-esteem can be reliably and dependably assessed has been presented. Is this a belief or fact?

Anxiety Check 2.4: Yes, they overlap.

Self-Review

1. Step 1, Stating a question
    Step 2, Reviewing the literature; gathering information
    Step 3, A hypothesis is made

Step 4, A study is conceptualized

Step 5, The data are collected

Step 6, The data are analyzed and interpreted

Step 7, A report is written

2. True, this is a null hypothesis

3. The study is measuring impulsivity among men arrested for assault and battery and men arrested for public intoxication

4. These are studies that attempt to speak about a population or client group—typically involving a large number of them—so as to well define who is in and who is not included in the group or population membership.

5. There are many ways you could have gone about this. Here are a few examples:

   - Students with at least a 3.5 GPA
   - Students with perfect attendance
   - Students who study at least 3 hours a night most nights
   - Students who take notes and ask questions in class
   - Students who turn in all of their assignments
   - Students who make As on their exams

6. Independent variables could include age, race, income, number of prior arrests, marital status, employment status, alcohol/drug use history, and so on.

7. Concept or construct

8. False

9. c. Bias

10. True

11. a. The hypothesis is too vague; there's no direction with any variable

12. b.

   Also a poor hypothesis. It would be better stated as a null hypothesis "There is no difference in the research ethics values held by MSW and BSW students."

   c. This is a workable hypothesis

   d.

   This is not a terrible hypothesis but could be improved by indicating if fatalistic attitudes decrease or increase survivability rates of persons with cancer.

13. False

14. Qualitative researchers typically do not feel that they must be fully informed about the literature prior to beginning their study. They may conduct some review of the literature but are not expected to master it in the same way as quantitative researchers do.

15. False

16. Yes, absolutely!

17. Qualitative

18. Quantitative

19. Qualitative

20. Depression is the dependent variable.

Chapter 3

Anxiety Check 3.1 Yes, those receiving the placebo might be more likely to drop out of the study. Those knowing they were receiving the new medication might think it was helping them more than it really was. The end result is that it would make the interpretation of the true effects of the drug difficult to determine.

Anxiety Check 3.2: While each IRB is independent from all others and able to make decisions based on their interpretation of policies and potential harm to the research subjects, I believe it is very likely researchers would still be required by their IRBs to obtain assent from person with Alzheimer's to participate.

Anxiety Check 3.3: The clearest dual relationship would come from Sophia, Bill, or Mrs. Simpson individually counseling inmates from the prison and then presenting them with evaluation forms of some type—especially if the inmates did not remain anonymous. If any of these three individuals are making large group presentations which are largely educational in nature and not so much therapy-oriented and if the participants can respond anonymously, then there is much less of a problem. There is no problem if they are largely unknown to the prisoners.

Anxiety Check 3.4: Prisoners are always a vulnerable population because their freedom of movement, activity, etc. is tightly controlled. What might be a minor incentive to a college student (say, $5) could be a major incentive to someone behind bars. In the past, prisoners have had terrible things done to them when they volunteered to be research subjects. See A. M Hornblum's (1998) book, *Acres of skin: Human experiments at Holmesburg Prison*.

Self-Review

1. True
2. True
3. False. Minors must still assent to participate
4. False. If there is no scientific merit, IRBS may refuse to grant permission for research
5. False. (Although IRBs will review these proposals much more closely to ensure there is no possibility of harm and that the research cannot be conducted any other way.)
6. False
7. Protocol
8. Anonymity
9. Confidentiality
10. True
11. Quantitative researchers usually report results in the aggregate as opposed to identifying individuals or quoting participants. Qualitative researchers use open-ended or unstructured interviews, so they are less sure of what will be revealed or disclosed to them than quantitative researchers. And, they cite the statements made by participants without personally identifying them.
12. False

Chapter 4

Anxiety Check 4.1: A subjective assessment reflects personal values or perspectives. I may think, for instance that I can tell when a person is lying. An objective assessment is when there is documentable evidence. For example, a roommate borrows a friend's car to go to the grocery store but the car's odometer reveals that he actually travelled 50 miles instead of 3 to the nearest supermarket. The odometer is objective evidence of the distance travelled.

Anxiety Check 4.2: One could count the number of times the child approaches another child on a playground for joint play or initiates conversation (e.g., in the cafeteria). In the classroom, one could count the number of times that the child offers to help a classmate or verbally contributes in a small group. 2nd bullet, record the length of time it takes for a child to go to sleep once placed in his or her crib or bed. 3rd bullet, the young woman could be given "assignments" to help decrease her shyness. For instance, she might be asked to not wear a watch and to ask five different people a day for the time. She could make 3 phone calls a day inquiring about a job. She could join an organization that has regular meetings and attend, volunteer at an agency on a regular basis. 4th bullet, the men could be asked to keep a diary or journal of the times per day they lost their temper and raised their voices or shouted.

Anxiety Check 4.3: Other behaviors that could suitable for tracking in an SSRD could include panic symptoms (especially if the child is being bullied at school), crying episodes, or temper tantrums,

Anxiety Check 4.4: Since the young man did show improvement over the course of a semester, there is no reason to believe the intervention is not working. Could it be strengthened by the assignment of a mentor or study buddy? That's possible. He may need someone paying closer attention to whether he is studying each night and submitting his assignments. However, there is no reason to assume that starting a new intervention and then another new one would be a successful strategy. No reason to move to the ABCD design.

Self-Review

1. True
2. False. Time goes on the horizontal axis
3. Two
4. ABAB
5. d. $A_1A_2A_3B$
6. Many peaks and valleys, not a straight linear line
7. a. They lend themselves to clinical practice
   b. They are not burdensome and they complement practice
   c. They are primarily visual and do not require statistical expertise
8. The major problem is one of generalization. Success with one client doesn't mean, for example, that the social worker is successful with all or most of her clients.
9. The baselines for subjects 2 and 3 are longer than for the first subject; intervention with the second subject is not started until it is shown to be effective with the first subject. Intervention with the third subject is not started until intervention with the second subject has also shown to be effective.
10. To determine if clients are making progress.
11. The major reason is probably lack of time to evaluate their practice, but other reasons include settings not amenable to single-system designs (for example, where there are short stays or rapid turnover of clients), and lastly, the inability to find suitable instruments to measure progress.
12. While both situations would be thought-provoking, unpredictable behavior in the B phase simply means that the intervention isn't working and that another one should be tried. Erratic activity

in the baseline could mean any number of things and this is where good questions are needed in assessment to understand when and where the undesired behavior occurs and what precipitated each occurrence.

13. Internal validity threats are history, maturation, instrumentation, testing, morality, statistical regression, and contamination/diffusion.

14. External validity is concerned with whether the findings can be generalized to other settings/populations.

15. The greatest threat to external validity is that it usually is not possible to involve random selection of subjects and therefore those in the study may not be truly representative of the client population.

Chapter 5

Anxiety Check 5.1: Yes, Sophia is correct

Anxiety Check 5.2: No, a classical experimental design requires random assignment to either the intervention or control group.

Anxiety Check 5.3: Without knowing more about the study, these would be dependent variables; they would show the outcome of the intervention. Think stimulus à response. The response is an outcome of the treatment.

Self-Review

1. No, it would be much more labor-intensive for Marsha to construct 80 different single-system research graphs and then have the possible problem of not being able to interpret them in a conclusive sense. Her focus is not on an individual client, but should be on whether the majority of the clients as a group received benefit from the intervention. Does she need to assess their depression weekly? Probably not. In a situation like this, the investigator would normally administer just pretests at the beginning of the study and posttests at the conclusion.

2. A control group and random assignment.

3. Extraneous

4. True. It would be an experiment even without pretests.

5. True. In 12 months or more children grow up, bodies change, even our thinking about various topics can shift.

6. False. This would be the threat of testing or practice.

7. True

8. True

9. False. This is a quasi-experimental design.

10. The time-series design or the time-series with control groups.

11. True

12. It is impossible with this design to rule out the threat of alternative explanations. With no control group, it is impossible to say that the intervention created the change observed at posttest.

13. Yes

14. False

15. False. These designs would be likely used because randomization was not possible.

16. False

Chapter 6

Anxiety Check 6.1: Those self-reporting that they needed more social distance had the greatest fear of AIDS. Those with high social distance scores also had the least empathy. That is, these two variables went in different directions.

Anxiety Check 6.2: Does it look like it measures empathy? And would that be face validity? (Yes to both). At a minimum, he should administer it to a sample of social workers or colleagues like those who could be presenters of the program to be developed to see if it has reliability in that sample. Then, he will need to consider how to establish its validity. I might either go for concurrent validity by administering it simultaneously with another empathy measure or find a group presumed to have low empathy and compare it to a sample of persons with high empathy to see if their scores are very different (known groups validity). Factor analysis would also be a possibility once a good sized sample was obtained.

Anxiety Check 6.3: My first thought is that the length of the instrument may cause some respondent fatigue with 81 items. Before deciding upon an instrument, one should look it over, read it carefully, and perhaps pilot test it. The HIV/AIDS Provider Stigma Inventory (HAPSI) contains 3 scales (Awareness, Acceptance, and Action) and many subscales. It is possible that Mrs. Simpson, Bill and Sophia might decide for their purposes to use only the Acceptance scale.

Self-Review

1. b. test-retest reliability
2. She would want to keep it; if it correlates with the other items it will improve the scale's internal consistency
3. You would be computing interrater reliability
4. Validity
5. False
6. False
7. False
8. False
9. False, validity could be affected in populations vastly different from the pilot or first sample—especially if vocabularies, ages, or cultural backgrounds vary a great deal from the first group.
10. True
11. Internal consistency of .83 is pretty good and she should be able to go forward with her plans to submit an article for publication. If you thought that she should add more items to get to 150%, then you don't have a good understanding of this material. Go back and read it again.

Chapter 7

Anxiety Check 7.1: It is leading in that it raises the issue of the respondent being unhappy. It is not balanced—respondents could be happy or unhappy in their current positions.

Anxiety Check 7.2: Yes, it is a loaded question. It presumes that the respondent has cheated or is cheating on exams—that may not be the case.

Anxiety Check 7.3: Sensitive information for students may be the same as for most adults: drug or alcohol use, involvement in sexual activities, illegal acts, cheating, lying, or dishonest acts—anything that could get them in trouble at school, home, or with the law.

Self-Review

1. True
2. False
3. False
4. d. It is vague
5. b. It uses jargon
6. c. For most people, this question asks for unavailable information
7. d. It uses inflammatory or loaded terms
8. a. It contains loaded terms
9. b. It is all-inclusive
10. d. It is vague
11. c. It is leading
12. Contingency
13. Because he is not sure how young adults cope with divorce, it would be better to use open-ended questions.

Chapter 8

Anxiety Check 8.1: 180 in a sample of 200; 450 in a sample of 500

Anxiety Check 8.2: Those not represented would be those mothers and babies in states where opiate-addicted babies are not at the highest level and in areas where there is no large neonatal unit. Those residing in the more rural states and nonmetropolitan areas would not have much chance to be represented.

Anxiety Check 8.3: No, the minimum sample for a population of 1,000 is 278 respondents.

Anxiety Check 8.4: At the 10:00 A.M. time you would miss those individuals who are working during the day then, at 11:30 P.M. you probably would miss those who work during the day and older, retired individuals. At 11:00 A.M. Sunday you would miss those who are attending church.

Anxiety Check 8.5: I would expect them to be homogenous—they all have something in common and that is what allows one respondent to lead the researcher on to another possible respondent having the same characteristic. They may be similar in several other characteristics but there is no guarantee of that.

Self-Review

1. True
2. Convenience—you also could have said available or accidental sample
3. Sample frame
4. True
5. a. stratified sample
6. True
7. True
8. False
9. Available, accidental
10. False

11. True
12. Snowball
13. Interviewer
14. False
15. We don't know the first random number William will begin with—that for the random number generator to determine.

Chapter 9

Anxiety Check 9.1: The survey would miss (under-estimate) the total number of homeless by not counting: those who choose not to be sheltered. This would include those who sleep in abandoned buildings, on park benches or in store fronts, sleep in their cars or in public restrooms, under highway underpasses, those who camp out in the woods, etc.

Anxiety Check 9.2: Such a survey may be biased in excluding individuals who, for instance, might not be able to read, who don't have Internet capability (if an electronic survey is being conducted), those who are working multiple jobs or long hours, those who are not fluent in English, etc.

Anxiety Check 9.3: A Post-it sticker with a handwritten note on it indicates a personal touch—that a real person is interested in the potential respondent's input or answers. This is in contrast to dealing with automated robot calls, large corporations that bombard individuals with mass mailings and are trying to sell a product. Also, a Post-It note is an unusual thing to find in a mailing and may whet the individual's curiosity to read more and lead them to participate in the survey.

Self-Review

1. Personal interview
2. True
3. True
4. True
5. d. 52%
6. The ability to observe the respondent and the surroundings (including facial expressions and reactions) and also the ability to present visual aids
7. Investigation of topics not previously well researched. Because little is known about the subject being investigated, sample size is not a major consideration and samples may be fairly small.
8. These are the advantages: relatively inexpensive, large number of respondents can be surveyed in a relatively short period, respondents can look up information if they need to, privacy is maximized, graphics and visuals can be presented (e.g., response sets to help with memory issues), can be completed when convenient for the respondent, respondents can see the context of a series of questions, there is no researcher present to bias the respondent's answers or to inaccurately record the responses.
9. False
10. Pilot test
11. False
12. False
13. c. Personal interview

Chapter 10

Anxiety Check 10.1: No, it is not close to an experiment because there is no random assignment. Cause and effect cannot be determined—content analysis merely reveals what is there in the document or record. It is unable to control other influences or variables.

Self-Review

1. False
2. He or she is limited by the fact that the data may not exist, or if it does, it may not be available for the years or locations in which the researcher is interested. There could be incomplete or sloppy records, or data that has questionable reliability. The researcher using archival data is limited by not being able to create new, original data.
3. True
4. c. secondary data analysis
5. False
6. True
7. They tend to be relatively inexpensive and don't involve contacting clients.
8. Lack of control over the source material/data—because it already exists. The researcher cannot reword questionnaire items to make them less vague or insensitive, and cannot probe like an interviewer to achieve greater clarification. The researcher also cannot introduce new variables.
9. Latent content
10. True

Chapter 11

Anxiety Check 11.1: Three features suggest that it may be a quantitative study. First, he created 10 multiple choice items for a measurement scale. Second, he developed a hypothesis, and third: he may have begun looking into the literature—at least he found and read a qualitative study.

Anxiety Check 11.2: Yes, this could be a qualitative study. D'aaron is a participant in the pawn world and taking notes allows him to record his observations for analysis at a later time.

Anxiety Check 11.3: He could engage in member-checking by asking either those who also work in the pawn shop to review his qualitative analysis or by asking a few customers of the store who bring pawn items in to review what he has written to see if it accurately captures their experiences and world-views. Also, prolonged engagement (e.g., employment in the pawn shop) would add to the trustworthiness of his findings. He could also try to triangulate his findings by including police or other individuals who come in looking for stolen goods that have been pawned.

Self-Review

1. a. quantitatively-oriented researchers
2. c. large sample sizes
3. d. concern with instruments and measurement
4. a. quantitative—could be secondary data analysis or survey
   b. qualitative
   c. quantitative

      d. qualitative

      e. quantitative

5.   You might select a qualitative approach: a) if you can't find an appropriate quantitative instrument to use, b) if you want to investigate a "hidden" or "hard to reach" population, c)if you want to study a phenomenon in its natural setting, d) when there is little or no literature or previous studies available on the phenomenon, e) when the topic requires greater sensitivity to explore it, f) when the investigator wishes to obtain the perspective of participants in their own words and actions and wishes to write a "rich description" of it, g) when the focus is on the process and not the outcome of a program or activity, and when the quantitative findings don't go far enough or need more explanation.

6.   True

7.   False

8.   False

9.   Theoretical saturation is when new data obtained by the researcher replicates earlier findings.

10.   Member checking involves going back into the field after data collection to verify material with one or more participants with regard to an interpretation or finding

11.   True

Chapter 12

Anxiety Check 12.1: Yes, see the shaded box in this chapter, Questions and Data Sources Useful in Process Evaluation

Anxiety Check 12.2: To purposely collect data on only the most successful clients to complete a program in the shortest time does not represent all of the clients' experiences. Unless it is identified as a purposive sample or "best case" scenario of what can be accomplished, it isn't good research and is terribly misleading. Provision of misleading information is a violation of NASW Code of Ethics and unconsidered unethical by almost every researcher.

Self-Review

1.   Patterns of use

2.   Formative evaluation

3.   a. narrative

4.   Consumer satisfaction

5.   Outcome evaluation

6.   Cost-effectiveness

7.   True

8.   That client satisfaction studies invariably produce high satisfaction ratings

9.   Patterns of use

10.   Time, resources, audience, purpose

11.   Let's start with a cost-effectiveness study. At a minimum, this type of study must operationalize who or what is considered a "success" and count those for some period of time (e.g., a year). Then this number is divided into the total cost for running the program for the same time period. A qualitative study does not do anything like that—and generally does not focus on expense or

number of graduates. In a qualitative study what would be more of interest would be the participants' experiences in their own words.

Chapter 13

Anxiety Check 13.1: A continuous variable is one where the next unit is predictable in a pattern of steady increments. So, if you weigh 130 today and go on a diet and lose a pound, you'll be at 129 and if you then gain four pounds you will weigh a predictable 133. A teen who is 5'10" who grows an inch will be 5'11." That's different from a variable that uses these categorizations: short, medium, tall where the next unit is not so standardized or predictable.

Anxiety Check 13.2: Yes, the report P (for probability) was less than .001 making it statistically significant well above the .05 criterion.

Anxiety Check 13.3: Yes, there are statistically significant differences among the three groups as indicated by the P (probability) being less than .001. The hypothesis is supported. The group that self-rated their chances of not returning to prison had the most years of prior work experience.

Self-Review

1. c. the mean
2. Nominal
3. Ordinal (because there is a directionality from high to low)
4. Attributes are the specifications or descriptive groups composing nominal variables. For example, the attributes of Marital Status might be: single, married, separated, divorced, and widowed. Or, more simply you might have: single or partnered. As a researcher you get to decide what the attributes should be for your variables.
5. b. bivariate
6. a. chi square
7. b. t-test for paired samples
8. c. one-way analysis of variance (because there are 3 groups and interval data)
9. False
10. d. both b and c are correct
11. c. about 12%
12. No, she has not created a nominal variable; she has created an ordinal variable.
13. The appropriate measure of central tendency would be the mode.

Chapter 14

Self-Review

1. False
2. To cut down on the amount of verbiage in a paper; no—not 10 tables except in an exceptionally long report where greater detail is requested or expected
3. True
4. False
5. True
6. False

Index

9 781793 507198